60°

45°

AUGUST
1975

UNITED
KINGDOM

IRELAND

London

NETHERLANDS

BELGIUM

LUX.

Paris

FRANCE

SWITZ.

PORTUGAL

SPAIN

Lisbon

ANDORRA

Gibraltar

MONACO

Corsica

Sardinia

Balearic Is.

HURRICANE

Is.

MOROCCO

TUNISIA

SPANISH
SAHARA

ALGERIA

LIBYA

MAURITANIA

MALI

NIGER

SENEGAL

BIA

-BISSAU

GUINEA

SIERRA LEONE

LIBERIA

UPPER VOLTA

IVORY
COAST

GHANA

TOGO

BENIN

NIGERIA

CHAD

EQUATORIAL GUINEA

SAO TOME AND
PRINCIPE

GABON

CAMEROON

CENTRAL AFRICAN
REPUBLIC

CONGO

ZAIRE

ANGOLA

St. Helena

MADE 18TH
PASSAGE OF
ATLANTIC
1972
WORLD RECORD

ZAMBIA

SOUTH-
WEST
AFRICA

BOTSWANA

RHODESIA

SOUTH
AFRICA

LESOTHO

SWAZILAND

Cape Town

Port Elizabeth

Durban

DECEMBER
1971

Tristan da Cunha
(St. Helena)

NORWAY

SWEDEN

FINLAND

DENMARK

FED REP

OF

GERMANY

GER
DEM
REP

POLAND

CZECHOSLOVAKIA

LIECH.

AUSTRIA

HUNGARY

ROMANIA

YUGOSLAVIA

BULGARIA

ITALY

ALBANIA

GREECE

Sicily

Crete

TURKEY

CYPRUS

SYRIA

LEBANON

ISRAEL

SAILED THE
DEAD SEA
DEC 1970

JORDON

Eilat

SHOT AT

EGYPT
(UAR)

SUDAN

SAUDI ARABIA

IRAQ

KUWAIT

IRAN

BAHRAIN

QATAR

UNITED ARAB
EMIRATES

OMAN

Massawa

YEMEN
(SANA)

YEMEN
(ADEN)

Fr. Terr. of the
Afars and Issas

Djibouti

ETHIOPIA

SOMALIA

UGANDA

KENYA

RWANDA

BURUNDI

TANZANIA

Dar es Salaam

COMOROS

Seychelles

Moroni

Majunga

MOZAMBIQUE

MALAWI

MADAGASCAR

U. S. S. R.

0°

15°

15°

30°

30°

15°

0°

15°

30°

The Incredible Voyage

The Incredible Voyage

Voyage

A Personal Odyssey

TRISTAN JONES

Foreword by John Hemming

SHEED ANDREWS AND McMEEL, INC.
SUBSIDIARY OF UNIVERSAL PRESS SYNDICATE
KANSAS CITY

Library of Congress Cataloging in Publication Data

Jones, Tristan, 1924-
    The incredible voyage.
    1. Voyages and travels — 1951-   2. Jones,
Tristan, 1924-   I. Title.
G465.J66   910'.41   [B]   77-7183
ISBN 0-8362-0703-3

I am a part of all that I have met.

Alfred, Lord Tennyson
"Ulysses"

Contents

Foreword

Tristan Jones set off on his Incredible Voyage with all the determination, exuberance, and even innocence of the first European explorers. His boats *Barbara* and *Sea Dart* were even smaller than the ships of the voyages of discovery. The first part of his remarkable adventure—from the Red Sea around the southern tip of Africa—sailed in reverse the voyages of Bartholomeu Dias and the Portuguese fleets that discovered this route to India. But it is when Tristan Jones reaches South America that his exploits remind me most strongly of those early explorers.

Having sailed on the Dead Sea, the lowest stretch of navigable water, Tristan Jones was determined to sail an ocean-going vessel on the highest waters of Lake Titicaca. It was a quest not unlike that of the Spanish conquistadors seeking imaginary lakes in the heart of the South American continent. The most famous of these lakes was that of El Dorado, the Gilded Man. This legend appears to have been based on fact. Until the late fifteenth century, one of the Chibcha tribes living beside the sacred lake of Guatavita near Bogotá used to anoint its chief and roll his body in gold dust. He would then enter a raft, make a ceremonial offering of gold and jewels in the lake, and finally jump in and wash off the gold dust. The magnificent gold museum in Bogotá has tiny golden replicas of the raft and its occupants during this ceremony. Tristan Jones would have enjoyed that museum—but all that he saw in Bogotá was the inside of a Colombian jail!

The Spanish conquistadors were obsessed with finding gold. They constantly interrogated or tortured Indians to learn where it could be found, and they were often told about the legend of El Dorado and the mysterious lake. Such rumors were enough to fire the imagination of these tough adventurers—after all, Hernan Cortes had just conquered the Aztec empire in Mexico and Francisco Pizarro made himself the richest soldier in Christendom from the spoils of the Inca empire. The Germans Ambrosius Ehinger and Nicholas Federamann plunged inland into Venezuela and Colombia from the Caribbean coast. Pizarro's lieutenant Sebastian de Benalcazar conquered Quito and the northern part of the Inca empire and then pushed eastwards into southern Colombia in search of El Dorado. When the first Spaniards sailed down the Amazon from Quito in 1542 they met Manaus Indians trading gold objects with the natives of the upper Amazon. The Manaus lived far up the Rio Negro and told the Spaniards that they obtained the gold from the upper reaches of their river—the homeland of the Chibchas. The legend persisted. There were rumors of a great lake called Parima or Manoa (after the Manaus) at the headwaters of the Orinoco. (Some explorer may have seen the plains that sometimes flood in this area.) Sir Walter Raleigh tried to reach this lake by sailing up the Orinoco, and other English, Dutch, and even Irish adventurers sought to approach it from the Amazon side.

Another elusive lake lay at the heart of the continent, not far from the place where Tristan Jones eventually reached the Paraguay river on the journey down from Titicaca. Indian tribes had told the Spaniards and Portuguese that if you sailed far enough up the Paraguay you reached some lakes from which it was only a short portage to rivers that flowed northwards into the Amazon. This information was essentially correct. But it grew, in the Europeans' imagination, into another vast lake that linked South America's two great river basins, the Amazon and the Plate-Paraguay. This lake was marked on maps right up to the end of the seventeenth century. It was thought to contain the lost City of the Caesars, home of the White King who controlled a mountain of silver.

Tristan Jones' attack on *his* personal El Dorado—Lake Titicaca—eventually caused him to sail right around the northern half of the South American continent, and also half way up the Amazon and down the Paraguay. He was following the routes of many of the first explorers. It is fascinating to learn from his narrative about the currents, storms, and other hazards that confronted those early sailors.

When Mr. Jones sailed north-westwards from Recife to the Amazon, he was following the route of the first Spaniards to discover Brazil. Vicente Yañez Pinzon, who had been with Columbus on his first voyage in 1492, took four caravels across the south Atlantic early in 1500. They struck land just north of Recife and then sailed along the route followed by Tristan Jones. They noted the mouths of two vast rivers, presumably the Pará and the Amazon, and they named the latter "Saint Mary of the Sweet Sea" because of its endless expanse of fresh water. Amerigo Vespucci (the man whose first name has been applied to the continents of the Americas) may well have discovered these two rivers a few months earlier, in late 1499. In a letter written in 1500 he described a voyage down the northeastern coast of South America in which "we saw two most tremendous rivers issuing from the land." Taking to their longboat, Vespucci and his men rowed up the larger of these rivers for two days, noting its dense forests and exotic birds.

Tristan Jones's attempt to sail up the Amazon reminds me more of explorers later than Amerigo Vespucci. The first Spaniards to sail or drift right down the entire length of the Amazon, from Quito to the Atlantic, did so in 1542 under the command of Francisco de Orellana. This great explorer obtained permission to return and attempt to colonize the river he had descended. He sailed in 1549 with three ships full of colonists with their wives and animals. But the venture ended in shipwreck for some and starvation among the swamps of the lower Amazon for Orellana and the others. The Amazon was the ruin of many later expeditions. The world's largest river defeated them, just as it forced Tristan Jones to turn back beyond Manaus. The only craft powerful enough to overcome the current of the Amazon are canoes paddled by teams of Indians, or ships with marine engines. Ocean-going liners sail right up the river to Iquitos in Peru, and I have been on some of the many antiquated boats that ply the upper rivers, to Pucallpa and other river ports.

When Tristan Jones determined to sail from the Amazon along the northern shores of South America, he was on the first coastline to be discovered by Europeans. It was Christopher Columbus, on his third voyage in August 1498, who first landed on the mainland of South America. His fleet anchored on the mainland opposite the island of Trinidad and examined some of the estuary of the Orinoco. During the next two years, other Spanish expeditions explored the coastline as far as the Gulf of Darien and the Isthmus of Panama.

Tristan Jones crossed the Isthmus, as Vasco Nuñez de Balboa had done in 1513—but he went through the Panama Canal, one of the first people to *sail* through under canvas. One advantage of traveling by yacht, particularly with a skipper as inquisitive as Tristan Jones, is the ability to visit remote islands. In this book we learn about such islands as Zanzibar and the Comoros in the Indian Ocean and Saint Helena and Devil's Island in the Atlantic. Tristan Jones is an adventurer entitled to cast doubt on the veracity of the claim by Henri Charrière, or "Papillon," that he escaped from the notorious prison on Devil's Island. But to me the most fascinating island Jones visited was Gorgona, off the Pacific coast of Colombia. He found that it was a functioning penal colony full of forgotten political prisoners, a terrible place, apparently beyond the reach of organizations such as Amnesty International.

Gorgona island was a port of call of Francisco Pizarro, one of the most desperate moments in that conqueror's tumultuous career. After the Spaniards had founded the settlement of Panama on the western shore of the Isthmus, they began to explore the Pacific coastline of South America. Pizarro was one of those explorers. On his second voyage along the coast of Colombia, in 1526, he wintered on the island of Gallo near Gorgona. Many of his men died of disease and starvation. Others were on the point of mutiny. The governor of Panama authorized any who wished to return to Panama. Pizarro issued a famous challenge: drawing a line in the sand, he dared his men to follow him across it, to the dangers of unknown lands to the south rather than the security of return to Panama. Only thirteen brave men elected to cross the line with their leader. They moved to the island of Gorgona, and from then onwards their fortunes improved. They sailed on to discover Peru; and a few years later Pizarro's conquistadors conquered and destroyed Peru's magnificent Inca empire.

Pizarro marched inland to seize Cuzco, the sumptuous capital of the Incas. He promptly sent scouts to explore Lake Titicaca. He had heard that the Lake was the origin of the Inca tribe in the legends of its creation. He knew that there were temples to the Incas' creator god Kon-Tiki Viracocha on islands in Lake Titicaca. There were also reports of the great complex of pre-Inca ruins at Tiahuanaco near the southern shore of the Lake. Pizarro's partner Diego de Almagro marched past Titicaca in 1535 on his way to investigate Chile, and there were soon many Spaniards settled on the fertile plain alongside the Lake. This was the main route for silver convoys from the silver mountain of Potosí—and the tribes living near Titicaca were a source of forced labor to toil in Potosí's deadly mines. The Jesuits had an important base beside Lake Titicaca, a college for training padres for their missionary empire in Paraguay. There was even a pitched battle in 1547 between rival factions of conquistadors, on the shores of the Lake close to the place where Tristan Jones sailed *Sea Dart* into Bolivian waters.

Beyond Titicaca, Tristan Jones descended the eastern foothills of the Andes, across Bolivia to the swamps of the Paraguay river. As he explains in this book, he was following the route of another early explorer: Aleixo García, the Portuguese adventurer who was the first European to see a corner of the Inca civilization. García was guided across South America by a horde of Chiriguano and Guaraní Indians who raided the Inca frontier some years before Pizarro invaded that empire. Tristan Jones launched his boat on the Paraguay in the Pantanal, the world's largest swamp, that spreads over many hundreds of square miles when the river floods. He descended the river along the route of yet another group of first explorers. In 1516 a Spanish fleet under Juan de Solís had discovered the Plate estuary—where Jones's saga ended. Ten years later the

Venetian Sebastian Cabot explored far up the Paraguay. Rumors of a fabulous lake in the interior inspired a series of later explorers, one of whom founded Asunción in Paraguay in 1539. So Tristan Jones, driven onwards to the goal of *his* lake, followed the routes of almost all the first explorers of South America. Had he lived in the early sixteenth century, he would doubtless have been one of them himself.

JOHN HEMMING
Director and Secretary
Royal Geographical Society
London   March 1977

Acknowledgments

To Marinus of Tyre, Pythagoras, Ptolemy of Alexandria, Saint Brendan, Madoc of Merioneth, Leif Ericsson, Ibn Batuta, Henry of Portugal, Vasco da Gama, Cristóbal Colón, Ferdinand Magellan, Juan de Solís, Aleixo García, Francis Drake, Walter Raleigh, Sebastian Cabot, Henry Hudson, Henry Morgan, Simón Bolívar, Bernardo O'Higgins, Horatio Nelson, Matthew Summers, Matthew Fontaine Maury, Robert Falcon Scott, Roald Amundsen, Ernest Henry Shackleton, Rudyard Kipling, Albert Einstein, and Machamachani, the Quipucamayo *of Taquila: Who made it possible.*

To Edward Allcard, William Andrews, Marcel Bardiaux, Peter Beard, Howard Blackburn, Chay Blythe, Alain Bombard, Starling Burgess, Humphrey Barton, Frank Casper, Francis Chichester, Alain Colas, Brian Cooke, Jacques Cousteau, Alec Crowhurst, Tom Follet, Loike Fougeron, Clare Francis, Alain Gerbault, Jean Gau, Robin Lee Graham, John Guzzwell, Blondie Haslar, Mike Henderson, Bill Howell, Eric and Susan Hiscock, Joan de Cat, William King, Robin Knox-Johnson, Jacques Le Toumelin, Robert Manry, Jacques Marin-Marie, Mike McMullen, Bernard Moitessier, Harry Pigeon, Dougal Robertson, Alec Rose, Joshua Slocum, Miles and Beryl Smeeton, Eric Tabarly, Nigel Tetley, Jean-Yves Terlain, Peer Tangvald, Kenichi Horie, Ryusuki Ushijima, Jean Marie Vidal, John Voss, and Otway Waller: Who did it their own way.

To Tansy Lee, 1866-1958, skipper of the sailing barge Second Apprentice: *Who taught me not to be afraid.*

To Arthur and Ruth Cohen, Bob and Ellie Grosby, David and Magee Shields, of New York, and Barry and Rosie Edgegoose, of London: Who stretched their hands into the darkness to help a wayside straggler.

To the people of the United States of America:
Who yet have the spirit to imagine the unimaginable.

To the land, the sea, the sky, and the poetry of Britain, which is my home.

PART ONE
To Strive

Those who dream by night in the dusty recesses of their minds wake in the day to find that it was vanity: but the dreamers of the day are dangerous men, for they may act their dream with open eyes, to make it possible.

T. E. Lawrence, from the suppressed introductory chapter of Seven Pillars of Wisdom

To Arthur Cohen

I had met the owner of Barbara, *Arthur Cohen, in early 1969 and it was arranged that I would deliver his boat to the western Mediterranean first. Upon meeting him, it was soon obvious that here was another of those encounters in my life which are practically inexplicable. Here was another adventurer at heart, a man who took life and molded it to his conception; tremendously energetic, resourceful and imaginative. Later, in Madeira, it was decided that Arthur would visit his vessel from time to time for short spells while the voyage across the Middle East was made, and that he would support the vessel. This he did until the South American attempt became obviously impossible for* Barbara.

There can be no saying who originated the idea of the crossing of South America. It has been a fixation of mine since at least 1962. How long Arthur had been interested in the project I do not know. Possibly earlier, because here was a man who had had the courage to make the first ever crossing of the Australian continent on a motorcycle decades before. Arthur joined the boat several times in the Mediterranean, once in the Indian Ocean, once in Brazil, and again in the West Indies. Whenever major decisions were undertaken it was always with complete frankness and I was given full rein in methods of tackling the voyages. Which was as it should be; after all it was my life on the line.

Arthur Cohen will always have my gratitude for giving me this further opportunity to tackle the impossible. I have desisted from mentioning him much further in the first two parts of this story, but his presence was always somewhere back there in real life, guiding, suggesting, arranging, encouraging. I reached Lake Titicaca shortly before Arthur died in Arizona. My one big regret is that he could not, as we had dreamed, join me there. As a small measure of my respect and admiration for him, I dedicate this part of the story to him; both the part he made possible and the part which was greatly assisted by his inspiration. He was a good man. A sailor through and through.

1
A BRAVE CONCEPT

Y SIXTEENTH TRANSATLAN-
tic crossing under full sail was fairly
uneventful, with the exception of
glancing off a basking whale about
six hundred miles to the east of Bermuda. I was in Arthur Cohen's yawl
Barbara, a sturdy thirty-eight-footer,
well found, Alden designed and
steady as a tramcar. Her only snag
was that having no dependable self-steering gear I had to
take on a crew for the crossing, which meant a vastly increased food bill and more care on the water consumption.
My crew were good sailors and excellent company, however, which more than made up for the drawbacks.

Anton Elbers was a fifty-year-old Dutchman, an ex-
Netherlands naval officer, while Dan Milton had been a
first officer in the United States Merchant Marine. Both
were members of the Corinthian Yacht Club, an organization which supplies amateur crews for sailing craft.

Anton, Dan, and I left Westport, Connecticut, with no
fanfares or other bullshit on 25 June 1969. *Barbara* was
ostensibly bound for a cruise of the Mediterranean; actually
her real destinations were much more exciting—the Dead
Sea and Lake Titicaca; for I was out to attempt nothing less
than the vertical sailing record of the world. These two
bodies of water, both remote, lie at an altitude difference of
almost 15,000 feet—the Dead Sea at 1,250 feet below sea
level, Lake Titicaca at 12,580 feet above sea level, almost
three miles up in the high Andes mountains of South
America. The distance as the crow flies between the two
bodies of water is about nine thousand miles. The distance
as a small craft sails is much, much greater.

Neither the Dead Sea nor Lake Titicaca had as yet ever
been sailed in a seagoing vessel; neither had ever been
reached by an ocean voyager and neither was properly
charted. No one to whom I broached the subject had any

idea how the voyage should be tackled, or which destination to make for first.

After studying the problem for almost two years I decided to tackle the Dead Sea first. This was by far the easier of the two destinations, for the only natural obstacle to overcome, once Israel was reached, was the Negev Desert, over which by now excellent roads had been constructed. The political obstacles, however, were much more difficult; for there was the ever-present risk of war breaking out between Israel and her Arab neighbors. I decided that I would hover around in the Mediterranean, awaiting the opportune moment to tackle the haul across land.

On passage to the Azores, *Barbara* had good winds from astern or on the starboard quarter and rolled along merrily, the only accidents being the breaking of the running poles twice and the loss of the taffrail log spinner, which was bitten off, probably by a shark or some other large fish. Apart from sighting three steamers en route, there was little else of note in the thirty-one-day passage from Westport to Setúbal, a small fishing port about thirty miles to the south of Lisbon, which has the finest seafood in Portugal.

Here, Anton and Dan left *Barbara,* while I continued on south to Gibraltar with Arthur and a friend, calling at Sagres and Cádiz. It was a fairly rough passage, a total of six days.

As it was rather late in the season and the Mediterranean is rather boisterous in the winter months, it was determined to spend those months outside the Strait of Gibraltar and make a slow, steady cruise down the coast of Morocco as far as Agadir, calling at some very interesting small ports. I then hove across to the Canary Islands with Arthur for two months, mainly to poke around the smaller, lesser-known islands of Gomera and Hierro.

In March of 1970, with a very lucky and unusual southerly wind, I made the passage from Gran Canaria to Funchal, in Madeira, in two days, met with Arthur, visited my friends on the ocean liner *QE2* and then set off for Gibraltar once more. On this passage I spent six days under spinnaker. So far *Barbara* had covered a total of 8,240 miles; 4,000 of these I had completed alone and the voyage had

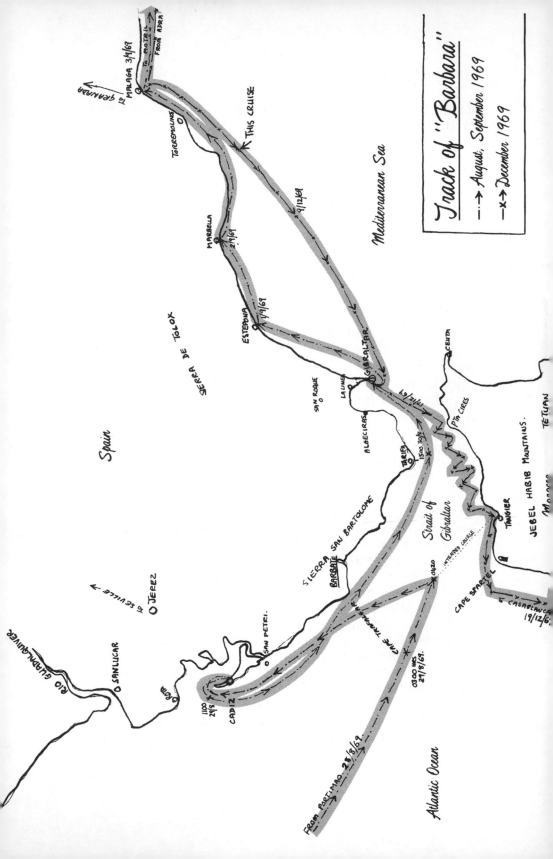

hardly begun! Now I decided to head eastward through the Mediterranean in the direction of Israel and my first destination—the Dead Sea.

All that summer and fall *Barbara* meandered through the Med—Ibiza, Corsica, Malta, Venice, Yugoslavia, the Greek Islands, the haunting, cholera-ravaged south coast of Turkey, one of the most beautiful coasts in the world, finally to Cyprus, where the authorities refused me entry on the grounds that I might be harboring cholera on board. The real reason, of course, was that I had visited Turkey, the ancient enemy of Greece.

Passing through Malta I encountered a young Englishman, Conrad Jelinek, who was looking for a lift to the Middle East, vaguely on his way to Nepal or God-knows-where. Although his appearance did not strike me as being very seamanlike—he had a sort of wild gypsy look—something in his manner did, and especially his sense of humor, so I took him on as general dogsbody and deckhand. Conrad turned out to be the ideal companion in a small sailing craft, quickwitted yet quiet, physically quite strong yet gentle, polite yet firm. He started his voyage a raw amateur; two years later he was able to navigate precisely by sextant, repair a broken main halyard sheave atop a buckling mast in a roaring gale, and make the most intricate splices. Often we would go for days in the ocean passage without saying one word, for none were necessary; we tuned into each other like two laser beams. He had an affinity for the stars; he was, I later found, as locked into nature as the wind itself.

I had searched the usual sailors' haunts on the waterfront of Valletta and Sliema, but had found no takers for voyaging to the Middle East and Red Sea. Why should the average yacht-swabbie bother to go on a trip like that when he could get on a vessel going to more "romantic" places such as the south of France or Yugoslavia, where he or she could show off his or her muscles or what-have-you to other likewise empty-minded morons, and maybe find some rich person to keep him/her/it over the coming winter? Eventually I was reduced to hanging a sign on the boat as she was tied up stern to in Sliema creek, refitting. "Crew wanted; usual number of limbs and senses; unusual trip; apply within."

Eventually Conrad turned up, breathless, having run halfway across the island upon hearing from another hippie friend of the vacancy.

"Ahoy there, anyone aboard?" he shouted. I was working in the cockpit within full view of him.

"No, of course there's no one on board except me. I'm an automatically inflatable rubber deckhand that the skipper winds up every morning before he goes over to spend the day in Tony's bar!"

He laughed. "Are you Tristan?"

"Yes, who are you?"

"Conrad Jelinek and I heard you were looking for a crew." His voice was well modulated with a good English Home Counties accent, not too affected. To the average ear the braying so-called Oxford accent is plain maddening after several days cooped up in a small craft (or anywhere else, come to that).

"Can you long-splice?" I asked, eyeing him closely.

"No."

"Can you tie a Blackwall hitch or a sheepshank."

"No."

"How about sewing, like for sail repairs?"

"No. I'm afraid not." His voice was by now downcast.

"Cook? Only has to be dead simple."

"No." His eyes squinted against the early morning sun behind me.

"Well, hell, man, what in the name of Christ *can* you do? Can you play the piano?"

"No," he grinned, "but I can sing and dance."

"Right, you're on, nip back wherever you kip, and get your gear on board this afternoon; I'm sailing tonight for Cyprus! How much gear you got? I don't want to see more than the same volume as you are yourself; bad for the morale."

He grinned again, let out a whoop, and was running off.

Being at the time rather "hippie" minded, Conrad had some vague idea about man's position in nature, but as yet he had no inkling of the awful struggle which must be maintained when man pits himself against the natural

forces of wind and water; nor did he yet know of the great
rewards, the sense of achievement, the beauty and the joy,
the pure hymn of the oceans. And yet his love for the sea
and nature was soon very obvious; his respect for me
showed very quickly by the way he made efforts to ignore
my idiosyncrasies. His courage and tenacity developed like
a fine tune played by a master on a Stradivarius violin. In
the event, it turned out that Conrad was a rare combination:
a born sailor and one of nature's gentlemen. These natural
attributes were mixed with the results of a Quaker
education—sobriety in the main and diligence in any effort.
In other words, he was worth his weight in gold. He was
never very talkative, yet when he did say something it was
almost always pertinent, and that, in the close confines of a
small craft, is a God-sent gift in anyone. He would sit on the
foredeck repairing sails or carrying out some other chore
for hours, with never a peep out of him, while I would be
down below knocking out an article for the yachting press
on my old beat-up typewriter.

We approached Haifa on the night of 12 November
1970, under the light of a full moon. All was calm and
peaceful and we chugged on under the thirty-six-
horsepower Perkins diesel engine, Lebanon under our gentle lee, a good fifteen miles to the east of *Barbara*. A soft swell
eased our beguiled apprehension when suddenly—
—zoom! Out of the dark nothingness on the moonless side,
a blinding light from an Israeli patrol craft lit us up.

"Heave to!" an electronic voice sang out. "Everyone on
deck!" I felt like I had been caught cracking a bank safe."
How difficult it is to feel innocent when you are! The
gunboat drifted around our stern, with her radar-
controlled guns pointed straight at us, the searchlights
obscenely probing every pore. "Identify yourself!" the voice
said.

It's not easy to remember who you are in these kinds of
circumstances. *"Barbara,* out of Westport, U.S.A., British
crew, sir, bound for Haifa from Kyrenia," my voice crashed
through the blinding light.

"Right, *Barbara,* you pass, you'll be met outside the port."
My eyes followed her after-gun, which in turn seemed to

follow my eyes. "Bon voyage!" shouted the electronic voice. The gunboat roared away at high speed in the direction of Lebanon. In *Barbara* tension collapsed like a rubber dinghy when you need it badly.

We plodded on through the beauty of the Levantine night towards Haifa. At the harbor entrance we were met and escorted in by the harbor police under the ever-watchful eye of the Israeli navy. As we slid in through the harbor entrance we could see sentries at every lamppost, while all the naval vessels seemed to be fully manned, in a state of active preparedness for anything.

By 1970 Israel had extended her enclave over Palestine and the Sinai. During the Six Day War she had shocked her Arab neighbors into a state of self-paralysis. She now commanded the Jordan west bank and the Sinai Peninsula. She had overcome, for the time being at any rate, the Arab attempts to cut her only line of communication with the East—the Strait of Tiran, at the southern end of the Gulf of Aqaba, Israel's outlet to the Red Sea. She was always vulnerable to the Arab guerrilla raids across her borders, especially from Jordan, but apart from the explosive pinpricks, often bloody and murderous, the situation, when *Barbara* arrived, was quieter than had been the case for some years, or was likely to be again, once the Arabs recovered from their Six Day War trauma. Now was the time for me to get to the Dead Sea, cross over the Negev Desert and slide down the Gulf of Aqaba into the Red Sea and so out into the comparatively safe Indian Ocean.

2
THE BELEAGUERED LAND

HEN *BARBARA* ARRIVED IN Haifa I had no idea about how to go about hauling the boat to the Dead Sea, or how to get the necessary permits. Like arctic navigation, it would all be "by guess and by God." When I walked into the harbormaster's office and told the clerks that I would like permission to transport my vessel to 'En Gedi on the Dead Sea, to cruise for a few days, they looked at me as if I was stark raving mad. Then, with a sheaf of forms about three inches thick to fill out, I walked despondently back to *Barbara* through the cold Haifa rain.

The weather in Israel during the winter, at least on the Mediterranean side, is very changeable, on some days cold and rainy with northerly winds, on other days balmy and sunny, with the wind blowing from the west, off the sea.

"When you run afoul of bureaucracy keep cool and go for a sail," I always believed, so I arranged to go about ten miles up the coast to visit the ancient port of Acre for a couple of days. I wanted to see the ruins and trace ancient battles.

After a sedate couple of hours' sail up the coast, Conrad and I entered the rock-littered harbor, ancient as Israel itself, and anchored out in the middle, for the port is shallow all round the jetties. In the hot afternoon we set to work, Conrad dismantling and easing one of the sheet-winches, which was stiff, while I touched up odds and ends of the cockpit paintwork. Around us several high-speed power-boats were setting up annoying bow waves, rocking the boat uncomfortably. Presently several people came swimming around the boat in masks and fins, shouting and laughing in a language which I took to be German. After a while they became bolder, coming right up to *Barbara*'s bottom and tapping. Tap, tap, knock, knock, bubbles, and gasps. Nothing could be more annoying.

"Get out the antifrogman gear, Conrad."

"Right, Skip. Which side?"

"There's a great big fat one right under the starboard side."

Conrad dove into the deckgear box and came out with a sign, a small plank nailed to a broomstick. He lowered it over the side, right in front of a particularly noisy and chunky swimmer. The swimmer turtled his way up to the sign, underwater, and stared at it through his mask.

"Bugger off!"

With an explosion of bubbles the swimmer surfaced, gasping and laughing.

"Gut afternoon!"

"Hello, mate!"

"You've just got to be English!"

"That's right, how did you guess?"

"I read your sign." He reached out his hand. I grabbed it and gave him a hearty shake. He couldn't stop laughing. "Let me introduce myself," he gasped, "Commander **Berenson**, Israeli navy, permission to come aboard?"

"Tristan Jones, Liverpool, Tramway Driver's Club. Of course, come aboard, we're just about to have a noggin. Sun's almost over the yardarm—watch the wet paint."

He climbed onboard and, seamanlike, headed forward, away from where the painting had been done. That impressed me right away. Here was no landlubber.

Although Commander **Berenson** must have weighed at least 180 pounds there was not an ounce of fat on him. The most striking thing about him was his eyes, mountain grey and piercing. Here was a man that anyone would think twice about tackling. He had been trained in the Royal Navy and a couple of years previously had taken part in the clandestine departure from Cherbourg of six gunboats which the French government had forbidden to sail to Haifa. Gedi was a sabra—Israeli-born—and like most of his kind was highly intelligent and ready for any enterprise, no matter how desperate or impossible it might seem.

Over a bottle of Johnnie Walker it was arranged that the Israeli navy would take me under its wing and get my boat to the Dead Sea. Not only that, but they would haul it to the Gulf of Aqaba. Previously they had hauled three small gunboats over the desert, but never before had a foreign, privately owned vessel been transported from the Mediterranean to the Gulf of Aqaba. Until now, there had been no need for it, for prior to the Six Day War a craft would have used the Suez Canal, and, anyway, who was crazy enough to attempt the passage of the reef- and pirate-ridden Red Sea?

Conrad and I hove out of Jaffa and returned to the naval base in Haifa aglow with anticipation. After three weeks of argument with the clerks in the port offices we had succeeded in bypassing all the bullshit.

On Monday, another day of sleet and cold wind, Gedi's friend, Adir, turned up. He was the boss of a haulage firm. He was small, thick, and very tough indeed. Nothing was impossible for him. He was accompanied by two others—Francois, a deep-sea diver, born in Marseille; and Jacob, a large, jolly truck driver with the biggest beer-belly I've ever seen. In 1937 Jacob had walked from Istanbul to Israel. He spoke no English, only a strange kind of Spanish handed down from the Jews who were thrown out of Spain in 1492—a very curious accent, but I could understand him. The cost involved in the haul was six hundred dollars.

By noon they had measured up *Barbara* underwater, welded up a steel cradle, conjured up a heavy mobile crane, extracted *Barbara*'s mast, lifted her out of the Mediterranean, and placed her on the cradle. This was in turn fixed to the bed of a giant tank-transporter, to which was connected a great diesel tractor.

The following morning, with the rain pouring down, the convoy set off for 'En Gedi. On Adir's ancient station wagon—incredibly shoddy, rusty, with one mudguard missing—he had a huge red flag streaming from the aerial. Behind it was the tractor pulling the great tank-transporter with *Barbara* sitting atop it. Conrad and I sat on the end of the flatbed keenly watching the wedges forced between *Barbara*'s hull and the sharp edges of the steel cradle.

We flashed our way down a modern superhighway from Haifa to Tel Aviv, through orange groves and market gardens, past ancient, dreaming Caesarea, Hadera, Petah Tiqwa, Lod, and Ramla. All the way the Israelis, an intensely curious people, stared at the strange load, many raising a cheer as we lumbered past. The Arabs sitting on the walls took no notice, or pretended to take no notice.

Every now and then, with the constant shaking, a wedge would fly out and the whole circus would halt. A combined Anglo-Israeli sledgehammer team would fall onto the culprit timber and bang it back into place. Jacob, with his immense strength, would give the wedge an extra slam for luck. Cars rushed past, horns blared, people yelled at the top of their voices. Fortunately for us, the road was flat and smooth.

At nightfall we reached Bethlehem. Adir suggested we spend the night there. Conrad and I were grateful, for it had been a long, tiring day of unaccustomed jolting, noise, and fumes. Besides, it was Christmas Eve.

The tank-transporter was parked by the bus station and we all regaled ourselves with food and beer. Adir and his gang, upon entering the clean, modern, self-service restaurant, made straight for the kosher section, while we British sailors, being gentiles, made do with any old thing. We had a fine time, with Adir spinning yarns about some of the salvage jobs he had performed for the navy. Later, merry on beer, Jacob sang songs of Istanbul, while Francois talked over the pop music scene with Conrad. Upon our return to *Barbara* I opened up a can of Christmas pudding from England which I had saved especially for the occasion, and everyone had a share. So we celebrated Christmas, chatting in five languages, in Bethlehem, in a land sacred to us all, with an ocean-going sailing craft. A very special occasion, in the cold desert air, under the stars gleaming in the velvet-black night sky. Adir told us that shepherds still slept in the hills.

On Christmas morning, we were up bright and early. Soon we were out of Bethlehem, driving along in the clear desert air. The climate in winter in this part of the Middle East is probably the finest in the world—dry, never above seventy-five degrees Fahrenheit by day nor below sixty-five at night. In the desert cacti bloom, and among the arid stretches kibbutzim, Israeli desert agricultural settlements, green and inviting, flash like shoulder decorations on a khaki uniform.

Our convoy trundled south, through Hebron's market gardens, out across the dry and forbidding hills of Judea. Then we dropped down and down, into the Jordan valley along a rough rock and sand track, until at last, in the bright of noon, we sighted the Dead Sea, glistening dully under a strange, low cloud. Above the cloud, away to the east, we could see the Moabite escarpment and beyond that, Jordan itself. *Barbara* was now at 1,300 feet below the level of the Mediterranean, lower than any other unsunken ocean vessel in the world. We had reached the first of our "impossible" destinations!

But the best laid schemes o' mice and men gang aft a-gley. The Israeli government, despite the best efforts of our naval friends, was adamant in its refusal to allow *Barbara* to be launched on the Dead Sea. The owner, back in Connecticut, knew little of our position, although I have no doubt whatsoever that Arthur would have been with us in our intentions. It seemed that further communication with Arthur would have been futile and delay in reaching the Red Sea would have been critical owing to the weather circumstances further south. I therefore settled for a short passage in a small sailing craft, provided through the good offices of one of our naval friends, from 'En Gedi to Masada.

3
THE DEAD SEA

HE DEAD SEA IS ABOUT AS strange a place as I have ever come across. It has a length of 47 miles and a breadth of 10, a surface area of around 360 square miles. The mean depth is 1,080 feet. It gets all its water from the River Jordan, which daily pours into it about *six million* tons, most of which is evaporated by the hot sun, forming a permanent low mist over the lake, a peculiar cloud, blue-white, the color of a dead fish's bel'y. The Dead Sea is the saltiest in the world, consisting of around 25 percent salts, compared to the ocean's average of around 6 percent. The water, if you swallow any, is nauseous; a tablespoonful will make you violently sick. This is because of the great amounts of chloride of magnesium in the salts. It also has an oily feel because of the calcium, of which it contains a high amount. When you wade out from the shore, you are swept off your feet as soon as the water level reaches your armpits; your shoulders are continually out of the water. When the water dries on your skin, it leaves a sticky feeling, as if you had been swimming in kerosene.

There is absolutely no life in the Dead Sea. No fish, no birds, nothing, except in the far north, where the fish brought down by the Jordan River die as soon as they enter the Dead Sea waters and are devoured by the few sea gulls. The rocky shore is littered with patches of asphalt, which float up from the bottom of the Sea. On the whole, it is one of the most arid, uninviting places on earth.

Curiously enough, geologists maintain that millions of years ago, during the Pluvial period, the Dead Sea was much bigger, stretching another 120 miles further north, with a level *above* that of the Mediterranean. It was capable of supporting life of every variety, but earthquakes and gradual silting filled up the former vast inland seabed.

The Dead Sea, as we call it, has been known by many

other names. To the Hebrews it was "The Sea of Arabah," to the Arabs "The Stinking Sea," to the modern Israeli "The Sea of Lot." The Old Testament comes to life here—Lot and Abraham visited these shores and the sinful towns of Sodom and Gomorrah were on its edge. The ruins are still there for all to see.

During the passage from 'En Gedi to Masada I had slight winds from the north, and in fact made the passage back to 'En Gedi using the outboard motor, for I was anxious to pass on with *Barbara* to the Red Sea.

I had taken an ocean-going vessel lower than anyone else on earth. Only government regulations had prevented her from sailing on the Dead Sea. Now all I had to do was navigate the boat to Lake Titicaca, three miles up in the far off Andes of South America.

The diesel tractor hauled *Barbara* once more over the escarpment on the edge of the hills of Judea to Hebron, then turned south and headed for Beersheba, a modern, very Western town plonked down by Israeli ingenuity in the heart of the desert. Here we saw our last supermarket until we reached South Africa, almost a year later.

Once through Beersheba we entered the Negev Desert and barreled off down the road to Eilat on a modern highway which passes for much of its length within five miles of the Jordanian border. In those days it was much subjected to raids by guerrillas, whose favorite trick was to suspend a grenade-festooned line across the road.

With brakes squealing, the trailer cautiously crawled around hairpin bends, *Barbara* sometimes heeling over twenty degrees and more. As dusk fell, we would pick out here and there the glow of an Israeli army campfire and, less frequently, kibbutzim, brightly lit, like liners on the ocean sea.

Conrad and I were by now becoming accustomed to each other's company; a difficult thing for two Britons at the best of times, especially when they hail from such disparate backgrounds. Especially when one of them has so very much to absorb from the other in a very short time. A serious undertaking, for our lives would be at stake.

"We must check over the engine before we leave Eilat," I

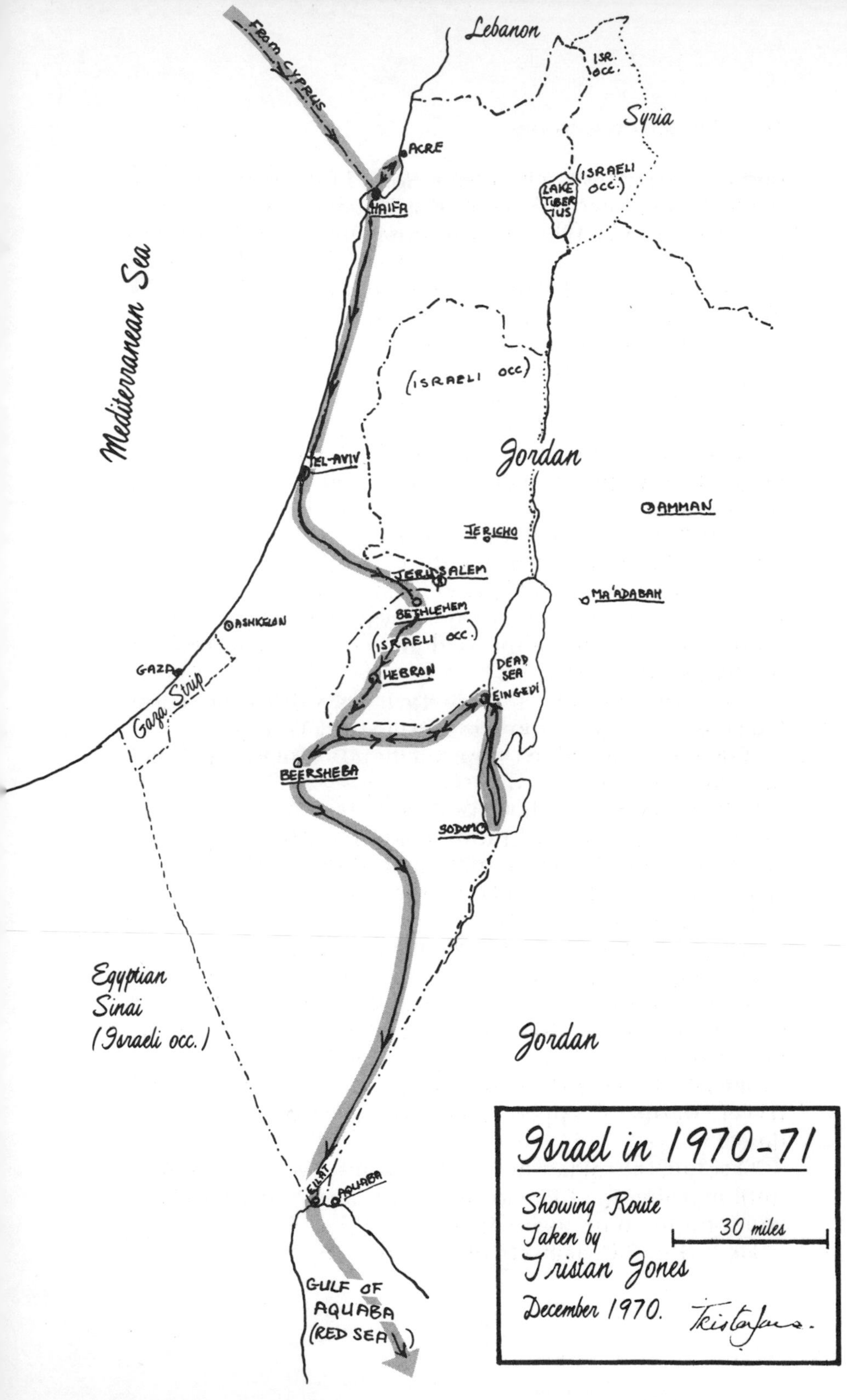

Lebanon

Syria

From Cyprus

ISR. OCC.

ACRE

LAKE TIBERIUS

(ISRAELI OCC.)

HAIFA

Mediterranean Sea

(ISRAELI OCC)

Jordan

TEL-AVIV

JERICHO

⊙AMMAN

JERUSALEM

BETHLEHEM

⊙MA'ADABAH

⊙ASHKELON

(ISRAELI OCC.)

GAZA

HEBRON

DEAD SEA

Gaza Strip

EIN GEDI

BEERSHEBA

SODOM

Egyptian Sinai (Israeli occ.)

Jordan

EILAT

AQUABA

GULF OF AQUABA (RED SEA)

Israel in 1970-71

Showing Route
Taken by

30 miles

Tristan Jones

December 1970.   Tristan Jones.

said to Conrad, as we bounced along in the gloaming.

"Just up my street; my van was diesel driven."

"What van was that? You never mentioned a truck before."

"Oh, didn't I tell you? My last job, oh, ages ago, was driving a small truck up and down the Thames valley delivering candy to tobacconists' shops."

"Jesus Christ!" I thought, "and this is the bloke I'm takin' into the Red Sea—a bloody candy-truck driver. Oh, well, why not? He seems to be doing OK so far." But I kept quiet as he continued, for on the back of the Israeli truck he was more talkative than I had ever seen him before, or since, come to that.

"And I used to do most of my own repairs," he continued.

"Oh, did you? That'll be handy, Conrad; all I know about a diesel is that it goes *suck, squeeze, bang, blow* and that's about it; they usually clap out on me anyway; can't stand them— noisy, smelly, and take up food and water space—I detest the blasted things!"

"My grandmother on my father's side came from Czechoslovakia just after the First World War—"

"Oh, fuck, go on, don't stop, tell me all about it; a real load of sailors they are."

"What about you?" he asked.

"Well, matey, on my granny's side I'm descended from Henry Morgan, the pirate, and on my father's side, from an illegitimate son of the Duke of Wellington."

"That's impressive, Skip!"

"Yes, a right pair of bastards we are, aren't we?"

He laughed again as he lit my cigarette.

By nine in the evening we were at the last Israeli army post before starting down a long stretch of road leading to Eilat and the sea. The convoy stopped at the checkpoint and Adir walked back to the rear, where Conrad and I sat on the trailer, warmly wrapped against the cool night air of the desert.

"Tristan, the soldier he say I tell you . . . you want to wait until morning for Army convoy with many guns, OK, but you want to go on now, OK too."

He puffed his cigarette nervously.

"The nightclub in Eilat, she close at 2:00 A.M.; maybe we go now, eh?" He threw away his cigarette and looked me straight in the eye. "It's a bit dangerous," he continued, "sometimes Arabs come over the border; but staying here all night . . ." He gestured at the lonely tents and the campfire.

"Well, Adir, it's all right with me to go on. We'll take things as they come."

He smiled. "You're not afraid to die at night then?"

"What's the difference, night or day? I once saw a man who was killed by peanuts in broad daylight."

Francois, who had joined us by now, after relieving himself at the roadside, explained to Adir what peanuts were. They looked at me quizzically, while Conrad sat there with a big grin on his face, for by now he was becoming accustomed to my odd tales at odd times.

"True as I'm sitting here on this trailer in the Negev Desert," I replied to their looks. "It was in Le Havre, in France, and they were unloading a cargo ship full of peanuts with one of those suction pipe things. Well, this bloke was walking under the pipe when—woosh!—it broke, busted clean open and down fell about two hundred tons of peanuts on the poor chap's head. They had to scrape him up with a shovel." I made a gesture of shoveling with my hand. "Now, which is better to die from, a grenade or bullet, or *bloody peanuts?*"

They were all laughing by now. Adir and Francois laughed all the way back to the lead car. Off we went through the barrier and out into the dark desert. Conrad was still grinning and glancing at me.

There was no sense in offering a slow target to any lurking terrorists, so we roared away at sixty miles an hour, Conrad and I holding on like grim death to the lurching, rolling trailer, straining our eyes in the darkness to watch the wedges, hoping and praying that they would not work loose. There would be no stopping on this stretch, fallen wedges or not.

So we crossed the pitch-black Negev Desert at high speed, until at last we sighted the light-loom of the Aqaba lighthouse away to the south across the rocky, moonlit plain.

Suddenly we were in the sandy streets of Eilat. We were on the shores of the Red Sea; we had actually crossed over Asia. We had passed from the sea of Ulysses and the *Odyssey* and we were now in the realm of the *Thousand and One Nights* and Sinbad himself. Later, as we watched the floor show in a shabby nightclub, I thought to myself, "Now all we have to do is run the Arab gauntlet for six thousand miles to Mombasa!" But I said nothing to Conrad. He was enjoying himself far too much for forebodings.

Early next morning we floated *Barbara* and said goodbye to Adir, Francois, and Jacob.

4
THE HOSTILE SEA

SRAEL SITS AT THE HUB of the Afro-Eurasian landmass. To the west she faces Europe across the Mediterranean. On two sides she is pressed between the jaws of Arab hostility—jaws held open by her army, like a stick in a crocodile's mouth.

To the south is the port of Eilat, Israel's only outlet to the Eastern world, which gives access to the two-thousand-mile-long Red Sea and the Gulf of Aden, along the shores of which the enemies of Israel sit in sulking hostility in all but three places.

Massawa and Assab, two of the three safe ports at the time we passed, were in Ethiopia, almost a thousand miles to the south of Israeli-held Sinai. Ethiopia at this time was ruled by Haile Selassie, King of Kings, Lion of Judah, descendant of Solomon and the Queen of Sheba. His authority extended for about five miles outside the two ports and as far as a bullet could travel from the heavily armed military convoys that made their way along the two road tracks which fell nine thousand feet down from the inland plain to the hot, disease-ridden coast.

Where the emperor could not rule, the Eritrean Liberation Front did. Supplied by arms and gold from the Far East by way of the People's Republic of Yemen, their ancient piracy, rooted in untold generations of bloody skulduggery, was, in 1970, called "revolution." In swift dzambouks and dhows they preyed on hapless fishermen and cached their weapons in ancient cisterns on the barren reefs of the Red Sea shores.

Massawa—the hottest inhabited place on earth, a stinking hellhole, the home of starvation and disease—was haven number one. Assab—just as hot, the worst port in the world—number two. Djibouti—an armed French oasis in a murderous desert—number three. From there it was two thousand miles on a straight course to the next friendly port—Mombasa!

In between, fanatics watched the shore with patient, inexhaustible hatred, waiting with bullets and sharpened knives.

Apart from all this, there was the wind, an *alien* wind that blew against us all the way for three thousand miles, from the northeast cape of Africa, stormy Guardafui, to two hundred miles south of the Sinai Peninsula. As if this wasn't enough, a contrary current flowed against us all the way from the Indian Ocean at an average of four knots, slap-bang on the nose.

"One thing's for sure, Conrad," I said as we sat on the jetty at Eilat, "the Arabs know we're here and they know where we're going. We must run the gauntlet from here to Djibouti and then from Djibouti to Mombasa. It's a hell of a long way."

As we talked an Israeli soldier lobbed grenades into the harbor, to guard against Arab frogmen.

"But surely, Tristan, with this northerly wind we should have an easy passage down to Mombasa?"

"This northerly will only last down to latitude twenty-seven. Then it's southerlies, and we're going to have to beat the pants off *Barbara* because the *north*-east monsoon out in the Indian Ocean turns to east when it enters the Gulf of Aden. Then it blows like hell through the Bab al Mandab straits, where it becomes a *south*-east wind, and that blows seven bells of shit straight up to the Sudanese border. This ain't going to be no bloody garden party."

"Bab al Mandab," Conrad said, "what does that mean?"

"Gate of Tears," I replied, "and the Arabs don't name places without reason. The old dhow skippers must have given it that name, trying to reach the favorable monsoon winds out in the Indian Ocean. They must have gone through bloody purgatory in those barren reaches, with the wind howling away like that. There's a *minimum* of forty knots of wind there in the winter months—continuous!"

"So you think it will be a rough trip, Tristan?"

"Hazardous, Conrad, bloody dangerous, in fact, and I tell you if you want to pull out, now's the place to do it and I won't think any the less of you."

"No bloody fear." His eyes lit up. "I wouldn't miss this little picnic for anything."

"Even the Arabs have a hard time sailing in the Red Sea," I commented.

"Yes, but that was in those Arab dhows," Conrad scoffed. "They must sail like cows—sideways."

"Don't you believe it. The Arabs *discovered* how to sail to windward, and they're still good at it. That's why they were in the East Indies while the Britons were still drifting around the English Channel in wickerwork coracles."

The Israeli soldier lobbed another grenade into the harbor, disturbing the tranquility of the hot afternoon.

"That change of wind at latitude twenty-seven north, that's interesting," I said, "because that's why the Pharaohs of ancient Egypt couldn't thrust their power further down into Africa. You see they could only sail with the wind, being square rigged. They never could reach the Bab al Mandab. For the same reason, the Romans only penetrated as far as the Sudanese border. But the Greeks, well, they must have somehow rowed against the wind, for they got down as far as Zanzibar. One of them, I forget his name, is supposed to have sailed right around Africa. Or maybe it was a Phoenician."

We sat silently for a few minutes under a palm tree, staring into the distance toward the far-off port of Aqaba, over the Jordanian frontier. It might as well have been on the moon.

"Conrad, we're all stored up, so we'll get water on board this evening and be off at first light tomorrow."

"Right, Skip. Any idea of the long-term plan yet, I mean the course we're going to take to get to Peru?"

"Peru? Let's not even think about that yet. I'll be content to fetch Mombasa in one piece. Once we get there we can make plans. I've got a load of charts coming there from London, both for the trans-Pacific route and for round the Cape of Good Hope."

"Big job, eh, Skip?"

"Yes, but you know, patience and perseverance. . .!"

The next morning I went around to the immigration

office and customs to clear out of Israel, then back onboard for a last check of all the sailing gear and the engine. Then we were off; first stop, Sharm el Sheikh, at the southern tip of the Sinai Peninsula, at present occupied by the Israeli armed forces.

The northerly breeze blows eternally in the Gulf of Aqaba, just as it did in the days of the Queen of Sheba, whose rowers strained against it to carry her north to King Solomon forty centuries ago.

Here we saw our first coral reefs since departing from Bermuda. They fringe the shores of the Gulf, their edges marked in color from turquoise to deep emerald green. Above the brilliant emerald loomed the bright orange glow of the desert coastal plain. Beyond that, the smoky blues and browns of the Sinai coastal mountains towered above the desert shore. Beautiful . . . and dead; not a bird, not a tree, not a blade of grass; nothing but lifeless, brilliant, hot color.

We pressed *Barbara* on under all working sail, roller jib, main and mizzen, running free and fast before the wind, bound for the Strait of Tiran. After a few miles the sea livened up, mounting steeper and steeper, and the steering became harder, for a shoal-draught boat such as *Barbara* will always try to slew much more than a deep-keeled traditional type of ocean runner. Conrad and I took two-hour watches at the wheel to ease the strain. I would not lessen the sails one inch, for I wanted to be clear of Aqaba waters by nightfall, when we would be safe from roving Arab craft.

"Pity we don't have a wind-vane steerer, Skip," gasped Conrad after a two-hour spell.

"Yes, and two million dollars, and a yacht in the Bahamas," I replied as I took over the kicking wheel.

"I'll have arms like King Kong by the time we reach Massawa," groaned Conrad, settling down in the shade of the sails.

"Suit your face, then, won't they?"

In the light of the false dawn early next morning, we slid through the Strait of Tiran, littered with coral reefs and wrecks, hardly any marked on the charts. We conned the boat through the coral and sandbanks by eye, thinking how

lucky we had been not to attempt it during the dark hours
and wondering if this was a portent of things to come.

On 10 January we passed out into the Red Sea, into
comparatively unrestricted waters. We had run one
hundred miles down—only nine hundred to go for Massawa in a straight line.

Over to the east, as we emerged from the Strait of Tiran,
lay Arabia and the plain of El Tihama. Beyond that the
Shafat mountain range rose up to the north. We could
almost hear the drumbeats of Lawrence's camel as he raced
north to Aqaba, to victory, disillusion, and despair.

So to Sharm el Sheikh, turning west on a broad reach,
along the southern shore of the Sinai. We hoisted the mizzen staysail, and with huge genoa, mainsail, mizzen staysail,
and mizzen straining like hounds, *Barbara* flew along like a
train. This was to be the last time we would have all fair
weather sail until we reached the Indian Ocean over two
months later. For the rest of that time we would beat directly into the wind, mostly under storm, or at least gale
conditions.

The anchorage for civilian vessels was at Mars-el-At, four
miles to the east of the naval base at Sharm el Sheikh, in
three fathoms, sand and weed, due south of a bloody
pneumatic dining hall! There on that stark, barren shore, the
Israelis had planted a caravan holiday camp!

Conrad and I rowed ashore and ate a meal with tourists
from a dozen countries, enjoying the ninety-eight-degree
heat of January. No one questioned our presence, even
though we were the first yacht to visit that area since before
World War II! No one remarked on the boat, even though
the last yacht in the whole of the Red Sea had passed
through more than ten years previously. I believe that if a
flying saucer had landed at el-At no one would have
blinked. A table would have been set out for the visitors and
they would have been sold souvenirs and allocated a sleeping caravan. I have no idea to this day why these people
were this way; however, it suited me fine, for I'm not partial
to fuss and palaver, especially before a difficult passage.

The organization of this holiday camp was a wonder to
behold. Vegetables and fruits were flown in from Tel Aviv

to the military airfield at Sharm el Sheikh. From our anchorage we watched Bedouin camel trains trundle through the caravan park, while overhead Israeli Mirage fighters waved around the steel-blue sky, keeping watch over the Egyptians away to the west, only minutes' flying time away. We stared at the sight, two phenomena thousands of years apart, yet there they were, for real, together in the desert.

"What time are we sailing, Skip?" Conrad asked.

"Nightfall. There's not much moon tonight, and I want to be well clear of Sinai by dawn. We'll keep a wary eye open for any Egyptian craft lurking about there. The navy base says they'll watch out for us on their radar for anything approaching, but that can only be effective for a hundred miles or so. After that, we're strictly on our own until Massawa, eight hundred miles further on, and most of that to windward."

"When do you think we'll fetch Massawa?"

"We'll allow for two weeks," I said. "That should be more than ample. There aren't any ports we can use before Massawa without risk of imprisonment or getting our throats slit. Any vessel which has passed through Israel has every Arab hand against her. The Red Sea is narrow, so there's not much sea room, not with the reefs sticking out from the shore sixty miles and more, and since the Suez Canal has been closed for a couple of years there's a good chance that the navigational aids are all out of action. Sandstorms will obscure the sky and make a joke of celestial navigation. We don't know what the currents are, nor their strength or direction. All we know is that most of the reefs and shoals are incorrectly charted. This isn't going to be a *picnic*. But we've one consolation—once we *do* reach the Indian Ocean, then the world's our oyster. Here, have a look at the map."

"Considering all these masses of reefs jutting out from the shores of the Red Sea, Skip, how about if we stick to the middle?"

"Fine, Conrad, as long as you know you *are* in the middle. But with high winds blowing sand all over the place, and us unable to get a fix, and these treacherous unknown currents setting us east or west or whatever for a whole day or night, it's not going to be easy."

"Yes, Skip, I see what you mean . . . but knowing you after these months I trust you to get us through, and I'm willing to take things as they come. If we come a cropper—well, we'll have at least had a go."

I looked at his dark eyes and sunburnt face. Here was a real find, a brave lad; fast developing into a true sailorman. Honest and straightforward with the heart of a lion. To watch the steady, gradual transformation from an insecure youth searching for his identity to a careful, practical man was for me an absorbing experience. Educated by Quakers in Buckingham, he had responded eagerly to my tutelage, even though I drove him hard at times.

"What's Quaker education like, then, Conrad?" I asked him, as he stowed food carefully in dry places around the galley.

"Oh, all right, I suppose. The place I went to was one of these more or less free schools, where you can do much as you please—you know, choose your own subjects and when to attend classes, all that kind of thing."

"Sounds more like a bloody Portuguese parliament to me. Did you learn anything?"

"Not much; and anyway, in the end it came to the same thing as most other people; the importance of being a success."

"What's success?"

"To most people, making money," he replied in a low voice.

"And to you?"

"To be part of the world. Why, what is it to you?"

"Getting into harbor in one bloody piece and knocking back a few pints in good company; keeping dry and three square meals a day."

"What about nature?" He was still very serious.

"Whose? Mine or yours?"

"You know, all this ocean and wind, the natural forces."

"Bugger 'em. Oh, they're all right, but most of the time all they've given me is a bloody hard, uncomfortable existence!"

"Then why do you do it?"

"Someone has to, doesn't he?"

"Masochism?"

"Don't give me any of your Austro-Hungarian Freudian bullshit!"

He laughed and shook his head. "You're crazy!" he said.

"Yes, I know, I always wanted a nine-to-five job; my secret ambition is to be a London bank clerk!"

"I can just see you walking over London Bridge in a derby hat, toting a briefcase; that would just suit you!" He grinned at me.

"I'd embezzle the bloody lot, mate, and have it away on my toes for Rio as fast as Christ would let me!"

"Mmm, me too," he replied.

"That's what comes of free schools!"

"Damned right, Skip!" He placed the last can of corned beef into a locker after carefully marking it on our stores list. "I'd go and live on a nature reserve myself."

"Yeah, Battersea Dogs' Home!"

"Oh hell," he replied, "where's the blasted case of beans?"

That evening, as soon as dusk fell, we bade farewell to our friends at the Israeli naval base, hoisted anchor, and slunk off into the gloom of the southern horizon to run the Arab gauntlet.

5
RUNNING THE GAUNTLET

UR FIRST NIGHT OUT WAS spent running free with the mainsail winged out on one side of the mast and the big genoa poled out on the other. The anchor was safely lashed down on the fo'c's'le, all lights were downed, the taffrail log was set out over the stern, a coffeepot was on the stove, and away we rolled, with the wind coming from directly astern, straight down from the high desolate mountains of the Sinai.

As *Barbara* sailed away from the coast the fetch of the sea increased, and with it our movement, so that by midnight we were wallowing violently. The sky was clear, with no moon, but Venus was setting in the west, twice the size she appears in normal ocean skies. Millions of bright stars gleamed overhead. It was all very beautiful, but we would have preferred overcast and even rain, for we were most anxious to avoid being seen by Arab craft, whether military or civilian. The Israelis had warned us in no uncertain terms what would happen to us if we were to encounter an Egyptian naval vessel.

About two o'clock in the middle of the night Conrad went below to make more coffee and reappeared shortly on deck.

"Lot of water in the bilge, Skip." He looked worried.

"OK, take over, mate; I'll take a look."

He took over the wheel and I went below to search for the leak. Searching a fully loaded boat thirty-eight-feet long while she wallows away, running off the wind, isn't much fun. You have to crawl through the bottom of the boat, raising floorboards and opening every small stowage compartment by the light of a flashlight. It needs all the perseverance and patience you can muster, as well as a cast-iron stomach and a thorough knowledge of the boat.

Whenever someone, usually standing on a jetty in the pleasant morning sunshine, looks down into my cockpit and after greetings and gossip about this and that says that he envies me because I don't have any cares or worries and can just take off into the setting sun without a problem in the world, I always smile to myself. What does this person know of the intricate preparation, the minute attention to the smallest details that goes into getting a small craft ready for the ocean. Overlooking even one significant point could very well result in disaster or even death. What does that person know of the careful, cautious attention paid to storing the boat with every possible item for any foreseeable accident or occurrence? What does he know of studying how to take out one's own teeth, or, if necessary, one's own appendix? The long-distance sailor is his own lawyer, doctor, engineer, plumber, carpenter, dentist, and diplomat. In many remote parts of the world navigational aids such as lights and radio beacons are nonexistent.

But try as he will to cover every detail before sailing, it often happens that the voyager can miss something, or that a defect can develop on the voyage, which was our case.

Barbara, being fiberglass, had had her hull distorted slightly while being lifted with the crane in Eilat harbor. The lifting cables had compressed the hull at the point where the engine-cooling water-inlet was located. The bolts holding the seacock to the hull had bent slightly, and water was now, after she had worked in the sea for several hours, passing in between the flange of the seacock and the hull at a good rate.

Apart from easing the motion by reefing down the genoa, there was little I could do for the moment. I carefully tapped in some caulking fiber between the seacock and the hull, very delicately, for to sheer one of the bolts would have been disastrous. This eased the leak to a trickle. I then sat down in the cabin and shut everything out of my mind but this problem.

To head back for the Sinai would have been one solution, but it would mean beating directly into the wind for two or even three days, and the motion of a sailing boat beating to windward is much more violent, for she is continuously crashing into headseas. This might cause the seacock to sheer from the hull. This was a chance I could not afford to take. Besides I'm always reluctant to turn back once on a course.

I fished out the chart from the navigation cuddy (where it was kept rolled up under cover to guard against spray) and inspected it. About fifty miles to the south of us lay two small islets, the Brothers Islands. If we could gain the protection of the lee of one of them, we would have a good chance to repair the leak in comparative calm and security. I looked up the islands in the *Admiralty Pilot for the Red Sea* and found that they were supposed to be uninhabited and that there was a lighthouse on the northernmost island, but the pilot book was dated 1952—eighteen years out of date. With the Suez Canal closed and hardly any shipping using the Red Sea, chances were that the lighthouse was now out of action. We scanned the south until dawn, but there was no loom (glare in the sky), no evidence of a lighthouse, nothing but the blackness of an empty night.

While Conrad pumped out the bilge to keep the water from sloshing around, I prepared to get a sunsight in order to fix, as near as possible, *Barbara*'s longitude, that is, the position of the north-south line on which she moved. It was no good taking a sunsight until the sun was at least twenty degrees above the eastern horizon, for in the heat of the Red Sea, even early in the morning, the amount of refraction and other distortion would lead to errors in obtaining the altitude of the sun and even greater errors in fixing our longitude. But in these latitudes, so near to the tropics, the sun rises fast, and by nine o'clock I had a good idea of our longitude (within five miles or so, allowing for distortion of the sun by the fine sand carried in the wind), and found we were directly north of the Brothers Islands, wallowing away at about four knots. The taffrail log indicated that we had sailed eighty-five miles so far; if there was no current against us or with us, this together with the longitude I had worked out, gave me a fairly exact position.

From this assumed position, I steered a course east-southeast by south, and after an hour the two islets appeared, gray shadows shimmering in the heat of the Red Sea. I decided to make for the northernmost of the islets and try to anchor on the southern side of it, out of the way of the wind and swell, which by this time had increased to a lively rate.

"Think there's anyone living there?" Conrad asked as we drank another mug of tea. *Barbara* was tossing violently by this time; the mid-morning wind, as usual in the Red Sea, was increasing to a full gale, whistling in the masts.

"I don't know," I said, "but there was no light last night. Chances are it's been abandoned. Anyway, the islets belong to Egypt. I can't imagine them having a military force of any size on them. They'd be sitting ducks for the Israeli navy if there was any trouble. No, Conrad, we'll have to take our chances because we must get this bloody leak fixed or we'll be pumping all the way to Massawa and that's days away to windward. Anyway, keep your eye on the level."

"Right on."

Steadily we drew nearer to the Brothers Islands. As I had no information about outlying reefs or depths, I gave the island a wide berth until we were at right angles to the south side of the rock. Then, turning sharply to port, on a broad reach in the strong north wind, we sailed in to the anchorage. I could not chance using the engine, in case any undue vibration might weaken the defective seacock bolts and shake them loose from the hull.

Keeping a sharp lookout forward for reefs and coral heads, we drew nearer. As we approached the islet I could see that the lighthouse appeared to be abandoned; rusty ironwork decorated the gallery, and there did not seem to be a soul around the iron-roofed huts standing near the column of the light.

"Doesn't seem to be anyone around, Tristan."

"Well, we'll soon find out—get the lead."

Conrad sounded *Barbara* into five fathoms of water. I luffed up into the wind (that is, faced the wind so the sails did not hold any wind pressure and shake loose). We were just about to drop the anchor when, suddenly, several figures ran out from the small buildings, crouched low. Some were in uniform, others in caftans, the long Arab "nightgowns" worn against the heat of day. They dove behind a low, whitewashed wall running across the hill, and opened fire. There must have been at least three machine guns and a dozen rifles all firing away from a range of about two hundred yards.

Bullets flew everywhere; Conrad, who had never seen a shot fired in anger before, turned and gaped at me in astonishment, gripping the anchor in his sunburned hands.

"What the fuck?" he shouted.

"Get back here, bloody fast!" I shouted, turning the wheel hard over to starboard, hoping the wind would catch the sails so they would fill and get us moving.

"Wh—what about the anchor, Skip?"

"Fuck the anchor! Get back here, you silly sod. Leave it on deck. For Christ's sake don't drop it over!"

But he was already back in the cockpit, crouched over and working the jib sheet winch. The firing continued in bursts. One round smashed into the pulpit, another clipped the mainmast just below the main halyard winch, two more passed through the mainsail.

"Bloody wretches!" murmured Conrad.

"Wretches be fucked—bastards!"

I peeped over the top of the cockpit, for by now *Barbara* was heeling over in the stiff breeze. There were no boats in evidence on the shore. After about five minutes, which seemed to us like an eternity, the firing faded and we zoomed away from the island like a cork out of a bottle, praying for more wind and cursing Egypt at the same time.

A couple of minutes later, crouched in the bottom of the steering well, our heads within an inch of each other, I turned round and found myself eyeball to eyeball with Conrad, sunburnt and sweaty, bearded and salt crusted. We stared at each other, then slowly the stares turned into grins, then smiles, then hoots and howls of laughter.

"Bloody bastards! Nightshirted, cholera-faced sons of bitches!" I roared.

Conrad quickly recovered both his sense of humor and his calm composure, but the Welsh blood was up in me and I sprang up to the mizzen shrouds and shook my fist at the far-off shore and swore blinding curses at Egypt, the Nile, the Pyramids, Nasser, Mohammed, the Aswan Dam, and anything else to do with that benighted country that I could think of.

"For God's sake, get down, Skip, they can't hear you."
Conrad was grinning. "What do we do now?" His calm voice
brought me down to thinking about our problems.

"Heave to as soon as we're out of their sight, then we'll
come back to the southern islet at dusk, get in the lee, make
a quick repair to the seacock and be off again by dawn.
There isn't anything on the southern rock, not even a hut.
Meanwhile I'll keep her going on this reach; you pump out.
And for God's sake, make us a cup of tea."

"Laced?"

"Just a little—no sense in getting half crocked here."

Off we went, with me sailing a straighter line than I've
ever sailed before, despite the heavy sea and the roaring
wind, out to the east, hoping and praying that there were no
Egyptian naval vessels around who might have picked up a
signal from our erstwhile friends on the island.

In two hours we had dropped the Brothers Islands astern
and hove to, that is, dropped all sails except the mizzen,
which we left up, or "bent," as we say, to hold the boat's bow
against the wind and the sea. All the time we kept a wary
lookout for signs of any vessel.

Sunsets in the Red Sea are a wondrous prism of color;
green sea, deep purple sky overhead, a blood-red horizon
shot with golden rays of sunlight. We wallowed away.

Just before dusk, having consumed a can of corned beef
and a pot of cold rice, I took a bearing on the southern rock
of the Brothers. We had approached very carefully just
near enough so I could sight it from the mast spreaders
after climbing up a twenty-foot mast with a hand-bearing
compass in a rough sea, and as darkness fell we made our
way in slowly. Coming up to the southern side of the rock we
were, of course, out of sight of anyone watching from the
main island. I couldn't use the engine, so it meant tacking to
the north in fairly heavy winds, making short boards so as to
remain obscured by the island.

"We won't drop the hook," I told Conrad. "We'll just
heave to in the lee, long enough for me to get a balk of
timber behind that seacock and, driving wedges between it
and the engine, force the seacock outwards, then tighten up
on the bolts. That should do the trick."

"Right, Skip. I'll watch her, but sing out if you need a hand."

"Keep your eye out for bloody Gyppos."

"Don't worry, I will!"

We dropped all sail behind the island, gently bobbing up and down about a hundred yards offshore, though distance is very difficult to judge in starlight. Conrad kept watch topsides while I disappeared below, with my heart in my mouth, and did the necessary. We then checked around the rigging and, apart from four bullet holes in the mainsail and a clipped pulpit and mainmast, found that things were good enough to tackle the windward passage to Massawa, about seven hundred miles as the crow flies to the south of us.

"Pity we ain't a crow, Skip," Conrad said.

"Bloody right, mate!"

6

AN ALIEN WIND

N 22 JANUARY *BARBARA* WAS two days south of the infamous Brothers Islands, and Conrad and I were becoming accustomed to long hours at the wheel, running free with the wind astern, which is always the hardest part of steering. But at least the leak was cured and we had plenty of food and fresh water, so all we had to do was keep her going south. We were forcing her hard, to get away from the Egyptian waters and the threat of discovery, and she was bowling along at up to seven knots in the high winds of the afternoon.

On the third day we sighted what appeared to be a low dark cloud stretching clear across the Red Sea east to west.

"Looks like a line squall," muttered Conrad, peering ahead.

"Line squall be blowed, that's a jet stream cloud. That's where the monsoon reaches up to the tropic. Shorten down the main, mate, I'll hoist the working jib. Then hold on to your hat, we're in for a dusting!"

"Christ!" he replied. "If you say that, it must be a bloody hurricane we're in for."

"*Hamseen*, mate!"

Sure enough, as we passed under the black cloud, the like of which I would not see again until I reached the River Plate five years later, the wind shifted completely around and we were soon headed into the teeth of a full gale. We stayed like that for another fourteen days and nights, in waters fraught with reefs, unknown currents, and the continuous threat of being sighted by pirates or terrorists.

The fourth, the fifth, the sixth days passed in weary labor, beating against steep seas and high winds, with the sand carried by the wind, a fine, dusty sand, seeping into every nook and cranny of the boat. By the seventh day I was beyond being merely concerned and had really started to worry. I had not had a good sight since passing the tropic, owing to the distortion of heavenly bodies caused by the sand dust.

"What do you think, Skip?" asked Conrad, calm as ever, his grubby fingers pointing at the sand-strewn chart. "Where do you think we are?"

"No idea," I replied. "All I know is where we're *not*, and that's in a good pub in London."

I looked at him, trying to appear unconcerned. "You stay on the wheel until dusk and I'll try to get another sextant shot or two. The sky seems to be clearing a bit, not so much sand around."

"And the best of luck!" he shouted.

"It's not just luck I need, it's a clear patch."

Miraculously, just as the darkness set in, I managed to get a snap shot of Polaris, low down on the northern horizon, with the waning moon rising in the east. A difficult job with the boat raring and pitching like a hobbyhorse in the short, violent sea, and the wind whistling away, but I had a fix. Down below, acrobatically guarding the sextant from being knocked in the companionway, I fished out the almanac, the sight tables, all the paraphernalia of the art of navigation, and set to work out the sights. I got a shock, for if they were correct, *Barbara* was slap-bang in the middle of the Suakin reefs, the most intricate maze of navigational hazards in the Red Sea! All around us were low coral reefs and islands, only a foot above sea level, with a full storm still blowing frantically aloft. The sea about *Barbara* was in a white frenzy. Not surprising, for we had inadvertently strayed right into the huge shallow banks of Suakin. On top of this I had no idea at all what the currents were doing. I sprang up the ladder.

"Right, Conrad, let's heave to, fast, or we'll be buying Sudanese real estate!" Just as I shouted, the jib rent asunder with a crack.

We handed down all the sail except the mizzen. A devil of a job, getting the jib in, for it was split right down the middle and flogging itself to death in the high wind, cracking like a machine gun. But patiently, tied to the pulpit with a lifeline, I managed to gather the flagging whips of sail and bundle it below.

Hove to, with *Barbara* jibing with a violent twisting motion, like a blind horse, we moved slowly astern. We unlashed the anchor on the bucking foredeck and stared into the frenzied blackness astern. If we sighted anything like a reef, I was ready to drop anchor, even if the violent snubbing of the chain dragged her foredeck off, or dismasted her, for that was our last chance of survival in that crazy, angry sea.

Somehow, faithful *Barbara* touched nothing all night. Surrounded by treacherous, jagged reefs, she slowly backed away through them. Dawn found us bleary-eyed but still alive, smashing up and down in shoal water, dirty yellow and menacing, with the steely blue sky of the desert glowing bitter orange all around the horizon.

"Holy smoke," said Conrad as, bone weary, he looked around him.

"Yeah, pretty sight, eh? Let's get the fuck out of here."

We set off, slowly working our way again into the wind, to the southeast, keeping careful watch ahead. I worked out, mainly by guess and intuition, our approximate position, and sure enough, after fifteen miles of backbreaking tacking, the Twin Rocks hove into view, jagged and murderous looking.

"Thank Christ we weren't here last night," I muttered.

We made our way to the waterless islet of Taller Saghir and somehow worked our way into its lee after an eight-hour struggle against wind and current. *Barbara* slid into calm water and we dropped the hook over the bow, with the gale blowing itself into a frenzy overhead. We lowered the sails, but left the burgee aloft as a sop to the double-devil Red Sea wind, which in short order tore it to shreds. Then we fell into an exhausted sleep.

Snug behind the low island reef, we let the gale blow all night and all the next day. The following day we fetched the islet, after taking careful sights of the sun. I found that it is, in fact, almost eight miles out of position on the Admiralty charts. The sea around it teems with fish and huge sharks, some of them up to fifteen feet long, while on the shore there are millions of sand crabs and a few skinny herons.

At all times during the daylight hours while we were at

this anchorage, one of us kept a careful eye open for any craft that might approach, and we were ready to hoist anchor at a moment's notice and clear off, for this was Sudanese territory.

In turns we explored the islet, rocky and barren under the blazing sun, and I left a note in a bottle on a cairn at the highest point. It is probably there still, if anyone is crazy enough to go look for it.

Next morning, refreshed, we set off to find our way out of this nightmare maze of reefs. I headed for the northeast, figuring that since that was the way we got in here, that was the way we would get out. I was right, for by late afternoon we were once again in clear blue water, having carefully and very slowly eyeballed our way out between the banks and reefs. We were again in deep water, and to us it looked beautiful, even if the gale was still blowing.

For another four days we drove *Barbara* heavily to windward, day and night, slam-banging against wicked short seas, carrying as much sail as we dared, our arms now as strong as steel rigging wires, through the hot wind and the eternal driving sand dust. *Barbara* shouldered the force of the sea, flung it aside, fought it, beat it, for on the twelfth day out of the Brothers Islands the wind dropped to a fair twenty knots and shifted around slightly to the east a few degrees, just enough so that we could belt on a close reach down a desolate, godforsaken, barren shore to find refuge and precious sleep behind the island of Difnein, the northernmost of the Dahlak Islands.

We were now within reasonable distance of Massawa, in Ethiopian waters, with a fairer wind after days of struggling and beating. In all those days we had never had a dry cockpit, and never, while underway, a moment's respite from the kicking wheel.

We raced a native dhow into Massawa harbor, but she was much bigger than *Barbara* so she beat us, but only just.

The distance from Mars-el-At to Massawa in a straight line is 890 miles. *Barbara* had sailed, according to the log, which, of course, takes no account of contrary currents, 1,824 miles on this passage, in sixteen days. Of this, at least a thousand miles was directly to windward. We were about

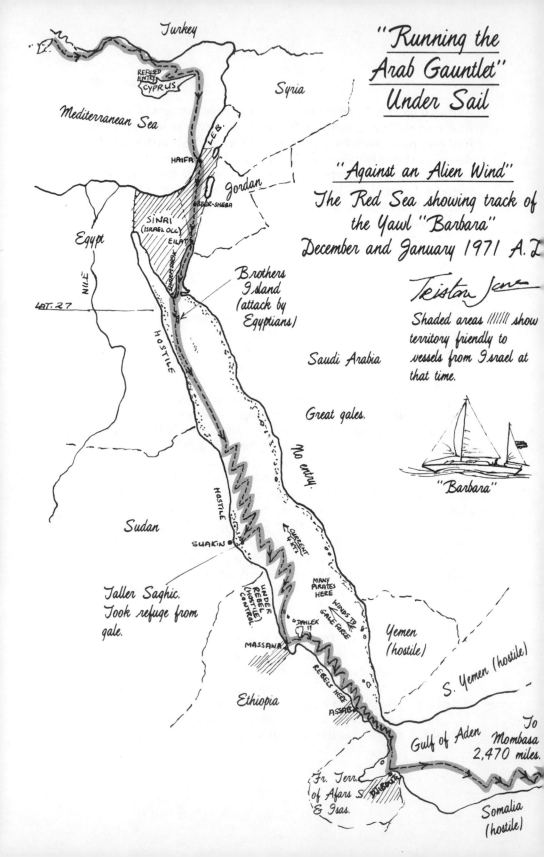

"Running the Arab Gauntlet" Under Sail

"Against an Alien Wind"
The Red Sea showing track of the Yawl "Barbara" December and January 1971 A.D.

Tristan Jones

Shaded areas ||||||| show territory friendly to vessels from Israel at that time.

"Barbara"

Turkey

Mediterranean Sea

REFUSED ENTRY
CYPRUS

Syria

LEB.

HAIFA

Jordan

BEER-SHEBA

SINAI (ISRAEL OCC.)

Egypt

EILAT

NILE

LAT. 27

ISRAEL BACK

HOSTILE

Brothers Island (attack by Egyptians)

Saudi Arabia

Great gales.

No entry.

CURRENT 4 KTS

HOSTILE

Sudan

SUAKIN

Taller Saghic. Took refuge from gale.

UNDER REBEL (HOSTILE) CONTROL.

MANY PIRATES HERE

WINDS TO GALE FORCE

Yemen (hostile)

S. Yemen (hostile)

DAHLEK I!

MASSAWA

REBELS HERE

Ethiopia

ASSAB

Gulf of Aden

To Mombasa 2,470 miles.

Fr. Terr. of Afars & Isas.

DJIBOUTI

Somalia (hostile)

halfway to the Indian Ocean and comparative safety. We had run the gauntlet this far without serious mishap. We had escaped death by Egyptian bullets and Sudanese reefs, so we had good cause to feel pleased. Also, in Massawa I received news that four more of my articles had been bought by magazines in England and Germany, which supplied extra funds to stock up for the passage to Mombasa, a passage I estimated would take another five weeks.

7
ETHIOPIAN INTERLUDE

 AILING INTO MASSAWA HAR-
bor, there was no doubt we had ar-
rived in Africa. Set in a great bay with
a narrow entrance, the town, steaming and dirty white, sprawled along
the south shore. Away at the end of
the bay, on a lush, green islet, stood
the winter palace of the Emperor
Haile Selassie, gleaming like snow in
the hot sun through a shimmering, stinking haze.

"Salubrious," said Conrad as he eyed the scene.

At anchor in the trembling heat lay several large dhows
from as far away as Iran and Egypt. Tied up to the long
quays packed with hordes of robed pilgrims waiting to pass
to and from Mecca and astir with bawling camels and braying donkeys lay the smaller dzambouks. Sleek, lower
sterned than the dhows, these lateen-rigged vessels are
among the fastest sailing craft on the seas. These are the
craft favored by the pirates, smugglers, terrorists, and other
"gentlemen of the trade" of the Red Sea.

We berthed alongside the harbormaster's office under
the watchful eye of a port policeman who, though bootless,
seemed to be conscientious enough, continually waving
away, with threatening gestures and loud curses, a battalion
of small, ragged, starved-looking children with huge round
eyes, bulging stomachs, and stick-thin legs. The harbormaster, a large, heavy man, lounged in an armchair, cooled by
two fans, while a continual procession of caftan-clad clerks
in sandals and turbans entered, bowing. A curt hand wave
and an initial scrawled on their forms sent them retiring
backwards through the doors, still bowing.

Speaking bad English, the harbormaster started off by
asking if *Barbara* carried any arms. Informed that she did
not, he then asked what stores she carried. I told him I had
enough to get me to Djibouti, where I hoped to restock. I
said that I hoped to be in Ethiopian waters only long

enough to obtain some cooking gas and diesel oil, also some fresh water.

He reflected that this was just as well, for it was dangerous to sail in these waters—banditry and guerrilla activity were rife. My safety could not be guaranteed in Ethiopia except in the ports of Massawa and Assab. Most of the rest of the coast was under the control of the Eritrean Liberation Front. He passed his finger across his throat in an unmistakable gesture, all the while staring at me with small, black, avaricious eyes. "Yes," I thought, "and if my kids were out there with those poor little beggars on the jetty and if I had to come in here bowing and scraping to a bastard like you, I'd be out there with the ELF, too!"

"Good bloke?" asked Conrad as I emerged from the office.

"Charming!" I replied. No sense in depressing him.

"I'll bet," he murmured.

The heat in Massawa was unbelievable. By midday it was well over 110 degrees in the shade. No breeze penetrated into the harbor. Squadrons of flies hovered over a thick layer of shit floating everywhere. Pilgrims by the thousands, along with their camels and other assorted animals, relieved themselves noisily along the jetties. The din was indescribable; all day and night the row went on, a cacophony of shouts, cries, wailing prayers, camel roars, donkey brays, beggars' pleadings, drums beating, as the dhows loaded up, never stopping. At night the decibels were vastly increased by the addition of blaring music from several sleazy rooftop nightclubs strung along the waterfront.

Across the river, through the thick heat haze, we could see huge mountains of salt awaiting shipment. Centuries ago the Roman army was partly paid in salt from these very flats.

The morning after clearing into Ethiopia, I took off inland to Asmara, three hundred miles away and nine thousand feet above sea level. This was the nearest place that butane gas could be obtained, unless I was willing to wait three weeks for supplies to arrive on the coast. I left Conrad to guard the boat and repulse the crowd of beggars, although he had adopted one poor, thin little starveling, all big eyes and protruding belly, feeding him twice a day on rice and protein—a tiny finger in a huge dike.

The journey inland was made in an ancient bus with open sides. It crawled along, heavily laden with passengers and goods inside and out, on the back and on the top. We were preceded first by an armored car, then a truck carrying about twenty of the imperial army infantry, then an army truck loaded with stores, then another armored car, then a group of soldiers on bicycles. After them wheezed and trundled the bus. The rear guard was brought up by two motorcycles with sidecars carrying machine guns, then a truckful of soldiers, all armed to the teeth, and another armored car. This was the thrice-weekly convoy from the coast to Asmara, without which the bus dared not proceed.

We climbed up and up the winding mountain road, until it became cooler and then positively cold. First we passed half-naked peasants on the road, driving camels, and natives wearing goatskin jerkins, and finally fully-robed Tigrean tribesmen, armed with ancient muskets and scimitars, tending herds of very moth-eaten looking cattle by the roadside.

The scenery on this route was sublime, green mountains covered in jungle, falling away into the distance. The relief from the coastal heat was fantastic.

At last the convoy sputtered and wheezed into Asmara, a large town built mostly by the Italians during their occupation of Eritrea in the 1920s and 1930s. A modern town, it even has some factories. The nights were cold, a complete contrast to stifling Massawa.

The next day, refreshed by a freezing sleep in a tiny hotel, I turned up at the bus station to find that the army had, by the emperor's command, been confined to barracks, and there was to be no escort back to the coast. The bus would return alone. Would all passengers therefore make sure that they carried a minimum amount of cash, jewelry, or other valuables? This did not concern me, for I was down to ten dollars anyway, and the only valuable I had with me was the bottle of butane gas.

Midway down the long, winding descent to the coast, a roadblock appeared, manned by some very fierce-looking

gentlemen, half of whom were clad in goatskins and ban-
doleers, the other half in khaki denims. All carried arms.
We were politely but firmly requested to step out of the bus
and lined up willy-nilly along the roadside, while two of the
soldiers passed along the line accepting contributions. I
handed over my ten dollars, comforting myself that the
show was worth every cent, while hoping they would not
"collect" my butane gas when they searched the luggage.
They did not, and soon we all reboarded the bus, with the
exception of one young man who stayed with the "freedom
fighters." I was afterwards told by another passenger, in
halting Italian, that this young man was probably the bandits' agent.

The bandits gave us a wave as we passed their roadblock
of felled trees and rumbled off down to the shit, flies, and
heat of Massawa.

That evening, back on board, I recounted the occurrence
to Conrad. It was funny, even if we had lost our only cash.
Fortunately the gas bottle connection fit *Barbara*'s system,
and we could cook hot food after living four days on cold
canned fish and meat with biscuits.

We stayed in Massawa for two weeks. During that period
we took off to the Dahlak Islands with six cadets from the
Imperial Navy. We took them at the request of the com-
manding officer, an Englishman, who told us that the only
Ethiopian navy ship had broken down in far-off Madagascar. She had been there for over a year and was not expected to return home for another year, if ever. We would
do the navy a favor by giving them some sea experience.

Together with the cadets, we sailed over to Great Dahlak,
a very barren island ringed round an immense lagoon teeming with fish. We spent a very enjoyable two days exploring
these islands, which had recently been visited and explored
by a British army team.

I met the chief of the island, who had been Lawrence of
Arabia's bodyguard and had, in fact, been with the mystery
man when he entered Damascus in 1918. He had a great
respect, even love, for the British, the "Ferenghi," as he
called us, and made us welcome.

The day before we left Massawa was Ethiopian navy day,

of all things. The Emperor Haile Selassie himself came down to Massawa with all his court to visit the ships of several different powers, including Russia and the United States.

The day before he arrived a very harassed-looking naval lieutenant climbed aboard to inform me breathlessly that the Emperor Haile Selassie was due to visit the port and would we make sure the boat was clean with no laundry hanging out.

Next day, early, all the dzambouks were cleared away from the jetties, all the pilgrims disappeared as if by magic, the streets were swept, all the tiny, starving beggars dissolved into thin air. God was in his heaven, all was right with the world—the emperor was coming!

He duly appeared about eleven o'clock, driving along the empty, unrecognizable waterfront in a Rolls-Royce, with his immediate family accompanying him. When he arrived alongside *Barbara,* the convoy stopped. He got out, hovered over by a huge bodyguard in a sparkling white uniform, a black, black man, probably Sudanese, so huge he seemed to be eight feet tall, bearing a great sword. Behind him stood another group of guards, all toting machine pistols.

With the emperor was the British naval commander, who introduced me to His Imperial Majesty. He was tiny and very stern looking and said to me in very good English (probably a relic of his exile in England in the thirties), "Captain Jones, I do not know what makes a man like you tick!"

I looked him straight in the eye and said, "Your Majesty, I don't know what makes a man like you tick!" He laughed out loud and climbed back into the Rolls.

That night Captain Bob Jones, United States Navy destroyer *Glennon,* visited *Barbara,* and we talked of John Paul Jones, our common forerunner.

8
GATE OF TEARS

T WAS NOW THE BEGINNING of February. Out in the far-off Indian Ocean the northeast monsoon would continue to blow until June, when it would change direction to the southeast. With the northeast monsoon we would have a fair wind, once out of the Gulf of Aden, to sail from the coast of Somalia to Kenya and Mombasa. From there, after restocking the boat with canned food, we would take off across the Indian Ocean to Ceylon, through the Strait of Malacca to Singapore, the China Sea, and then on across the Pacific with the north Pacific current, to South America and Peru, where lay my eventual destination—Lake Titicaca. A long, long voyage and if taken at one swallow, a daunting prospect even for the hardiest and most accustomed mariner.

But first I had to navigate *Barbara* down through the southern gullet of the Red Sea, the terrible Bab al Mandab, then out, all the time with the wind dead ahead, through the Gulf of Aden. Except for the French port of Djibouti, we would have hostile territory on each side of us clear down to the Kenya frontier, for we were tainted men with the mark of Cain—we had visited Israel, a deadly crime in Arab eyes.

Outside the main Ethiopian ports of Massawa and Assab chaos reigned. Swift dzambouks, some with powerful auxiliary engines, swooped down on the coast through secret channels, through uncharted reefs, laden with arms, money, and men for the Eritrean Liberation Front, which was trying to wrest the whole seaboard from Emperor Haile Selassie. Manned by fanatical Yemenis, they fired eagerly upon anyone not of their own ilk. Part of a wide-ranging Moslem plot, they were trying to seal off the southern end of the Red Sea, thus closing Israel's windpipe to the East.

Ashore, their protagonists, the Imperial Ethiopian Army, were just as trigger-happy, recognizing not the slightest difference between a Yemeni gunrunner and a foreign cruising vessel. Their guiding rule was, "If you don't know what it is, destroy it."

Outside the dangerous coastal passages the wind howls from the southeast, whistling its way through the Bab al Mandab. The current gives way before the wind, setting up a steep, nasty sea that slams northwards at a violent five knots.

In Massawa we filled the water tanks, then spent many hours in stuffy, sweaty offices filling out forms that no one would ever look at. At last we cleared out and were off.

The distance from Massawa to Assab is 270 miles direct. Slamming to windward, and thus doubling the distance, it is around 500 miles. On the morning of the first day out of port a full gale broke loose out of the south, and we sought the lee of Shumma, a horseshoe-shaped reef, to cower there before the fierceness of the hottest seawind in the world.

Presently, as the sun passed over the meridian, the wind increased until by early afternoon it was a full raging storm. Conrad and I took turns keeping anchor watch, sitting in the shade of a large umbrella which I had purchased in Massawa. North Sea sailors have a saying that the three most useless things in a sailboat are a wheelbarrow, an umbrella, and a naval officer. This time we disproved that old saw, for the umbrella was a great blessing in the scorching hot sun of the Red Sea. We were, however, grateful we did not have the other two items aboard.

Just after noon Conrad sang out that the anchor was dragging. In the blasting, searing wind, I took a quick bearing on the ends of the reef and confirmed that it was. Directly astern lay the jagged end of one side of the horseshoe reef. If we touched that, *Barbara* would be lost. I slid down the companionway to start the engine and stepped right into a foot of water. We were leaking again. Or so I thought.

To hell with the water in the bilge; first we had to save the boat and clear out of the lagoon into the storm. We could figure out the leak once we were out in clear water. I started the engine just in time, for the anchor chain parted as it sputtered alive. Without attempting to recover the anchor in that raving wind, we slowly made our way out through the rugged, narrow entrance of the lagoon, into the frantic white sea. Once out there we hoisted the mizzen and hove to, for I knew there was nothing to leeward of us for a good forty miles.

Having stopped the engine, I hopped below. The first thing I did was taste the water, for I had a horrible hunch; the water level had not risen since we had dragged the anchor. One lick of a finger confirmed my suspicions—it was fresh water! *Fresh bloody water* in the Red Sea! Somehow we had sprung a leak in our fresh water tanks! Together, frantically, Conrad and I ripped up the floorboards of the cabin sole and checked the cross-connection pipes, which supply the galley tap. There, right at the cross-connection, were teethmarks! The pipe had been *bitten through*. Sweating, I looked up at Conrad; his face was white with despair.

"A rat, a fucking bloody rat!" I screamed. " It must have come onboard in Massawa. Jesus Christ! How much spare water we got in jerrycans?"

He jumped up the companionway to check. "One two-gallon bloody can up here. None that I know of down below."

I pored over the grubby chart with a sweaty finger. After reading through the *Admiralty Pilot,* I found that the nearest fresh water lay 220 miles to windward, at a small hamlet called Edd on the mainland coast. Edd might, or might not, be in the hands of the ELF.

"We've two choices," I explained. "One, we can die of thirst by trying to reach Assab direct. We need two pints a day at least in this heat and we're a week out of Assab. If there is any unforeseen delay or accident on the way, then we've had it, for there's nothing ashore, it's all bone-dry desert! And it hasn't rained here in a century. Two, we can make for Edd and take our chance on being shot if the ELF is there. If we beat real hard and use the engine we can be there in forty-eight hours."

"OK, Tristan. I'm with you on that!" he replied. He was badly rattled. The thought of death by thirst is just about the worst prospect a sailor can imagine. It must be the most painful, awful death of the lot. Two years before I had spent a week in a rubber dinghy alone in the mid-Atlantic, and by the time I was picked up by a Portuguese man-of-war I was delirious with suffering, with a grossly swollen tongue, unable to speak or think properly, almost dead in intense agony, with the most hellish hallucinations. In this Red Sea heat we would dry out twice as fast; three days would be enough to finish us off, very painfully indeed.

"What do we do if we find hostiles at Edd?" he asked quietly.

"If we're certain they are hostile, then we bear off and drain the engine circulating water system. It'll be muddy and taste bloody awful, but it'll keep us alive for a few more days until we maybe sight a ship or reach Assab."

Carefully rationing out fresh water from the jerrycan, we beat for three days against hard winds and seas and finally entered the uncharted, reef-strewn anchorage only hours after we had drunk the last of the spare fresh water. The beach was crawling with armed figures. We dropped the hook and waited for the worst. We had no way of knowing if they were ELF or the Imperial Army, for they both dressed alike in rags of the most startling variety.

"What do you think, Conrad?"

"Scruffy lot, aren't they?"

Eventually a boat pushed off from the beach crowded with armed men who soon identified themselves, in halting Italian, as members of the Imperial Army. We'd had the devil's luck, for they had ejected a strong force of the Eritrean Liberation Front only the day before we appeared on the scene! Rotting bodies on the shore bore witness to their story.

The water we found in the brackish well on shore was green and tasted like no other water on earth, but it sufficed. At least it was better than thirsting to death, or being killed by an ELF bullet or worse, for the Yemeni Moslem is a master at the slow, lingering demise of any prisoner he happens to take.

Four days later we reached Assab, after a long, slow beat to windward. Conrad and I were almost too weak to work the sail; we were sick as dogs, unable to swallow any food and shitting green slime.

The first thing we did in Assab was smoke out the rat. He was a real monster, over three feet long from the tip of his nose to the end of his tail. We bunged up all the openings except one ventilator, then set fire to rags soaked in olive oil sitting in a biscuit tin down below. The thick smoke panicked the rat out of the one ventilator we had left open, and as he emerged we knocked him on the head. Cleaning up the inside of the boat after the smoke-out was much more difficult, especially in heat of over 120 degrees.

Assab is just about the worst port I have ever been in, and that is really saying something. The wind and the sea roll straight into the port, which is open to the south. The shops are empty (not that we had any money), and beggars by the hundred crowd the quay. Bureaucracy rides rampant in the dark, stuffy offices of the harbormaster, the chief of police, the customs, the agent for foreign vessels, and the—who the hell knows what he was, but he was carrying out his function in full splendor from behind a pile of papers a foot deep and an impressive array of rubber stamps and all the other paraphernalia of stupidity and futility that always collects in these places, the world over, from Stavanger to Callao, Assab to Vladivostok.

Tied to the jetty bollards by eight heavy mooring lines and held out from the jetty by our two remaining anchors, we pitched and tossed in Assab harbor for three days and nights, waiting for the wind to abate enough for us to attempt the passage of the Bab al Mandab. When it did drop it dropped altogether, so that eventually we made the passage under power in a flat calm! We slipped through the channel between the small islands known as the Seven Brothers and the coast of the French territory of the Afars and Issas, in order to avoid any interference from Yemeni forces, who were at that time, with Russian connivance, demanding control over all vessels using the Bab al Mandab.

At long last we were out of the Red Sea, the "Sea of Hazards."

In 1971 the French still held what used to be called French Somaliland, later to be known as the Territory of the Afars and the Issas. A mountainous, sizzling waste of rocky desert inhabited by two of the most warlike tribes in Africa, it had been seized by the French at the turn of the century, so that they could control the railway up through the mountains to the rich coffee lands of the Ethiopian plateau. The British presence at Aden, across the Gulf and athwart the lucrative trade from Europe to India, had also prompted French intervention.

The French were still there, reluctantly. Written into their treaty with the indigenous tribes was the clause that they would leave the Territory within twenty-four hours when requested to do so! But the Afars and the Issas, still naked savages, were continually at each others' throats, the Afars supported by the Ethiopians and the Issas by the Somalis. France held the bloody ring in between, with a large garrison of foreign legionnaires, mainly Germans, entrenched in Djibouti, the only town of any size.

Djibouti lies on the southern side of the Gulf of Tadjoura, an extensive arm of the Gulf of Aden reaching right into the coastal mountains. The tidal currents here run up to twelve knots, while the winds are either nonexistent or very vigorous. Here, yearly, in May, blows the *hamseen,* or fifty-day gale, out of the west. When this starts all navigation stops.

As *Barbara* entered the port in mid-February, it was calm—a hot, muggy, misty deadness. Even at dawn, as the sun rose, the metal fittings on the boat were too warm to touch. We anchored off the customs house, made breakfast, then rowed ashore to the end of a mile-long jetty. Marching past a line of palm trees planted every ten meters with Gallic precision, we entered the harbormaster's office and introduced ourselves.

We were met with incredulity. It was not possible! The last yacht to call in Djibouti had been in 1952! Excitedly, a phone call was made to the Club Nautique, the local French boat club, consisting mainly of French army officers. We were driven to the town and the shops by Jacques Herry, their commodore, who was also the minister of the interior. As we trundled round in an aging Citroën, it was evident that the French had achieved a lot here in fifty years. The town was clean and well ordered, with many small, shady parks. There were a number of fine restaurants and shops that looked well stocked and elegant. Conrad and I enjoyed coffee on the terrace of an *estaminet* overlooking the main square, abustle with Arabs and tribesmen heading for the market, yashmaked women, and wild-and-woolly-looking Somalis, all crowding through the square under the gaze of immaculate French gendarmes.

The following day one of the members of the Club Nautique, a colonel in the foreign legion, drove us up into the mountains of the interior, very stark and lifeless, for a view of the city and the Gulf. On the way back he showed us how the French stop the Afars and Issas from raiding the suburbs. There was a strip of ground about three hundred yards wide all around the town littered with broken glass and beer bottles. There must have been enough beer bottles there to have supplied the French army from Napoleon's time to now. The strip stretched for about six miles in a great arc, right around the inland edge of Djibouti. The tribesmen, being barefoot, didn't dare cross it! The two roads into town were controlled by heavily armed legionnaires. The huge parade grounds outside the gates were full of camel trains and horsemen, as well as fierce-looking mountain men, awaiting permission to pass the gates. The scene was full of color, full of movement, with great crowds of people squeezing in between the vast area of broken beer bottles.

Jacques Herry, chatting aboard *Barbara*, warned me that there was a grave risk of arrest in Somalia, if we should have to call into any port there. The German consul to Djibouti had, about six years previously, been wrecked on the coast near Berbera, and he was still being held in jail on a charge of spying.

To reach Mombasa *Barbara* would have to skirt the coast of Somalia for almost twenty-five hundred miles. Most of that would be beating to windward; Cape Guardafui, at the tip of the Horn of Africa, is notorious for its storms. The chances were fifty-fifty that we would not need to enter Somalia, but just in case I decided to cover myself.

I went around to the office of the Somali consul and, after waiting for several hours, was finally conducted into that gentleman's presence. He was from what had been previously known as British Somaliland and had been educated at Oxford. He was very black, very civil, and intensely interested in cricket. I invited him out for a sail in the Gulf the next day. Obviously honored, he accepted with alacrity.

The following day was heavy with heat; there wasn't a drop of wind on the mirror-smooth, fast-running Gulf. Fishing boats on the horizon seemed to be suspended in crystal space. We chugged out under power, with the Somali consul getting greener by the minute.

Half a mile outside the harbor he begged to be taken back into port. He would sign, immediately on our return, a laissez-passer for the whole coast of Somalia; he would even give us letters of introduction to his friends in Mogadishu—even a note to the president—if only we would take him back. So we did. Within an hour after tying up at the jetty, I had the permits and the notes. What he didn't know was that Conrad was up in the fo'c's'le, throwing his weight from side to side so that *Barbara* would get a sickening roll on. That had been arranged as soon as I saw how allergic to sea-moving the man was.

Strange, for Somalis are among the finest seamen in the world, and in high demand as crew on merchant vessels. But those are big ships, of course, a completely different thing from a small sailing craft rolling away on a dead flat sea.

We stayed in Djibouti about ten days and, having at last received funds from London, stocked up the boat for the long passage to Mombasa. We also carefully watered, adding chlorine judiciously, for the water supply could not be guaranteed for purity, and we did not want more "Massawa fever." We set to every morning before sunrise, repairing gear, mending sails, applying a bit of varnish here and there, checking, eternally checking, all the gear, overhauling the engine and rerigging worn lines.

By ten o'clock it was too hot and muggy to work down below, so we did topside work until noon. After lunch I would go into town to visit Jacques, or read up information on East Africa at the admirable public library, or visit my friends at the foreign legion bar. Conrad would head for the only hotel in town, where there was an excellent swim-

ming pool and some gorgeous *mamselles*. My time was spent
in more serious ways—studying the future courses. To cut a
long story sideways, our spell in Djibouti, a civilized, green,
clean oasis in a sea of ignorance, was like passing from hell
to Hyde Park. It saved our sanity.

Late in the afternoon on the second of March we worked
Barbara out of the shimmering heat of Djibouti and headed
east, escorted for the first five miles or so by practically all
the small craft in the Club Nautique, one of them busy
making a film of our departure for French television. Then,
as dusk fell, we were alone, heaving to the swells of the Gulf
of Aden.

In the morning the east wind got up and stayed against us
all the way to Cape Guardafui. To reach that Cape we beat
for just over one thousand miles through the water, although the distance direct is only about six hundred miles.
A strong, westerly going current was against us and there
was a short, steep sea. For ten days and nights we pounded
away, standing in close to the deserted, barren, mountainous shore of Somalia during the day in order to avoid most
of the current and to take advantage of the fact that on a hot
desert coast, near the shore, the wind, during the heat of the
day, always *tries to blow onshore* at right angles to the coast. In
other words, the nearer you are to the shore the more the
wind blows at right angles from the sea, instead of from
ahead. Also, the desert coasts, being generally in more remote parts of the world, are usually poorly charted, so it's
nerve-racking, eye-straining exercise, continually searching ahead for any possible outcrops or shallows not shown
on the charts. At night, of course, there are no lights and so
you must stand off five miles or so, which means your boat is
out in the strength of the current, and so gets set back for
miles during darkness. This applies to any desert coast
when working against the wind in a sailing craft.

But when you're going *with* the wind and the current, it's
an entirely different story, for you may stand well out of
sight of land, picking up a landfall now and again as it
pleases you, and whiz away free as a bird, just as *Barbara* did
once she passed Cape Guardafui and headed south. To
anyone considering making passages along a desert shore

in the tropics the facts stated here are most significant. They were borne out on my passages with the wind and current off Morocco and Somalia, and against the elements off Egypt, the Sudan, Ethiopia, Northern Somalia, and the Atacama Desert of the west coast of South America.

Barbara pounded the whole length of the Gulf of Aden for ten days—*fourteen thousand, four hundred minutes*, with around *twenty-eight crashes every minute* against the eternal monsoon wind—but eventually we fetched Cape Guardafui. We weren't quite sure at the time, for the light was extinguished, but when the moon rose we saw it, high, white, and ghostly, only two miles away on our starboard bow, and in two more hours we were out, into the Indian Ocean. Out of the narrow seas at last, after almost a year in the claustrophobic Mediterranean and the Red Sea. At last we could look at an horizon and know that there was nothing to hit for thousands of miles. As we wore the cape, shortened down in a boisterous sea and heavy wind, we peered into the eastern horizon. "India's over there!" we cried, pointing directly east. "Australia's that way!" and "Antarctica's down there!" What a relief! After a total of twenty-nine days of hammering to windward for nearly three thousand miles, we were running before the wind on our own course. If we wished, we could approach the coast, or we could stand off a thousand miles; we could shorten sail or pile it on. At last we had *command* of the wind and were free as an albatross in the wide oceans of the world; we had run the Arab gauntlet! After twenty-nine days of hammering into the wind and current, with shut hatches and a continually wet cockpit, in sizzling heat, our bodies racked by saltwater blisters, bashing along in confined waters, between unsurveyed reefs, off hostile shores, we had the whole bloody Indian Ocean to play with!

Just then the old, bullet-scarred mainsail, straining before the full blast of the monsoon wind, split with an explosive crack at the head. But what did we care? *Barbara* was dancing to the ocean seas and going like blazes for Mombasa, fifteen hundred miles to the south, with a fair wind all the way! We let the old mainsail flap and flutter aloft all night, for she'd earned a stern-wind. In the early morning we would hand it and bend on the new spare mainsail, which I had carefully saved for just this moment.

Several days later, after bowling merrily along in the twenty-knot wind, I had the ineffable delight of being exactly on the equator at noon on the day of the equinox. This meant that for several moments the sun was at a point precisely above my head and its altitude was ninety degrees all around the horizon. A curious experience, which might happen once in a navigator's lifetime. I suppose this must be the most accurate way of fixing the latitude. Of more interest to me, however, was our distance from the coast, that is, our longitude. I obtained this by shooting the new moon and Venus, while Acrux gave me a fair latitude, for the Southern Cross had hove into sight.

"Good position, Skip?" Conrad asked as I clambered topside to take the wheel.

"I don't know about good, chum. Accurate, yes, but we're not bound for a pub!"

Running before the wind, even with the wind on the quarter, is a thousand times more pleasant than beating. The movement of the boat is steadier and smoother, steering is much easier, the cockpit stays dry, and the monotony of the passage can be broken by undertaking the thousand and one tasks that always need doing in a small sailing craft. You can even write letters. I wrote three articles on our passages while running down our southing to Mombasa. Every now and again we would steer to the southwest, just to take a look at the coast, playing cat and mouse for the devilment of it. One day, about two hundred miles south of the equator, we saw the first trees we had seen on the shore, with the exception of Djibouti, since we had left Israel—six thousand miles of desert coast without sighting one green tree! This was a clump of palm trees near the coast hard by Barawa, and we gazed at them for long minutes through the binoculars. A green wonder!

When we reached the latitude of Mombasa, on the evening of the twenty-first of February, we changed course to the west, for we were sixty miles offshore. With the wind now on *Barbara*'s starboard beam we headed in, accompanied all through the brilliant moonlit night by a huge whale shark, longer than *Barbara*, which swam alongside of us, about forty yards off, slowly and peacefully, without for one moment bothering us in any way, but scaring both Conrad and me absolutely shitless.

"Well, lad, you wanted to get close to nature—there she is."

"I don't mind, Skip. When you get over the first fright it's fascinating," he replied.

"First fright? I'm just getting to my fifty-first! Look at the size of that bugger!"

The whale shark left us as the lights of Mombasa hove into view dead ahead. We slowed down, then hove to under mizzen for the night, about three miles off the port, to await the dawn, taking turns to catch short snatches of sweet sleep, dreaming of passages ahead.

9

MEADOWS OF GOLD

N THE EARLY MORNING WE made our way into the vast harbor of Mombasa, picking our way between the reefs. This was easy, for the buoys are well maintained and, more important, in position; in Africa, a most unusual situation. We had good reason to be pleased with ourselves —*Barbara* had made the passage from Djibouti of 2,400 miles in twenty-one days. Considering that a thousand miles had been directly against the wind, this was pretty good going. Since we had left Israel we had spent forty-two days at sea and sailed 4,230 miles— an average of slightly over 100 miles per day. The boat was in fairly good shape still, despite the continuous hammering to windward and Egyptian bullet scars, tattered sails and badly chafed sailing gear.

I determined to spend two or three weeks in Mombasa. First, to rest a while; second, to refit the vessel; and third, to await the delivery of charts from London. These charts were necessary to make the passage east from the Seychelles Islands to Peru, more than half a world away.

Our reception by the port police and customs in Mombasa was the best and most civil that we received in the whole of Africa. I anchored the boat off the Yacht Club, but the monsoon wind drives right into this roadstead of Kilindini, and I determined to get permission to shift to the Old Harbor. Besides, I had seen the fleet of dhows in that port, and they intrigued me so much I just had to get in among that floating feast of splendor.

On the afternoon of the first day in port I signed on Alem Desta as second hand. The son of a Tigrean chief in Ethiopia, he had flown down to join *Barbara* for a few months, as I had promised his father in Asmara he could do. Slight, thin, and very black, he was a Coptic Christian, eighteen years old. After his spell with *Barbara* he was destined to join the Imperial Ethiopian Navy. He had obtained an Ethiopian seaman's passbook. Its number was 00001. It was the first one ever issued in the huge empire of Ethiopia, making Alem Desta their first professional seaman. I trained him in navigation and seamanship. Very intelligent, he had been busily learning English for the past few months. With us he learned seaman's English and no end of salty phrases.

One morning, bright and early, we shifted *Barbara* round to the Old Harbor and anchored her among about fifty of the big oceangoing dhows lying before the white, gleaming town of square buildings, looking like a cubist painting in bright color, sprawling along a green hill, waving with palm trees. Over the dhows clambered brown sailors in white loincloths, wailing the chants of Iran and the East Indies. It looked for all the world like a scene out of *A Thousand and One Nights*.

All along the shoreline there were ramps and small jetties alive with humanity—merchants in turbans, beggars in rags, women in yashmaks, and thousands of dock porters and coolies, unloading small fishing craft and scrambling up the ramps with immense loads on their shoulders.

Alem scoffed at the dhows, for he despised Moslems and he knew that the dhows, unlike *Barbara*, had no engine. I explained to him that these men were real sailors, descended from generations who have plied the seas for thousands of years. Mombasa is one of the oldest ports of the world. Its seamen were making ocean voyages before the Phoenicians or the Vikings knew what a ship was; they were making voyages to India and China thousands of years ago. It was from here that knowledge of the compass and the rudder reached the Arabs, enabling them to seize control of the Mediterranean for centuries.

"They still bloddy Moslems; they eat dog," said Alem.

"Bullshit!" I replied.

The actual Arab town of Mombasa was founded by Hussain-ben-Ali, who was thrown out of Oman, on the south shore of Arabia, about A.D. 1000. When he arrived in Mombasa there were large towns already on the Kenyan and Tanzanian coasts, one of which was even known to the

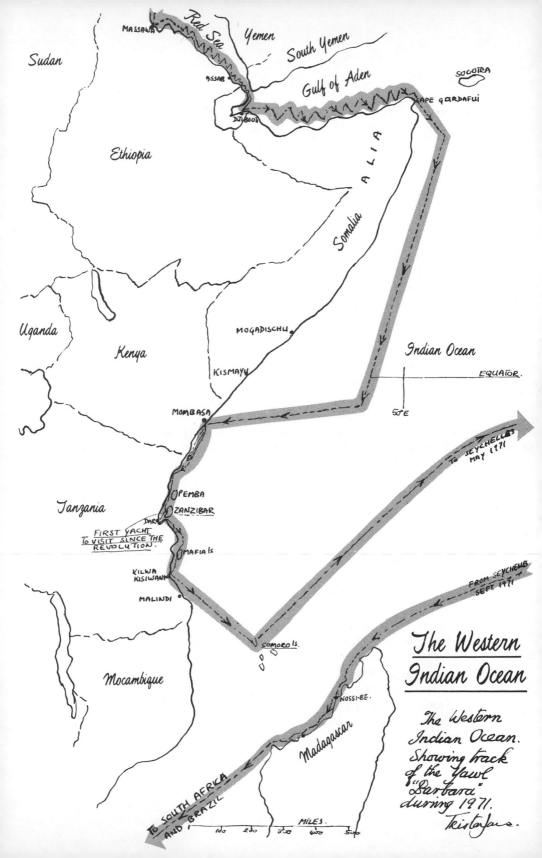

The Western
Indian Ocean

The Western
Indian Ocean.
Showing track
of the Yawl
"Barbara"
during 1971.

Tristan Jones.

ancient Greeks—Rhapta, the capital of the land of Azania, which traded with India, Persia, and Europe.

The Indian Ocean itself was known to the ancient Greeks as the Erythaen Sea, which means Red Sea, while in recent times Roman coins have been found at various places on the coast, indicating either that Roman sailors penetrated this far south in the days of their empire, or that people from this coast were in touch with the Romans.

In the Greek *periplus,* or pilot to the Indian Ocean, little information is given about the ancient inhabitants of the Mombasa area. They were exceedingly tall and exported gold, tortoise shell, and ivory, palm oil and rhinoceros horn, the latter used to this day as an aphrodisiac in places as far apart as Egypt and China.

Ptolemy of Alexandria, in his geography of Africa, also reported that the natives here were tall and handsome, but that Bantu people were coming down from the interior. The trade in slaves from this coast to the Middle East and China is millenniums old. The Arab name for black people is *zanji,* for coast their word is *bar*; thus derives the name Zanzibar. For centuries Mombasa was part of the domains of the sultan of Zanzibar. Slavery was still legal within the sultan's country until 1912, though the British Royal Navy kept a vigil for almost ninety years against the export of slaves, surely one of the most humanitarian activities ever persisted in by the armed forces of a great power—in this the Royal Navy shines. Many thousands of men lost their lives in the antislavery service, from disease and drowning. This is a story yet to be told. Of all its heroes—Drake, Raleigh, Collingwood, Vernon, Nelson—these are the ones the Royal Navy should be proudest of. Unhonored and unsung, they fought against the vilest trade for close on a century, a sailor's fight, in sailing vessels mostly; short, bloody encounters in remote seas off unhealthy shores.

The correct name for dhows is really dzambouks. They are on average about 150 feet in length, with fine bows and high sterns. Built for the most part of cedar or mahogany, the wooden hulls are oiled, for the only paint visible is around the stern on the gaudy scrollwork carved right around the counters. They have a mast which appears to be short for the length of the hull. The mast has no standing rigging, being stepped right into the keel and leaning forward. On the mast a great long boom is hoisted. This boom consists of several lengths of straight tree branches lashed together and grows progressively smaller in diameter towards the outboard end of the boom. This is a clever reefing system, for when the wind pipes up harder, one by one these small branches snap, thus shortening the lateen sail, reducing its area little by little from the upper, outer head downwards. When the rough weather is over they resume whole sail by sending the smallest member of the crew, usually a boy, up the boom to relash the broken sections!

The dzambouks are generally a family concern, and the members of the crew are usually of the same kin. The skipper is often the oldest member of the family, and he navigates by keeping a star on a certain latitude and by the look of the sea surroundings. In case of doubt he carries an ancient leather scroll, which he unwinds each morning of the voyage and which tells him how things should look and how the wind is and how the sea should run. Amazing, but they make their destinations, and have done so for three thousand years or more, so regular are the conditions in the Indian Ocean, where the monsoon blows like clockwork. They sail as far afield as Singapore, Calcutta, the Gulf of Persia, and Egypt. They are part of an ancient trade-route system which crosses the Sahara on the one side and the Himalayas and Tibet on the other, which reaches from the Philippines to the Zambezi River, and which has been in operation since the known dawn of history. Even the Chinese had contact with this coast; Ibn Batuta gives an account of a conversation with a Chinese captain in Zanzibar in 1320 who told him that as a young man he had made a voyage to a land "so many days east of China they were unaccountable." They brought back *gold* and *silver*, and there were high mountains and a holy lake. Was this a voyage to Peru before 1320? Where else, many days to the east of China, would he have obtained gold and silver?

Conrad and I, having made friends with the captain of an Indian dhow from the Malabar coast, visited the vessel. Alem would not go; being a proud Coptic he was afraid of contamination or worse. Down below we found a cargo that would make the average steamer look like a garbage barge. In a hold about fifty feet long by twenty wide were stacked hundreds of hand-woven carpets. There were piles of rich brocades, and at one end six camphor-wood chests full of ivory—all illegally obtained, of course, here in Mombasa. The timbers of the vessel had obviously been rough-hewn with an adz, but the bilges were almost dry, and apart from the smells of Indian cooking in the open brazier on deck, there was little odor in the hold. The captain's small cuddy, or cabin, aft, was decorated with brocades, a bamboo mat, and several silk cushions. I was interested to find that much of the rope used is made onboard, being twisted from the raw hemp on a rope-maker's wheel set up on the foredeck. The sails were of cotton, much packed and patched, and almost grey with age, but obviously cared for with love. The crew consisted of the captain, six deckhands, a cook, a carpenter, and two small boys, all belonging to the same family hailing from Calicut, in India.

The method of treating the bottom of these crafts is interesting to the western sailor, for it is ages old. They beach the craft on the tide, or careen her if there is none, then kill a dozen goats or sheep and collect the fat, which they mix with sulphur. They then paint the hull with this foul brew, after burning off the growth on the ship's hull. They assured me that this antifouling was effective for a year in the Indian Ocean and the Red Sea, and that they got very little trouble with teredo worms.

The method of burning off the growth was quite simple. They built a fire under the hull and shifted it along as the weeds and barnacles cindered. The ashes were rubbed off with a flat piece of wood. Of course, the men sat around as the small boys did the work. But that's the way in the East.

"Them Moslems—they bloddy lazy men," said Alem.

"Shut up!" Conrad told him sternly.

We visited the Mombasa Yacht Club. While it had obviously been of great importance to the settlers during colonial days, it was now a mere shadow of its former self. At the club, I was told that it would be risky to approach either Pemba or Zanzibar, as the Maoist revolutionary government there did not look kindly upon private yachtsmen.

"Well," I remarked to Conrad on the way back onboard, "we'll tackle that problem when we come to it. But Zanzibar; that really intrigues me. Always wanted to visit that place. I never did have the chance—until now!"

The next day we borrowed a car from a kind yacht-club member and drove inland to the big game reserve at Tsavo. Conrad was in high delight as we passed by lions, elephants, hippos, and giraffes. It was good to get away from salt water for a couple of days, up into the coolness of the highlands. Alem was bored. All that interested him was glaring at the Kikuyu game wardens. Mount Kilimanjaro glistened away to the south of us as we drove up to Tsavo, along one of the oldest trade roads in Africa. In the Tsavo game lodge dining room I had a narrow escape when a spitting cobra dropped from a rafter directly above my head! It was killed by a white settler who attacked it with a broom. He then congratulated me on being the luckiest man in Africa. I headed for the bar for a stiff one. After the Red Sea, a spitting cobra was all I needed!

On the way back to the coast we passed through the ancient port of Malindi, which is very picturesque, constructed mainly according to old Arab Omani architecture, with the sleeping benches ordained by the Koran provided for homeless people outside the walls. However, the harbor is very poor, a mere roadstead behind a reef, with the Indian Ocean swells driving straight in. I would not fancy lying there in a vessel for long.

Next day, having restocked our canned and dried foods and water, we made plans for a passage down the coast to visit the Comoro Islands, rare islands indeed, well off the beaten track of steamers, but very much frequented in the days of sail. With several weeks to go before the arrival of the southeast monsoon, we decided to take off for the Comoros, only 1,250 miles away. I wrote to London to redirect the overdue charts to the Seychelles.

Setting out from Mombasa on the twenty-fifth of April, we beat down the coast for forty-five miles, then bore away into the channel between Wassin Island and the mainland. Here, there was a very fair anchorage and the reefs were full of unusual shells and exotic fish. Conrad had a field day splashing around, while I took a look around the village and chatted with the schoolmaster, a most civil gentleman whose main concern was that he had no books. I supplied him with some paperbacks, well worn, for which he was most grateful. In return, he gave me some fresh fish and a goat, which we barbecued and consumed that night on the mosquito-infested shore. The most interesting thing in Wassin to me, however, was the great number of outrigger canoes, brought here for repair from all parts of the African coast.

The canoes are actual evidence of Polynesian influence in Africa. They first appeared in Madagascar when a great invasion took place from Java, forty-five hundred miles away to the east, about the year A.D. 400. The invaders conquered Madagascar, then for centuries raided the African shore for slaves and booty. They even penetrated inland, and several years ago evidence of Polynesian influence was found as far away as Morocco. From this it appears that the ancients, and in particular the ancient navigators, were by no means short of the knowledge of how to get from one part of the world to another. The outrigger was unknown in Europe or Asia when it arrived in Africa.

After a couple of days in Wassin we beat steadily down the coast into Tanzanian waters and entered that country at Tanga. However, as we were tired and wanted to rest before tackling the Zanzibar channel, with its strong currents and winds, we did not go ashore.

Next day we headed for the small islet of Mazwe, tiny and jungle covered. Here we met some fishermen who were grateful for a few cigarettes. They told us that they had been on the islet for three months, catching turtles on the vast coral reef which stretched out northeast of the anchorage. Simple, pleasant folk, they crowded excitedly around our tape recorder while we played the Beatles. Their favorite was "A Hard Day's Night"!

Alem watched them suspiciously, hovering in the background.

Back in the stifling hot cabin in *Barbara* I inspected the chart of the coast further south. To go outside of Zanzibar Island would mean a two-hundred-mile detour out into the full forces of the monsoon, whereas to pass through the Zanzibar channel would be much shorter and perhaps quicker. Whether it would be safer only time would tell. I decided to try for the channel.

We beat all day against the southeast monsoon, in a nasty sea, and by four in the afternoon it was obvious that we would never clear the reef-ridden channel by nightfall. There were two alternatives—either turn back to Tanga or make for Zanzibar harbor. Turning back is against my principles, so, risky as it was, I decided to head for Zanzibar and to hell with the consequences. Besides, I'd already been in some countries where entry is, to say the least, awkward—one that springs to mind right away is Albania. At any rate, I had found that if you treat people the right way they are pretty much the same the world over, regardless of their politics. I was carrying no arms; I was out to exploit no one; and my only politics were, and still are, a good wind and a good craft. What could they do to me? As usual, before taking a major decision when anyone else is with me, I held a council of war. Both Conrad and Alem agreed with my thoughts, so we changed course and headed for one of the most fantastic and beautiful harbors in the world—fabled Zanzibar!

10
ISLANDS FORBIDDEN AND FORGOTTEN

 E WERE RECEIVED COLDLY but correctly. We found empty shops and a great scarcity of food. We found blaring loudspeakers on every corner and Chinese militarism all over the place. We found the Zanzibar Hotel, once obviously a place of great splendor, now a shoddy, run-down shadow. But the town, the ancient Arab town, was as it has always been, filled with interesting houses and cool courtyards set in tiny alleyways. The country's major export is cloves, and the smell of it is overpowering in the port. Here in Africa it goes to make toothache tincture, while in Indonesia it is mixed with tobacco to give a mild high to the smoker.

Zanzibar has been a city for over a thousand years. It was first built by the Shirazis, who sailed down from Persia around A.D. 1050, then the Omanis, who took over around A.D. 1100 and held power until 1963, when independence was declared. The following year, 1964, the Arabs were massacred. Since then Zanzibar has been a Maoist bridgehead in Africa, where revolutionary forces are trained and arms and money enter the continent. Although it is supposed to be in union with Tanzania, it is so in name only.

The first night in Zanzibar, Conrad and I dined with the minister of the interior, while Alem sulked onboard. The minister agreed, eventually, that the century of British tutelage had, in fact, been the best thing that could have happened to the island. He ended up begging us to stay for the May Day celebrations, to be held in the Mao Tse-tung stadium the next day; but I'd seen enough of 1984 during the past few hours and made my excuses. We would sail for Dar es Salaam the next morning. I'm glad we did, for during the celebrations fourteen men were executed in the stadium for running guns into Zanzibar.

68

The passage over the channel to Dar es Salaam was short and sweet and by late afternoon we were at anchor off the old Yacht Club, which is now the Police Social Club. Nevertheless, we were invited to a dance that night and had a great time. Next day we wandered around the old German-built town, grateful for the exercise, and had a meal in one of the many Indian restaurants.

From Dar es Salaam we sailed direct for the Comoros, taking eight days to cover the distance of 953 miles, aided by steady southeast winds of about twenty knots. From 200 miles away we picked up the high volcano of Comoro!

We had good sailing, again close hauled. Life was much easier now that Alem had caught on to the rudiments of steering. Now we could go into three watches—three hours on and six hours off. After the watch on-watch off up until Mombasa, this was luxury indeed.

The Comoro Islands, lying near to the center of the northern entrance to the Mozambique Channel, are a group of four islands—Grande Comore, Mohéli, Anjouan, and Mayotte. In 1971 they were administered by the French government as an overseas territory. Except for Mayotte, they are volcanic in origin, with mountainous summits.

The islands were known to the ancients as the Islands of the Moon, and they were the southern limit of the vast medieval Arab empire. After the European entry into the Indian Ocean, before the ports of South Africa and Mozambique were developed, they were the main victualing place for ships on their way from the Cape of Good Hope to India and the East. The beef and fruit of the Comoros were renowned throughout the sailing world for their quality. The islands were also notorious for the warlike nature of their inhabitants, each island continually carrying out raids on the others. This state of affairs lasted until the French took over in 1890. With the demise of large sailing vessels, the importance of the islands disappeared, and for decades, they have been an isolated backwater in the Indian Ocean. A tourist industry is just starting to build up.

The harbor at Moroni, the capital of the Comoros, has a tiny entrance that dries out between the tides, making it impossible for any vessel which draws more than three feet. So *Barbara* remained out in the roadstead, heaving for days to the swell of the ocean.

The port is very picturesque; the inhabitants wear long djellabas and tarbooshes during their prayers and ablutions. Along the waterfront are thirteen mosques in a row. One gentleman in a long robe and tarboosh introduced himself, in bad English, as Mustafa, ex-sergeant, British army! He had served in the Eighth Army under Montgomery in Egypt. He hailed from Zanzibar, but had wisely got out of that country when he saw the handwriting on the wall for the Arabs, whom the blacks, on taking power by a margin of one vote, slaughtered to a man.

From Mustafa I found out about some very strange customs on the islands. For instance, a baby born under the sign of Aquarius is cast outside to die. The cost of a wife is about two years' wages, while the cost of the wedding party, which is a *must*, is about five years' wages. Under Moslem law the husband must provide a roof for his wife, so he gets into debt for about thirty years—and this on an island only thirty-five miles long by fifteen miles wide with a population of 100,000 souls and very little arable land. Maybe that's the reason for chucking out the Aquarius babies.

The fishing off the Comoros is fabulous. One of the rarest fishes in the world is found here, the fossil fish *coelacanth,* which was first caught by local fishermen in 1938. It was so rare that the University of Paris used to pay two thousand dollars for a specimen. One evening Conrad and I saw two of them, caught that day, lying in the refrigerator of the French inspector of forests for Moroni Island!

Making rope out of coconut fibers is one of the local industries. All along the shore we heard the click-click as hundreds of women, sitting in the shade of palm trees, beat the sticky fiber into separate strands. A lot of the girls had white clay smeared over their dusky faces, for it was Mohammed's birthday and these people are very devout Sunni Moslems.

Five times a day the men and boys came down to the shore to face, not east, but north to Mecca, raising their arms to

Allah and falling on their knees with their faces to the ground before him. After praying, they relieved themselves at a spot just below the prayer ramp, squatting for hours, shitting away with enraptured faces. Just below *that* spot hundreds of bathers submerged themselves, clothes and all (at this end of the port the men, then the boys, then the girls under the eagle eyes of their mothers, and lastly, on the seaward end of the foreshore, the women). They managed to perform these three vital activities—praying, shitting, and washing—as if they were completely unaware of the presence of any other soul.

"Bloddy Moslems," said Alem, spitting over the side.

Only the men and boys go to the mosque, which is not a place for females. And so lives one-fifth of the world.

I decided to wait for the end of the rainy season here in the Comoros, patching sails, reading, and writing some articles. We could live cheaply; coconuts and fish could be had for taking. For a month we cruised the islands with Arthur, ending up in Mutsamudu, from which we headed north for the Seychelles Islands, on our way east at last!

11

INDIAN OCEAN PARADISE

T WAS NOW EARLY JUNE AND in the Indian Ocean the southeast monsoon was still blowing, ideal for carrying *Barbara* north to the Seychelles. There I intended to collect the charts ordered from London and continue across to Ceylon and Singapore. From there, in the spring of 1972, I would make my way across the South China Sea and the Pacific Ocean to Peru, where I hoped to haul *Barbara* across the Andes from the coast to the highest navigable water on earth, Lake Titicaca. With luck I would be in Peru by December of 1972. How was I to guess, at that time, sitting in the remote little harbor of Mutsamudu, that I would not arrive in South America until a year later?

From Mutsamudu, with a lively quartering wind of twenty-five knots average, we made the run of 1,050 miles to Victoria on Mahé, the main island of the Seychelles, in exactly ten days. As a landfall, I chose the tiny coral island of African Islet, about 100 miles west of Mahé. I was very eager to visit this remote spot, for its bird life and seashells were among the most interesting on earth. Also the equatorial current runs west at an unknown and variable rate, and I did not, in case of inclement weather, wish to be set down on the Admiralty Islets, a long, low chain of reefs stretching north for 150 miles, situated to the southeast of the Seychelles. Rather, I preferred to pass to the lee side of them and sail up around the northern end, where African Islet was situated.

Alem was fascinated to watch me working on the charts, especially the coastal ones.

"Hey, Skip, that bloddy good; who make charts?"

"They are made in London, in a big office."

"How do they know about Africa?"

"They sent ships out a long time ago, to draw all the bays

and rivers and beaches, so that other ships could sail along safely."

"Maybe they got one of my home?"

"Very likely. If they do I'll send you one after you get back there."

"Where is that island? The one over there?" He pointed a hand at a headland of the continent.

"That's not an island; look, that's this part of Africa here which sticks out into the ocean. It looks like an island, but it's not really. It's because it's higher than the rest of the shore, which we cannot see because it's so low. Actually it is joined on to the rest of Africa."

But it took months for him to grasp this. He found it extremely difficult to believe in what he could not see and yet he was a fanatical Coptic Christian, who sincerely believed in about a thousand different saints, some of them the most improbable beings I've ever heard of. He also believed fanatically in the innate superiority of the Amhara over the Afar; and of the Afar over the Issas; and the Issas over the Somali; and so on *ad infinitum,* the members of each new tribe encountered always being added to his list at the bottom. In other words, despite months of our hammering away, arguing against his ideas, he was a prig. This attitude among tribes in Africa is by no means unusual. The Zulu thinks he's much better than the Xhosa, the Kikuyu despises the Masai. There is no such thing as an "African" or a "Kenyan" or a "Tanzanian"; these are terms introduced in the colonial period and now used by the smart politicians to their own advantage. Below the social level of a postal clerk, that is to say about 80 percent of the population, these terms are hardly even known.

On the third day out, bowling along at top speed, I was taking Conrad through the motions on a noon sight, when he dropped the sextant. Our only one! It clattered on deck, and I stepped on it quickly to keep it from falling over the side. The index mirror fell on the deck. Cursing our luck, I took the two parts down below and using a matchstick and marine glue, refixed the mirror. I straightened the index arm as best I could, then, using a larger mirror to calculate the amount of distortion, figured out what allowances should be made in the altitude readings. After several hours of patient fiddling (not an easy thing to do in a thirty-eight-foot boat crossing the ocean at speed), I was reasonably sure that the sextant would serve to give us at least a rough fix. I decided to navigate with the results I had obtained. Eight days later, in the afternoon, I sent Conrad aloft to the spreaders to look out for land, and there, dead ahead, right where it should have been, waving away on the horizon, shaking its head like a randy highland bull, was our single palm tree. Conrad was astonished. I pretended not to be surprised, as navigators will, but secretly I was prouder of picking up that single tree in the vast wastes of the Indian Ocean than I have been of any other single feat of celestial navigation.

We stayed at African Islet for two days, tucked in behind the mile-long reef, anchored in dead flat water, with the monsoon blowing overhead and the immense ocean seas crashing onto the low reef a few yards away.

There were thousands of birds nesting on the reef—frigate birds and terns, so tame you could actually touch them, so rarely had man visited the reef. The number and variety of the seashells on the shores of the islet were a marvel, and we spent many delightful hours inspecting them. Conrad caught three good-sized fish, and we smoked them on the sandy beach to the music of the seas roaring over the reef.

It was interesting to speculate what could be done if we were ever shipwrecked on such a waterless island. I came to the conclusion that I would set up as many surfaces as I could, even the seashells themselves, facing the wind, and try to catch whatever moisture possible. Given a large surface area, it might be possible to collect enough moisture to stay alive. Of course, the ideal surface would be clear plastic sheeting, but not everyone carries such an item when they're cast ashore.

On this particular passage, from Mutsamudu to Victoria, we caught several of the most delicious eating fish in the oceans, the dorado. It is a very beautiful fish, emerald green with a bright golden belly. Immediately after it is caught it can be eaten. Fried in butter, it tastes delicious. On ocean

passages I always trail astern at least three lines with different sized hooks. For a lure, out in the blue seas, a small piece
of rag will suffice, for the average ocean denizen is not a
very wily creature and is attracted by anything that looks
even remotely edible.

By this time, Alem had integrated himself well into the
company and was busy learning all the things sailors have to
learn—knots, splices, bends, hitches, steering, basic
mechanics, mathematics. He was also learning, though very
slowly, that for a sailor the most important virtues are
patience and a good sense of humor, and that physical
strength takes a definite second place to intelligence and
perseverance.

We fetched Victoria (sailormen do not arrive at a place,
they *fetch it to them*) on the twenty-second of June and found,
to my great disappointment, that the charts from London
had not arrived. We would have to hang around the islands
for a while to chase them up by letter. As we were short on
cash, I decided to make for La Digue Island, where we could
fish and live cheaply. Our total expenses during the six-
week period we stayed there were exactly five dollars.
Without touching our precious boat stores, we lived on fish,
fruit, and coconuts. While Alem and Conrad fished and did
the onboard boat chores, I wrote some more articles, hoping to make some money. Whether we went east or west, we
were still more than half a world away from Lake Titicaca.

Before leaving the Dead Sea, back in Israel, I had written,
purely on the offchance, to the Peruvian Yacht Club, asking
them their opinion on my chances of hauling *Barbara* up the
coast from Callao across the Andes to Lake Titicaca. I had
sent them details of her dimensions and weight and mentioned that I had hoped to be in Callao no later than December 1972. Now, six months later, their reply, channeled
through my London forwarding address, finally reached
me. It contained some disturbing news. They considered it
impossible for a vessel of her weight to pass; high up in the
Andes was a bridge over a chasm which was only supposed
to take a load of eight tons deadweight total. *Barbara* herself
weighed about twelve tons. With the weight of a truck
added this would make about twenty tons total! Also, there

was a very low tunnel, with a passing height of only ten feet. However, if I could ascend the Amazon River for over two thousand miles from the Atlantic to a place called Pucallpa, on the eastern side of Peru, there was a twelve-ton crane and a track, very rough but passable, up into the Andes, which eventually led to Puno, on Lake Titicaca.

I contacted Arthur, now back in the States, and put it to him that we should change direction. He agreed.

I dug out the atlas and pored over it. This meant turning right around and making a voyage of eight thousand miles in order to ascend the Amazon before the river rose in March of next year. It meant passing around the Cape of Good Hope. It also meant taking a chance that the crane would still be in operation when and if we reached Pucallpa.

For two more weeks we enjoyed the idyllic Seychelles while I turned the problem over in my mind. We visited the island of Praslin, where the coco-de-mer, the old "fruit-of-the-tree-of-life" grows. The island is supposed to be the remnant of the Garden of Eden. Indeed, it is a true tropical paradise, one of the very few genuine ones, with no insects and ideal temperatures all year round, and plenty of fruit and fish.

At last, I made my decision. We would head, as fast as we could, for the Amazon. We had enough stores for six months, the boat was in good condition, and we were raring to go. We would make a dash to get to Pucallpa, *ten thousand* miles away. It was now August, and we would have to make the distance in less than six months! As it was, I already had a chart of the northwest coast of Madagascar and another of the South African coast from Durban to the Cape of Good Hope. Most likely, I could get a chart of northeast Brazil in Capetown. I made for Victoria, said farewell to my friend, Edward Allcard (who used to cruise with regularity around Cape Horn in his old German forty-footer, *Sea Wanderer*), and stocked up with fresh vegetables and water. Then we were off. First stop, Coetivy Island, two hundred and fifty miles southeast of Mahé, where *Barbara* was the first yacht ever seen. The locals, coconut pickers to a man, stared at us in wonder as we tacked through the reef.

In antique French the overseer explained how their only

excitement came when a ship would pass the island, far out on the horizon, maybe once every two or three months. All two hundred inhabitants would turn out, running joyfully down to the beach to watch as the smudge of smoke passed by them. At night, if a ship passed, they would light a huge bonfire, kept in readiness, so the ship would know they were there. Not as a navigation aid, understand, but just so the people on the ship would know that they *were there*. This tale affected me greatly. I thought it was one of the saddest, loneliest places I had ever been to.

"Them people stupid," said Alem. "They don't know nothing."

We did not stay long in Coetivy, for the cyclone season was just starting. We exchanged a few yarns with the islanders and passed on, heading for the Cape of Good Hope and the Amazon. All thirty-eight feet of us.

1969: Tristan relaxing at the helm of the *Barbara* in the Canary Islands after his sixteenth trans-Atlantic crossing.

Tristan in Gibraltar, December 1969—an ordinary tourist, enjoying the sights. This was the last time he wore a tie for nearly six years.

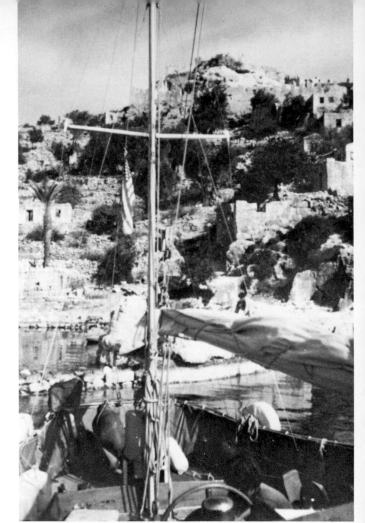

Barbara docked at Antalya, Turkey, October 1970. "...haunting, cholera-ravaged south coast of Turkey, one of the most beautiful coasts in the world...."

Hauling *Barbara* across Israel to the Dead Sea: the first time a foreign, privately owned vessel had been transported from the Mediterranean to the Gulf of Aqaba.

Barbara being lowered into the Red Sea at Eilat, December 1970

The rat caught on *Barbara* after biting through the water tank hoses. "He was a real monster, over three feet long from the tip of his nose to the end of his tail."

Tristan searching for land from the mast of *Barbara*.

Tristan, Conrad Jelinek, and Alem Desta in Kenya, just before the passage of *Barbara* to the Seychelles, via the Comoros Islands

The prolific vegetation of Brazil on display at an herb stall in Belem.

Barbara under power going into the Amazon.

Despite poverty and disease, there was great warmth and affection between ragged Amazon parents and their pitifully hungry children.

Typical dwelling place of an Amazon jute farmer, with Tristan wading in front, braving snakes and piranhas.

Turning-back point for *Barbara* on the Amazon. A morbid place, "rotting crosses of an old-time rubber-collectors' graveyard, overgrown by the conquering jungle, alive with mosquitos and piums...."

View of Devil's Island from St. Joseph's Island

PART TWO
To Seek

"Flog that man, Mr. Christian!"
"But, Sir, he's dead!"
"Mr. Christian, I said flog that man!"
> *Captain Bligh, Royal Navy*
> *On board the frigate* Bounty
> *From Royal Navy folklore*

12
A ROUND OF CYCLONES

ETWEEN COETIVY ISLAND and Madagascar's northernmost part, Hellville, there are 610 miles of ocean. Around the area are several groups of low-lying coral islands, none of which are lit at night. These include the Farquhar Group, the Cosmoledos, Cerf, and St. Pierre Islands. During the day you can see the palms that grow on most of these coral islets, but at night it is impossible to know how near they are until you hear the surf beating against the reefs. With the treeless islets, this is also the case in the daytime. If you can hear the surf, then you are lost, for it is a lee shore. With the wind blowing onto the reefs, together with the westerly set of the Indian Ocean current in those latitúdes, your craft is likely to be thrown onto the jagged coral and you will be in for a diet of coconut and fish for several weeks, until the next craft comes along—if you're lucky.

The best thing to do is head aṣ far to the east of this archipelago as is prudent, and this is what we set out to do in *Barbara*. For the first two days we had good southeasterly monsoon winds, from thirty to thirty-five knots, and we were covering 144 miles a day, but on the third day we got our first cyclone. It came up on the shoulders of clouds black as the back of a fireplace, full of menacing thunder and lightning. Within an hour we were battling winds of seventy knots with tremendous seas. In order to miss the reefs we had to stay as close hauled as we could so as to make southing; for to give way and drift southeast would have set us right down on the hazards of Farquhar.

We reefed down to working jib, one-third of the main, and the mizzen, and kept on going, hard. The storm slashed and howled; the Indian Ocean, relatively shallow, rolled up into tremendous mountains of dark blue, heaving water. It was as if God himself was having a fit. But in *Barbara*, though uncomfortable, we were not unduly fearful; our gear was good and we had learned to be very patient. My main concern was not to lose ground to the west; as it was, we cleared the easternmost reefs by about fifteen miles. As soon as I knew we were well clear of the Farquhars, we handed the working jib, which by this time was straining like a brewer's cart-horse, and hoisted the storm jib so as to let her ride easier. And so we passed through our first three-day cyclone.

From the foregoing no one should imagine, if they have never experienced a full-blown storm at sea, that the ocean voyager becomes blasé about it, or that the living fear of Christ does not enter into his soul and emerge down his spine to his balls. Because he doesn't and it does. Every time. At least in my case. Most of the ocean voyagers to whom I have talked about this agree with me, but there are some who tend to play down their true feelings. Curious that women never do; they are one hundred percent truthful when it comes to admitting fear. I suppose some guys still have the remains of shore-side machismo in them. Not me; when I shit I shit, and I don't give a damn who knows it. If they think any the less of me for being honest about it, then let them take off and navigate in a rip-roaring cyclone, with certain death under the lee in the black, stormy, rain-lashed, uncertain depths. Let *them* peer, eyes aching with want of sleep, into the darkness in a heaving, crazy, thundering hull in God's vastness; let them strain their ears away from the roaring wind and try to pick out the sound of surf on the deadly reefs. *Then* they can look down their noses, if they like. But don't let them tell me they were not afraid up to a certain point.

I say a certain point, because there comes a time when, without any diminution of the dangers, you get beyond fear. You come to realize that it interferes with logical thought and isn't solving anything. You've done all you can do to avoid disaster, now you are in the hands of God. When this moment comes, a man feels the greatest peace of mind that is possible for him ever to experience. At that moment he realizes that death is not terribly important, even though it is inevitable, and that he has lived his life as well as he could in his own way. If this is the end, then fair enough, he's lived this life, now for the *next*. Then some regret; not at the thought of losing your life, but because you have *put* yourself in that situation. You determine to survive. *In extremis*, survival is the result of being angry with yourself for being a bloody fool!

I have very often been in a situation in which I did not think I would survive, but, by God, I would go on trying—I was going to play the bloody game right down to the bottom line, because it's *fun*. Also it's very interesting. Also, for the time being, *it's all we have*.

The storm eased off for one day and then we got another cyclone. By the time we wore around into the lee of Cape Ambre we were, all three of us, like half-drowned dogs. In the second cyclone, with plenty of room under the lee, the wind rose so high I decided to run before it under storm jib alone. Between two very sure fixes we covered 178 miles in twenty-four hours, running northwest before the wind, with roller-coasting seas threatening to overwhelm the stern every three seconds. We had to struggle with the wheel the whole time, arm-breaking work, for a shallow-draft boat like *Barbara* will always try to broach, or turn sideways to the wind, and then she would lie in a trough between hellishly high seas and be overcome and turn turtle.

Alem, while all this was going on, had to be prodded and cajoled into action, for his natural inclination was to give up easily. This took a lot of energy from me.

At last we got under the protection of Cape Ambre, in fairly flat water, with the sun shining. We took every blanket, every sheet, every book, every chart out of the cabin and dried it in the sunshine. Everything in the boat was thoroughly damp, for we had taken quite a number of seas over the stern. At least a dozen times the cockpit had been filled, with the helmsman, roped to the binnacle, up to his waist in water and seawater pouring down the companionway, so that we would have to pump out by hand for an hour, five or six tons of seawater at a time.

I took *Barbara* into a well-protected bay, Nosy Mitsio, and dropped anchor. The weather, with the cyclone passed, was beautiful—green hills; deserted, sandy beaches; clear, clean sea; plenty of fish; a blue sky with the monsoon clouds scudding overhead. The boat's gear still was in good order. What more could a man want? A pretty girl? Well, this was Madagascar, where live the most beautiful women on God's earth. Majunga, the chief port, was only two hundred miles away. We could wait. Meanwhile, we got the gear dry and the boat shipshape. I'm a great believer in arriving at a port as if we had had nothing but gravy-sailing all the way, regardless of the distance. There is no point in looking bedraggled. It's not pretty and it's impolite to the onlookers, if there are any, if there aren't it's impolite to your vessel.

We had a good, fair-wind sail down through the island to Majunga. As there was much tide there, I determined to clean the bottom.

At the harbormaster's office, I found my old friend Christian Joubert. He was from Brittany, and I had known him when that beautiful, friendly French peninsula was my old stamping ground. Many a cargo of home-distilled whiskey straight from the Hebrides I had landed at L'Aberwrach right under his very nose. Now here he was, lording it over a tropical port, living like the bloody Kublai Khan himself. He was delighted to see me and arranged for *Barbara* to be leaned against a tug while the tide went out so that we could clean the bottom.

The bottom of Majunga harbor is the most foul-smelling mud it has ever been my misfortune to be up to my knees in, full of minute crabs, which would, when we sank into the soft mud, ooze over the top of our sea boots and nip our legs. Despite the stinking, hot, muddy slime, we scrubbed off all the grass, barnacles, and growth that had accumulated since we left Israel, nine months earlier. Then we slapped on the antifouling, a thick, red copper paint which you must be very careful not to get into your eyes, lest you be blinded.

We cleaned off the propeller, smeared it with thick grease, and inspected all the underwater fittings, particularly the rudder pintles and the seacocks. Then we painted on a new waterline of blue. Soon *Barbara* looked as pretty as a well-loved boat can look. But not half as pretty as the lasses in Madame Chapeu's, the premier *établissement* of Majunga. Half-Polynesian, half-Arab, they were a sight for sore eyes. Famous throughout the Southern Hemisphere, Madame Chapeu's was the biggest whorehouse I'd ever seen—until I reached Belém, in Brazil. Alem, overcoming his Coptic bias on this occasion, had a ball.

13

THE CRYSTAL COAST

USTRALIAN SAILORS HAVE a term—"seeing the country and meeting the people." What it really means is going on a good run ashore, having a few drinks, visiting different bars, and making friends, mostly with all the pretty girls that cross your bows. That is exactly what we did in Majunga; for I had earned enough cash to have some to spare, and a bored sailor is a bad sailor. We ate well, for the restaurants are cheap; we drank perhaps a little too much, for smuggled booze is cheap; and we made a lot of friends, fair and dusky. So many, in fact, that when we came to leave, Christian, the harbormaster, actually accused me of not having learned one damned thing in fifteen years!

From Majunga we cruised slowly down what is surely the loveliest cruising ground in the world (or so I thought until Lake Titicaca). The air is so clear that it seems you can touch the Massif Centrale, a range of mountains two hundred miles away. In the mornings the limpid sky and the sea appear to be joined together, so that it is impossible to see the horizon, and all the time you are floating in the clearest water I have ever seen. The bottom at sixty feet is as plainly visible as the floor under your feet. It was as if the boat was afloat in a crystal bowl. The silence was so delicate, a shimmering, trembling silence, that it seemed that the slightest noise would shatter the world around you into a million pieces.

Barbara would ghost along in the lightest of zephyrs, and we would creep around the deck, whispering so as not to shatter the magic. There were hundreds of islands off this coast, most of them uninhabited, full of birds and luxurious vegetables. Sandy, untrodden beaches, coral reefs aswarm with fish, safe anchorages, and the best sailing imaginable, all under the lee of Madagascar, with the monsoon coming off the land and a dead flat sea.

We were in no hurry, for ahead of us lay the long, stormy passage around South Africa and the Cape of Good Hope. It was still only September, the southern spring. It would be best to dally until November before tackling one of the roughest sea passages in the world, the thousand-mile run between Durban and Capetown.

I found out a curious thing while we were visiting these islands. It is always my habit when in remote parts to visit the chief elder of any community. At Nosy Vahalia, because I had nothing else suitable, I took the chief one of my old navy shirts—the old collarless type with a tail fore and aft. The chief, an ancient about ninety years old, was beside himself with delight. These folk are Moslems, and he intended to wear the shirt to the mosque. He first gave me coffee and a cheroot to smoke, then sent for chickens for me to take back. When we awoke onboard out at anchor the next day, we found the cockpit full of vegetables, fruit, and fish. We had enough food for three weeks and it did not cost one cent. When we went ashore we were escorted like princes to other villages, where we were received as honored guests.

Slowly we ambled down the coast of Madagascar for three hundred miles. This is my favorite kind of cruising, among small remote islands, on a weather shore, with a backdrop of mountains. I have known it in Norway, in Turkey, in Madagascar, and in Panama, and it never fails to enchant me. I could stay in that sort of place forever. Maybe I will end my days somewhere like that, perhaps in southern Chile, an area which has always fascinated me because of its thousands of islands and unspoiled natural beauty. For my last voyage I can head out into Drake's Passage and see and feel the winds of the world as they whistle around the Horn. And my soul can soar like an albatross above the seas of the southern passage, returning north only to seek out the lonely islands and shielings of the Strait of Magellan and Tierra del Fuego.

During this slow passage down the coast of Madagascar we fished a deal and caught many stingrays, the wings of which make delicious eating, something like Dover sole. We also caught dorado, for this is one area where that ocean fish comes in near to shore. The rocky shores were alive with landcrabs, and these, too, made good eating, while on the coral reefs were enough crabs and crayfish to keep us gorged for life. Ashore there were limes, lemons, small oranges, tomatoes, breadfruit, wild pig, and goats. There were few insects, none at all on the islands. Every night we would barbecue on the beach, and the glare of the firelight revealed thousands of landcrabs watching our antics with curiosity. But they were harmless, and would scurry away as soon as we moved towards them. They were ugly-looking devils, gray and hairy, and seemed almost obscene to us; then we remembered that we were brown and hairy too, and that the crabs probably thought the same about us, except for Alem, who was very black and almost hairless, and terrified of the crabs.

The Mozambique Channel is a thousand miles wide. At the time we sailed it there was a full-scale civil war going on in the then Portuguese colony of Mozambique. We decided to give that country a wide berth. After our last call in Madagascar, *Barbara* sailed 1,468 miles to Durban, encountering four storms en route, two in the Mozambique Channel and two off the coast of South Africa. The worst one was about one hundred miles northeast of Durban, off the coast of Zululand.

Between storms, which in October are regular in this area (we were passing from the cyclonic system into the temperate zone), we had glorious sailing weather. The Indian Ocean is the bluest of all, a deep aquamarine color, much darker than sky blue. The winds, in between tempests, are steady north of the tropic, and there is much more bird life than in the Pacific or the Atlantic. This is because the many reefs and islets are widely scattered, and while this makes for navigational hazards, it means that there are many isolated specks of coral and land for the birds to visit.

I think the Indian Ocean is probably the most interesting area for tropical cruising. Unfortunately, very few yachtsmen pass through this part of the world. Vast areas of these seas are unknown to western small craft. Most of these isolated pinpricks are natural wildlife reserves, as, for example, Aldabra, with its huge turtles, and Bassa de India and Europa Island in the Mozambique channel, two completely untouched and unspoiled coral reefs teeming with sealife. The inhabitants of the area are, in the main, some of the friendliest and most hospitable people that you could possibly wish to meet. The few outsiders living among them are surely amongst the most colorful characters anywhere; most of them operate small cargo schooners and steamers between the islands, collecting copra. In particular, I recall one French lady, skipper of a small steamer in the Comoros, who, pistol at hip, kept the whole male population of Mutsamudu hard at loading her vessel for days on end, with never a murmur of complaint. At the end of the day she would drink a bottle of the best whiskey without turning a hair, at the same time preserving her French savoir-faire and elegance.

The history of this part of the ocean is interesting. The Arabs penetrated as far south as Madagascar in the fourteenth century, looking for gold in the Zambezi River and slaves from Mozambique. In the fifteenth century the Portuguese, led by the courageous Bartholomeu Dias and the indomitable Vasco da Gama, finally, after decades of patient and steady exploration down the west coast of Africa, rounded the Cape of Good Hope to the East Indies and China, establishing an empire which did not dissolve until 1975. The Portuguese also built a chain of forts right up the East African coast and, until the British stumbled into the area after the Napoleonic wars, controlled most of the trade in this huge area.

Until the British defeated the French at Trafalgar, there was a running struggle for control of the sea route around the Cape of Good Hope between these two countries (the Dutch having dropped out in the mid-1700s). Finally, the Cape became a British base for the fleet, another Gibraltar, and the French islands of Mauritius and La Réunion were taken over, thus safeguarding the approaches to and from Europe and allowing the British to take over India.

During this time the Cape of Good Hope became a very important sailing route, with ships richly laden passing to and from the East and Europe. With the trade, as always in the days before the steamer, came the pirates, the freebooters, and for well over a century Madagascar was the lair from which they would pounce on the East Indiamen on their way to and from the Cape. To this day in the Comores and Madagascar, a steamship, indeed any foreign vessel of any kind, is called a "mannowarri," which comes from the old British term, "Man o' War." A foreign seaman is known as a "goddami," for until the nineteenth century "goddamn" was a favorite British expletive. On Madagascar "goddami mannowarri" means a sailor from a foreign ship! This is part of the Swahili language in that area.

On the passage down the Mozambique Channel, which took sixteen days, we blew out the sails a number of times, so that by the time *Barbara* reached Durban, there were more patches on some sails than original sail.

The great storm of Zululand was a lulu. The Agulhas Current runs south down through the Mozambique Channel, but the axis of the current is close to the African shore, about twenty miles offshore, roughly on the 100-fathom line, where the continental shelf drops off into the deeps. Off Cape St. Lucia, in Zululand, however, the axis of the current approaches close to the shore. Now on the axis of the current, and on the seaward side of it, the seas are so steep, with a full gale or storm blowing against the current, that a small craft cannot survive for long, if at all. Therefore, it is wise to stay close to Cape St. Lucia and that is what we did, hoping to slide past before a "southerly buster" came along to shake us up. One hit us smack on the nose just as we reached the Cape—a real beauty, a real ripsnorter. It was the twenty-first of September; later, after we fetched Durban, I found out that the windspeed at the airport that day had registered eighty-two knots.

So there we were, with huge breakers assaulting the coast of Zululand under our quarter a couple of miles off, unable to make much offing because of the tremendous seas of the Agulhas Current. Right through the middle of this hellish mess runs one of the busiest shipping lanes in the world, with huge tankers and cargo vessels passing at the rate of one every half-hour. We couldn't go in, we couldn't go out, and we couldn't stay put.

As the storm increased towards late afternoon, I calculated that if we hove to under mizzen, with the current
pushing us one way and the wind pushing the other, we
might *just* stay put while the tide was running out. However,
as soon as the tide changed, we would be forced to try to
make the offing, come what may. So for six hours, until well
after dark, we hove to. Then, about midnight, with the wind
slacking off a touch, we started to work our way out, slowly
and very delicately, against huge seas, across the steamer
track at right angles, to the edge of the continental shelf. We
had bent on the storm trysail—a small, heavy-canvas, trian-
gular sail rigged in place of the mainsail, except that it is
loose-footed, that is, not hanked onto the boom. With this
sail and the storm jib, we crept across the face of the wind
and sea. I say crept, but in actual fact, in those seas, we
bounced around like a bronco, all three of us lashed to
sturdy fittings with our safety harnesses. It was useless to try
running the engine, for half the time the stern of the boat
was clear out of the sea while the other half of the time the
bow was digging in deep, so that the sea washed straight
over the topsides. We put out a strong light and hoped that
the steamers would see us in time to avoid us. To the
mariner, and especially the single-handler, the gravest
danger in all oceans is other craft, particularly the monster
tankers, for they are so large that from the bridge, with the
way ahead obscured by a foredeck as big as Yankee
Stadium, the helmsman cannot see anything closer than
three miles away. At night he can see nothing at all that is
not further than three miles away. The tanker trusts to her
radar, and in confined seas, such as we were crashing
around in, her officers usually pay strict attention to the
radar. But human nature being what it is, there is always the
chance that for a few minutes the officer of the watch might
be drinking coffee, or reading the football results, and not
paying attention to his screen. If a tanker like that touched
Barbara, she would not feel the slightest shock in those seas.
We would sink immediately.

But that night off Zululand the tanker sailors were alive
and well and at least four of them changed course to avoid
us. Watching their radar screens, watching this small mys-

terious blob out there in the frantic sea, they probably thought we were a small fishing boat that had failed to make port, or that we were stark raving mad. When we had made enough offing (and there was no doubt at all when we had, for the movement was violent, the boat actually being tossed up in the air off the tops of the seas), we started toward shore again, across the steamer track. For three days and nights this nightmare continued until, very weary indeed, we found the wind abating down to about force seven. Handing the mainsail we beat our way into the narrow entrance of Durban harbor, over a hundred miles to the southeast of Cape St. Lucia, down a wild, storm-beaten shore. Finally, we tied up in Durban alongside the Point Yacht Club. The first pint of beer was the best I have ever tasted. The second was even better.

14

FROM THE SUBLIME TO THE RIDICULOUS

N DURBAN WE WERE MET by the port police and allotted a berth at the Point Yacht Club. It was late at night, so I waited until next day before tackling the shore entry formalities, which in South Africa are complicated, for this is, despite all the efforts to conceal the fact, a police state. Every move, in any direction, is carefully watched and recorded. This is not immediately obvious and it takes some time to sink in. Not in our case, however, for we had Alem aboard and Alem was an African, a *black*.

The first fireworks went off at the immigration office, where I presented the passports. At first, I was received cordially and politely, for the white South African can be the pleasantest of people, the most genial of hosts; but as soon as Alem's picture was discovered all this changed. I was told that he would not be allowed to stay onboard a small craft such as *Barbara* with two white men. In South Africa it is unlawful for members of two races to live in the same place.

"But where would he live?" I protested.

"In the African township," I was told.

"Where is that?"

"Fourteen miles inland."

"But he doesn't speak Zulu or Xhosa; he is not a Bantu—he has nothing in common with the Bantu. He is Hamitic."

"No matter, that is the law."

"Then if that is the law, the law is bloody stupid!" Did they mean to tell me that a man who was fit to be at sea with me in all weathers, who did his duties and did them well, who was as civilized as any other sailor under the sun, whose father I had promised I would treat as my own son, did they mean to tell me that he was not fit to use the same shower or shithouse? That he was not fit to sit at a table with me in a restaurant? That he could not use the same cinema? What the bloody hell was all this about?! But it was the law of the land and the immigration and police, who by now had joined the scene, were adamant: "You can't allow the other races to mingle with us, they're just not ready for it, not in this country."

"Look!" I said, for by now I was getting riled. "Look, I don't give a damn about your politics. What happens between your blacks and whites and Indians in this country doesn't matter a hoot to me, but what happens to my bloody crew *does*, and if he can't stay onboard the boat, if he has, by your laws, to go fourteen miles, walking [for there's hardly any public transport for Africans], to the township to get a meal or a bed, if he can't even use the Asiatic shithouse at the Club, if he can't get even a meal at the back door of the Club, then I'm off. My boat is in a bad state, we've weathered several storms, we're short of food, and the Cape of Good Hope is a bitch at this time of year, but if this is the case, if you can't bend one fraction of an inch, then bugger it, gentlemen, we will leave and I'll tackle the Cape and the South Atlantic to Brazil direct. But I tell you this, and this is my word, that if we are forced to do this near suicidal thing, I will make damned sure that sailing men the world over know exactly *why*. You can do what you like about it—arrest me, arrest the boat; chuck us out, lock, stock, and bloody barrel, but don't expect me to stand by and watch one of my crew treated like a blasted subhuman; because I won't and he isn't."

By now the chief of the port police had joined us, a big, florid Dutch South African. He looked as if he could crush me and I have no doubt that he would have been quite happy to do so.

"Careful now," said the immigration official, "there's such a law as the Suppression of Communism Act."

"Communism! What the hell are you talking about? Just because a skipper won't let his crew be messed about with? Bloody communism! You must be joking. Anyway, if that's the way it has to be, then I'm off, and I repeat, I'll scream blue murder about this for the rest of my life and make damned sure that every sailing man from Valparaiso to Gibraltar knows exactly what happened. Good morning!"

I made for the door, shaking.

"Now just a minute, Captain." The police chief lowered his tone down a few notches. "Just a minute. There's no point in leaving in a huff. I'll tell you what we'll do. This *Kaffir*"—a favorite Boer word for a black, similar to "nigger"—"we'll register him as an Asiatic. Yes, that'll do the trick. Let's see, we can say he comes from the Maldive Islands. They're Indian and the goliwogs there are black enough. No one'll know the difference. Then he can use the Asiatic facilities, washrooms, toilets, restaurants. That's the answer."

And so it was that we bent the rigidly entrenched South African laws of apartheid, just a very little, but *bent* them—Alem got his meals, his films, and his shit, too. It used to rile me at lunch time when we would go to a little cheap restaurant for meat pie and chips. Down the center of the restaurant was a line of refrigerators and soft-drink machines. Alem would have to stand to eat on one side of these, while Conrad and I sat down at a table on the other side. What stupidity! What narrow-minded, blind, futile, foolish, short-sighted, half-witted, fuddle-brained, irrational, senseless, ridiculous poppycock! But the meat pies were delicious and Alem even enjoyed them standing up!

The morning air in Durban is fresh and cool. We would rise early and work hard until one o'clock, when the heat becomes oppressive. Tall, white apartment buildings line the waterfront, fading away into the distance beyond the Yacht Club. Between the Yacht Club jetty and the skyscrapers there is a wide highway, with traffic roaring along from one set of traffic lights to the next.

All around the port there are great cargo ships, oil tankers, grain and sugar carriers, for Durban was then, with the Suez Canal closed, a very busy port. Out in the roadstead, beyond the harbor entrance, were as many as twenty ships lying to anchor, awaiting berth in the port.

Barbara was berthed hard by the public boating ramp, alongside a dozen other ocean-cruising craft, most of which had been in Durban for more than a year, their owners working ashore to earn enough to carry on around the Cape of Good Hope to the West Indies or Europe. Most of them had come from Australia or the Pacific, for this is one of the ocean-cruising world's focal points. Practically every yacht that crosses the Indian Ocean on her way to Europe, the United States, or the West Indies calls there. *Barbara* was back in the mainstream of world cruising, having been, since leaving the Mediterranean, off the beaten track. During the time the Suez Canal was closed, she was the only small craft to pass from the Mediterranean to the Indian Ocean by way of the Red Sea. Gradually we were joined by a few other sailing craft arriving from the east, awaiting the southern summer before tackling the redoubtable Cape of Good Hope.

"What have we got to do here, Tristan?" Conrad asked.

"Well," I said, "first of all, the engine's got to come out. It needs an overhaul badly and it looks as if this is the only place we can do it between here and the headwaters of the Amazon."

We headed round to Wilson's yard under sail and moored the boat steady. Four huge Zulus lifted the engine out with the aid of a small crane, four bottles of beer, a couple of puffs of dagga (a narcotic that grows in Zambia), and some chanting. Out it came, and we set to painting the engine compartment bilges, scraping and varnishing topsides, and repairing the sails. In a month, with the engine replaced, gleaming with paint, topsides revarnished and sails all repaired, we were ready to tackle the Cape. I was anxious to reach the South Atlantic quickly, in order to get to the Amazon before the rainy season commenced in March. We still had five thousand miles to go to the coast of Brazil; then another four thousand to reach Pucallpa and the Promised Land.

During the time we were refitting, Alem returned to the misty highlands of Ethiopia, for his father had died and he was due to enter the Imperial Navy in January. We shook hands at the airport, looking each other straight in the eye. He was going back almost an ocean sailor, with some salt in his blood and the breeze in his ears. He could swear like a sailor by this time, too. Also, far more importantly, he had learned a lot about tolerance.

Conrad took a week off to explore the bar of the River St. Johns, in the Transkei. Meanwhile, I explored the bars on the Durban waterfront, thinking that I would have enough river trips to last me quite a while during the next few months. I would tackle rivers when I came to them; I certainly wasn't going looking for them in Africa.

On the fourteenth of November, revictualled and refurbished, we sailed out of Durban harbor to tackle the thousand-mile run around the Cape of Good Hope, the Cape of Storms, as Dias originally called it. We were heading for the Atlantic, our own ocean, the waters I had been born upon, in a British tramp steamer off the island of Tristan da Cunha, forty-six years previously. I felt like I was heading for home.

ROUND THE CAPE OF GOOD HOPE

O N THE LONG THOUSAND-MILE passage from Durban to Capetown, *Barbara* encountered four storms in ten days. This is usual for that time of year. The prevailing westerlies on their way around the world collide in those latitudes of the South Atlantic with the Agulhas Current, which heads south from the Indian Ocean. Tremendous seas are set up, great steep slopes and valleys, with white water blowing off the crests, the spume whizzing over the topsides, cold and bitter after the warmth of the tropical Indian Ocean monsoon. For the first few days Conrad and I felt the strain of being back on two watches, heaving against the wheel day and night. But, as with everything, it was just a question of becoming accustomed to the effort, and within four days we were into the routine, enjoying the wild sailing between the storms.

Again, as north of Durban, the Agulhas Current sets up enormous waves to seaward of its axis, so the best thing to do is stay near the coast of South Africa, if possible inside the shipping lane, yet far enough offshore to avoid hazards such as riptides or uncharted rocks. This is a wild coast, littered with wrecks of merchant ships that have strayed too close. But at least the coast is fairly well lit, and by taking careful bearings you can navigate safely at night, even in the roughest weather. The problem is that, having to sail fairly close to the mountainous shore, say within six miles, you are subject to sudden gusts, katabatic winds which swoop down from the high peaks of the Drakensberg range in gusts of up to one hundred miles per hour. At night, too, there is the ever-present danger of collision with one of the hundreds of merchant ships that charge past the Cape every twenty-four hours.

Off Cape Agulhas, actually the southern point of the African continent, we got the worst blow of the whole voyage. A terrific wind was blowing straight onshore from the southwest. We were down to trysail and storm jib, slowly heading south, when a huge sea, looking like a moving mountain, just picked up the boat and threw her over on her port side. I was perched on the companionway ladder, taking a bearing on Cape Agulhas light. Conrad was lashed to the binnacle with his safety harness, an immensely strong belt of canvas webbing and nylon lines with a breaking strain of two thousand pounds. Suddenly the boat slammed over on her side, plunging the cross-trees of the mast on the port side down in the sea. The boat lay sideways at an angle of ninety degrees from the upright for at least two minutes, though it was difficult to gauge the exact period. I was thrown against the corner of the coachroof and the companionway, breaking three ribs. The cockpit was awash with cold sea water and the wheel binnacle, the sturdy steel column on which the wheel was mounted, was bent. The compass, rigidly secured to the column with thick brass bolts, was knocked right off and fell into the cockpit. Conrad's safety harness, with its breaking strain of two thousand pounds, snapped like a piece of cotton. All I heard him say was "Fuck!" as he went flying. Luckily he managed to hug the binnacle, at the same time dropping into the bottom of the steering well. After what seemed like a century *Barbara*, shuddering like a stuck pig, slowly came back to her sailing angle. We had survived a knockdown. I was in intense pain, but managed to rescue the compass from going over the side.

"Come on, mate, up you get!" I grabbed Conrad, hauled him up somehow, and relashed him, half-drowned and unconscious, to the starboard jib-sheet winch and cleat with the main halyard. All this in a roaring, cold, wet, stinging chaos of wind and salt water. But I was thankful it was my ribs which were stove in and not *Barbara*'s.

"All right, Skip?"

"Guess so, Conrad," I gasped as I heaved the wheel back on course.

On the morning of the twenty-seventh we were in greenish seas and although we could see nothing in the low clouds and overcast skies, we knew that we had worn the worst. We were now in the South Atlantic, so we bore away to the northwest, still reefed down to trysail and storm jib, crashing into gigantic swells, but, with the wind on our port beam, going like a train. The boat had held up; now we were making for the Cape of Good Hope.

"Bit roughish last night, eh?" said Conrad, grinning.

"Boisterous," I commented, wincing with pain from the broken ribs (I had wrapped my chest tightly with some spare sailcloth).

In the mid-afternoon, when the horizon cleared, the Cape loomed up on the starboard bow.

"There she is!" shouted Conrad, "the Cape!" His gloved hand pointed toward the bow.

"Whereaway?"

"Dead ahead!" He looked at me surprised. "Slap-bang on the nose, Skip, I couldn't have done better myself!"

"Well, where in Christ's name did you expect it to be, astern? Now go down below and rustle up some tucker!"

Somehow, Conrad managed to conjure up a hot meal of porridge and beans.

"There you are, Tristan," he handed a tin plate up through the companionway. "Get yourself wrapped round that."

There we were, still in one piece, back again in the Atlantic! Since *Barbara* had left it to enter the Mediterranean she had sailed very close to fourteen thousand miles in twenty months. She had crossed a desert; she had made her way through reef-strewn seas. She had sailed through the most politically dangerous waters on earth. And now she was bound for the western hemisphere to tackle the mightiest river current of all, the Amazon.

With three broken ribs I would have to rest a few days in Capetown, even if it meant a delay in reaching the Amazon, four thousand miles away. I'd sold a couple of magazine articles, so there was enough cash to stock the boat up for the Atlantic passage and a bit left over. I moved to the Hotel Elizabeth at Crown Point, and for the first time in eleven years I lived ashore for a few days, resting, reading, mainly about the Amazon and Brazil, and spending a few hours each evening in the convivial bars round about. My stay was enlivened by a visit from two gentlemen purporting to be journalists, one of whom assiduously photographed me from all angles in the hotel lounge, while the other asked me about my impressions of South Africa, in particular, apartheid, and the opinions other countries had on the subject. They didn't fool me for one minute; a sailor can smell a policeman a mile away to leeward. Needless to say, I gave them the God's honest truth of my own opinions with great pleasure.

"What does the outside world think? In the main they think you're bloody fools; even if your intentions are good, only you think so."

When my ribs mended, Conrad and I went overland to the Cape Nature Reserve to see the statue of Vasco da Gama. As we approached the spot along the well-paved road, we came to a sign pointing down a rough track, written in Afrikaans and English: "Statue of Vasco da Gama" and below, "Asians and Colored only." A little further on was another sign, this one pointing down a smooth roadway with cut grass borders that read, "Whites only." I insisted that Conrad turn the car right round and head for the docks. We finished storing up, filled the water tanks, and said goodbye to a lot of friends. We were ready to get off this beautiful land, so spoiled by a sickness that only the most drastic change will cure.

Had she taken the right course after the Second World War, South Africa could have been the leader of the whole of Africa. She had the power, the know-how, to drag the rest of Africa out of its turbidity; she could have led Black Africa into the twentieth century. Instead, blind, deaf, and bloody dumb, she awaits the inevitable—a bloodbath, or, with luck, the survival on sufferance of a small European enclave at the southern end of a beautiful, tragic continent.

We bore away from lovely Table Bay on the nineteenth of December with a fine southerly buster blowing *Barbara* into the South Atlantic, bound for Brazil, 3,300 miles away. At last I was on my way to tackle the great, mysterious continent that had fascinated me from childhood and for whose independence from Spain three of my forebears had fought, well over a century before.

16
ANOTHER OCEAN CROSSING

OR THREE HUNDRED MILES from Capetown, steering northwest, we had southerly winds, strong to gale force, right on the stern. We made good distances, for we were refreshed and able to keep up all working sail. The skies were overcast, but this did not worry me—we had the winds of the South Atlantic before us, and if I did not know my exact position for a few days, it would do no harm. The South Atlantic is not like the Indian Ocean; there are no isolated reefs to hit, at least south of the equator. We were heading out of the shipping lanes, and we could just let *Barbara* rip away into the horizon. This is the best kind of ocean sailing, with a clear way ahead, plenty of food and water onboard, a sound vessel and gear, and moderate weather. Sailing like this, you feel as free as a bird on the winds of the wide ocean. We set the foresail and the mizzen so that the boat would steer herself with the wind on the quarter during the day. We steered her by night until we were well clear of the shipping lanes, then we let her steer herself day and night, while we took three days off from the torture of the tiller.

On Christmas Day Conrad uncorked a bottle of Cape wine. With a canned chicken and a Christmas pudding, we celebrated and toasted absent friends and loved ones, while the boat danced away on the sweetest, kindest ocean in the world, for north of the Tropic of Capricorn the South Atlantic hardly knows what a gale or a storm is; the winds are steady southeast and very rarely above twenty knots.

"Good sailing, Tristan." That was his Christmas greeting to me.

"Merry Exmas, mate."

On Boxing Day, the day after Christmas, we raised, for the first time in over a year, our spinnaker. It stayed up for four days in a wind so steady you could balance a teacup on the compass. Sailing under spinnaker is very wearying, for you must watch it all the time; but the speed set up was so good it was worth the effort, and we stuck it out, two hours on, two off, for four days, making six to seven knots. Meanwhile, the fishing was good, and we caught at least one bonito or dorado every day, thus conserving our canned fish and meat. We popped the fish straight into the pressure cooker, regardless of the time of day, and yaffled it greedily. The best fish restaurant in the world cannot duplicate the taste of fresh ocean fish boiled in a little salt water, with curry paste smeared on the top, eaten as the boat heaves and lifts to the blue ocean swells on her way back into the tropics, away from the cold cruel waters of the Cape.

After four days on the spinnaker the strain began to tell. The first week out of Capetown we covered almost a thousand miles, so we handed the spinnaker and rigged up the genoa and the main ("wing and wing" as we say), with foreguys holding the boom forward and a running pole, also guyed forward, holding the genoa out. Then we ran away for another thousand miles, with not a thing in sight, not a bird, not a ship, nothing but the odd fish which we brought in on our lines. Nothing but the heaving sea swell and clouds, wispy and young in the morning, heavy and pregnant with rain in the evening. By this time I was getting very clear sights, which gave me as exact positions as I could obtain from the dancing deck of a sailboat making seven knots. On the sixteenth day out, having sailed 1,537 miles, we sighted St. Helena Island, high and misty in the distance, and made for the anchorage on the north side of the island, James Bay. Here we dropped the hook in the swell, had a good sleep until evening, then went ashore for a few beers in the "standard" pub, where we chatted until closing time with the friendly locals, who speak an accent very close to early Victorian west-country English, though most of them are colored folk of African descent. They were, or seemed to be, more British than either Conrad or me. Their main anxiety seemed to be that England might hand the island over to South Africa. I can't say that I blame them.

The second day in St. Helena we went to see Longwood, the beautiful house where Napoleon lived during his exile on the island before his death. From the way the islanders talk you would think it all had happened only yesterday. It was a treat to be in such an English place, and a real pleasure to go up to Mrs. Baines's grocery store on the little village high street, for all the world like a small-town main street somewhere in the English Counties, and enjoy a leisurely talk with this genial lady, whose little shop, stocked with such British necessities as Earl Grey tea and Guinness stout, Oxo beef cubes, and Rose's lime juice, is like the promised land after the watery wastes of the South Atlantic.

We did not delay at St. Helena more than three nights, strong though the temptation was, for the Amazon floods would not wait on our dalliance. Sadly, we bore off for Recife, in Brazil, almost seventeen hundred miles away.

Again, we had good winds and a following sea. Again for days on end, *Barbara* was wing and wing, rushing away to the northeast; and thereby hangs a tale, for on the whole passage we sighted only one other craft, and she almost caused us complete disaster.

On the morning of Sunday, 16 January 1972, the latitude 11°40′ south, longitude 21°10′ west, we sighted a small craft out on the western horizon. *Barbara* was still wing and wing, with all the sails well braced, making about seven knots, surfing on the rolling seas. Steaming parallel to us was the Taiwan trawler *No. 22 Chin Ying Chang*. After half an hour she made towards us at high speed, heading for a point directly ahead of *Barbara*; then, of all things, she *dropped her nets*. Right directly in front of our bows, only two hundred yards away! She had the whole of the South Atlantic to work in and she dropped her nets *two hundred yards ahead of a sailing boat running down wind*! Right in the middle of the huge South Atlantic!

"Stupid sod!" said Conrad as he ran forward to let go the braces.

Conrad and I moved faster than we had ever moved before. Down foreguys, bring the genoa round on the port side, come round to bring the wind onto the starboard side and sail parallel to the bloody fool, then come about on the starboard tack and head westward round the end of her fishing trawls, great steel nets that would have torn *Barba-*

ra's hull to shreds. The crew, a motley gang of scarecrows, lined the trawler's rail, grinning and waving. It's the first time I ever roundly cursed a Chinese in the middle of the ocean.

"They can't hear you, you know," said Conrad.

"No, but I can and you can!"

With three days still to go, we crossed over the continental shelf of South America on the twentieth of January. You can always tell when you are above the continental shelf, for the seas alter their rhythm. They are no longer as regular and steady. The rhythm of the sea becomes jerky and unpredictable. On the twenty-first we sighted our first birds. On the twenty-second the sea discolored slightly; and on the twenty-third we spotted Olinda lighthouse, our landfall, dead ahead, eight miles off. We hove to for the night, for we had no chart of Recife and it was obvious, even if only from the name (Portuguese for "reef"), that there would be hazards to avoid on the way in.

We had a nice bonito for supper, as we lay to under mizzen, with an oil lamp swinging from the main boom; then in turns we kept watch for the night, four on, four off. Finally at six o'clock the land, low and green, showed up clearly, and we wended our way into Recife harbor under short sail and tied up by the customs house. We had made the 3,340 miles from Capetown in thirty days. From the Seychelles, where this particular leg had started, *Barbara* had sailed 6,000 miles in just three months. I had made my seventeenth Atlantic voyage under sail! Conrad had made his first. It was the same for both of us.

17

A GOOD RUN ASHORE

HE TWENTY-THIRD DAY OF January, 1972, was a Sunday, so there were no customs or immigration officials on duty in Recife as we slid into the harbor. We couldn't land until *Barbara* had been entered into the country properly, so had to wait till the following day to explore the port. We didn't mind; contrary to popular belief, after a long ocean passage there is a certain reluctance to rejoin the disordered and seemingly illogical hurly-burly of a landsman's life. This is, of course, in contrast to the steady, well-regulated routine of a sailing vessel on a long passage, where the only problems, usually of a minor nature, have to do with the sails and rigging, the navigation and minor defects which appear from time to time in the boat's equipment.

Alone, or with a good mate like Conrad, there are few, if any, personality problems; life is all harmony with the sea and nature. Even now, after all the ocean crossings I have made, I find myself reluctant to approach the shore when making a landfall after a few weeks at sea. I get to such a state of peace with myself that I do not want to enter into the maze of problems which human intercourse brings with it—the pretense, the hypocrisy, the vain attempts to communicate, the whole bag of tricks brought about by people trying to chase their own asses. But of course this is a passing phase, and as soon as I am back in the stream of humanity for a few hours it goes away.

We watched the locals parade along the waterfront in their finery, milling throngs of brightly clad lads and lasses of all shades of color, ladies in their Sunday best, men and boys in all stages of attire from brief bathing shorts to full-dress tropical whites, all chatting away, happy and jolly as only Brazilians can be. As for us, when the sun went down, we cleaned up the cabin and the galley, ready for the official visits in the morning. Then we made supper, had a short shot of Scotch bought duty-free in South Africa, and turned in to sleep fitfully within earshot of blasting music from a nightclub twenty yards away. But I was happy, for I had at last reached the continent wherein lay my destination, far away in the west, across untold stretches of jungle and mountain, beyond the world's mightiest river, up among the clouds.

Early next day the officials came onboard, for in this part of the world folks bestir themselves very early, so as to get as much done as they can before the sun gets too high. We were duly entered into Brazil, with curious looks of course when I gave our destination as Pucallpa, Peru. But by this time I was accustomed to curious looks; I'd received them in Venice, in Israel, in Djibouti and South Africa—a few more wouldn't make the slightest difference.

Recife used to be called Pernambuco. In the heyday of sail it was one of the crossroads of the world, for it lies right on the northeast corner of Brazil, where the ocean currents and winds change direction. It grew to be a large city. Then sail disappeared, leaving a great port with very little trade. The only other vessels we saw during our stay were an Italian freighter and a Japanese trawler. The night life of the town is still geared to receiving fleets of ships, so you can imagine what a whale of a time the crew of the *Barbara* had. Instead of three days, as originally planned, we stayed two weeks.

The city consists, like New York, of several islands connected by bridges. The part of the city immediately backing the port, about four square miles in area, is called La Zona. It consists mainly of bars, cheap restaurants, cathouses, cinemas, exhibition dens, dance halls, massage parlors, gambling saloons, and barber shops, all wide open day and night and all very cheap. It was a sailor's shore-going paradise. There was absolutely nothing that you could not get within a five-minute walk of the boat. During the two weeks we stayed there we had all our meals cooked for us, all our shopping done regularly, the cabin and galley cleaned, and the topsides scrubbed numerous times every day. Yet I do not recall the same lads or lasses being on board for two days running. If there was ever a place where you could fuck yourself to death, free, gratis, and for nothing, Recife was it. There must have been, and I'm not exaggerating, at least ten thousand available women and boys within half an hour's stroll from the boat. It was enough to bring the most intrepid voyager to heel!

"Mmm," said Conrad, after his first trip ashore.

At our favorite bar the patrons took a shine to us, so much so that they even provided voluntary escorts to guide us safely around the town. We had no fear of any harm, no matter how much *cachaça* we drank. This *cachaça*, by the way, is firewater distilled from sugar cane; it makes West Indies rum or Polish vodka taste like fizzy lemonade. More than a moderate sip of the stuff was enough to blow our heads off, while a shot would make us reel. When the delights of the lower port began to pall, we walked up to the pretty little tree-lined square by the cathedral and listened to guitar concerts under the clear, cool, starry tropical night.

"Nice to get away for a rest," said Conrad, sipping his beer.

"It's not a rest you need, mate, it's a bloody nursing home!"

The local yacht club treated us royally, giving *Barbara* a free berth for the length of her stay, and even laying on a dinner in our honor. In return, we took a load of kids from the Recife orphanage out for a day's sail. They get very few foreign yachts visiting Recife, which is a pity, for it is certainly one of the most friendly and hospitable places I have ever called at, and I'd jump at the chance to fetch that port again, even if I were ninety years old and had to rumble ashore in a wheelchair. If there is a place in heaven for sailors (and there must surely be), it will be just like Recife, except the heat will be less intense and the air drier, for the humidity there is enough to make you wringing wet with the slightest effort.

It was at Recife that at last Conrad finally overcame his Quaker education. When the time came, we left with genuine regret, for we had found a lot of friends at all levels in the town; and though it's true that some of them would never in a million years be invited to tea at Buckingham

Palace, I'd invite them onboard any boat I was in and be proud to do it too.

"Is Belém anything like Recife, Skip?"

"God help us if it is," I replied.

With a crowd of at least a hundred people to wave us off, we bore away out of Recife harbor and headed west-north-west, along the coast of Brazil for a thousand miles. From Cape São Roque (the northeastern corner of South America) onwards, we had the current with us and the wind right up *Barbara*'s ass, so we had a rollicking good run and made the passage to Salinópolis, on the mouth of the Amazon, in nine days flat. On this run we were amazed to see, far out in the offing, sixty miles offshore, what appeared to be a man sitting on a kitchen chair with a sail aloft. It turned out to be a bamboo raft, called a jangada, which is a type of fast sailer used by the local fishermen. It was about fifteen feet long, but from a distance it was impossible to see the actual platform of the raft. As a result it looked just like a chair under sail; one of the most curious craft I have ever seen.

As we neared the mouth of the Amazon the thunder and lightning storms became more frequent. The whole of the eastern horizon blackened in a terrible way, looking like the threat of Jehovah, then the wind dropped and you could almost feel the electricity in the air. Next the wind came in a terrific gust, then the rain, tumbling down so thick we couldn't see the compass three feet away. The sea turned white with the wind blowing spume off the surface, and it looked like the end of the world was at hand. Then, suddenly, it was over. The sky lightened, the wind dropped to normal and all was steady. All in a matter of minutes, and this happened every hour or so. It was a mite disturbing at first, but, as usual, we soon got accustomed to it.

On the night of the eleventh of February, my calculations putting us sixty miles east of Salinópolis, we changed course inshore, and at 5:00 A.M. on the twelfth we raised the light of that point, on the southern shore of the world's greatest estuary. We stood off, and hove to, to wait the dawn. We had arrived at the mouth of the Amazon, the greatest of rivers. Now all we had to do was enter the mouth and ascend the river for twenty-three hundred miles. Easy! So we thought, but I was in for the lesson of a lifetime. If I'd had an inkling of what was to come, I'd have turned round and high-tailed it for the West Indies right away.

18

THE AMAZING AMAZON

INCE *BARBARA* AND I, ALONG with Conrad Jelinek for most of the way, had departed from Westport, we had covered more than thirty thousand miles of sea and ocean. A good third of that had been to windward. Hove to off the dangerous, wreck-strewn, sandbank-littered mouth of the Amazon, over a thousand miles from Recife, our last port of call, I fondly imagined that our long saga was close to a finish.

I little dreamed that it would take two more years of slogging effort and over another ten thousand miles of sailing and harrowing struggle before I would finally reach my destination, Lake Titicaca. Nor that this would eventually be achieved in another craft than *Barbara*. Reaching the Lake would not be the apogee of my odyssey; I would finally wind up doing nothing less than a complete crossing of the huge continent of South America in a sea craft—the first such exploit in the annals of navigation!

I was blithely unaware that I would be brought to grips with the mightiest sea-current in the world—the cold, gray, pitiless, unforgiving Humboldt—which surges up the west coast of South America. As we lay there, wallowing in the South Atlantic swell, waiting for the ocean tide to finally overcome the rush of the mightiest river on earth, I had no way of knowing that in order to regain the ocean after reaching my destination, I would have to tackle yet again the snow-sheathed Andes, nor that I would somehow have to cross the most inhospitable region on the face of the globe, more terrible than the arctic, the fetid Chaco desert and the biological riot of the Mato Grosso swamps—the Green Hell in the heart of the South American landmass!

Neither did I know that after all this I would find myself back in the South Atlantic Ocean after conquering some of the greatest natural obstacles known to man, after navigating uncharted and dangerous rivers for more than two thousand miles in a twenty-foot sloop! Nor, thank God, did I foresee that I would come closer to a miserable, hungry death than I ever had before, nor that there would be times when I would dearly wish that I was back in the good old days, frozen into the ice north of Spitsbergen or whale-wrecked in mid-Atlantic.

I naively and firmly believed that it would be a simple matter pushing up against the current to Pucallpa, and that from there on it would be merely a question of logistics in order to reach Titicaca. Logistics? In South America? What a joke! *Now* I know! But happily I had no inkling of this at the time we hoisted the mainsail and headed into the largest river estuary on earth.

The River Amazon is about four thousand nautical miles long from its source to its mouth. It drains an area bigger than the whole of the continental United States. It starts as a trickle in the bleak Andes from Lake Vilafro, high up in Peru. There it is known as the Apurimac. Coming down from the mountains on the eastern face of the cordilleras, it garners the waters of thousands of streams. The Apurimac, ever growing, ribbons its way for a thousand miles north-ward from the desolate mountain massives to the edge of the dense jungle where it becomes the Ucayali. Another thousand miles winding through hot, humid, steaming jungle, inhabited by some of the fiercest tribes in a fierce continent, it emerges into the relatively civilized Iquitos area, where it becomes the Solimões, which name it keeps, as it pours, ever wider, ever stronger, first north and then east, until it reaches Manaus, over one thousand miles from the ocean. Here it becomes the Amazon. At Manaus the Amazon is *eighty* miles wide! At the mouth it is *two hundred and eighty* miles wide! Sitting in the mouth is Marajó Island, which is bigger than Switzerland! It is estimated, by God only knows what pedantic mathematical genius, that the Amazon carries enough mud to sea *every* year to create an island *four hundred and eighty miles* long by *four hundred and eighty miles* wide and five thousand feet high off the seabed!

The average speed of the current in the dry season in the middle of the river is six knots; but when the sun moves south over the equator for the austral summer, it melts the snow on the high Andes peaks. Then the river becomes a mass of roaring water speeding along at fifteen knots, and the level of the river increases on average about thirty-five feet! Thousands upon thousands of square miles of jungle terrain are flooded, and an inland sea *bigger in area than the Mediterranean* exists until the waters again subside. Due to the annual inundations, either in rising or declining flood, mighty trees, some over two hundred feet high, great chunks of land, and masses of jungle undergrowth fall into the river forming floating islands, some *more than five miles long*, which charge downstream at the speed of the river itself.

As the mighty mass of yellow water reaches the sea, its volume is so great that it actually holds back the ocean tide until around fifteen minutes before high tide on the full moon, or spring, tides. Then the ocean overcomes the river and a wall of water up to fifteen feet high roars up the Amazon northern mouth. This vertical wall of water, moving at around fifteen knots, is the dreaded *pororoca,* which no small craft can hope to encounter and survive. We had avoided this hazard by entering the River Pará, the southern mouth.

This, then, was the mighty water system that *Barbara* set out to tackle. As the tide started to run in, we headed in with it, and were swept thirty-six miles in four hours—nine knots! All working sail up in the northeast trade wind! Bouncing from chop to chop in the muddy yellow waters, very badly buoyed, we could only guess at the channel. On most sandbanks, the masts of sunken steamers and sailing schooners stuck up as guides. It was like rushing pell-mell through a ships' graveyard blindfolded, for our echo-sounder, an instrument for measuring the depth of water, had given up the ghost long ago. Conrad swung the lead to test for depth, while I struggled against the hard wind astern and heavy chop to keep a straight course. In the middle of the estuary, twenty miles inside, we couldn't see either bank; in fact we were a good thirty-eight miles inside the river before we sighted any land at all—low jungle, a thin ribbon of trees, featureless.

When the tide turned again we soon knew it, for although we were sailing at seven knots through the water, we started moving *astern* at about five knots. I headed carefully inshore, sounding all the way and dropped the anchor, to await the next ingoing tide. It was heavy work. And so, patiently, in four tides, we covered the 120 miles from the ocean to Belém without mishap. But we were lucky, for upon inspecting the rudder in Belém I found that the violent action of the short choppy current had actually broken off three of the five rudder pintles, and the fourth was just hanging by a thread. If we'd lost the rudder in that sea, we'd have been in a pretty pickle, for I had nowhere near enough money to afford a tow, or a new rudder. As it was, when I arrived at Belém I was down to about two hundred dollars. Since undertaking the long voyage from the Seychelles, I had had little opportunity to write and earn cash. It was vital to beat the Andes flood. Nothing could delay us, for we had only another two months in which to make two thousand miles against the river current.

At Belém, we moored in the quaint old fishing port of Vero-Peso (which means "watch the weight"). The town was the marketplace of a vast area of Brazil, with boats negotiating the river for hundreds of miles to bring goods, fruit, fish, livestock, manioc, beans, coffee, to the Belém waterfront.

The heat at Belém is not too oppressive as it is tempered by rainstorms as regular as the clock from noon until sunset each day. It was a marvel to see how the market, abustle with thousands of shoppers and vendors at 11:45, was completely deserted and empty by 12:00. The town has some very beautiful old houses from the colonial Portuguese period, and a very well stocked zoo. We found the locals friendly, but had quite a bit of trouble repelling a few overenthusiastic *cachaça* drinkers. However, after we had thrown a couple headfirst into the Pará current, the rest got the message and we weren't bothered as much. The fishport was busy day and night, and very noisy, so after careening *Barbara* against the wall to clean and paint her bottom, we motored round to El Condor, an anchorage at the mouth of the Tocantins River. Here, after a night of blaring music, laughter, and screams, we discovered that we were, in fact, moored only twenty yards from the biggest brothel in South America, if not the world! They had a "staff" of at least five hundred! But the Madame, when we called for a beer, treated us exceedingly well and arranged for a cooked meal at seven each evening. This was a great honor, for the Brazilian does not usually eat dinner until around ten at night. The meals were good, too, great thick steaks and manioc at a most reasonable price. The girls kept an eye on the boat for us when we went into town for stores and lined up on the veranda to wave goodbye when we set sail upstream.

"See you soon!" shouted Conrad.

"Some hopes," said I.

We called back into the main town of Belém to pick up Arthur, who accompanied us, with a friend, on the long monotonous haul upstream as far as Manaus.

The way to push against the Amazon for the first five hundred miles or so is to set off in the mid-forenoon, when the trade wind pipes up, preferably with the incoming tide, and try to keep to the leeward side of the river, close to the shore. That way you avoid most of the current and get the full benefit of the wind; though you must be careful, for you are on a lee shore all the time. We were always ready to drop the anchor on a second's notice. The first four days' run, about two hundred and fifty miles, led through Os Estrechos (The Narrows), a twisting, turning maze of small, but deep channels through an archipelago of islands, some of which are so extensive they take hours to pass. With the bends in the river, we were not able to use the sails much, and had to resort to the engine, using up half of our precious fuel supplies. But as soon as we emerged into the Amazon itself, we found we could use the mizzen, the stays'l, and the genoa. We could not use the mainsail, however, because we had to rig a canvas awning to guard against the intense heat and the heavy downpour. We also used this awning to catch rain for fresh water, as the river water is too muddy to drink.

All along the river, on the shores and on the islands, a jungle of high tropical trees, enshrouded in climbing lianas, dominates a sub-forest of dense undergrowth so thick the eye can only see a yard or so into it. This undergrowth is crawling with insects and teeming with animal life. Above, among the higher branches, the screaming howler monkeys and a thousand different species of birds join in a fantastic Devil's chorus. Near the shores, and especially in the stinking, fetid marsh lagoons, in swamps thick with mosquitoes, lurk alligators by the thousands and fearsome piranha fish by the millions, always ready to attack any kind of food, animal or human. The water also swarms with snakes, many of them very dangerous indeed. In the relatively open spaces, which at first sight seem to be safer than the thicker undergrowth, prowl the jaguar and the anaconda, the latter growing to a length of thirty feet and able to coil itself around a man and squeeze him to death in less than five seconds (and have him digested by sunset too!).

Most of the Amazon basin is only a few feet above water level. Except for the trade centers at Belém, Santarém, Manaus, and Iquitos, the population is scattered, hungry, sordid, and miserable. As we negotiated the Estrechos passage we saw people so ignorant, so abysmally primitive, that they did not even know how to fish! This I had never come across before. They just lounged around, scantily clothed, mostly black or a mixture of black and Indian, half bitten to death by insects, the kids with the swollen bellies of severe malnutrition, the adults listless with the apathy of awful poverty. And yet they were living on top of a river full of fish—full of good, life-giving protein!

The Amazon is alive with fish, including catfish up to ten feet long. There is also the manatee, a mammal which suckles its young and moans at sunset like a woman in orgasm. The origin of the mermaid legend perhaps?

The Estrechos Islands cover an area bigger than Western Europe. It is low, swampy, and swarming with insects. The population is mainly black, the descendants of slaves. The average income, when we were there, was *twenty-five dollars* per year! And yet, I could not help noticing, as we passed within a few feet of their miserable bug- and disease-ridden hovels, that each one had flowers growing in rusty old tin cans on the open front stoop; nor could I not notice the

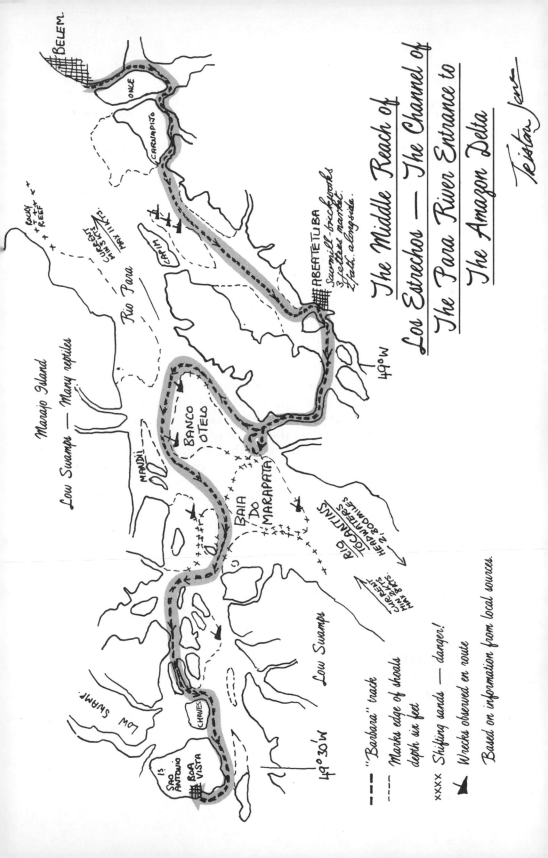

The Middle Reach of
Los Estrechos — The Channel of
The Para River Entrance to
The Amazon Delta

Tristan Jones

BELEM.

ONCE

CARNAPITO

ABEATETUBA
Sawmill—brickworks
3 fetied market.
Yachts alongside.

49°W

CAPIM

Rio Para

Rocky
REEF
CURRENT
UNKNOWN
MAX 11 KTS

Marajo Island

Low Swamp — Many reptiles

MANDII

BANCO
OTELO

BAIA
DO
MARAPATA

RIO
TOCANTINS
HEADWATERS
1000 MILES

CURRENT
UNKNOWN
MAX 11 KTS

Low Swamp

CHAVES

LOW SWAMP

SAO
ANTONIO

BOA
VISTA
15

49°30'W

- - - "Barbara" track

- - - Marks edge of shoals
        depth six feet

xxxx   Shifting sands — danger!

⚓   Wrecks observed en route

Based on information from local sources.

obvious affection between the ragged, starved parents and their pitifully hungry children.

We pressed on up the Amazon for two weeks, calling at Obidos and Santarém, mostly under sail, using the engine only when there was no wind at all. At Obidos (the furthest the Atlantic tide reaches into the Amazon, five hundred miles from the ocean) we found an old building, which during the days of the rubber boom at the turn of the century used to be a hotel. French ships, on their way up to Manaus, used to call there. The place contained, in the only cellar I ever saw in Brazil, thousands of bottles of vintage Bordeaux wines going at the rate of twenty U.S. cents a bottle. Conrad and I stayed there for two days instead of one, the wine was so good.

"Cheers, may you live long and die happy!"

"Bottoms up mate! And may the...skin...of...your ass...never cover a bloody banjo!"

Steadily we sailed on up the mighty river. The scenery hardly changed—a monotonous prospect of thick jungle on the low shore, except around Almeirim, where there is the only range of small hills in the whole of Brazilian Amazonia. Our food supplies were in good shape, and we were catching a fish every other day or so; but the continuous strain of concentration at the wheel in the fluky winds and currents for twelve hours a day was beginning to tell. With the heat and humidity during the day and the insects at night, it was a wonder that we kept going as well as we did; but we managed to reach Manaus in just thirty-five days from Belém, mostly under sail against a six-knot current. By now it was the end of March. I was concerned, for our delays in South Africa and Recife and Obidos had eaten up precious weeks. We still had a thousand miles, maybe more, to go to reach Pucallpa. We stayed only one day in Manaus, though we wanted to stay more, and shoved off upstream against the eternal current. With only a month to beat the current and the floods, we had no margin for dallying.

19
HARD TIMES

HE RIVER CRAFT OF THE Amazon are interesting. Down in the delta there are many sailing craft. These are usually double-enders, about forty feet long, flush decked, with one gaff sail and a small head-sail. At first sight they appeared to be crudely built, but upon closer inspection we found that they were in fact very well put together, considering that they are built by rule of thumb, without the use of levels or, as far as I could see, any kind of measuring device. The Amazonian is a natural carpenter and shipwright, and it is a marvel to see him chopping away with only an adz, a tool which looks something like a sharp hoe, but with a very short handle. The timber they use is, of course, excellent—guaqui, a kind of teak, and ironwood, a very tough timber indeed, which they use for frames.

When *Barbara* entered Belém, not knowing the depths, she ran hard aground on the mud of Vero-Peso port. With the tide running out very fast there was nothing to do but prop her up until the next tide came in. Quickly Conrad swam ashore to collect balks of timber, of which there were many lying on the jetty. Scooping them up, he started throwing them in the water to float them over to the stranded boat. Most of them promptly sank, for they were ironwood. The locals howled with laughter at our ignorance!

From Belém up river most of the traffic is carried by strange-looking power craft called *yates.* These are sailing boat hulls beautifully built and meticulously cared for, up to a hundred feet long, fitted with giant diesel engines, usually of Japanese make. A lot of the sailing gear and rigging is still carried, complete with very pretty ropework and bunting; and the boats are kept spotless, for the old Portuguese marine excellence shows through in the Brazilian.

Further upstream, beyond the rapid narrows of Obidos, beyond the furthest tidal point, sail completely disappears and we only saw *yates* and dugout canoes. These latter are a marvel of symmetry; the locals cut them out of a single log, by eye, in perfect form. They are propelled by one or two very broad-bladed paddles, which also serve to steer the craft. Because they are not very stable, however, it is quite an art to navigate a dugout, though we never once saw one capsize. Near the few towns the dugouts were equipped with small outboard engines. It was a peculiar sight to see one pass, loaded high with a whole family, some chickens, a pig, baggage, all shaded under big black umbrellas, on its way to market.

Soccer football is almost a religion among the Amazonians, and we would sometimes see a whole team, in complete playing gear, plus spectators, with flags and banners gaily flying and a band of musicians, paddling away in a group of dugouts, heading for a competitor's village.

At nightfall we headed into the bank to moor, for it is too hazardous to navigate in the dark. We sailed right up to an overhanging tree, secured a long line, then dropped out into the stream again to cast the anchor. We had to hold the boat out away from under the overhanging branches lest hordes of great ants, an inch and a half long, drop onboard. These ants, the sauba, would have eaten the whole boat overnight! Also there was danger of snakes dropping onboard. As it was, we used to paint the mooring line with kerosene to discourage them from slithering onboard. Other dangers, if we stayed too near the shore, were jaguars, for they can leap long distances, and we didn't fancy making a meal for one of them!

While we were moored well out in the stream, floating islands would often come along and jam under the anchor line. Soon others would join that one, and if we were not lively we would have a hundred tons of Amazonian jungle bearing down on our anchor. As a result, we had to keep watches through the night, clearing the mass of vegetation away from the hull every hour or so. Up in the trees the howler monkeys made the most God-awful racket imaginable, screaming like tortured troglodytes.

After mooring to a tree we rigged up the mosquito net over the hatch and closed the hatch and all other openings into the hull; for as soon as the sun set, the onslaught of the mosquitoes began and continued with unabated fury, for about three hours, but sometimes all night. In the close, confined cabin, with all openings shut tight, it got very muggy. Every time one of us went topsides to clear the anchor line, a battalion of mosquitoes rushed in and set to work. Rubbing tobacco juice over any exposed skin helped to keep them away.

"Nasty little sods," spat Conrad, as he beat them off.

"They can't hear you, you know," I retorted. He grinned and remembered the Chinese trawler in the South Atlantic.

During the daytime, when the mosquito retired, the piúm fly took over. What a little monster! About a quarter of an inch in diameter, it is very black, almost like a horse fly. Beneath its ugly little body hangs a sack. It lands on exposed skin and sucks blood until the sack is about as big and red as a strawberry, then takes off, making a noise like a wet fart. There's no sting, and if you're not careful, in the course of a day you could bleed to death.

Vampire bats were a threat at night, too, but the mosquito net guarded against them. These ugly little devils hang upside down in the trees by the thousands. The face of the vampire bat must be the most evil-looking thing on earth. Sometimes they attacked in daylight, swooping down on the boat, fluttering straight into our faces, with malicious grins on their disgusting mouths, eyes glittering with wickedness. Conrad stood on the poopdeck swatting them with the cricket bat. Often he knocked up a score of a dozen or so, splattering their heads. Nothing like a good bit of English willow for a vampire bat! Some of them had a two-foot wingspan!

In the water were snakes and piranha fish. These latter are vicious, and can attack and consume a horse in a few minutes. Another danger is more subtle. It is a small fish, an inch long, which makes for the orifices of the body, usually the sex organs, and enters and penetrates into the urethra. There the little bastard opens a kind of hooking device. The only way he can be extracted is by operating, cutting the body open and lifting the little sod bodily out. We never once saw an Amazonian pissing in the river west of Manaus, and we were told that the reason is the little hook fish can actually swim up the piss stream and enter the penis orifice. Upon inspecting the hull intakes just before we emerged from the Amazon, we found thousands of the buggers, dead, in the engine intakes and cockpit drain hull fitting.

As *Barbara* slowly made her way upstream we had to use the engine more and more, in addition to every puff of wind. As we pushed along, the current got stronger and our speed less and less. By mid-April we were reduced to a crawl of no more than a knot. Our food stocks were low, we were now down to a sack of rice and a can of tea. There was not much time to fish, for all our energies were concentrated on making our way upstream. We were both suffering badly from malaria and loss of blood and lack of sleep caused by incessant insect attacks. However, we kept going, for our destination was upstream. On the twenty-fifth of April, our fuel supply was down to five gallons and this I determined to hoard against any future emergency. Our speed slowed to a mere crawl against the seven- and eight-knot current, though, when we had any wind, we would sail like blazes. Finally, just above the small, miserable settlement of Codajas, we started to *espia*, or haul the boat from one tree to the next. Soon we were covered with black scars left by the piúm fly, oozing pus, our bodies burned and dehydrated, but we kept going. First we took a six-hundred-foot, one-hundred-fathom nylon line upstream in the rubber dinghy (try rowing against a seven-knot current) to another giant tree crawling with six-inch-wide mygale spiders, and tied it to the tree. It was a two-man job, for these trees have a girth up to eighty feet around. Then we went back to *Barbara*, let go of the tree we were already tied to, and hauled her up to the next tree. And so on, for hours on end in the steaming heat. Sometimes we would see as many as a dozen sucuriju, water boa constrictors, fifteen feet long, hanging around waiting for a tasty morsel and sometimes the highly dangerous jararaca snake, whose bite can kill in less than three seconds.

"How's nature boy today?" I asked Conrad.

"Fascinating, isn't it?"

"Yes, like a bloody execution chamber!"

One of the few pleasant sights were the gorgeous butterflies, of which there are over seven hundred species of the Amazon. The biggest, the morphos, has a wingspan of a foot and is the prettiest insect I have ever seen, colored a deep scarlet and gold. When the sun set, the yellow Amazon would turn a glittering gold color. To see the emerald parakeets and the scarlet butterflies fluttering around in a deep azure sky at sunset almost made up for all the hardships.

Day after day we slaved at the *espia,* struggling with our remaining strength against the roaring waters of the Amazon. Struggling in the stinking mist, across shore-side swamps, in the awful eternal smell of rotting vegetation, in the unceasing din of insects chirping, monkeys howling, trees crashing mightily, and always the river, the everlasting *brutal*, roaring current as it swooshed down thousands of miles to the Atlantic Ocean far away. Sick with malaria, our bowels scored with painful dysentery, scarred with running sores from pium bites, desperately in need of solid food, we pitted ourselves against the continent, with only the sailor-man's will to fetch the destination keeping us alive and moving.

By the fifteenth of May, after sixteen days of hard slog, we had progressed exactly 160 miles. The river was rising by the hour, threatening to overflow the banks; already vast areas of the jungle were flooded. Soon, even the *espia* would not be possible, for we would be swept into some swamp and stranded there, rotting, dead, forever. By now our main source of nutrition was to cut the rough bark from the cow trees and drink the thick, gooey liquid that oozed out, the color and consistency of semen. Once we caught a manatee and boiled it in the pressure cooker. Another time we spotted a capybara, a huge rodent, about as big as a pig, eight feet long, and chased it downstream. After losing a hundred precious yards, we fell on it with a machete, harpoon, spear, and a hammer. We cut steaks off the huge, rat-like, hairy monster and ate them voraciously. We knocked a cebidae monkey off a high branch and, finding him very skinny under the fur, cut off his arms and boiled them. The sight of his shaven arms sticking out of the pot, with hands like those of a newborn baby, will stay with me the rest of my life. He had another hand on the end of his tail, for grasping the high branches. We didn't eat his tail, though we were tempted.

The fight to keep the sauba ants off the boat was everlasting. These ants are insatiable and will eat anything organic, including wood. They are so powerful, I was told, that on one occasion at least they were known to have dug a tunnel under a river as broad as the Hudson off Manhattan in order to get at the vegetation on the other side! The only sure way to get rid of them, once they establish a foothold, is to blow them up with gunpowder or burn them with gasoline. Of course, neither of these solutions was practical on board *Barbara*, so we tethered four chameleons on a long line, topsides. These lizards, about eight inches long, with great long tongues, flicked up the ants as they climbed or dropped onboard. They were well fed and we were safe from ants.

Our trailing lines were a nuisance, continually getting tangled in vegetation. We caught tucunaré, a pretty fish, with an eye-like spot on its tail and good eating; but we had to be careful, for there are stingrays in the Amazon, a wound from which, in our weakened condition, might have killed us.

As slow as a wet Sunday, we crept up against the rushing waters. Then, on the twentieth of May, we finally came to a halt. The scene was morbid. We tied up by the rotting wooden crosses of an old-time rubber-collectors' graveyard, now overgrown by the conquering jungle, alive with mosquitoes and piúms, and held a council of war.

This is the custom of sailor-men when there are vital decisions to be made, when there are valid alternatives, each one of which might be fatal. All the cards are put on the table, all the bullshit discarded, and the odds are carefully and honestly calculated.

With aching hearts, after an hour's argument, we both conceded that we had lost this round. The Amazon had beaten us. We would have to turn back. This was the most painful decision I had ever made, for in twenty-five years of voyaging in small craft I had never failed to reach my destination except once, when dismasted off Greenland in 1962. We had pitted our puny craft against the wildest continent in the world, and we had lost. All the hard sailing across half the world, all the risk-taking up fourteen hundred miles of the uncharted Amazon, all the suffering—the heat, the loss of blood, the grinding effort, hard physical and mental effort, the hunger—all the discomfort and isolation from the civilized world, all the wear and tear on the boat and her gear, had been to no avail. The Amazon had beaten us.

Before we cast off to make for the ocean fourteen hundred miles away, I got out our bedraggled, worn, insect-eaten atlas of the world, its pages falling apart with damp-rot. In the sweaty cabin I inspected it, while Conrad desperately tried for another fish in the roaring, rushing waters outside. As I looked at the map of South America I could hear the brushwood scraping the sides of the hull as it pushed past on the current.

It was no good; I was down to a hundred dollars. This was enough to take us to Grenada, in the West Indies, just under three thousand miles away. *Barbara* could not make it to Pucallpa. She was too big to be hauled up from the Peruvian Pacific coast to Lake Titicaca. I would have to get hold of a smaller boat. However, I resolved that this was not going to be the last round; that I would reach my destination whatever the cost, whatever sacrifices had to be made, and however long it took. Defeating the Andes and reaching Lake Titicaca now became to me like the quest for the Holy Grail. All right, so I had lost this round. I would get out, recuperate, and try again, and again, and *again*, if necessary.

Conrad, thin and very sick looking, came from the companionway clutching a tiny aramaça sole, which he had dredged up from the river bottom.

"Here we are, Skip, not exactly Escoffier material, but—"

His feet and arms were covered with pium sores. He was in rags, but he looked pleased. Here was solid food, enough to keep us going for another two or three days. As we scoffed down the aramaça, bitter tasting and tiny, dreaming of luxuries like milk and bread, butter and beef, he said, "What do you reckon, Skip?"

"After we get this little bugger digested, mate, we're casting off and heading midstream," I replied. "We'll float down to Manaus and pick up some grub. We've had it, Conrad, it's no good kidding ourselves, this bloody lot has beaten us, and the sooner we get to civilization the better. We did a tremendous thing, tackling this goddamn river after a sustained fast passage from the Indian Ocean, but it's impossible. Of course, we could await the next dry season in Manaus, but that's at least eight months away, and what are we going to live on? There's sod all left in the kitty after this hundred bucks is gone, and it's going to take weeks before Arthur can get anything through to us or I could earn anything from any writing I can do. No, the best thing is for us to get the hell out. We'll retire ungracefully, because by the living God I haven't finished with this blasted continent yet!"

"You're a determined bastard, aren't you?"

"It's a question of professional pride. I've never failed to fetch my destination yet and I'm buggered if I'm going to miss this one."

"What good's it going to do you or anyone else, whether you reach your wretched lake or not?"

"It'll show some of the cynical, fainthearted sods on this earth that nothing is impossible, that if you put your bloody mind to something you should keep at the bastard until you win."

"Sounds like something out of Kipling."

"And what's wrong with that?"

"Ever tried striking a match on a bar of soap?"

"As a matter of fact, yes. When the outside temperature is down to sixty below, it's easy. Up in the Arctic—"

"Oh, Jesus, Tristan, here you go again. Now I know what you're doing in this stinking hellhole; you're bloody well thawing out!"

"OK, mate, let's set this bloody vessel adrift. Atlantic here we come!"

"With God's help!" said Conrad, climbing up the ladder.

"Amen to that!"

We let go the *espia* line and worked our way out into midstream, defeated, bitterly disappointed, but still defiant. I shook my fist at the direction of the Andes. "You won this one, you bastards!" I cursed. "But Christ, I'll beat you yet!"

20

BLOODY BUT UNBOWED

NCE IN MIDSTREAM WE FLEW down the Amazon. There was no need to put up more sail than the jib or genoa and the mizzen, just enough to overtake the current and hold steerage way. There was much less danger of colliding with huge tree trunks or floating islands, for we were making the same speed more or less, and if we did catch up with a trunk, we would just scrape it gently and steer away.

This was as well, for we were in a pitiful state, with our strength ebbing fast; but we kept going day and night until we reached Manaus and food supplies. In fact, the second day going downstream I got the inspiration to tie up to two trees, huge pama trees, which still had the strange, oblong, red, cherry-like fruit, good to eat, on the branches. The two trees, each about 150 feet from roots to top, were crawling with ants. We let the four chameleon lizards loose on them and in two hours there was not one ant left alive.

As the trees, floating downstream at a speed of about seven knots, swung round and round in the swirling current, so did *Barbara*; and as we approached civilized country, or rather waters, for this is a world of water where everything in the flood season lives afloat, we must have presented a very strange sight—two bedraggled scarecrows patching sails on a thirty-eight-foot ocean boat moored to two monstrous jungle trees. Lashed alongside the trees we were in no danger from collision, for the branches ahead on one tree, astern on the other, cleared the way for us very handily indeed. So we went on day and night for almost a week, until at last we came to Manaus, where we joyfully worked our way alongside the huge floating dock installed by the British during the last century.

A few days of good, nutritious food soon put us to rights, and we were well enough to visit the wonderful opera house, where the greatest singers in the world used to entertain the rubber barons. Astonishing, when you consider that to this day there are no roads connecting this city with the outside world! But then Manaus is full of surprises, such as the tramway system which was built before any in England—the second in the world in fact. This system trundles merrily along until it comes to a full stop at the jungle's edge. Beyond that terminal there is nothing but rain forest for thousands of miles.

I chose to emerge through the dangerous nightmare of the northern Amazon mouth for two reasons. If we took the longer, safer detour through the Estrechos to Belém, it would add almost six hundred miles to our passage to the West Indies, and I had stores sufficient only for six weeks. Secondly, no other yacht had ever navigated this treacherous channel before, and I wanted to show the blasted Amazon that I wasn't completely beaten. This may sound a bit like bombastic foolhardiness, but after our defeat it was balm to my soul to tackle the "Dragon's Mouth," the most difficult way of going out.

At Manaus we received antibiotic shots courtesy of the army, mosquito repellent from the harbormaster, and water purification tablets from the British Booth Line, which maintains steamer services between Manaus and the outside world. In very short order our swollen legs, caused by thousands of pium fly bites, shrank to normal, our stomachs recovered, and our strength returned sufficiently for us to tackle the downstream passage to the mouth. On the tenth of June we started off for the ocean. After restocking at Manaus I had exactly twenty dollars. This would have to suffice until we reached Grenada.

Lashed to trees afloat on the current, we hurried downstream at a speed of twelve knots. The passage downstream from Manaus to Macapá, inside the northern mouth, took us only five days—a distance of close to *nine hundred miles!*

On our way downstream we found the *formiga de fogo*, the fire ant, running amok. These little devils swarm over the ground by the millions. They do not accidentally encounter a human ankle; they purposely set out to attack it, and their sting is like red-hot needles. The Brazilians avoid them by sitting with their legs on a stool, the legs of which have been smeared with copaiba balsam, made from a tree leaf. This is the only thing which will keep the fire ants at bay. They swarm like a moving carpet anywhere that humans gather.

Now that we were moving easily downstream we were able to observe the wildlife at our leisure. It was a great pleasure to see thousands of beautiful, snowy white egrets wading among the reeds onshore, giant woodpeckers and vultures by the squadron. On the remote stretches of the river we made landfall by sighting a group of wheeling vultures and making for the spot directly below them. I often wondered if this was the first time an ocean-going yacht had been navigated by means of vultures!

As we whirled downstream we saw bits of pumice stone which had been washed down all the way from the volcanoes of Cotopaxi and Sangay, high up in the mighty Andes of Peru and Ecuador, three thousand miles away. The Indians on the river edge believe the pumice is solidified river spume; most of them have never seen a rock, much less a mountain. I fished out a piece of pumice and hung it around my neck, vowing not to rest until I had returned it to where it came from.

In some parts of the river, among the extensive islands, there are great mobs of turtles which lay their eggs on the sandy beaches during the low-river season; but now, in the flood, all this was hidden from us, and all we could see were birds of many colors—japini, yellow and black, by the thousands, egrets, and tsiginia, a kind of pheasant, and a hundred different types of parrots and parakeets screeching overhead. In the heat of noon, the whole forest would go deadly quiet, for in the jungle all life sleeps away the hot afternoon, with the exception of the piúm fly, who is always at his bloodsucking work, and his cousin the motuku, who unlike the piúm stings like blazes and sticks his proboscis into your flesh in a most reckless way. There are, I am told, over seven thousand species of insects in the Amazon Basin. It is estimated that over fifteen hundred of these species have a sting and pose a danger to humans one way or the other.

Later, in a radio discussion with Major Blashford Snell, head of the Scientific Exploration Society, I was asked what I thought were the most dangerous jungle animals. Without hesitation I replied "the insects," for they never cease to attack. The large animals, such as the African lion, or the jaguar, or the hippo, will only attack when provoked or when hungry; but the insect *never* stops attacking. He never hesitates to sting. He almost never seems to sleep. The insect is the most dangerous threat of all.

By the river banks we often saw alligators, especially where the banks were eroded and there were roads. They were up to twelve feet long, nasty-looking brutes.

At Macapá we anchored, just for the hell of it, right slap-bang on the equator, swinging to and fro from the southern hemisphere to the northern for two days. Then, satisfied with having crossed the line more than a hundred times and exhausted with the humid heat of the place, we took off for the hundred-mile drift down to Curuá Island, the last refuge before the huge, open, unmarked, stormy northern mouth. The current rushed downstream against the wind, throwing up a steep, choppy sea which made the Block Island Sound Race look like a child's paddle game. Then, in the far-off distance, as we squared away up a creek and tied ourselves to trees with eight stout mooring lines, we could hear a low rumble that sounded like the guns of war. As it came closer it got louder; then suddenly, with a deafening noise, the *pororoca* passed upstream, a vertical wall of yellow water, invading and vanquishing the Amazon itself as it roared past the mouth of our creek at fourteen knots or so. In the space of five minutes, *Barbara* rose forty feet in the air, like a slow elevator. One minute we were among the roots of trees, the next among the topmost branches. We were playing a cat and mouse game with one of the most dangerous stretches of water on the earth. This was my last kick at the Amazon; a risky gesture of defiance.

We had to wait for the waning moon before chancing a rush offshore, but when the time finally came we went out of Curuá Creek as fast as we could, with all sail up, close hauled and the engine pushing, so that with the combined speed of the outgoing tide and current, which was about eight knots, plus our six knots, we flew out of there like a bat out of hell at fourteen knots, close to twenty land miles an hour. There was no indication at all as to where the dozens of sandbanks lay, just a mass of heaving, choppy, dirty yellow water which seemed to go on forever. Indeed it almost does, for the force of the Amazon current is felt as much as 350 miles out in the Atlantic Ocean. Within *six hours* of weighing the anchor at Curuá, we had made *120 miles* out into the ocean offing, safe from the *pororoca*. We continued due east all night, once again joyfully lifting to the ocean swells.

We were back in the Atlantic—*our* Atlantic—the wide, deep, blue spaces, safe at last from the thousand and one hazards of the Amazon. We were home again. True, we were in a rather sorry state, for dysentery had returned, and with it weakness. Spasmodic malaria was a problem, we were thin as rakes, and the boat's gear was shoddy and badly frayed; but when we turned course northeast for Cayenne, in French Guiana, we had the current with us and a beam wind of about thirty knots. And so we sailed, free again in the ocean, pushing *Barbara* to the limit in the boisterous rollers of the north Brazilian continental shelf. We were still in yellow water, brackish to the taste, but at least we were free of the shackles of the Amazon and headed for the civilized, safe West Indies and the twentieth century.

21
PENAL PARADISE

HE DISTANCE FROM CURUÁ Island, in the northern mouth of the Amazon, direct to Cayenne is just over 360 miles. By the route we covered, standing well out to sea before altering course to follow the coast, we sailed 490 miles. We encountered the usual squally and thundery weather that prevails on the lee shore of any tropical landmass, accompanied by heavy rain showers; but the winds were mostly steady in between squalls, usually around twenty-five knots. Over the continental shelf the seas ran high. The northeast coast of South America is subject to frequent underwater volcanic eruptions, and the second night out we felt one of these, a dull, shuddering shock that passed through *Barbara*'s hull. If you don't know about the possibility of earthquakes on the sea-bottom hereabouts, it can be an unnerving experience, something like a depth-charge explosion. As with earthquakes, the sea-bottom changes shape, and this part of the Atlantic Ocean is one of the most unstable in the world, continually changing its depth; as a result, maritime charts for the area are rarely correct. Adding to the problem is the fact that the seawater is very much discolored by the effluence of the Amazon; these yellow waters prevail all the way to Trinidad, more than a thousand miles up the coast from the Amazon Estuary!

These waters are alive with sharks, mainly of the hammerhead variety, which would accompany us, eyeing *Barbara* hungrily, for days at a stretch. Little did they know how hungrily we were eyeing them and waiting with the harpoon for one to approach too closely.

It is wise to keep well away from the coast of northern Brazil and French Guiana until it is time to turn in, and then it is best to approach your destination at right angles, so as to minimize the possibility of grounding on an uncharted shoal thrown up by a recent seaquake. After four days' good going, we did exactly that. I had a British Admiralty chart of the approaches to Cayenne harbor. But when we reached the indicated position of the outer channel buoy, we found in its place heaving Atlantic rollers sweeping right over a shallow sandbar. There was nothing in sight but the low, green coast, a thin line away to the south. With no indication at all of any channel, we hove to in the swooping seas, about a mile north of the shallows, to await the night and get bearings on the lighthouse, and to watch for someone to show us the way in. This is the regular procedure; but when you're half-dead with malaria, malnutrition, and dysentery it is an embarrassment, to say the least. We were relieved when a small shrimp-fisherman appeared in the late afternoon. With a big grin on his black Guianan face, he led us in through the newly dredged and buoyed channel, the entrance to which was about nine miles away from the position shown on our chart. The chart had been brought up to date only nine months before.

Tired and weary, we tied up in Cayenne, the capital of French Guiana, ate some beans for supper, and turned in. In the morning, awakened early by a knock on the coach-roof, I emerged to find my old Norwegian friend and sailing buddy, Peer Tangvald, perched on the side deck, all sunburn and smiles. We had last met nine years before on the coast of Norway, and now here he was, with his beautiful French wife, building a sixty-foot ketch to sail around the world. He took me, still weak with dysentery, to see the hull, which he had completed, and we discussed the rigging of the new boat. We talked ten to the dozen in the shade of the rough boatshed he had built over the hull as protection from the scorching sun and bucketing rainstorms. During lunch, which was the first decent meal I had had since leaving Manaus, we got around to the subject of my voyage. Peer listened sympathetically as I explained my defeat on the Amazon and my need for a smaller boat to tackle the job from the Pacific coast of South America. He then remarked that he had seen just the boat I might like during a recent visit to Barbados—a small, very sturdy, well-rigged twenty-footer, British built. Her name was *Sea Dart*. Originally she had been constructed to tackle the northwest passage, between Alaska and Greenland. Peer had heard from the present owner that the original builder had put so much money into constructing the hull that he had gone broke. Peer was certain this was the boat for me, but as it had been several months since he had seen her in Bridgetown, Barbados, there was no way of knowing where she was. Maybe she had already passed through the Panama Canal, for Peer had heard that her present owner intended to sail her to British Columbia.

I took note of all this, and passed on to other subjects. Peer invited us to eat at his table as long as we were in Cayenne, but told us that in our condition the best place for us to go to get out of the oppressive heat and humidity of Cayenne was Les Iles du Salut, the old French penal colony, of which Devil's Island forms a part! The air was better there, and there were fewer insects. There was also good anchorage and we would be much cooler.

Peer then took us around the town, showing us the more interesting parts from the old days when it was the home of fifty thousand convicts. He also lent me thirty dollars, then showed us the best and cheapest places to buy food. The islands were only twenty-eight miles from Cayenne, and by early evening we were at anchor in the convict-built harbor of Ile Royale, which, in the old penal days, used to be the headquarters of the prison system on the islands. Here we intended to stay for ten days to try to get both ourselves and the boat together to enter the spick-and-span yachting world of the West Indies, only six hundred miles away.

We found the islands delightful. There are three—Ile Royale, Saint Joseph, and Ile du Diable. Devil's Island, where the French government used to exile political prisoners, is the smallest and the most difficult to approach, being surrounded by swift currents and rocks. All three of the islands are covered by coconut trees which glisten in the sun, while the climate is the best we had come across so far in the western hemisphere. There were plenty of fish, and ashore, wild pigs which were easy to hunt. The only thing preventing these islands from becoming a first-class holiday resort was the lack of sandy beaches.

On Saint Joseph and Ile Royale we explored the ruins of the old prison. The most impressive sight was the mural painted in the old convicts' prison showing Jesus breaking the prisoners' chains. Most of the cells are still barred, and we saw how the convicts used to sleep, on long wooden benches, with their wrists shackled to the edges.

Two days before we were due to leave, I suggested to Conrad that we ought to try and anchor off Devil's Island and look around. After a very tricky wind through the maze of rocks we finally anchored right in front of Dreyfus's seat. I went ashore, but found little of interest. Most of the buildings were in ruins, smothered by an undergrowth of thick creepers. There were droves of wild pigs, however, and we had plenty of meat to eat that night on the rocky shore, under the stars. We later found that *Barbara* was the first yacht ever to succeed in anchoring there.

If Henri Charrière, the man known as Papillon, was telling the truth when he stated that he escaped from Devil's Island to the shore of French Guiana with the aid of a bag of coconuts, then the tides and currents thereabouts must have changed drastically in the last few years. The way the sea moves he would have been lucky to end up in Tobago to the northwest. It is impossible for a swimmer to make the passage, no matter how strong he is. The current runs always offshore, whatever the state of the tide, and is never less than three knots. The island is twelve miles from the continental shore. Every time the tide runs out, the current increases to six knots, running west-north-west. During conversations I had with the lighthouse-keeper on Ile Royale, himself an ex-convict, he maintained firmly that only one person had ever escaped from the islands, and that was a trusty during the Second World War who was on night sentry duty in the port. He surreptitiously calked his sentry box, made a sail for it, and navigated his tiny craft to Trinidad, where he was received with open arms and inducted into the Free French Navy! The lighthouse-keeper was certain the escapee's name was not Henri Charrière. In addition, he showed me the old solitary confinement cells on Ile Saint Joseph, which surround a natural pool of seawater, and stoutly maintained that all the prisoners were let out of their cells in the heat of the afternoon and allowed to lounge around and swim in the pool! Certainly a very different tale from Papillon's. But the old rogue told a good story, so let him lie in peace.

Another interesting story the lighthouse-keeper told me was that under the chapel, from 1937 onwards, a full-scale counterfeiting plant was in operation, which was not discovered until the Germans occupied Paris. One fine day the SS were counting through great piles of one-hundred-franc notes when they found two with the same number. They got on the trail, which eventually led to the Devil's Island chapel, and the game was up. It was estimated that over two million dollars' worth of forged notes were exported to France from the Convict Islands between 1937 and 1940!

The convict population of the islands was around six thousand men. The lighthouse-keeper told me that at night, towards the end of the war, it was not the convicts who were locked up, but rather the wardens who locked themselves up in their barracks. The convicts had the run of the island, at least on Ile Royale. They even organized a gambling casino and a nightclub, starring gay members of the community.

Well nourished on wild pig, coconuts, and fish, we weighed anchor, a mite regretfully, for this had been a most pleasant interlude, and headed for Grenada, the most southerly of the West Indies. We reached the island in eight days. We had fine winds and kind seas and were physically much better, but mentally we were feeling the strain of the hard, continuous effort. The morning we sighted Grenada, I wrote in my log: "Misty to the northeast, I am sick at heart. I do not think I can take any more now."

22

WEST INDIES PEEPSHOW

HE SCENE IN GRENADA WAS astonishing. There were about two hundred yachts in the harbor, for this is the southern end of the West Indies Islands sailing circuit. Most of them were charter vessels; worried-looking skippers and crews dashed around in a continuous frenzy of activity, polishing, varnishing, painting, collecting stores, chasing up customers.

Some of the charter skippers were old acquaintances from the days when, like myself, they had been sea-rovers and cruising men. I was astonished to see how thoroughly they had adapted themselves to the rat race of the charter industry. A few, however, were still sailors enough to be able to converse about other subjects than money, varnishing, obtaining ice, varnishing, money, getting customers, varnishing, where to obtain the cheapest supplies, varnishing, and money.

One or two asked about our trip, and when told they expressed little reaction, but soon returned to the tramways of their trade. In general, charter skippers have little sense of adventure; they are at the tail end of a long line of communications which stretches back to the agency offices in the big cities of the U.S. Quite a few of them, in conversation with me, expressed nothing but disdain, even contempt, for the islanders, forever complaining about how lazy and inefficient they were. Some, particularly the British, had retired from one rat race to another, hoping to play the colonial only to find, to their bitter disappointment, that the "fuzzy-wuzzies" now had minds of their own.

The most pitiful were the ones who had sailed down from the States or over from Europe, carrying their mores with them (in the case of the Americans, the money-work ethic; the Europeans, the class-leisure bullshit). Here, lost in another world, they clung to each other in narrow, tight enclaves. They had tried to bring the suburbs of Philadelphia, Manchester, and Paris with them to the tropics, and when it didn't work they were puzzled.

On the other hand, the native Grenadians looked upon these strange white people with their opulent boats as a bottomless source of money. Their sole ambition was to extract as much of that money in the shortest possible time with the least amount of effort. The Grenadians' attitude was one of surly resentment. Their faces reflected an attempt at inscrutability which was, to us at least, after our experiences with the outgoing Africans and lively Brazilians, discouraging. There was no attempt on their part to be friendly or reciprocating. We encountered only a sulky lack of trust, a wall of hate.

By the time we arrived, this state of affairs had reached the highest echelons of power in the island. When Mr. Gary, ex-Union Leader, wheeler-dealer, mob-rouser, the "Napoleon of the Nutmegs," finally gained power, he imposed extortionate mooring fees on all yachtsmen, regardless of whether they were using his island as a moneymaking base. He even imposed a tax on anchoring anywhere around Grenada. In response, the charter fleet and cruising craft, en masse, weighed anchor and cast off lines, ready to shift their base elsewhere. Emperor Gary finally relented and the boats returned to their moorings.

While bemusedly observing these proceedings, I was busily writing articles to raise funds, at the same time refitting *Barbara* and making plans to find another boat. I made inquiries all over the islands, as far north as Saint Thomas, in the U.S. Virgin Islands, about *Sea Dart*, but to no avail. With the proceeds from several articles published in Europe and Australia, we moored comfortably at Grenada Yacht Services, at a jetty where fresh water and electricity were available, the first we had seen since leaving Malta two years previously.

After a month in the torrid environs of Grenada, I'd had enough, and sailed for the islands further north, first, to look for a small vessel tough enough to tackle South America and secondly, to get away from the poisonous, gossipy atmosphere of the Yacht Basin.

About two days before I left Grenada, Conrad approached me on the jetty, looking serious.

"Do you need me any more, Skip?"

"No, why, want the day off?"

"No, I mean for any more sailing. I was thinking, what with you looking for a smaller boat, there won't be much room for two, will there? Anyway, I'd like to get back to England for a spell. My girlfriend's getting pissed off with only getting a letter now and again, and I'd rather not lose her...and my father's agreed to put up the money for a boat of my own." It was the longest speech I had ever heard him make.

"What will you do?"

"Charter in the Greek Islands, if I can find a suitable craft, maybe to skin-diving groups; but I'm not sure yet."

"Well, OK, mate, I'll put up a plane ticket for you."

"Great, and if I can't sail back I'll fly back."

"Better than swimming, anyway!"

"Thanks a lot, Tristan."

"That's all right, and don't forget to keep your bloody boat's bow to windward of your destination; and for Christ's sake, never drop the sextant again!"

He laughed. "I'll never forget that little jaunt, never!"

"I should bloodywell hope not!"

The following day he took off. We shook hands, showing, in the British way, as little emotion as possible. (He eventually found his boat, his wife, and his skin-divers, and is now very successfully chartering out of the West Indies, no doubt entertaining his guests with tales of a certain crusty old salt and the mad voyages they made together.)

In October 1972, I set off for the islands of the Lesser Antilles group, making my way easily in the steady trades which prevail in that area to Saint Vincent, Saint Lucia, Martinique, Guadeloupe, Antigua, and finally, the Virgin Islands. Here, on U.S. territory, I returned *Barbara* to Arthur. It was a sad parting. Since leaving the United States two and a half years earlier, she had covered more than 38,000 miles. She was now in fair condition again, and I was very sorry to see the last of her, even though it is not in my nature to be sentimental about a boat. We had been through a lot of adventures together and she had never let me down; but she was too big to get to Lake Titicaca, so she had to go.

With the money in hand, I returned to Grenada and bought a thirty-four-foot yawl that had been sitting in the Yacht Basin for some years. She had some dry rot in her frames, but otherwise was in good condition. I renamed her *Banjo II* and set to work to refit her, replacing three frames and two deck beams with good solid teak; then I returned to my search of the islands. On the first day out in *Banjo*, I called at the small island of Bequia, just to the south of Saint Vincent. There, swinging at anchor in the beautiful bay, was *Sea Dart*, tiny, only seventeen feet on the waterline, but well found. I immediately rowed over and scanned her. She was obviously well maintained, with very sound gear and a wind-vane steerer. Her sails were in good trim and her topsides looked perfect.

I knocked up the owner, who showed me around below. We discussed the hull; he informed me she had three keels. I put down a deposit, and two days later she was mine. Meanwhile, I sold *Banjo II* at a reasonable profit. I now had a vessel suitable for the attempt on the Andes.

Sea Dart was built by a small yard in England. I was told she was intended to make the northwest passage between Alaska and Greenland; as a result her scantlings, or specifications, had been greatly modified, and she had been built with great care, of the finest materials, mahogany marine ply. She was built to the Debutante design, which was a popular class of weekend sailer, originally intended for cruises in the English Channel. From England she had sailed in 1970 to Barbados, where she had been sold to a young American who in turn sold her to me. He had intended to make a passage across the Pacific to Australia, and had spent a considerable amount of time and money preparing her for the voyages. The hull and rigging, sails and deck fittings were in perfect condition, while the boat's equipment down below was also in good order. The hull was sound, being sheathed in twenty layers of Cascomite, a silk and rubber coating that protects the bottom from the ravages of the teredo worm, a tropical borer which is the scourge of wooden vessels. Her navigational equipment was impeccable. In short, *Sea Dart*, with a space only twenty feet long by seven feet wide, was better equipped, with more sound gear, than many craft twice her size. She had, for instance, over three hundred charts of the Caribbean and the Pacific stowed away under the berths! She cost me $5,000 U.S.

With no inboard engine she did not, of course, have a radio, nor a refrigerator, nor electricity; but these things are all luxuries, unthought of in sailing vessels fifty years ago. Besides, the simpler the gear, the less work maintaining it, and the more time for voyaging.

In comparison to *Barbara*'s, the living cabin was tiny, but the builders had still managed to fit in three six-foot berths, a small table, sufficient lockers to carry three months' supplies for one man, and a minute, kerosene-operated galley stove. There was no head or sink, but two buckets would suffice for those needs. Her sail locker was forward, crammed with good, almost new sails; aft, she had a locker full of long lengths of good line and enough paint to last, on a normal cruise, for two years.

I spent two days making an inventory and checking the gear. I bought sufficient food to last a month. Then I took *Sea Dart* out on trials and sailed the ass off her one afternoon.

On the evening of 10 April 1973, after seven months of recuperating from the Amazon disaster, I sailed from the West Indies, running free, with the main swung out one side and a (for *Sea Dart*) huge genoa poled out the other, the trade wind dead astern. As little *Sea Dart* lifted boisterously to the Caribbean seas, the island lights dropped slowly astern, below the stars, in the clear tropical night. I was again reaching for my destination and my destiny—now it would be a fight to the finish!

The galley of *Sea Dart;* compared to *Barbara,* it was tiny, but still commodious enough to fit three berths, a small table, sufficient lockers to carry three months' supplies, and a kerosene-operated stove.

Tristan at work inside *Sea Dart,* writing articles for sailing magazines, "sweltering in temperatures of over a hundred degrees, with the boat pitching and rolling...."

Three hundred miles out to sea, off the coast of Colombia. The little land bird kept Tristan company for three days, sleeping on the coach roof and turning up on the back stays at noon to be fed.

Tristan, exhausted, off the Gorgona prison island, Colombia, October 1973. "There was no noise whatsoever, no talking, no shouting, just absolute and utter silence."

Sea Dart aboard the truck crossing Peru.

Sea Dart at 14,800 feet above sea level, with Misti Volcano in the background, being smuggled across Peru on the flatbed of Salomon's ancient Ford truck.

A Quechuan Indian band at Puno, Peru

Indian dancer at Puno, Peru

Destination reached: with a prayer of thankfulness to all the Gods of the Oceans, *Sea Dart* is lowered into the waters of Lake Titicaca.

Natives at Lake Titicaca. Silent, barefoot, dirty, they gaped in astonishment at this apparition from another world: a boat from the sea!

The first photo of an ocean-going vessel taken from behind a llama. *Sea Dart* sailing on Lake Titicaca at three miles above sea level.

Balsa-reed craft at Taquila, Lake Titicaca. A half-ton of reeds, bound together with cords, it is one of the safest and stablest crafts afloat.

A pre-Inca tomb on Lake Titicaca. Built of stones, without mortar, yet fitted snugly together, the skeletons inside were standing up, with their faces pointed directly east.

Sea Dart securely fastened to the flatbed of a Bolivian train ready for the haul to Puerto Suarez, on the Brazilian frontier.

Huanapaco in Buenos Aires, fully recovered after the ordeal in the Mato Grosso. "In addition to a sense of humor, he had the patience of Job." Only a man conditioned to the pitiless life of the Altiplano could have endured what he did.

PART THREE
To Find

We're 'ere because we're 'ere,
Because we're 'ere because we're 'ere;
We're 'ere because we're 'ere,
Because we're 'ere because we're 'ere!

Royal Navy lower-deck song,
World War II.
Sung to the tune of
"Auld Lang Syne."

23

OF CABBAGES AND KINGS

LTHOUGH THE WEST INDIES Islands are not a great distance from the South American shores of Venezuela and Colombia, very few yachtsmen visit those two countries, or indeed, any of the other countries which border the Caribbean, with the exception of Mexico. There are several reasons for this. One is the language difference; except in Belize and the Panama Canal Zone, the tongues used are mainly Spanish and Indian dialects. Another reason is that the sailing conditions are not as easy and uncomplicated as in the long, thousand-mile Antilles Islands chain, which arcs north to south at right angles to the prevailing easterly trade winds. A third reason, related to the second, is that navigational aids, such as radio beacons, buoys, and lighthouses, are few, except in areas such as Curaçao and the Canal Zone. A fourth, and perhaps decisive factor, is the many occurrences of *piracy*, especially in the area of Colombia.

On the Venezuelan coast there is frequent traffic in and around the Margarita Islands and Tortuga, a thriving sailing-fishing community, which means that you are generally not too far from help, should anything untoward crop up. But on the Colombian coast this is not the case. Colombia is the main producer of "soft drugs" in South America. Much of this is smuggled out to the United States by small planes, while much else is taken out by small craft, mainly to Puerto Rico, where it is passed on to the great cities of the United States. The coast of Colombia is, therefore, in the hands of racketeers and gangsters. Strangers are not at all welcome.

On shore in both Venezuela and Colombia, corruption is rife, and thievery is the order of the day. You must be very careful where you decide to enter or to anchor on these shores and be prepared to defend your vessel and the members of your crew.

145

Caribbean Sea

W. INDIES

CURACAO
GRENADA
STA MARTA
CARTAGENA

PANAMA

V E N E
Z U E L A
R ORINOCO
G U I A N A
SURINAM
FR. GUIANA
DEVIL'S IS
CAYENNE

BUENA
VENTURA
BOGOTA
C O L O M B I A
GORGONA

QUITA
ECUADOR
SOLIMAS

MANAUS R. AMAZON
REACHED POINT
1340 MILES FROM
OCEAN

BELEM

EQUATOR

"BARBARA"

RECIFE
From
INDIAN OCEAN
JAN 72.

PUCALLPA
R. MADEIRA
R. TAPAJOS
R. XINGU
R. ECANTINS

B   R   A   Z   I   L

REACHED 16,000 FT +
ABOVE SEA-LEVEL

R. BENI
LAKE
TITICACA

LIMA

AREQUIPA
LA PAZ
COCHABAMBA
ORURO
MATTO
GROSSO
THE
"GREEN HELL"

BRASILIA

ANTOFAGASTO

G   R   A   N
C   H   A   C   O
P A R A G U A Y
SAO PAULO
RIO DE JANEIRO

Pacific Ocean

ASUNCION

Atlantic Ocean

SANTA FE

VALPARAISO
MENDOZA
ROSARIO
URUGUAY
To ENGLAND
AUG. 76.

BUENOS AIRES
MONTEVIDEO

A   R   G   E   N   T   I   N   A

South America

1000 MILES.

BRITISH
FALKLAND IS

The brightest spot on the southern side of the Caribbean Sea is the former Dutch colony of Curaçao and Aruba, at the western end of the island chain strung along the coast of Venezuela. Here there are modern ports, duty-free shopping facilities, honest officials, and clean, safe streets. Curaçao was the ideal jumping off place for an exploration of the little-known, notorious coast of Colombia, and it was to these islands that I directed *Sea Dart*'s course after departing from Bequia.

The winds on the coast of Venezuela are moderate to heavy; that means anything from twenty-five knots to forty knots. The winds are steady while the current, as far as Curaçao, runs west. It then changes, describing a counterclockwise course to the north of Panama, south to the Gulf of Darien, then eastward along the coast of Colombia. From Curaçao onward I would have the current mainly against me at rates up to three knots. This did not worry me, for I was in no particular hurry.

As *Sea Dart* rolled and bucketed west-south-west from Bequia, running free with the sails boomed out each side, under control of the very effective steering gear, I had plenty of time to fill in the plan I had roughly sketched out in the West Indies. This was no simple matter, for it involved a lot of research into the history, geography, climate, ethnography, volcanology, even zoology of the area. A sailor should research every area into which he goes in a small craft. I always do; I never go in completely blind. If a mariner sometimes surprises you with his erudition, you must bear in mind that in the remote parts of the seacoasts of this earth, upon his accurate researching, upon his detailed assessing of the risks, very often *his life hangs*.

My plan was first to explore the southwest shores of the Caribbean Sea, the least known, bordering on sweltering jungle shores, inhabited mainly by Indians, one of the least-explored parts of the Western Hemisphere. This would take until July or August. Then I would pass through the Panama Canal and make ready to tackle the long, long beat to windward against the Humboldt Current in September. In other words I would, on my way to Lake Titicaca, five thousand sailing miles to the south, make a two-thousand-mile detour in order to satisfy my curiosity about the Darien Gap.

During my stay in the West Indies, I had gained information on the Humboldt Current from every source I could think of. Earlier, in the Maritime Museum in Barcelona, Spain, I had read an account of a voyage which mentioned that every seven years the current reversed itself. When this occurred, the reversed current was renamed "The Holy Child." I had searched and inquired in a number of places, as far apart as the British Museum and Lima University, for information on the years when this had occurred, and everything indicated that there was a sporting chance that it would again happen in 1973. If it *did*, then it would happen about September; and, instead of having to buck the current for almost two thousand miles direct, it would be *with* *Sea Dart*, thus making an inestimably easier trip.

My researches into reversal of the mightiest ocean current of all made me realize that Pizarro, the conqueror of the Incas, had had the devil's own luck. After getting his small fleet together in Panama, he had in fact sailed down on the reverse current, the "Holy Child," to land in what is now Ecuador. Had this not been the case, it would have taken the Spaniards much, much longer to reach the Inca Empire. Atahualpa, the emperor, would have been forewarned by their slow approach and have been ready for them. The Spaniards would probably have been massacred, and the history of the world would have taken a completely different course. More than likely the Spanish would not have gained access to the treasures of the Andes, with which to finance their conquests, and the nations of Northern Europe would probably not have been spurred into colonial conquest in order to counter the growing threat of Spanish domination of Europe.

Of course, this is all conjecture, but the scenario is clear. In such ways have the ocean currents of the world guided man's history. Looking at the maps of the old Spanish and Portuguese empires, it is quite evident that the latter were far better sailors, much more adept at going windward. The only possessions of Spain which involved any lengthy hauls against the wind were in the Pacific, on the western side,

places such as the Philippines and the New Hebrides. However, it is evident that when these were not approached
from the Peruvian coast, with a long, downwind run across
the Pacific, they were tackled around the Cape of Good
Hope and across the Indian Ocean with the aid of Portuguese pilots!

As *Sea Dart* barreled through the islands and rocky reefs
off the Venezuelan coast, my thoughts turned to these
fascinating matters—the old Spanish trade route across the
Atlantic from the Canaries to Puerto Rico and Cuba, then
down across the Caribbean to Cartagena and over to Portobelo, on the coast of what is now Panama. From there
overland, through sweltering coastal jungles along narrow
beaten paths by mule, up, up, and over the mighty Andes
passes, for over a thousand miles, to the highlands of
Bolivia, where lay the golden treasures of the Incas and the
silver mountain of Potosí. The journey took about a year.
Considering the primitive conditions, the lack of good
navigational knowledge, the scarcity of ports, the nonexis-
tence of tropical medicines, the attacks by pirates,
privateers, and others, not to speak of savages and cannibals
in the interior of Panama and Colombia, the journey was an
incredible feat in itself. Though the rape of the Inca Empire
is repugnant to me, I cannot help but have great admiration
for these conquistadors. They deserved every ounce of Inca
gold that ever reached the shores of Spain, though their
motivation was not only gold—they were also possessed by a
religious fanaticism unequaled before or since.

The main outlets in America for the Inca treasures were
Cartagena in Colombia and Portobelo in Panama. For two
centuries precious gold and silver poured through these
strongholds; for two centuries the naval might of Britain,
France, and Holland was directed towards obstructing the
flow or seizing it. In the course of this struggle hundreds of
sea battles were fought, thousands of men perished, empires were founded, and in the course of seeking alternative
routes of attack against the treasure, tremendous sea voyages were made, the oceans of the world were navigated,
and vast areas were opened to the knowledge of western
man. In remote villages on the bleak and waterless coast of

Peru, a crying child is still quieted with the threat, "Sssss...El Draque viene!" "Hush, Drake is coming!"

In the early nineteenth century, following the rot of Spanish power in Europe and the success of the American and French revolutions, the Creoles (European-descended South Americans) revolted against Spain. Assisted by English veterans from the Napoleonic wars, Simón Bolívar in the northern part of the continent, with the aid of his Irish, Scotch, and Welsh regiments, routed the Spanish. Meeting with San Martín from the south, he established the patchwork of comic-opera republics now known as Latin America. A misnomer if there ever was one, for the vast majority of people in these countries are Indians whose lives continue in the old pattern, a struggle against hunger and cold, against the rapacity of the *patrón*, the landowner. Ignored almost completely by the Creoles, unaffected by scores of "revolutions," they live, for the most part, the same way they did the day that Pizarro strangled Atahualpa back in 1533. What should be called Indio-America is known as Latin America, even though, with the exception of a few towns and cities, it's about as Latin as the Taj Mahal!

Wedged into the tiny cockpit of *Sea Dart*, peeling potatoes, sewing a sail, or taking a sight, I thought a lot about these matters. Years before I had visited the coast of "Spanish" South America in a British warship, but had encountered only the British communities and the Europe-oriented Creoles in the towns. Now I was going to visit the *real* South America, although I had little idea what I was in for, or how it would change my ideas of the world and history.

The entire continent lying to the south of *Sea Dart* was in many areas still as mysterious as when Columbus first sighted it at the end of the fifteenth century. Little did I know that I would stumble on evidence that would indicate that mariners from the Middle East had been in contact with South America at least two thousand years before Columbus was born! A great continent, it is little known both to outsiders and to the people who live in its cities, whose eyes still gaze with longing toward London, Paris, Lisbon, Rome, and Madrid. Their refusal to see what is directly under their noses is the main cause for all the strife and misery, all the hunger and destitution of a continent groaning under the weight of huge urban populations.

On the north coast of Colombia lies a thin strip of coastal jungle inhabited, for the most part, by the descendants of African slaves; they are mainly fishermen and rice farmers. It is from these people that the crews of pirate vessels and the drug smugglers are recruited. Inland, on the rainy mountainsides, live the Indians, still in the mule-back and blanket stage of civilization, inscrutable and severe. In the highlands live white descendants of the Spanish and other European colonizers of the past centuries; the country and mountain people are a fine group of intelligent, thrifty folk. In the cities lives a collection of murderous thieves and rogues. This was the country I was now bound for.

24

COLOMBIA—IN AND OUT

Y THE TIME I SIGHTED Curaçao Island, on the sixteenth of April, I was very satisfied with *Sea Dart*. I had tried her under all points of sail in winds up to thirty-five knots, and I had turned her round to test her against the heavy seas on the Venezuelan shelf. She performed like a thoroughbred, surprisingly forceful for her size. Of course, she was much livelier than *Barbara*, but that was to be expected. However, try as I might, I could not get her to lay over more than thirty degrees from the horizontal, even in the strongest blows. This was partly due to the fact that I had bent her aluminum mast in a slight bow with the masthead truck bent aft on the theory that with the luff of the mainsail bent, as in the Arab felucca rig, the mainsail would spill the wind much sooner than if the luff was straight. This is important when you are on a mountainous coast, where there is always the risk of sudden heavy gusts (katabatic winds) coming down off the cold peaks to replace the air which is rising off the warmer sea. As I was on my own, the steering gear would be in command of the course for much of the time, and I did not want a sudden gust to blow the boat over.

The addition of the bowsprit had improved her sailing a great deal, for it meant I could carry a big genoa which reached back to the cockpit winches. Going downwind, I could pole that out, and with the main booming out on the opposite side, she would whiz along, sometimes at a frightening rate, jumping from sea to sea. At one point, on the coast of Venezuela, off the Islas Los Roques, with three very clear landmarks to take bearings on, I found that she was surfing at *ten knots* in a thirty-five-knot wind. This is a dangerous speed for such a small craft, but I fully intended this passage to Curaçao to be in the nature of a trial, for I was in for a desperately difficult voyage and I had to be absolutely sure the boat was capable of meeting all my demands.

I found the cabin very cramped after the comparatively spacious accommodations on *Barbara*. I cooked in the tiny companionway, with my knees under my chin, using a pressure cooker over a one-burner kerosene flame. When enough steam had issued out of the escape valve, I opened the pot, ate right out of it, then washed it in sea-water. The only problem was the violent movement of the boat; if I wasn't careful, potatoes and rice, sardines and corned beef slopped all over the cockpit. The few times it happened I scooped it up and ate it anyway, for I always have a clean cockpit, no matter what the rest of the boat is like. Going to windward, however, it was almost impossible to cook, for the pressure cooker continually jerked off the stove because of the heavy movement against the ocean swell.

I swooped down onto Willemstad, the main port of Curaçao. Dusk was approaching, the swift, tropical dusk. I bore up into the entrance on a beam reach and almost collided with a very low road bridge, only yards around the headland. I managed to bring her up, all standing, to await the bridge's opening. On the shore a crowd of grinning and shouting youngsters told me how much they appreciated the spectacle.

Once in the port I was shown a very rocky berth alongside the main waterfront. As soon as the port official disappeared, I worked *Sea Dart* around into a small side canal used as a fruit market. Although it was very noisy, especially in the mornings, with the arrival of the fruit vessels from Venezuela, it was most colorful. The fruiters were a friendly, cheerful lot who loved to hear a story, and we got on well. I bought their fruit and they guarded *Sea Dart* when I ventured into the narrow streets between the old, Dutch-colonial houses for a cheap meal. The harbormaster was an old acquaintance from the Dutch navy, whom I had last seen in Holland in 1947. Time and again he warned me about the risks of cruising the Colombian coast, but after my Red Sea jaunt I was fairly confident that I could get in and out of Colombia without too much grief.

At the duty-free port in Curaçao I bought a camera for

$127.63 and canned food enough for three months. I evidently loaded the boat up too much, for on the five-hundred-mile run to Santa Marta, west of Curaçao, I found that she pounded much more. Nonetheless, I made that run in five days, sighting the headland of Cabo de la Aguja at seven in the morning on the twenty-fifth and getting alongside, after a day-long struggle with fluky winds, in the late afternoon. I was once more in South America, a thousand miles from the West Indies, almost two thousand miles from where I had last stepped on the continent at Cayenne, in French Guiana. I was once more on the continent where lay my elusive destination, far away to the south, across thousands of miles of lofty barren peaks, in the cold misty heights of the mighty Andes. In fact, Cabo de la Aguja is where one spur of the tremendous barrier reaches the sea. As I looked at the steaming, barren, volcanic mountains beyond the sleepy little town dozing at siesta in the late afternoon sun, as it has done ever since Simón Bolívar died there, I envisioned that terrible backbone with snowy peaks up to twenty-two thousand feet above sea level extending all the way down to Tierra del Fuego and Cape Horn, four thousand miles away. And then I looked at little *Sea Dart*—a mind-boggling comparison.

I lay down on deck, under the shade of the awning, to await the opening of the harbormaster's office. I had taken off my deck shoes, which I stowed by the foot of the mast, and I went to sleep, for I was tired, having been awake most of the night keeping an eye out for fishing craft. There was not a soul in evidence anywhere, except a policeman on the dock gate, nodding away in his little shelter. When I awoke, the shoes were gone! There was still no one in sight anywhere. I had been asleep no more than five minutes. The scene was still the same; a hot, dusty wind blew over the dockside; a dead dog, swollen and stinking, bumped against the jetty piers a little way down; the guard still nodded over his rifle; the sun still scorched the burnt mountainside; the little town dozed on—but my shoes were gone, the only ones I had. Welcome to Colombia!

I spent only one night in Santa Marta, for it is, as ports go, and especially South American ports, a deadly dull place (although the meal that night in a waterside restaurant was very good and cheap). On my way back to the boat I passed a streetside stall and bought my shoes back; they only cost me a dollar and a half. The hawker was friendly, polite, and didn't bat an eyelid throughout the whole transaction. In the morning, before sailing, having bribed the guard to watch the boat, I went to see the house where Bolívar died, a most impressive Spanish mansion, with a cool courtyard and wonderful furnishings. I collected the boat's papers from the immigration office, which cost only a "tip" of three packets of cigarettes, and took off for the run, now against the current, along the coast, 170 miles to Cartagena. Having worked my way out well clear of the coast and settled down to my sea chores, it was not until late in the afternoon that I discovered that my spare anchor line had been stolen from the after dodger, the lock of which had been expertly picked. I was learning, all right. This time I wasn't going to buy it back. I spent most of my waking moments on this passage thinking up ways of protecting my vessel from a race of people whose national sport is stealing!

The following day, although well out to sea, I passed the mouth of the River Magdalena, one of South America's most important, for it was and still is, the main traffic artery in a country where communication between cities is immensely difficult because of the deep valleys and lofty mountain ranges. I knew very well I was passing the mouth even though it was raining hard, for the color of the sea changed dramatically from blue to muddy brown despite the fact I was over twenty miles from the coast.

On this passage, and on subsequent ones all the way to Portobelo, I showed no lights at night and kept a wary eye open for small craft. Whenever I sighted small craft, especially small power craft, obviously faster than *Sea Dart*, I dropped all the sails and hove to, if possible with the bow facing the "suspect" until he was well over the horizon. That way I presented the smallest silhouette. With the light gray color of the hull and topsides, there was little danger of my being noticed from more than three miles away.

Sailing into Cartagena was exciting. There is a long, yet well-marked, channel which loads into a lagoon artificially created by the Spaniards in the 1700s. By joining together several islands with underwater walls, they allowed small craft in and out at high tide and prevented the entry of large men-of-war. All around the lagoon, and surrounding the old, European-style town, are immense fortifications, some of the most extensive I have ever seen, built of huge stone blocks. The average life expectancy of the slaves engaged in constructing the fortifications of Cartagena in the sixteenth and seventeenth centuries was around five months. The hot, unhealthy climate killed them off, as much as the savage treatment meted out by the Spaniards. For stealing extra food a slave was thrown into one of the fortress moats, which were purposely stocked with sharks.

There were one or two American vessels at the Yacht Club, much bigger than *Sea Dart*, secure under the eyes of a very tough-looking armed guard, who strutted along the jetty. At the head of the jetty, beautifully situated in one of the oldest of the miniature Spanish forts, was a very exclusive restaurant where the price of a dinner was roughly equivalent to eight months' income for a Cartagena dock worker.

With *Sea Dart* safely tied up under guard, I made my way up to Bogotá, the capital of Colombia, six hundred miles inland, at nine thousand feet in the sierras. I was curious to see the city, but more important, I thought I might be able to obtain a small outboard motor there. I had no power unit on *Sea Dart* and would surely need one to get her through the Panama Canal. It would also be very handy if I was becalmed, as had happened a couple of times, and for getting into and out of ports against a contrary tide or wind. There were none small enough in Curaçao, none at all in Cartagena; but various people at the Yacht Club had told me that I might be able to buy one in Bogotá. A reasonable enough assumption in a country with a population of over twenty-two million people and a coastline of over a thousand miles total length.

With my traveler's checks safely tucked into my money belt, my papers and passport in order, my visitor's tourist card and my ticket, I took the plane for Bogotá. Within five minutes of leaving the airport in that city, I had been relieved of the hundred dollars cash I had in my wallet, together, of course with the wallet. This happened at the airport taxi stand. No hustle, no bustle, no shoving or pushing; very quietly and expertly my wallet was lifted out of my inside jacket pocket, despite the fact that I was wearing a leather jacket buttoned up to the neck against the cold!

When I arrived at the Hotel San Francisco, I discovered the loss of my ready cash. I explained the problem to the management, who were kind enough to book me in anyway. After dinner I shut myself in my room.

Early next day I cashed the traveler's checks, five hundred dollars. By this time I had located a dealer who had a couple of four-horsepower Johnsons in stock. One would be just the ticket for *Sea Dart*. I left the money changer's office and started to cross the road against a heavy stream of nine-o'clock traffic. On the mid-street island, between the two streams of traffic, I was suddenly surrounded by five men, two pistols were shoved into my ribs, one on each side, and I was relieved of not only the five hundred dollars, but also my passport and tourist entry visa card. There wasn't a thing I could do about it, for in Bogotá a human life is not worth a nickel, let alone five hundred dollars. The thieves disappeared as if by magic into the traffic. Standing on the opposite side of the street was a policeman. I told him what had happened and that my money, passport, and papers had been stolen. When he asked me for identification and I said I had none, he promptly arrested me for not having any!

They don't mess around in Colombia. I went straight into a cage situated in a cellar, beneath which ran an open sewer. In the cold of Bogotá, nine thousand feet above sea level, there were no blankets and no food unless you paid for them. For five days, I froze and starved; finally I emerged to be thrust into a room full of hooded men—*La Cámara de Encapuchados*, the DST, or secret police. Eventually I was tossed out into the street with no explanation and no apology, despite the many protests I had made in my good Spanish about the state of affairs.

Physically, it didn't mean much, but the injustice of the whole thing rankled. I met men in that jail who had been inside for over four years without accusation or trial; and there was little likelihood of their going to trial, as the judges were on strike! I met a lad of sixteen who had been arrested the previous year for eloping with his girl friend, also age sixteen. He had been rotting in these cages over an open sewer for twelve months, dependent upon other prisoners for food. His family would not feed him because of the shame he had brought upon them! An American boy in close confinement in a tiny cell on a marijuana charge told me through the door that he had been inside that cell for four months without trial. This in a country whose top officials were, I was told, for the most part, intimately connected with the soft-drug traffic. Unfortunately, because of interference from a particularly sadistic bastard of a guard, I did not get his name.

As soon as I was out of the hellhole of the *Casa Pequeña*, I headed for the British consulate. The staff expressed little surprise at what had happened, but very efficiently issued me another passport. After a delay of two days to arrange the transfer of my remaining funds from England, I headed back to the coast, by railway this time, which is much cheaper than by air, although the journey takes well over two days.

Back in Cartagena I stumbled onboard *Sea Dart*, hoisted sail, and cleared off out into the lagoon, to anchor in an isolated creek and await the early morning breeze. "When in danger or in doubt, hoist the sail, and fuck off out." Never have truer words been said, especially in Colombia. Other countries send all kinds of teams to the Olympic games; Colombia sends a team of pickpockets!

25

A FORGOTTEN COLONY

S I SAILED *SEA DART* OUT of the Boca Grande, the main channel of Cartagena harbor, I thought of the scraps of information I had picked up in the course of rambling around the oceans of the world concerning a Scottish colony that had been established on the coast of Darien, in the malaria-ridden jungle swamps of southern Panama, early in the eighteenth century. In the past I had come across references to the colony in old books and had listened to people talk about the mysterious "New Scotland" in Central America. Apart from vague and sketchy references, the story belonged to the realm and tradition of Celtic Twilight.

Some years before, poring over old Admiralty charts of the Gulf of Darien, I came across two clues as to the possible site of the Scottish fortress. On the chart were two names in Spanish among the reefs and deep indentations on the southern Caribbean coast of Panama: Punta Escoces (Scotch Point) and Bahía Caledonia (Caledonia Bay). Caledonia is, of course, the old Latin name for Scotland. Could these two names have survived centuries after the site was abandoned? I decided then that if I ever found myself in the area, I would take a good look around.

From Cartagena to the Gulf of Darien is about 230 miles, an easy run for *Sea Dart*. However, with thundery rain lashing down and sheets of lightning striking all round my small boat, I took it easy, anchoring behind small islands each night. The electric storms of Darien were really something to experience. They frightened the living shit out of me. As many as twenty flashes of thick lightning struck the sea around the craft. It usually lasted from about ten at night until four in the morning. I strung a thick battery cable from the stainless steel backstay over the stern, hoping it would act as a lightning conductor in case the boat was

struck. Alone in a tiny craft, I did not stand much chance of
surviving if she blew up or burned out, for I could not
afford the loss of speed that would have been the penalty
for trailing my rubber Avon dinghy astern. Lightning is
frightening enough onshore; at sea in a small craft, coming
down in the water, it is a nightmare. Once I met an Australian in New Guinea. He had sailed a small craft over from
New Georgia, in the Solomon Islands, to Port Moresby. In
the manner of the Aussies he had stowed about 150 cans of
beer in the bilge. As he was sailing over the Solomon Sea,
another storm bedeviled area, lightning struck the masthead. The flash ran down the mast and he thought the end
of the world had come. However, there was no explosion;
instead, the beer cans welded together and he had to spend
days chipping them out of the bilge!

I found safe anchorages in the San Bernardo Islands, off
Isla Fuerte. I also found friendly fisher folk here, blacks. I
anchored in such shallow water that I was able to wade
alongside the boat and clean the bottom off with a long
scrubber. This is a boon to a nonswimmer like myself,
because otherwise it means having to go over the side lashed
to the boat with a strong line.

The final run over to the Panamanian coast necessitated
an overnight sail of about a hundred miles. I set the course
direct for Punta Escoces, where I hoped to feel my way in
behind the prominent headland and find protection from
the strong wind. Despite the fact that I set a course twenty
miles to the north of the point, I finished up thirty miles to
the south of it; the strong current, running south, had set
me off fifty miles! During the course of this passage, I spent
one of the weirdest and most frightening nights of my life,
with the wind howling, the rain sheeting down, and forked
lightning stabbing the sea all around me for hours. I
smoked two packs of cigarettes and made tea, hot and
strong, five times during the night. To be in a small craft
without any radio aids to navigation, with no possibility of
getting a sighting of a star or anything else to help fix your
position, in an unknown current shoving you towards a low,
unlit jungle shore inhabited by savages, sailing into wet,
black nothingness, with thunder crashing overhead and

lightning flashing all around, is a very nerve-racking experience.

In the morning the wind dropped and the sky cleared up quickly, as it does in a tropical rain belt. Ahead lay the high land of Cabo Tiburón (Shark Cape). To be absolutely sure where I was, I lay off until noon when I got a good latitude. With the risk of Indian attacks, I could take no chances here.

Under the lee of Cabo Tiburón is the tiny port of Limon, the Colombian frontier post. No road connects Panama with Colombia; the mountainous terrain is far too precipitous. Connection is by sea, a few small canoes that hug the coast. I lay in the lovely, hot bay overnight, took a shower under a shore-side waterfall, and collected bananas from an old plantation which had fallen to the onslaught of the jungle.

The following day I sailed thirty miles up the coast, close-hauled, and bore around Punta Escoces, which appeared to be nothing but a small promontory, about three hundred feet high, behind which lay a shallow bay. I carefully wore around into this bay, sounding as I went with the lead, for the chart I was working from had been surveyed in 1857! As coral grows at a fast rate, there would have been vast changes since the chart was made. Slowly I worked my way into the calm, clear water behind the headland and dropped the anchor on top of a sandy patch of sea-bottom. Below, I made myself a sandwich of biscuit and corned beef, then did a few chores before the tropical sun went down. I didn't light a lamp, for I didn't want to attract attention, human or insect.

At first light in the morning I was awakened by an Indian tapping on the topside. He was dressed in a loincloth and had blue paint on his cheeks. In a tiny dugout rested his bow, several arrows, and his woman, beautifully dressed in what appeared to be a sari-like silk dress. Over her shoulders she wore an exquisitely embroidered shawl, or *mola*, down which her dark tresses flowed. A gold ring, an inch and a half in diameter, running through her nose, completed the ensemble. They looked friendly enough, and by the time I had given them a cup of tea and exchanged greetings in Spanish, which they understood to a certain extent, they were even friendlier. They smiled and chatted to each other in low voices.

Later, we went ashore in their dugout and entered the cleanest native village I have ever seen outside England. The paths between the cane and straw huts were swept, there were no weeds or bushes to harbor insects. The women were all spotless and were busy washing clothes by the edge of a stream on a flat rock. The men were gathered in the middle of the central square, surrounding a man who looked to me to be about ninety years of age! I was later to find that he was, in fact, the same age as myself! This seems to be a characteristic of the Cunas. Feeling a little like Stanley meeting Livingstone, I greeted the chief in Spanish and presented him with some cans of corned beef. He replied fluently in Spanish and told me his name was Turuna Ana. I asked him if I could pass around cigarettes, and he said yes, and his followers accepted them gracefully.

I told the chief that I was alone, looking for the ruins of an old fort—Escoces. Had he ever heard anything about Escoces? No, he hadn't, but there were a lot of old stones and a ditch over there at Coco, just this side of the point. I asked him if I might take a look at this place, and the chief detailed four younger men to accompany me. We had walked for about a mile along the shore-side path when I almost fell headlong into a ditch, a perfectly straight moat cut through the coral! I took one look at the smooth sides of the eight-foot-deep moat and knew that I had come to the right place. Excitedly, I traced the moat along its star-shaped path into the shore and then back again to the sea. On the escarpment I found piles of cut stones all around the periphery of the central hill. The mosquitoes made only a brief examination possible, but it was clear to me that I had found Fort Saint Andrew. So it was not only a legendary tale told in the cold, misty Hebridean nights; Scotland had once had her very own colony here in the feverish swamps of southern Panama!

(Later, upon my return to Europe, I went to the British Museum. There I discovered that the Scottish Jacobites had sent out an expedition to Panama in 1698 with the idea of

building a road across the isthmus and charging tolls to the
Spanish for using the road to bring treasure across to the
Caribbean. As Catholics, they had fondly imagined that the
Spanish would welcome them and perhaps even help them.
Instead, they were besieged for a year after the fort was
built. Despite frequent and bloody Spanish attacks, however, they did not surrender until they were practically
starving. So impressed were the Spaniards with their defense that they allowed the Scots to march out carrying their
arms and colors and even provided them with ships and
stores with which to make the long ocean passage home.
Several offshoots of the main settlement had been established, but had subsequently disappeared.)

I returned to the village and talked with Turuna Ana. He
had heard tales of strange-looking people living to the
north, on the other side of the coastal mountains. These
people did not speak Cuna, and though half-savage, they
worshiped three gods—a father god, a son god, and a
mother god. Of these three, the mother god was the most
important. Soon as I heard this I determined to go and have
a look at these folk. Several times Turuna Ana mentioned
the phrase "Cabellos Rojos"—"Red Hairs"—when talking
about them.

After spending a very pleasant week among Turuna
Ana's Indians, watching the women weave and the men
hunt and fish, I weighed anchor and set off north to Bahía
Caledonia. A study of the chart, which was the only guide I
had, indicated that this was probably the best place to start
looking for the Cabellos Rojos. I intended to strike inland
from there. It shouldn't take me more than one or two days
to sight our friends, or so I thought. Little did I know the
Darien jungle and mountains!

Two of Turuna Ana's hunters accompanied me to
Caledonia Bay, a short day's sail from Coco against wind
and current, in very restricted waters. The chart of the area,
which had guided me across the Gulf of Darien, was very
small-scale, and did not show the reefs and shallows. My two
Cuna friends kept a good lookout while I conned the boat
into the shallow, rock-strewn inlet of Caledonia, or as the
Indians called it, "Cali-da." Both my friends were around

twenty-four; though it was difficult to judge their ages. One, as near as I can write it down, was called Hawili; I promptly named him Willie. He was to accompany me over the Sierra de Darien. Turuna Ana had assured me he was a good tracker and fearless. The other, rather tall and lanky for a Cuna Indian, was called Cha-dia. He became Charlie-boy. His job was to stay with the boat while Willie and I pushed inland. Charlie-boy was an expert fisherman. As we beat up to Caledonia he caught several fair-sized dorados with my lines. The lines and tackle, all still fairly new at this time, delighted him, while the fish he hooked delighted all three of us.

With Willie I could converse in pidgin-Spanish, of which he had a rough knowledge; with Charlie-boy it was a question of grimaces, gestures, grins, and loud hollers. We found this very funny, and our laughter frightened the flamingos in the rushes on the shore-side.

I anchored at the head of the bay, under the lee of a small isle. To avoid calamity in case of a rare shift of wind, I laid out the big hurricane anchor at the end of a forty-fathom line. Then the three of us set to making an excellent supper of dorado and rice. The mosquitoes were a nuisance to me, but didn't seem to bother my "crew." I made milkless tea for them, which they relished, smacking their lips and making the Cuna sign of approval, which consists of throwing the hand, palm inwards, violently up in front of the face. At night, when the reception was best, I tuned my transoceanic radio to listen to the BBC news. This fascinated them, and I realized they had never heard a radio before. Willie said they had heard of radio, but that neither he nor Charlie-boy had ever listened to one. They did not seem to enjoy modern music, rock, soul, and so-forth, but classical chamber music captivated them. It was all I could do to persuade them to turn in, for I wanted to make an early start with the false dawn.

At first light next day Willie and I set off on what I thought would be a two- or three-day stroll into the mountains. However, it turned out to be a twelve-day struggle in some of the most difficult terrain I have ever encountered. Before leaving I asked Charlie-boy to look after my "canoe," which I told him was my mother, my father, my sister, my brother, and my home. Obviously affected by this, Charlie-boy grabbed my hand and, speaking through Willie, promised to look carefully after *Sea Dart*.

The first day's march, westward over the dip between two peaks about two thousand feet high, was fairly easy, even though we had to cut our way through dense undergrowth with our machetes, or cutlasses, as we mariners call them. I carried enough canned food for a week plus a margin of three days, as well as some bronze screws, copper nails, and sailcloth for presents. Willie carried rice, sugar, salt, tea, and five gallons of water. As it turned out, we did not need the water, for there were plenty of streams right through the area, and rain showers at that time of year, June, were frequent and sometimes very heavy indeed. In addition, I carried a mosquito net, and Willie the working jib to use as a tent.

Near the coast the insects were prolific, particularly the mosquitoes and a type of tiny sandfly which was about the most persistent, voracious little bastard it has ever been my misfortune to encounter. They even penetrated through a cotton shirt. At first, the heat made life very difficult, but as we climbed up over the first coastal range, then the second, the air got cooler. The going became more difficult, however, and even very dangerous, with the land broken up into innumerable ravines, overgrown with thick, thorny undergrowth.

On the third day Willie and I passed over a ridge between the peaks of two mountains about five or six thousand feet high and found ourselves looking down on an extensive valley, about fifteen to twenty miles wide, stretching northeast and southwest far as the eye could see, covered in an emerald carpet of jungle. I passed the binoculars to Willie; I wanted to see if he had seen what I had. Very soon he grunted, "*Humo!*" Smoke! Pointing to the east, I passed a finger overhead as the sun travels and asked, "*Días, cuanto?*" He showed three fingers, and we set off towards the smoke, using the tiny dinghy compass I had with me to get a bearing. The distance to the fire from the saddle must have been no more than twelve miles, but it took us exactly three days to cover it. Enroute we must have walked, climbed, cut, slashed, and stumbled at least thirty miles, fording with difficulty fast, roaring streams, avoiding swampland, forever on the lookout for snakes and other jungle creatures.

One night, lying asleep in a small clearing by a stream, Willie snake-bellied over to me and put his hand over my mouth. Pointing to an overgrown hillock in the distance, he whispered, *"Cabellos Rojos alla."* My hand went to my cutlass, but Willie grabbed it and shook his head. We wrapped ourselves up tightly in the sail and the mosquito net and slept uneasily till the first light of dawn.

The Cabellos Rojos trailed us all the next day, never more than fifty yards away. We followed a rough track towards the clearing where their village lay. When we arrived in the clearing it was completely deserted. Willie signaled me not to approach the huts, which were oblong, with tilted roofs, perched on short stilts and made of wood branches and grass. He took the presents from me and laid them on the ground—six cans of my precious corned beef plus the screws and copper nails. In the bright sunshine, my few presents looked tawdry and worthless. Willie then led me to the outside of the clearing, well away from the huts. Then he sat down, gesturing me to do the same, and we waited, patiently.

After an hour of listening to what sounded like birdcalls, the bushes on the far side of the parade ground parted and five men walked out. They were much taller than the average Indian, clad in short aprons over their cocks, armed with bows and arrows and what seemed to be blowpipes. Around their necks they wore little bags. On their ankles were short feathers. Otherwise they were naked. Two of them had bright ginger hair; another had hair of a tawny hue. They held their hands palm out, walked over to the gifts we had laid out, and looked at them silently. Then came the same gesture of approval I had seen the Cuna use on the coast, a wave of the hand like a fan in front of the face. Willie got up and casually walked over to them. One by one he put his hands on their shoulders and with his forehead touched their foreheads. Then he beckoned me to do the same. I put a brave face on and approached them.

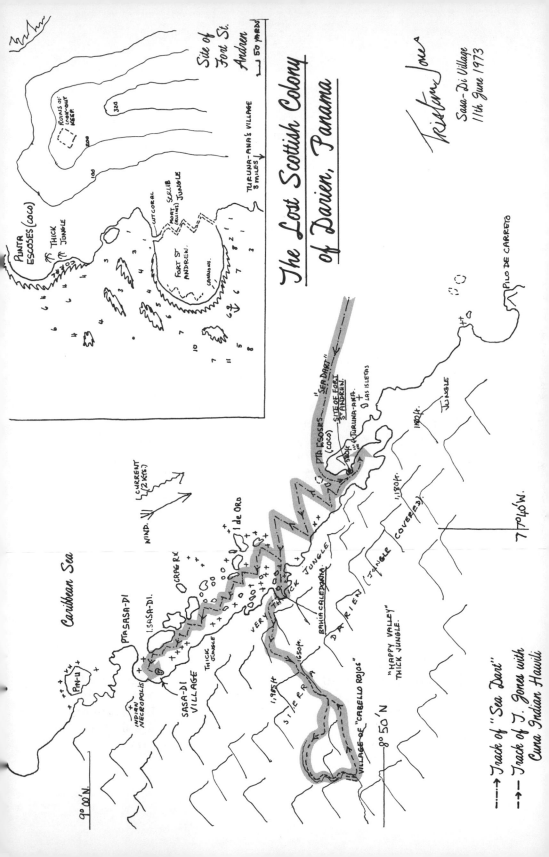

The Lost Scottish Colony of Darien, Panama

Tristan Jones

Sasa-Di Village
11th June 1973

Site of
Fort St.
Andrew

└─ 50 yds ─┘

Ruins of
Look-out
Keep

Punta
Escoses (coco)

Thick
Jungle

CUT CORAL

MORE (RUINS)
SCRUB JUNGLE

FORT ST.
ANDREW

CANNONS

TURUNA-ANA'S VILLAGE
3 MILES

PILO DE CARRETO

"SEA DART"

PTA ESCOSES
(COCO)

SITE OF FORT
ST ANDREW

TURUNA-ANA

Las Isletas

JUNGLE

1,180 ft.

Caribbean Sea

CURRENT
(2 KTS?)

WIND

I. de ORO

OCRAG RK

PIASASA-DI

I. SASA-DI.

AN-U

INDIAN
NECROPOLIS

SASA-DI
VILLAGE

THICK JUNGLE

VERY THICK JUNGLE

1,950 ft.

1,650 ft.

THICK JUNGLE

BAHIA CALEDONIA

JUNGLE (COVERED)

D   A   R   I   E   N

S   I   E   R   R   A

"HAPPY VALLEY"
THICK JUNGLE.

VILLAGE OF "CABELLO ROJOS"

9° 00' N.

8° 50' N.

77° 40' W.

---·→ Track of "Sea Dart"

———→ Track of J. Jones with
Cuna Indian Hawili

Their red hair was cut in a sort of pageboy bob. Two of the men had bones stuck up their nostrils; all had scars on their faces and bodies.

As I went through the forehead touching routine, I saw that three of them had light blue eyes! They had a unique smell from rubbing themselves with the leaf of a strong-smelling plant to repel insects. After much gesticulation and smiling over the copper nails and canvas, I opened the cans and ate some corned beef, to show them what it was. They fell on it and cleaned out the rest in short order, but kept the empty cans.

Willie told me that he could understand some of their words, but for the rest it was a matter of sign language. After the tribe filtered back into the village from the forest, I tried to make them understand that I came from far away and that we wished to stay the night, then return over the mountains to the coast. To this they agreed and showed Willie and me into an empty hut. Inside, crudely painted in a sort of blue dye, was a cross and over it the figure of a woman with a halo around her head!

That night we ate iguana, with roots and rice and Indian beer. Due to a tender stomach, I did not inquire too closely as to how the beer was made; what did intrigue me was when one of the older men showed me a rough pair of tweezers made from a twig of creeper. With this they plucked out their beards! Indians with beards? Red beards?

The women ate separately from the men. They were dressed modestly, more or less in the style of the Cuna Indian women, but without the *mola*. Some of them had the high cheekbones of Indians, as did a few of the men; but the majority of the eighty people in the village had no sign in their faces or bodies of Indian ancestry. The only clues were the ornaments in their houses and the way they laced into the beer, for in an hour most of the men were either blind-drunk or maudlin. Again I dozed cutlass in hand.

At dawn, still feeling very apprehensive, Willie and I took our farewells. The headman indicated that two of the Cabellos Rojos would accompany us as far as the divide of the Sierra de Darien. They knew the forest trails, and our route back was much easier than the way we had come.

When we parted, on the ridge, we gave these two men most of the remaining corned beef.

It took Willie and me another three days to reach the coast, scrambling over the thorn-covered gullies, several of which were so deep and wide they required a detour of many miles to get round.

Emerging at last from the jungle, we found *Sea Dart* lying peacefully to anchor, surrounded by a fleet of Cuna canoes. Charlie-boy was fishing from the bow, chatting with his friends, who had paddled up against the current all the way from Coco to find out how we were getting on. Charlie-boy had caught many fish and dried them by hanging them on the rigging in the sun.

On the following day the whole fleet of Cuna canoes, led by *Sea Dart*, sailed back down to Punta Escoces to anchor in front of the sparkling clean village, under a backdrop of high, misty blue mountains. To the north of us, far away, as we feasted on roast fish and coconut, the moon rose over the old Scottish stronghold, a monument to the wanderings of that hardy race of folk.

On the fourteenth of June, 1973, I started off to sail up through the chain of islands strung for 150 miles along the southern Caribbean coast of Panama. The Spanish name for the islands is Las Muletas; the Anglo name is the San Blas Islands, after the Cape which marks their northern end. In the heyday of the Spanish Main, when all the Inca gold was being channeled through the ports of Cartagena to the south and Portobelo to the north, this group of islands was the lair of pirates and privateers, British, Dutch, and French. With their fast, shallow-draft brigantines, they entered the reefs and, safe from the lumbering, deep-drafted Spanish men-of-war, found refuge among the friendly Cunas, who hated the Spaniards as they hated, and still do, anyone who dares to interfere with their women.

The Spanish never succeeded in subduing the Cunas, and to this day they maintain a great degree of autonomy from the central government of Panama. With animals and fish plentiful and easy to catch, in an area relatively unaffected by hurricanes, their lives, along with those of the gauchos of the South American pampas, are probably the most carefree and uninhibited of any on the two American continents. Their houses, though made of primitive materials, are well constructed, solid, and clean. Their needs are simple, their diet sufficient. While they have started to build schools, and in the northern islands there are even a few outboard motors, they are extremely wary and suspicious of Western amenities.

The islands are small, no more than a mile or two long, with white sandy beaches. Beyond the beaches palm trees wave in the trade wind. Beneath the palms are scattered the huts of the Indians, mainly along the shores. Some of the villages are populous, with as many as a thousand huts. The paths between the huts are spotless. Pigs and other animals are kept in compounds away from the huts.

Sailing among the islands is straightforward, as long as you keep a sharp lookout for shallows and reefs. Again, as in many of the remoter parts of the world, navigation charts are both inaccurate and misleading. But with the water so clear that the bottom of the sea can be seen at sixty feet, keeping out of danger is a matter of common sense and vigilance.

I took my time sailing up through the archipelago, anchoring off small islands at night, but calling at the larger villages on the way. I spent a week in the town of Mulatupo, which even has a thatch cinema! Another large town, built of Indian huts, is Playón Chico. On the hills above is an extensive Indian pantheon, where for centuries the Cuna dead have been put to rest in wickerwork baskets hanging among the trees.

The only sign of western intrusion in all the San Blas Islands is at the far northern end, where two Americans have established a tiny, informal hotel. The cold beer there is wonderful! The most northerly of the group, Porvenir Island, has a small airfield and the beginnings of a miniscule tourist industry. For impecunious yachtsmen this is a good place to refit on a round the world passage. There is a former American army base on an artificial island close to Porvenir where stores and supplies may be obtained cheaply through the owners of the hotel.

The whole coast of Panama from Cape San Blas west to

Colón is full of historical interest. On my first night out I anchored in Nombre de Dios Bay, where Francis Drake, the greatest sea dog of them all, lies buried in the sea-bed "slung between the roundshot," after having been brought low, not by the guns of proud Spain, but by the bite of an anopheles mosquito!

The closer to Colón I moved, the more Spanish was spoken. As *Sea Dart* approached the Canal Zone, the people changed from Indians to blacks and mestizos, or a mixture of black and Indian. At Portobelo are several wonderfully well preserved Spanish fortresses, built to protect the long inlet and old royal wharves and warehouses from the depredations of English seamen. Many of the old cannons are still in position in the walls. The warehouses are still intact and are situated on old brick wharves at the end of the jetty, with the royal coats of arms still hanging over the huge doors. The roofs and floors are in good order, despite three centuries of heat and rain. In these warehouses a great proportion of the treasure looted from South America was stored before shipment to Spain. The people of present Portobelo, a poor fishing village of just a few huts, are black. I will always remember them as among some of the most friendly and kindly folk I met in all my wanderings in the Americas.

To the west of the deserted old fortress of San Fernando is the hospital operated by the U.S. government during the building of the Panama Canal. In the hills behind the hospital are the remains of extensive quarries from whence came the vast quantities of granite used in the construction of the harbors and walls throughout the canal project. The fishing off the fortress was very good and I managed to hook a fair amount of red mullet. The climate in Portobelo is reasonable, never much above eighty-five degrees, which is probably the reason the hospital was built here. Mosquitoes and sand flies, however, make life a misery, day and night.

It was for this reason that I decided to make for the Canal Zone instead of refitting topsides in Portobelo. With a fair wind on the beam, *Sea Dart* hammered off to the west-north-west, fetching up at the entrance to the great Canal at noon on the ninth of July. *Sea Dart* had sailed 2,098 miles since leaving Bequia, and was now ready to pass through to the Pacific Ocean and attempt to overcome the Humboldt Current. But first she would have to be careened on the Pacific side, where there is a tide, for the bottom had fouled with all kinds of marine growth in the warm, clear, fertile waters of the San Blas Islands.

I sailed the boat into Cristobal harbor, inside the U.S. zone, and brought her gently alongside the customs house. I was immediately ordered off by an official, a small, fat, balding man in a gray suit, with ballpoint pens poking out of his breast pocket. *Sea Dart* was not allowed to come alongside. I would have to anchor off and come back with my papers in my dinghy (this notwithstanding that the harbor water was thick with fuel oil, gooey and black, which would ruin my rubber dinghy). Once again I was back in the cloudcuckooland of bloody bureaucracy!

26
SMALL BOAT: BIG DITCH

T THE CRISTOBAL YACHT Club I was allotted a berth after *Sea Dart* had been measured for passage through the Canal. Once again I was in the mainstream of ocean yachting. I met a few old friends who were hanging around and others who knew of me, so I was not short of company. It was a real pleasure to meet these mariners, for, contrary to accepted ideas about single-handers, we are not, as a rule, loners when on shore. We love to swap yarns and compare experiences. Listening to long-distance voyagers, I always pick up lots of practical information, as well as bits of esoterica. Indeed, it was in this way that I had first heard the rumor of the lost Scottish colony in Darien.

In Cristobal I was particularly lucky to meet up with the fifty-foot sloop *Nuits St. Georges* out of La Rochelle, France, on her way to Tahiti. On board were a retired architect and a naturalist, excited at the prospect of visiting the Galápagos Islands. I also met with the forty-foot *White Horse of Kent*, the first ferrocement (reinforced concrete) vessel I had seen at close quarters. She had been built by her owner, Colin Usmar, in Capetown. She was solid and full of good gear, but, like *Sea Dart*, without an engine, so Colin was busy negotiating for a tow through the Canal. He was an Englishman from Dover, a bricklayer by trade, who had emigrated to South Africa, built several houses, and with the proceeds had constructed the *White Horse*. Colin was accompanied by his Rhodesian wife, Lynn. Together we spent several evenings in the club bar swapping yarns and planning *White Horse*'s crossing of the Pacific to Australia. As they were sailing on short funds, Colin was anxious to get to Australia in order to earn money bricklaying.

People have asked me how they can make a living while sailing long distances. There are several ways, but you have to be good at them. First, have a special trade, such as bricklaying, plumbing, electricity, or radio repair. Or, second, be a dentist; they are in demand and are permitted to practice almost anywhere, which doctors and lawyers are not. Third, be a writer, although this is most difficult, especially if you are in a small craft undergoing a long voyage in out-of-the-way areas. The problems of day-to-day existence alone are enough to take up your full time. On top of that is the problem of maintaining communication with editorial contacts in several countries. The effort is almost too much; to sit in a tiny cabin, sweltering in temperatures of over a hundred degrees, with the boat pitching and rolling, is almost unbearable. Then again, when I am writing for magazines, there is usually a long time lag of several months, in some cases over a year, between completing a work and receiving funds.

The city at the Caribbean end of the Panama Canal is divided into two zones of startling contrast. It is something like I imagine East and West Berlin to be. Cristobal, in the Canal Zone, is surrounded by manicured green lawns and flower beds and full of air-conditioned houses set in their own grounds, clean streets, and eager servants. Colón, the other half, is full of sprawling slums, shabby tenements, and smelly, rubbish-littered tracks crawling with disease, vice, and apathy. The two zones are divided by a railroad line patrolled by the Zone police, who are, I was told, the highest paid police force in the world.

The Canal Zone itself is a strip of land either side of the waterway stretching right across the isthmus, dividing the Republic of Panama into two parts, and guarded by chain-link fences. The Zone contains, as far as I could make out, thirteen military bases! The inhabitants of the Zone, all U.S. citizens, live in a style grander than that of the old British colonials in India during the days of the Raj. They have PX privileges, duty-free shops, cinemas and clubs, which no one who is not military or employed by the Canal authorities is entitled to use. They live in an air-conditioned cocoon, oblivious to the suffering, starvation, ignorance, and disease on the other side of the chain-link fence.

The origins of the Canal are interesting. It was first

dreamed of by the Spanish conquistadors in the sixteenth century, but, as with many of their dreams that involved actual physical labor, it came to naught. In the nineteenth century, Ferdinand de Lesseps, the great French engineer who built the Suez Canal, attempted the task. For nine years a great labor force struggled through the difficult country, mainly digging by hand, before giving up exhausted. A narrow ditch of only a few miles was all there was to show for the expenditure of $440 million and twenty thousand lives, the latter primarily the result of yellow fever.

The French dealt with Colombia, which owned Panama at that time. When the Americans, after transferring their Pacific Fleet around Cape Horn to the Atlantic during the war against Spain in Cuba, decided to cut a canal, they approached Colombia. The Colombians refused the terms offered, so the United States stirred up a Panamanian revolt against Colombia—the first of the famous covert operations (if we discount the mysterious and highly suspicious blowing up of the battleship *Maine* in Havana harbor in 1898).

Supported by U.S. Marines, the Panamanians succeeded in gaining their independence from Colombia. The day after the final bugle notes died away, a treaty was signed giving the United States "perpetual rights" over the Canal Zone, with "equivalent sovereignty." Nevertheless, Panama, by the terms of the treaty, retained "titular sovereignty" over the Zone.

The Canal took ten years to build. It was a gigantic undertaking, a marvel of engineering and medicine; in the space of three years malaria and yellow fever were brought under control. Whole sides of mountains were moved, millions of tons of stone were cut away, and the two oceans were at last joined. There are three sets of locks, each 110 feet wide and 1,000 feet long, on the Caribbean side. These take ships 85 feet up into Gatun Lake; on the Pacific side are three more locks to take them down again to the level of Balboa Channel.

In drawing up the regulations for a sailing craft passing through the Canal, the Canal Authority had a bureaucratic field day. First, the boat has to be measured by an inspector, complete with notebook, forms, and tape measure. Back at the office the clerks get to work on the inspector's findings, converting his linear measurements, by some exotic formula of their own, to tonnage, and it is upon this tonnage that the fee for the passage is based. Next, the mariner is given a time and a date for starting the trip. After that he is given a thick wad of printed instructions. The vessel has to have solid, sturdy deck cleats, and four 200-foot mooring lines. In addition to a skipper and a pilot, she must carry four line-handlers—two forward and two aft.

On the thirteenth of July, a Friday, I was due to go through. My cruising friends had already passed through, so there was no chance of their acting as line-handlers for me. I combed the club for volunteers, but as the weather was wet, none were forthcoming. The club barman, half jokingly, suggested that I telephone the local seminary, as he knew a monk who liked sailing. This I did, and Brother Francis promised to arrange for three of his cohorts to come down with him in the early morning.

Late Thursday night I received a message stating that my passage had been postponed until Sunday, the fifteenth. I phoned Brother Francis to see if he and his friends could possibly make it on Sunday.

"Oh, no," he said. "That is our busiest day at the monastery. I'm terribly sorry."

All day Friday and Saturday I searched for four volunteer line-handlers, for I could not afford to pay the professionals. Finally, very early on Sunday morning, with the rain still pouring down, I found the answer.

A steady dribble of young hippies passes through Panama. At that time their main base was the laundry room of the Cristobal Yacht Club, where they slept among the washing machines. They were mainly Americans, on their way to South America or just wandering around. I tore off up to the laundry and shook the first lad I tripped over. He was most enthusiastic about a trip through the Canal and promised to come along at 5:30 A.M. with three friends.

They were the most unlikely yacht crew I'd ever seen. Well over six feet tall, they had beards down to their chests. Bangles and beads jangled as they hefted their huge

rucksacks into *Sea Dart*'s tiny cockpit. They were too big to
fit below in my cabin, so they sat on the deck for breakfast,
which they wolfed hurriedly down. Then, while I arranged
the mooring lines and other gear, making ready for the
arrival of the pilot, they went forward to practice yoga or
talk about Buddha or whatever hippies do on a drizzling
morning. They were so big that when they moved forward
Sea Dart's stern came up out of the water!

After half an hour the pilot appeared. A more complete
contrast to the rest of my crew cannot be imagined. He was
in his fifties, with a crew cut and peaked cap, rimless glasses
and piercing blue eyes. Shaking the rain off his shoulders,
he asked me where the *Sea Dart* was.

"There," I replied, pointing down at my tiny boat, whose
deck was well below the level of the top of the dock.

He stared down at my craft for a moment, then said,
"This? Goddamn it, I thought this was your dinghy. Why
don't you just truck her over on the railroad?"

"Can't afford it."

"Hell, I'm not taking this goddamn kid's toy through, for
Crissake!"

"Then I'll have to head out again and sail round Cape
Horn, won't I?"

"Aw, Jesus Christ, OK. Let's get goin'."

"Why don't we hang on the slack for a few minutes, until
the rain stops? I've got some coffee made."

We talked in the cabin over coffee for a while, about
places and people. He was a friend of Christian Joubert, the
harbormaster of Majunga, in Madagascar, half a world
away. A couple of years previously he had piloted through
the Canal an old friend of mine, Sir Percy Wynn Harris, on
his way from the independence celebrations in Gambia,
West Africa, to Australia.

"What speed can you do, Cap'n?" the pilot asked me as we
stepped topsides.

"Depends on the wind, but she's a pretty lively goer."

"Wind?"

"Yes. Ain't got a motor yet."

"Jesus H. Christ! OK, Cap'n, seein' as it's you we'll sail the
goddamn thing through. Holy fuck, I'll even take you into

the locks *before* the steamers."

So it was that *Sea Dart* became the first vessel ever to sail through the Panama Canal. With a fair northeasterly we made good time and I worked out a grand system for sailing into the locks and fetching up short with no problem. The four giant hippies lined up across the tiny deck amidships acted as a sail. When we got halfway into the locks I shouted, "Down," and they dropped prone on the deck, and there we were, automatically reefed down. We were probably the only ocean-sailing craft in the world to use hippie beards as sails! By this means I had enough speed to turn the boat right around into the wind and bring her to a complete stop right in the middle of the lock. Then the line-handlers cast the long lines ashore and the dock workers walked the boat down, stern first, to the end of the lock. The great steamers followed *Sea Dart* in, the entry gates, huge and ponderous, closed, and the water level rose, throwing *Sea Dart* every which way but doing no harm, for she was securely tied in a position in the middle of the lock where she could bump nothing.

We retained the wind all through Gatun Lake, a beautiful stretch of water dotted with small islands, on which are located the country houses of Canal executives, set among waving palms and smooth lawns.

Sea Dart kept the wind all the way to the Pedro Miguel locks, at the Pacific end of the Canal, finally shooting out of them like a greyhound after a rabbit. I fetched up off the Yacht Club at Balboa just before dusk. I had crossed from the Atlantic to the Pacific by one of only three water routes, the others being around Cape Horn and the Northwest Passage from Greenland to Alaska. Eventually I was to find a fourth—from the Pacific to the Atlantic, clear across South America!

27
STRAINING AT THE LEASH

T WAS NOW THE TWENTY-fifth of July and time for me to start preparations for the task of beating against the Humboldt Current. At Taboga Island, a few miles off the mainland, there is a good eight-foot tide. Combined with a nice flat sandy beach and *Sea Dart*'s three keels, it meant that I could sail in, drop the anchor, go down with the tide, and sit nice and dry for several hours each tide. The best beach is on the southeast side of the small island, and although the climate is hot and muggy and the horse flies are a continual pest, it's a good place for a voyager who is not too well off. It doesn't cost anything to get the boat high and dry. The locals are friendly, and it's near enough to Panama City to go to and fro in the ferry to collect supplies.

By the end of the first week in August, I had cleaned and repainted *Sea Dart*'s bottom with antifouling paint, given the sides a fresh coat of blue-gray paint designed to camouflage the boat an horizon color, repaired all the sails (an ongoing chore), sorted out and restowed all the internal gear, and started storing five months' supplies of canned goods. In case *Sea Dart* was swept away from the South American Pacific littoral by the strong Humboldt Current, I would have to head out across the Pacific to the nearest ocean islands—the Tuamotus, *four thousand* miles to the west! I had to carry sufficient food and water for this contingency.

The consensus of opinion in the Balboa Yacht Club among people who had experienced the strength of the Humboldt was that a small craft with a short waterline length, incapable of maintaining a speed of more than four knots, would not be able to overcome the Humboldt. If I was forced out to the Tuamotus, then I would follow that course. From those islands I would have to make another

very long ocean passage of two thousand miles, southeast to
Easter Island, then another two thousand miles to Juan
Fernández Island, off the coast of Chile and from there
come back up north with the current to the coast of Peru.
This had been the traditional route from Panama and the
West Coast of North America in the days of sail, for much
larger square-rigged vessels. The ocean island route, however, meant a total distance of ten thousand miles! In a
vessel the size of *Sea Dart*, this would mean almost continual
hard sailing for around six months. I would not arrive at
Callao, in Peru, until February 1974. The Andes snow
would be melting, the rainy season would be in full swing,
the mountain tracks would be soggy deathtraps, and I
would be stuck waiting on the coast for another eight
months before I could haul across the Andes. In effect, I
would be delayed a whole year reaching Lake Titicaca.

So, it was worth the risk to go headlong into the current
and cut all corners. The distance direct from Taboga to
Callao is around seventeen hundred miles. Against the
prevailing southerly winds and current, with *Sea Dart* continually tacking, I estimated the distance to be about thirty-
five hundred miles.

The Humboldt Current was due to slacken off around
the beginning of September; I would start my long beat
then. At the reduced speed it should take *Sea Dart* around
nine weeks to reach Callao. That would mean arrival at that
port around mid-November. Once there, I had until New
Year's to cross the Andes; a margin of six weeks. It was well
worth the risk to take the direct route, even though the
navigational hazards were obvious, with heavy rains off the
coast of Colombia and fogs off Peru. It would mean a
continual arduous beat to windward, weeks of crashing into
high seas on one of the most inhospitable coasts in the
world—first the low, swampy jungle shores inhabited by
cannibalistic Indians, then the foggy, unprotected Atacama
Desert. Diligently I studied all the information available
about this route. I knew what I was in for; but I also knew
that if I was to make up for my defeat on the Amazon, I
would have to overcome the Humboldt. With grim determination, I prepared *Sea Dart* and myself for what is proba-

bly the most difficult passage in the world for a single-handed small craft.

Each weekend for a month I went over to Balboa to obtain food, collect a new mainsail sent out from England, and glean what bits of information I could about the area I was heading for. Everyone I talked with doubted that I would succeed in defeating the Humboldt. I thought I had a fifty-fifty chance. Whatever the outcome, I was determined to reach my destination, even if it took the rest of my life. My pride had been wounded in the Amazon. After all the struggling for almost three years, after all the storm-fighting, all the sleepless long hours of a hundred nights, all the planning and plotting, all the tackling of hazardous odds, I had been defeated.

I had started the voyage as a kind of humorous gesture to point out the ridiculous direction in which ocean cruising was heading. By offering huge sums of money, big business and the communications media had made a mockery of the sport, turning what is and always has been an effort of individual or group endeavor into a rat race of frenzied competition. In the ocean there are only two competitors—the vessel and nature itself. Anything else deprives mankind of one of the last truly personal encounters between man and God, or whatever it is that makes our universe tick. What had started off as an amusing venture three years before had now become a deadly serious matter—*a pilgrimage to my pride*!

By Saturday, 8 September, all was ready. Counting on one can of meat or fish every two days, together with one can of vegetables every three days, plus a half pound of rice each day with half a pint of water, I had five months' supply of food. I also had two cartons of a new type of compressed food presented to me by a U.S. Army colonel in the Special Forces who was at that time training in the Canal Zone; he wanted me to try it and send him a report. I jumped at the chance. Solid protein, for free! The rations turned out to be very good, though tasteless. Consisting of meat fibers, fruit, chocolate, and sugar all mixed up together and tightly compressed, they were similar to pemmican, which the Eskimos make in the Arctic.

I also had onboard charts of all the islands in the main groups clear across the Pacific to Australia. If I was forced out into the ocean, I would be prepared. This came to a bundle of around eighty charts. I had spares for the rigging and sail repairs enough for five years of normal cruising, plus kerosene sufficient to last for six months, a new Johnson outboard engine, four horsepower, and a gallon of gasoline for use in an emergency. Also, and most important, I had first aid gear, including tooth-pulling equipment and sterilized scalpels, pain-killers and other medical aids. Previously, I'd had to pull three of my own teeth when alone in ocean crossings, two of them with an ordinary pair of mole grips. I was not going to be caught short this time! Toothache is the worst pain of all when you are alone and a thousand miles from the nearest dentist.

The way to pull a tooth at sea is to stick your head in a porthole in the companionway and, reaching your arm around inside the boat, try to pull the tooth through the opening with the tooth extractor. Without anesthetic, this is a painful process. A half bottle of brandy helps, in two doses, one before and one after. Going to windward, it's easier to get the tooth loose because the jerking of the boat helps. The key is to keep your arm rigid inside the boat. You do this by lashing it taut to a fitting, perhaps the handhold rails inside the companionway. The hardest part of the whole operation is to resist self-pity, for this, like fear, only interferes with solving the problem. Hating the tooth helps, though.

28

A NEAR DISASTER

N SUNDAY, 9 SEPTEMBER 1973, I weighed anchor in the roadstead of Taboga Islet, as Pizarro had done centuries before, and shaped a course for the island of Pedro González, in the Perlas Group, still in Panamanian territory. The thirty-seven-mile run, downwind, took almost all day, and I entered the small anchorage off the tin-roofed village just before dusk and dropped anchor on the sandy bottom. After the usual evening mosquito onslaught, I rowed ashore in the dinghy and, with my last remaining Panamanian coins, knocked back a couple of beers in the shanty-store. The place was a marvel of stowage, with dried and fresh goods of all descriptions piled on the creaking floor: beans, coffee, rice, yucca, kerosene, gasoline, butter, bread by the sackful, candles, all littered around willy-nilly, like a midshipman's locker, all on top and nothing handy! There were bunches of dried fish, coils of rolled tobacco hanging from the roof, a dozen or more children, ass-naked and black as a bobby's boots, crawling and fumbling over the makeshift counter of butter boxes, grabbing handfuls of fishhooks. Tall, lanky, hard-muscled fishermen and their chubby, lively wives, dressed in Derby Day jockey colors, were knocking back foaming cans of beer. I retired to the stoop, slapping the mosquitoes, and swapped yarns with a few of them. I told them tales of the Irish Sea, so far away, and they told me of fields blooming with marijuana plants, hills and valleys of Panama Red over yonder on San José Island. They declared they were much better off now that they could carry the stuff over to the mainland and earn more money than they ever had before. They told me how three gringo yachts had arrived in San José three or four years previously and never left. Sea plants grew on the boats' bottoms like the Hanging Gardens of Babylon, and the gringos themselves

were permanently stoned out of their minds, but very good people. And happy, *muy buenos amigos*!

The next day I slipped from Pedro González and headed south. Once clear of the Perlas Islands the wind changed to light airs from the south. It would stay in the south, dead against me, all the way to Callao, but I wasn't to know that as I watched the hills of San José Island drop below the horizon.

On the second day, trailing five fishing lines astern, including a two-thousand-pounder with an eight-inch hook baited with a dorado's head, I caught a hammerhead shark. He was twelve feet long and fought like a wounded steer. I had to rig up a block forward, lead the thick nylon line through the snatch then back to the jib sheet winch, and haul away on the ratchet. He was a tough bugger, and it took me three hours to get him alongside. A fierce, ugly devil, he had a head like a sledgehammer, with an eye at each end of his peens. *Sea Dart* sat so low in the water I had to get his head high enough out of the water to kill him. I dared not approach him with the gaff-hook as he was kicking hard and snapping at the boat like a demon. Securing the line to a cleat, I sent the snatch block, with the bight of the fishing line roved through it, up to the masthead on the topping lift. Then I let go of the line from the cleat and there he was, tugging away at the top of *Sea Dart's* mast, as if at the end of a giant metal fishing rod. Again I hauled away and slowly he came up, but his weight canted the boat over about thirty degrees. In this fashion, I got his length up out of the water. I didn't dare go near him, for he was kicking like a mule.

After three hours he quieted down enough for me to whack him over the head with my long tree-felling ax (which I always carry in case I ever need to chop the rigging loose after a dismasting). A couple of solid crashers at his brain and he was dead. I plunged a butcher's knife into his ribs and hacked out a couple of good thick steaks. The best parts I popped into the pressure cooker and boiled in the shark's own blood, one after the other, until I had enough protein to last three days. The rest I had to ditch. A terrible waste, but with no refrigeration or ice there was nothing else I could do. This was the first of *fourteen* sharks, eight of them hammerheads, which I caught in the Humboldt, and which helped supplement my food rations. The others were gray sharks, not quite as tasty as the hammerhead, but less ugly and twice as dangerous to get onboard. As I passed on to the south, and finally over the equator, I hooked more and more fish—dorado, grouper, and swordfish.

After passing Santa Elena, on the coast of Ecuador, two degrees south of the equator, it was almost impossible to cook, the seas were so high. I was reduced to eating raw fish. Raw shark steak can be a bit off-putting; you have to teach yourself to ignore the taste and count the proteins. I also pickled a lot of fish in three gallons of lemon juice, thus making ceviche, which was quite good.

As I sailed south, the current got stronger and it began to get rainier by the time I was in latitude four north, about three hundred miles off the Pacific coast of Colombia. This is the second heaviest rainfall area in the world, with an average of three hundred inches per year! It bucketed down, sheets of it, replenishing my water tanks but also obscuring my vision to the point where I could not see the compass five inches before my eyes. However, it also worked to my advantage, for it obscured me from the eyes of any possible pirate, of which there are many in these waters, working out of Buenaventura, the asshole of the world, headquarters of the drug-smuggling rings.

In the Bight of Buenaventura, *Sea Dart* had to struggle hard against contrary light winds and strong currents. By the twenty-ninth of September, twenty days out of the Perlas Islands, she was only six hundred miles to the south of Balboa. That night, she almost foundered. I had stood out on the south-westerly tack in a warm, pissing rain, with a southerly wind, about twenty knots, close hauled. The sea was getting up, and the boat was hammering like the reverse gear on a Canadian Pacific steam engine. About two o'clock in the morning I was thrown bodily onto the cabin roof. The boat had turned completely upside down. I could plainly see the bloody ocean, all wet and phosphorous, *below* the companionway. A second later, *Sea Dart* righted herself with a dreadful, banging slam that shook every bone in my body. I was thrown forward like a puppet doll, against the forward bulkhead. Then, very seamanlike, she came up into the wind and sat there, waddling in the boisterous sea.

As I came to my senses, I could hear a banging and clattering overhead, a steady, violent thump, thump, thump on the deck. "Another bloody whale!" I thought. Bruised and battered, I scrambled aft, then remembered that I had no dinghy to jump into. I was up to my knees in water, sloshing around. Fortunately, all my charts and books were stowed well up the boat's side. Out in the pouring rain, in the black, warm, sticky, persistent rain of the Bight of Buenaventura, I grabbed all the stays and shrouds to see if they were all right and worked my way forward. The scene was a shambles.

Whatever *Sea Dart* had collided with must have been very solid. To this day I am not certain whether it was a whale or one of the huge tree trunks washed out to sea from the rain-soaked jungles of Colombia. I suspect it was a whale, simply because the currents run up from the south and in this area flow north along the coast. Anyway, it was a whopper. *Sea Dart* had tripped right over it, stern over bow, and the shock had dragged the bowsprit right out of the foredeck, snapping two inch-thick securing bolts, each six inches long, and leaving a hole in the marine-ply deck that I could put my head through.

I lowered the mainsail and rigged the trysail on the boom, to keep her head up to the wind. This took about an hour, for I also had to lower the flogging genoa with the thumping bowsprit on its foot. How I ever got it onboard with that thirty-pound lump of wood and phosphor-bronze metal swishing around, threatening to clout me on the head, I'll never know, but eventually I managed it, all the while sitting on the bow, lashed to the forward cleats on the heaving, pounding foredeck.

Next, I pumped the boat out, two hours on the hand bilge pump, out in the cockpit. Up and down, up and down, for what seemed like a century in the dark, wet, night, angry at not being able to sail to windward, for I knew the current was pushing *Sea Dart* back all the time she was hove to, probably at anything up to three knots, out into the ocean.

When I got her reasonably dry inside, I set about rigging up a makeshift, or jury, bowsprit. Lashing a strong line around the inboard end of the sprit, I passed it down through the hole torn out of the deck, around a snatch block lashed to the anchor-chain-securing ringbolt in the forepeak, and hauled away on the line passed around the unused jib-sheet winch. Then I lashed another line around the middle part of the bowsprit and secured both sides to the pulpit stanchions. With luck, this would hold the bowsprit long enough to get me somewhere. Then I bunged up the holed deck with sails and shirts and over the lot rigged a canvas patch, which I quickly nailed right onto the deck. That was enough to keep out most of the water that might come over the bow. Then I went down below to look at the chart and plan the next move.

I didn't dare go into Buenaventura. It was notorious as the worst port in the whole world. What, then, were the alternatives? I dared not head for the Colombian coast, one of the most hazardous in the world to approach; I had been warned that the reception from the inhabitants might be anything from an invitation to marry the chief's daughter to an invitation to step into the cooking pot. Heading back to the Perlas Islands and losing a hard-gained six hundred miles was also out. To go on until I reached the coast of Ecuador might be feasible, but with such a crazily rigged bowsprit I would not be able to carry the big genoa in any strong wind, and it might take weeks to make Esmeraldas, the nearest port. There was one other alternative: the Colombian prison island of Gorgona! In Cartagena, I had heard rumors about a small island to which political prisoners were exiled, never to be seen or heard of again. I had been warned by several Colombians to keep clear of the place; now it seemed the only possible shelter I could reach in reasonable time where I could find enough protection to repair my badly mauled *Sea Dart*. Anxiously, I hoisted sail and bore away through the rain for Gorgona.

29

A REAL-LIFE DEVIL'S ISLAND

SPENT THE NIGHTS OF September twenty-ninth and thirtieth on deck, steering by hand, peering at my jury bowsprit, hoping to God it would hold, and longing for a break in the early morning sky which would enable me to shoot the stars and maybe the sun and thus give me my position. At dawn, through a break in the towering cumulus skies, I got a snap shot of Venus setting in the west. Through another break, shortly afterward, I shot Sirius, the Dog Star. A few minutes later I knew where I was: 3° 35′ north, 78° 20′ west of the Greenwich meridian. From there I could plot my course and head for Gorgona and shelter, for by now it was blowing a good twenty-five to thirty knots out of the southwest, so much so that I changed the genoa for the working jib to ease the strain on the jury rig. I sailed *Sea Dart* as hard as I dared, through one thick rain shower after another, southeast, until just before dusk I saw a tiny, far-off gray shape out ahead on the horizon. All night long I beat for it, with the wind blowing directly from the island and the current holding me back, but I kept at it, hour after wet bloody hour, until at four in the morning I was near enough to see a tiny, glimmering light. Next day, I beat up to Gorgona in hard winds, not daring to strain the forestay too much: at five in the afternoon of the first of October, I gained the lee of the island and cast the danforth anchor over the side. I was numb with exhaustion and famished. On the beach, about two hundred yards away, a group of uniformed men armed with rifles and handguns were covering me, while another small group pushed off the shore in a longboat.

They came onboard with landlubbers' clumsiness, kicking the deckfittings with their boots, a fat sergeant first, pointing his rifle awkwardly at my head, followed by another gentleman, also fat, in a handsome uniform upon

188

which were displayed rows of medals that would have put
Haile Selassie to shame. His cap, U.S. Army general's style,
had so much gold braid that I wondered why he didn't wear
a gold cap with khaki braid. He spoke in rapid Spanish,
much the way an hidalgo might speak to a roadsweeper.

"From where do you come?"

"Panama, *Señor*."

"Nationality?"

"British," I replied, thumbing at the tattered ensign aft.

"Where are you going?"

"Salinas, Ecuador. But I have had some damage. I need
assistance."

"Very good. You will be allowed to remain here for
twenty-four hours only. We can give you no water, or food,
and you must not speak to any of the prisoners. The guards
have instructions to shoot if you do." He almost smiled as he
said this.

"I need help," I told him. "I need someone to hold the
knight-head bolts down below while I tighten the nuts."

"We can lend you a man, but you must not speak with
him."

"But *Señor,* how will he know which bolt to hold?"

"My God, such questions." He turned to leave, obviously
affected by the roll of the boat for he was turning green
under his red face.

"Sergeant, see that he only passes working instructions to
the prisoner and make sure he gives him nothing. Take me
ashore!"

Dusk descended and rain poured down topsides. I settled
into the cabin to clear up the mess left by the pitch-pole. To
my great relief, I found that the only food spoiled was a bag
of sugar, twenty-five kilos, wet through. I laid as much of it
as I could out in plates and pans to dry in the hot, humid
atmosphere, then opened a can of sardines and a packet of
biscuits and sat down to eat them and fell fast asleep.

About three hours later I woke up. *Sea Dart* was still
rolling merrily away, for there was no protection from the
ocean swell at that sad island, only a little from the prevailing wind. I set to making a permanent repair to the bowsprit
fixings. First I cut a marine-ply patch to cover the gaping

hole, then made a pad for below the deck to hold the bolts. By the early hours of the morning I had patched the deck, using self-riveting rivets (a must in any seagoing yacht), and straightened the bolts by bashing them with a hammer. Then I screwed in an inch-thick mahogany patch to the deckhead, or ceiling, of the forepeak, the tiny compartment in the bows of the boat. By false dawn I was ready to tighten up the bolts, and promptly fell asleep again.

I woke to find the sun beating down with mid-morning ferocity. I emerged from the cockpit and looked at the beach. At either end were huge piles of rocks, each about half the size of an ordinary sack of potatoes. Between each pile were two lines of men, each carrying one rock. One line was heading for this end of the beach, dumping their rocks on the pile, while the other line was going to *that* end of the beach and dropping their rocks on the pile over there. There must have been at least five hundred men engaged in this futile, insane promenade. The prisoners wore only a pair of pants. They were all burned brown with the sun; judging by their hair, I guessed the racial makeup to be mostly white. Every five yards along this crazy cakewalk was a guard armed with a rifle. Every now and then the guards would encourage someone who had stumbled or faltered with the rifle butt or the muzzle tip. There was no noise whatsoever, no talking, no shouting, just absolute and utter silence.

After a while the longboat shoved off towards me. Manning it were two soldiers in khaki uniforms, a sergeant, and a moron. The sergeant had a revolver, which he waved around menacingly. The moron was armed with a rifle; his tunic was festooned with two belts of ammunition. Between them stood a prisoner with closely cropped hair, dressed only in striped trousers, a man of about thirty-five, intelligent looking. For the first time in my life I felt ashamed of my freedom.

They came onboard, making a lot of racket. I noted with surprise that the moron was barefooted.

"What is your wish?" grunted the fat sergeant.

"I need someone to go forward, down below, to hold the nuts on the bolts which I will pass through the holes in the

deck, and to hold them with this wrench—*esta llave!*" I
pushed the wrench under his nose, so as not to tax his brain
too much. "And hold the nuts when I shout out."

"*Muy bien*. But apart from this you must not talk to the
prisoner!"

"Right, sergeant. Why don't you make yourself comfortable on the side facing away from the beach and have a drop
of whiskey?"

I passed them my last remaining bottle of Scotch. They
sat under the sun awning, sipping the spirits. I winked at the
prisoner and went below. I sat down on the forepeak and
started tightening up the bolts. The job was tedious, for the
threads were three inches long and the wrench was too big
to turn the bolt more than one flat at a time. Each time I
gave a turn I gave a tap, and soon the prisoner got the idea.
Between each tap he would say a few words. He shall be
nameless because presumably he is still there, on that mad
Devil's Island, in the hot sun and the pouring rain, moving
that insane heap of rocks across the beach.

He told me he came from the Cali area. He was married,
with a daughter. He had been in prison for eleven years. He
was now thirty-six. He had been a trade union organizer in a
textile plant in Cali. He had been falsely accused of guerrilla
activities. One day the police had arrested him and that was
that. He did not know if his wife knew where he was,
because she never came to visit him. He had been in Cali
prison for one year; for the remaining ten years he had
been on Gorgona Island. All the prisoners were *políticos*,
and he knew of only a few who had ever been tried in a
court. He himself had never stepped foot in a court, neither
did he know if he had been tried in absence by military
tribunal. The only food in Gorgona was fish caught by the
prisoners and rice. They were all kept in separate solitary
cells and were not allowed to talk to one another. The
penalty for talking, outside the kitchen gangs, was six
months solitary. Several men had tried to swim the fifteen
miles to the mainland. Most had been brought back and
shot on the beach; no others were believed to have succeeded in swimming the shark-infested current. If they did
reach the shore they would not survive; the government

paid good pesos for any convicts brought in by the Indians. The prisoners worked on the "beach party" from seven in the morning to six in the evening, with two half-hour breaks. He had no hope of getting away from Gorgona in his lifetime, because even if there was a revolution in Colombia he was sure the guards would kill all the prisoners before any rescue could reach them. There were too many tales to be told, too many stories of terrible brutality, torture, rape, for the guards ever to let them be rescued. As far as anyone knew, there was no record of their imprisonment anywhere; as far as their families were concerned, they might as well be dead.

After it was over the soldiers left with the prisoner. He smiled as he stepped onboard the longboat and waved his hands behind his back as they rowed ashore.

The look in his eyes will always haunt me. As he stepped into the boat, he glanced at me for just one fleeting moment. In that look was a world of torment and suffering.

By four in the afternoon I was ready to sail. The prisoners were still at their backbreaking toil on the beach. I felt the eyes of every one of them on me as I hoisted the mainsail, weighed the anchor, and bore off that beach of misery and despair. As *Sea Dart* lifted her head to the seas, I lit my anchor lamp so that those on the beach could see its glimmer long after they had lost sight of the first free man they had seen in many years. As for me, even with another two thousand miles to beat to windward in wet, cold discomfort, with hardly a cooked meal for weeks to come and unknown hazards all the way, I left Gorgona knowing that *I was the most fortunate man alive*.

The sugar never did dry and I was forced to ditch most of it.

30
AGAINST THE HUMBOLDT

 LEFT GORGONA ON WEDNES-day, 3 October 1973, and for twenty-eight days solid beat against contrary winds and currents until I was forced into Salinas, Ecuador, to top up *Sea Dart*'s water tanks. I dared not take the risk of being swept out into the Pacific Ocean with less than three month's supply at a half-pint a day. I had learned well the lesson of 1967.

My average distance covered *through the water* in twenty-four hours during this period was around fifty miles; but because the Humboldt was continuously pushing little *Sea Dart* back, the average distance covered *over the ground* was no more than seventeen miles! A sailing boat going into the wind never sails directly forward; there is always a sideways movement called leeway. In addition to the leeway caused by the wind, there was also one caused by the current. I would sail on the starboard tack, southeastward, into the coast for twenty miles. About a mile offshore I would come onto the port tack for twenty miles, then again to southeast for twenty miles. After covering a total of sixty miles, I would find, after fifteen hours' sailing, that I had moved only twelve, or at the most, fifteen miles, to the south! At night I could not risk going too close to the unlit coast, which is very badly charted. In many areas the actual coastline is anywhere up to eight miles out of position on the charts. There are many uncharted rocks and other offshore dangers. Therefore I would have to stand well offshore during the night, in the full strength of the current. Many a time I found that, after sailing hard all night, in the morning I had been pushed back to a position further *north* than the one *Sea Dart* had reached the previous dusk!

The further south I sailed, nearer the equator, the stronger the current became. Off Punta Galera the fog closed in and the temperature got colder. On the equator, I found myself wearing three sweaters and a pair of thick woolen trousers; this was the full Humboldt Current, coming straight up from the Antarctic. The hot tropical sun evaporating the cold sea-water was responsible for the fogs. There was no rain, and the few times I did see the coast through the fog, it was bleak, dry, desert shore, with barren mountains towering above it and Pacific Ocean swells breaking on the rocky coast. Many times it broke on rocks which were completely absent from my charts!

After twenty-eight days of continuous hammering into the wind, day and night, I had moved directly south only 240 miles. And yet the total distance actually sailed between Gorgona and Salinas, by the taffrail log, was *1,408* miles!

As *Sea Dart* passed into the full flood of the Humboldt, animal life increased. I was almost always in the company of seals, walruses, and pelicans. The walruses would swim up to about ten feet astern, grunting and snorting through their mustaches like old, pensioned British army sergeants.

In this part of the world, on the Pacific coast of South America south of the equator, it never rains. The last rainfall on parts of the coast was before living memory. And yet the sky is always overcast, the sun a pale, fuzzy disk of white light. The horizon is often obscured, and it is impossible to get a sight except on very rare occasions, usually at dusk, when the wind increases its twenty-knot average to something like thirty knots. The weather is like clockwork: fog from midnight to around 4:00 P.M., with the wind in the south blowing up the coast; then a gradual clearing as the wind strength increases to a peak around 9:00 P.M., when it gradually slows down again. The fogs are sometimes so thick that it is impossible to see the foredeck of a twenty-foot boat from the cockpit—a distance of about ten feet! To try and get inside the current, near the coast, I listened for the sound of the breakers against the terrible rocks. As soon as I heard any thunderous noises in the distance, I brought the boat about and bore away out into the ocean again. A nerve-racking job, to say the least. The boat pitched and pounded into the great Pacific swells, with a movement very much like that of a double-decker bus accelerating to forty miles an hour and stopping dead every five seconds. Anyone who has had the experience of beating in a craft of *Sea Dart*'s size will know what I mean. It was wearisome, exhausting work, especially when the movement became too violent to permit any cooking and I had to eat raw food.

By the time I pulled into the tiny harbor of Salinas under the shadow of the bluff and bold Cape Santa Elena, I was concerned, for it was now the end of October and so far, in almost two months of hard sailing, I had only covered half the distance to Callao. If *Sea Dart* didn't reach Callao by New Year, she would be stuck on the coast waiting for the next Andes dry season before I could haul her across the mountains. I decided to stay in Salinas for three days, long enough to water the boat and arrange with the Ecuadorian navy to guard her while I went up through the mountains to the beautiful inland capital of Quito at the invitation of the British ambassador, Mr. Peter Mennel, who had heard of my approach and had sent an invitation to me at Balboa.

Invitation in hand, trying comically to regain my land legs, I walked up the sandy beach of Salinas and called at the office of the Ecuadorian naval commandant. He courteously arranged an anchorage right in front of the harbormaster's office, where the boat could be watched while I was in Quito. However, I would have to go to the immigration office to enter the country correctly. With my passport I went to the immigration office and found a creature who was the stereotype of the legendary South American bureaucrat—fat belly, cheroot, snaky, avaricious eyes, greasy, smarmed down hair, and an unctuous smile. Yes, I could enter the country, he said, but as I had come in a private vessel I would have to pay a one hundred dollar entry fee. Unfortunately, all I had in the world was five hundred dollars.

"But I'm only here to collect some fresh water and to go to see the British ambassador. I'll only be in the country for three days!"

"Ah, then come to see me when you return from Quito, *Señor*."

Upon my return from Quito (one of the most interesting cities I have ever visited, almost pure Quechua Indian, but with many fine Spanish colonial relics, such as the beautiful cathedral), I called on the immigration officer. He insisted on the entry fee, otherwise I would not be allowed to leave. Finally I paid him one hundred of my last remaining five hundred dollars. I also asked for a receipt. No, unfortunately, the cupboard was locked today, he could not give me a receipt; but I was free to go and he would forward it on to me in Peru, care of the British embassy. A sentry close by fingered his rifle. Dusk was an hour away. I had to get out. He pocketed the hundred dollars with a smirk, and I was allowed to leave. I never did get a receipt, but at least my water tanks were full, even if I did have to haul each load in a jerrycan for about two miles along the beach.

31

HARKING BACK A BIT

T HE PASSAGE ALONG THE coast of Ecuador and Peru was—apart from the discomfort, strain, arduous sailing, and nerve-racking navigational conditions—of great interest to me. *Sea Dart* was slowly but surely plodding her tortuous way past a part of the Western Hemisphere which I believe to have been known to the ancient Asiatic and Middle Eastern world. That is, known to the Chinese, the Asiatic Indians, the Phoenicians, and probably the Persians long, long, before either the Norsemen or Saint Brendan, Prince Madoc, stray European fishermen or Columbus stepped on the shores of North America.

Ptolemy, the famous Greek geographer who lived in Alexandria around A.D. 141, made a map of the world, a *mappa mundi*, by copying a map made some decades before by a fellow Greek, the first known mapmaker, Marinus of Tyre. On his map, Marinus had shown a great ocean to the east of China. On the other side of this ocean, he placed a fairly straight coastline joined at the top to the east of China and sweeping first east and then south all the way to the Antarctic, where it went west. On this long, southbound, straight coastline, Marinus placed three prominent capes. They were located in approximately the position of the three most prominent capes of the South American west coast—Cape San Lorenzo, Cape Santa Elena, and Cabo Blanco. The first two are in Ecuador, the last in Peru. Marinus knew where those three capes were! He placed them just south of the equator and on what is now longitude eighty-one west. For this we have Ptolemy's word, because he admitted that he had copied Marinus's map. But during the interval between Marinus and Ptolemy, the idea got about among geographers (who knew the world was a globe, despite later fables) that there could not be inhabited

197

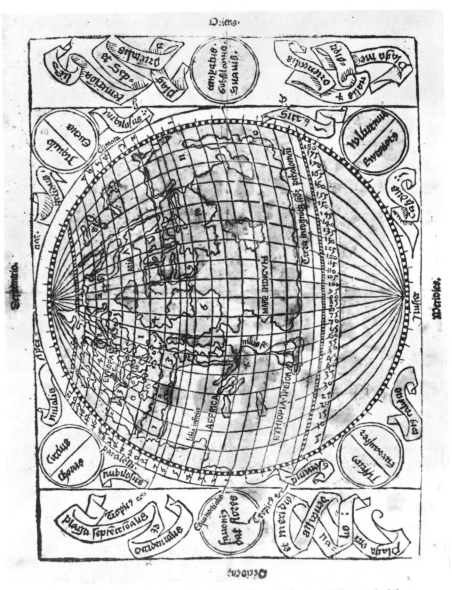

A woodcut map produced in Nuremburg about 1493, copied from a map made by Ptolemy in the second century A.D. This in turn was copied from the *Mappa Mundi* made by Marinus of Tyre. Map courtesy of the Rare Book Division of The New York Public Library; Astor, Lenox and Tilden Foundations.

land over more than 180 degrees of the global surface. The reason for this was that they did not understand the nature of gravity and thought that anyone going to the other side of the earth would drop off!

Ptolemy, too, believed this, so on his map he made the Pacific Ocean (or, as he called it, *Sinus Magnus*) much smaller, by moving Marinus's continent much farther west, closer to China. However, at the same time, he retained Marinus's three capes in the same latitude, just south of the equator.

Ptolemy wound up with a long straight coastline, except for the three capes, running south from the northern end of China at just about the longitude of the present International Date Line.

From this information I can only conclude the following:

1. Marinus knew there was a continent on the eastern side of the Pacific Ocean.
2. Marinus also knew that there were three prominent capes on that continent, just south of the equator.
3. He knew there was a river to the south of the three capes, which he named "Maiiu" (the Quechua word for river).
4. Given the above as correct, then Marinus at least two generations before Ptolemy must have known of a voyage to that continent by someone who had made the round trip.
5. If Marinus knew of such a voyage, then that voyage must have been made *across the Pacific*, because neither Marinus, nor Ptolemy, on their maps, showed the east coast of America, only the west coast.

Given that such a voyage was made, it must have been carried out by following the Pacific counter-current, which flows from west to east, about five degrees either side of the equator. This is contrary to the currents further north and south, which flow from east to west. For example, if you throw a sealed bottle into the sea at Sarawak, in Borneo (a place known to Greek mariners), it will eventually finish up in the area of the Pacific off the coast of Ecuador.

If the Phoenicians, the Greeks, the Egyptians, or the Persians had left Borneo and followed the equatorial counter-current, rowing or drifting against the light breezes, they, too, after a very long voyage, would have arrived in Ecuador. Getting back to the Indian Ocean would have been no problem, for the current further south, together with the easterly winds, the Trades, would have blown them back to the west.

Chinese artifacts of great age have been found on the northern coast of Ecuador.

Ibn Batuta, the famed Arab traveler of the fourteenth century, wrote of a conversation he had with a Chinese junk captain in Zanzibar. The captain told him that, as a young man, he had made a voyage to "a land of gold" to the east of China, "so distant that the days of the voyage were un-countable."

The Indian legend of Manco Capac, the founder of the Inca empire, states that he was born on an island called Guaya off the coast of Ecuador and that his parents had been shipwrecked there, having sailed from "where the sun sets."

Again, the legend of Kon-Tiki-Vira-Cocha says that he left the Inca empire from the southern cape of the three shown on Marinus's map, just about where Paita is today. The Inca legend says that he appeared out of the "spume of the sea" in the south. It could be that a ship from the Middle East, having reached the three capes, pushed on south against the Humboldt Current and was wrecked on the stormy coast of Chile. That would explain white, bearded men coming from the south. What would be more logical to mariners than, after exploring the country for several years, to build a boat to sail home and then to make their departure from nearer the equator, in much milder latitudes than where they had been shipwrecked?

I do not dispute Thor Heyerdahl's contention that there is a connection between the balsa craft of North Africa and those of South America, nor that Kon-Tiki and his follow-ers may have been in both places, but I do believe that there is far more likelihood that this voyage was made across the Pacific (along an *already known* sailing route) than across the Atlantic. There is, up to now, not a scrap of material evi-dence in the West Indies or Brazil, of pre-Columbian arrivals from across the Atlantic. The Phoenicians evidently did not know of the Canary Islands! Yet they knew Borneo!

All this evidence—the maps; the ocean currents; the otherwise inexplicable appearance in South America of advanced states of civilization, such as the Tiahuanaco temple builders; the discovery of Chinese-looking pottery on the Ecuadorian coast; the amazing resemblances between the Mayan pyramids and those of ancient Egypt; the now certain knowledge of contact between the civilizations of Peru and those of Colombia and Mexico; the sudden appearance among primitive Andes Indians of what appeared to be supermen, white and bearded—points to trade and contact from the west, from Asia and the eastern Mediterranean.

We know that shipbuilding in the Middle East, even before the time of Ptolemy, was well advanced, and featured cedar hulls and copper fastenings. We know that Persian and Phoenician, not to mention Greek, knowledge of astronomy, geometry, and even geography was far more advanced than was thought some decades ago.

A Greek cargo ship salvaged from the Mediterranean north of Kyrenia, Cyprus, gives evidence of seaworthy construction. She was built well before the time of Christ; decked over and in the hands of a Phoenician sailing master, she would have been quite capable of a transoceanic voyage from the Red Sea to Peru. It would have been long, it would have been hazardous, but what was that to a race of sailors who had already reached Iceland, visited the Azores, and sailed right around Africa?

As *Sea Dart* bashed and crashed her way against the swift Humboldt, I had very little sleep. For hours I sat in the cockpit, hunched up against the bitter cold, listening for the sound of breakers on the rocky shore. For hours I thought of this fascinating, puzzling succession of clues. (I had not yet, of course, heard of the Aymara legends of Manco Capac and Kon-Tiki, but I *had* seen Ptolemy's map, one wet afternoon in the British Museum, when, idly looking through a large folder of ancient maps, I suddenly found myself gazing at a rendering of Ecuador made in A.D. 141.)

Did Columbus see the Ptolemy map? Scion of an ancient

Jewish family, a family originating in Phoenicia, he probably had.

Did Columbus believe the world was much smaller than it is?

If he saw the Ptolemy map and gave it credit, he surely did.

Was Columbus looking for China when he crossed the Atlantic?

If he'd studied Ptolemy, probably not; he would have been looking for Cattigara, the land of GOLD to the east of China! The origin of El Dorado. He must have heard of, and possibly read, the account of Ibn Batuta's meeting with the Chinese mariner who had been to Cattigara.

The ancient Greeks knew the circumference of the world to within ninety miles. Marinus knew of the existence of a continent where America is now. Ptolemy, however, made *the great geographer's error:* because he could not believe that people could live on the other side of the globe, he took hold of the coast of America and moved it to approximately the mid-Pacific, thus shortening the world's circumference by about a quarter. I do not, for one minute, believe that Columbus ever thought he had reached China; he probably thought he had reached the eastern side of Marinus's and Ptolemy's Cattigara. Because Ptolemy showed Cattigara to be much nearer to China, Columbus must have believed the world to be about one quarter less in size.

In the cold and fog, *Sea Dart* beat into the ocean swells for what seemed an eternity. When the fog cleared for rare moments as I sailed near the ghostly shore with the breakers roaring like thunder, I would glimpse the headlands and know I was looking at land that the Phoenicians and the Greeks had seen. (Three years later my beliefs about ancient contact between the Middle East and South America were reinforced. In the map section of the New York Public Library, I gazed at another copy of Ptolemy's map; on it were the same capes I had seen, the same shoreline. The same lake on the same latitude as Titicaca—the jaguar-water, home of the sun god!)

32
CALLAO!

HE VOYAGE AGAINST WIND and current from Salinas to Callao took from the sixth of November until the twenty-fourth of December 1975; a total of forty-eight days. Forty-eight foggy, cold, damp days; forty-eight cold, foggy, damp nights. I do not think I had more than two hours' sleep at a stretch during the whole passage. In those forty-eight days and nights, my little boat, seventeen feet along the waterline, sailed just over two thousand miles through the water, though the straight distance between the two ports is about seven hundred miles.

Only on a few afternoons was I able to get snap noon sights of the sun through the foggy overcast and thus to confirm that slowly, agonizingly, I was approaching the port. Some noon positions almost broke my will, for they showed that *Sea Dart* had been pushed by the unforgiving Humboldt to a position further north than where she had been the day before. It was like trying to climb an escalator running downhill much faster than you are climbing! Once or twice, in moments of exhaustion, when depression crept in, I was tempted to give up the struggle. I thought how easy it would be to head out across the Pacific Ocean. Much, much easier to head for warm, blue water, sunny skies, out for five-thousand-odd miles across the ocean than to tackle the cold, gray, overcast, swift-running, malicious Humboldt, with its rough seas and barren shores.

Sometimes when the fog cleared and I was close to the coast, I could see, beyond the empty desert, the Andes frowning loftily. I would look at poor, brave, battered, tiny *Sea Dart* and wonder what the hell I was doing, challenging the might of nature with her frail little hull. But then I would imagine, on the other side of the tremendous peaks, the Amazon and the way it had so *perfunctorily* cast me aside from my course. And I would grit my teeth and think, "Right, you bastards, turn me back, will you?" I would peer at the tiny bit of South America that I could dimly see and try to tighten the jib-sheet in even further, determined not to give the bloody old Humboldt one fucking inch more than it could steal from me.

The further south I sailed towards Callao, the weaker the winds became. About three hundred miles north of my destination, I took hold of the tiller and steered the boat by hand. A wind-vane steering gear needs a good wind to enable it to operate accurately. Below a wind speed of eight knots, it becomes very erratic and untrustworthy. Now steering a boat by hand alone for over a month is no joke. It cuts off time for anything else, including sleeping. Very often I found myself falling fast asleep at the helm. I would wait until the wind piped up a bit so she could steer herself, then leave the tiller to make a meal. Sometimes I'd have to wait for a day or two. But I never let her come up in the wind and drift back even one yard. I refused to give the Humboldt *one centimeter* more than it was already taking from me. A couple of times, nearing Callao, the wind dropped entirely, leaving a dead flat calm. By now I was used to the Humboldt weather signs and could see it coming a good while before the actual calm. While I still had a wind, I would work my way inshore and find a shallow area near the coast. There I would anchor and sit in the swell, waiting for a wind.

On one of these occasions I saw a sight I hope I never see again, at least not in a tiny craft like *Sea Dart*. I was anchored off the Guanape Islands, in the lee of one of the barren islets. The sun, for a change, had penetrated the thin fog overhead. I fell asleep as soon as the anchor dug in, for I'd not slept for four days and nights straight. Suddenly I was awakened by a noise which sounded as if the boat were grounding on a sandy beach. I hopped up topsides, thinking the anchor had dragged and she had drifted ashore. I looked over the side, then under the boat. There was the biggest jellyfish I have ever seen, floating with an undulating movement under the keels, trying to lift the bloody boat up! He was twenty-five feet wide, from tip to tip and colored a scarlet red.

I grabbed the anchor chain and heaved it in quicker than I'd ever done before. Miraculously, *Sea Dart* slid over the top. I got the hell out of there, but not before noticing other rays, even bigger, some emerald green, some blue, some scarlet. Never had I seen this before, nor do I ever wish to again. The Humboldt when you're heading south is bad enough without 1,370 square feet of stinging monster trying to tip your boat over!

Steadily the beat went on, day after weary day, steering the boat in light winds, patiently, with every ounce of cunning, straining every nerve, every corpuscle, draining every last drop of energy. At long, long last I reached Callao Bay. I entered the bay all alone, for the Peruvian fishing fleet had been forbidden to work because of the scarcity of pilchards that year, which was a blessing for me. Navigation was difficult enough without having to thread my way through several hundred fishing craft.

My attention was attracted by a small white dot which soon transformed itself into a full-bloom sailing yacht. She was, the crew of *Calypso* informed me after lining up to give me a rousing cheer, the flagship of the Peruvian Yacht Club, and she had come to escort *Sea Dart* into harbor. They had heard of my approach. I had been sighted several times by watchers on the shore, and there had been a running commentary on my progress broadcast over the local radio station for several days. I was astounded; I had no inkling that anyone even knew I was anywhere near Callao. But it was good to be in company again after being alone so long and a comfort to know that, should the wind die, I could get a tow into port. The four-horse-power Johnson outboard was still in its wrappers, the gallon of gasoline still unused. I had not ever bothered to mount it after the initial test.

At 6:15 on the evening of the twenty-fourth of December 1973, I arrived at Callao. This was the end of the ocean passages between the Dead Sea and Lake Titicaca. It had taken almost exactly three years to sail from the head of the Red Sea to Callao, a distance, if we count the search for *Sea Dart*, of more than 40,000 miles.

The Peruvian Yacht Club is a fine building, a relic of the great days of English influence on the west coast of South America. It was full of mementos from the heyday of the sailing ships which traded with Peru and Chile, bringing out manufactured goods from Britain and Germany and returning to Europe with guano, the birdshit of untold generations of wheeling seagulls, with which the islands of the eastern Pacific were literally covered. The trade declined after the development of artificial fertilizer during the First World War, but the club remains a going concern.

The members of the club included a number of Anglo-Peruvians who showed me great hospitality and friendliness. Underlying their bonhomie, however, was a bitterness against the Peruvian military government, which, uniquely in South America, was tending towards a kind of socialism, trying to redistribute the land among the peasants and giving industrial workers more share in the running of the factories.

So gloomy was the situation for the members of the middle and upper-middle classes that within an hour of my arrival I had three offers to buy *Sea Dart* from gentlemen who were desperately trying to find some way to transfer their money out of Peru! Everyone was intrigued by my plan to haul her across the mountains to Lake Titicaca, but they were also pessimistic about my chances of obtaining permission from the military government. The government had taken an extremely anti-gringo posture. In South America "gringo" means anyone who is white and not from the communist bloc; it has nothing to do with the original Mexican epithet for a citizen of the United States, which in South America is *"yanqui."*

The commodore of the club arranged to have *Sea Dart* hauled out with a small crane. When I returned to the boat after dinner, I found that the club attendants had completely scraped the bottom and applied one coat of antifouling paint. She was, from the waterline down, like new again! This gesture was unforgettable.

I slept soundly that night, with the boat sitting on her keels on the jetty of Callao, content at long last to be so near my goal and remembering Christmas Eve three years before, when I had slept in Bethlehem with my boat on another continent, but under the same bright star of hope. After all those thousands of miles of pressing ahead under sail, I was again ready to tackle the continent of South America and raise my boat nearer to the stars than any ocean vessel had ever gone!

33
KINDRED SPIRITS

ARLY ON CHRISTMAS DAY, with my head still fuzzy from the previous night at the Yacht Club, I woke to find an invitation to a party at the house of the British naval attaché. Donning my best bib and tucker, and after a quick slug of the dog that bit me, I made my way to Lima, where I was made most welcome by Commander Stephen, Royal Navy, and his family. I spent the day lounging by their garden pool in a very English-looking garden. At first I felt like a visitor from Mars, but a few drams quickly put me to rights again.

As the day wore sedately on the garden attracted diplomats from other western legations, with their wives and families. I was graciously introduced all round, and the topic of conversation for a while was my haul to the Lake. The general consensus was that such a project was impossible. Apart from the physical hazards this late in the season, with the rains starting on the mountain passes, it would take at least six months to obtain all the necessary permits from the government. Six months and a small fortune in bribes! Again, as in so many other places where I had encountered westerners, I detected a look on their faces which showed quite plainly that they thought I was stark raving mad. There were two exceptions—the British, who have a fondness for eccentricity, and the American naval attaché, who immediately grasped what I was doing and offered to help in getting contacts ashore after the holiday was over. But even they were doubtful of my chances of reaching the Lake.

Well fed and tanked up, I was dropped off on the Callao waterfront by the embassy car. Shaken by the discouraging news I had heard at the party, I walked slowly back in the direction of *Sea Dart*. After all the struggle to get to Callao, I was now going to have to fight a whole mass of bureaucracy,

South American bureaucracy, just about the worst in the world—a continual mad-hatter's tea party, a crazy blizzard of paperwork, a marathon of marching in the heat from one dingy office to another, from one garlic-breathed manipulator of paper clips to the next.

In most parts of South America the siesta is religiously kept, and doubly so on Christmas Day. The tawdry waterfront streets of Callao were deserted except for an old car full of military police. Although the sky was overcast, the heat was stifling. It was the height of the southern summer, and although the air temperature at sea was around fifty degrees, ashore it was closer to a hundred. I walked about a mile along the shoddy, ill-kept, broken pavements. The heat, the humidity, the stench from the inefficient drains, the doubtfulness of my prospects, coupled with thoughts of Christmas in Wales, produced a Celtic Black-Dog mood in me. The swinging doors of a particularly scruffy little bar beckoned with all the seductiveness of Ulysses' sirens. In I went, following the ancient, time-honored tradition of the sailorman: "When you're pissed off ashore, piss up, and leave your craft at the jetty."

The place was filthy, dark, and at first glance, deserted. From behind a greasy bead curtain an old lady emerged—emaciated, gnarled, and obviously displeased at being disturbed from her reverie and rosary.

"*Buenas, Señor, qué quieres?*"

"*Una cervezita, Señora, por el amor de Dios.*" They use the diminutive a great deal on the Peruvian coast, indeed, throughout all of Peru, Bolivia, and Chile.

She handed over a small bottle of beer, grimy and hot, the froth spilling over onto the bar counter.

After several bottles the place began to lose its Inquisitional look. Swig by swig, it gradually took on the cheery glow of an English pub—a fireplace, a Christmas tree in the corner, horse-brasses over the bar, merry fishermen knocking back a few for the next trip, a perky barmaid, and a guv'nor who was good for credit.

"Psst...psst." The Latin American signal for attention. I looked at the grimy, dim end of the bar. A figure stumbled out of the black shadows. A small Indian wearing a battered fedora, tattered black jacket, filthy shirt. Bleary, almond eyes glittering black in a mahogany carved face. An ugly face, an honest face, a man's face.

"*Buenas, amigo; gringo?*" he staggered nearer, belching.

"*Sí, amigo*, bloody *gringo*."

"*Americano?*"

"*No*, bloody *británico*."

"*Marinero*...sailor?"

"*Sí, marinero*."

"*Que barco*...what ship?"

"Bloody hardship!"

"*Grande?*"

"*Sí, amigo*, fucking *gigantico!*"

"*Adonde va tu barco*? Where's your ship bound?"

"*Lago Titicaca!*"

"*Cómo? No se puede!* That's not possible!"

"With my ship it is. With my ship, anything's possible!"

"How? The Lake is three hundred miles inland, over the mountains." He was knocking back beer like a Grenadier Guardsman in great, gusty swallows. "How big is your ship?"

"Seven meters long. She's a sailing boat, and I've come half-way round the world to get to that bloody Lake, but it looks hopeless." I explained to him the situation, step by step, me sorting out phrases from English to Spanish and he sorting them from Spanish to Quechua. Suddenly, a big grin cracked his carved wooden face.

"You got no problems, no problems at all." He belched and almost capsized, grabbing the bar just in time. I noticed how firm and strong his hands were, for the bar almost shattered under his tight grip. "Listen, my name is Salomon, and I come from Puno, up there on the shores of the Lake. I am a truck driver; the *only* one who can make it down to the coast. If I can't make it, nobody can, and when my *dinero* is all gone, by God, back to Puno I go, and we put your little boat on my truck and we go together. You're my friend, you're a good *hombre*, the British always keep their word, we go together with *mi novia*, my girlfriend, and we have—*carraco!* Holy shit!—a *good* time."

"*Un momento, amigo*, you've got a truck? You come from

Puno? You're going back? When?"

"*Mañana*; first I drink this." He slapped down a great wad of filthy *sols* on the counter. Then he farted, belched, and hiccuped at the same time. He swung his free hand up and out into the air. "We go over the mountains, up in the sky, like the condors!" He hiccuped again.

"Listen, *amigo*, seriously." I caught hold of his greasy *chicha*-, soup-, and beer-stained collar. "Listen, when can you come for my boat?"

"*Mañana, mi palabra*." He grabbed my hand and shook it.

"How much?"

"Look." He grabbed my hand again and put his other hand on my shoulder. His stink was enough to cause the complete evacuation of New York if he ever got within ten miles to windward of the Verrazano Bridge. "We're friends, huh? We drink together, yes? We eat together, no? You pay this, you pay the gasoline, and you give one hundred fifty dollars for Salomon, no? Yes?"

"Done." I shook his hand tightly enough to crack his bones. One hundred and fifty dollars for a seven-hundred-mile haul!

"*Palabra inglés*? English promise?" He looked almost grim as he said this.

"*Palabra británico, en la vida de mi madre,*" I replied.

"Then we do it, *amigo, mañana!*" He took another staggering swig at the beer, belched, farted, hiccuped, grabbed the counter with one hand and scratched his crotch with the other.

"But Salomon, what about permits? I haven't got permission to import the boat. She's a foreign vessel. We have to go to the customs, to the port authority, to the police."

"*Amigo mio*, the only things you *got* to do—you know what they are? You know what they are, my *amigo ingles*? *Shit and die!* Customs—port authorities—immigration—police *esos marricones!*" He belched again and threw out his arms in the Peruvian gesture of eternal contempt.

"Papers, forms, rubber stamps, what do they do, *amigo*? They bring back my truck when I go over a cliff? They help you in a storm? Shit! and anyway," he leered craftily, with a slow wink, "anyway, I have a brother-in-law in the port authority. We get papers all right! *Mañana! Temprano!* Early!"

The Almighty, in his wisdom, sends some strange angels to the rescue of distressed sailors, but he certainly never sent one as strange as Salomon, nor as drunken, nor as dirty, nor as vulgar, coarse, raw, rough, and laden with obscenities. But he also never sent one as truthful, as honest, and as brave. Neither did he ever send one at a more propitious moment! Salomon, the Angel of the Andes, many will be the times I will drink to your health in the seaports of the world!

34
A SPLENDID RECEPTION

E BRITONS CALL THE DAY after Christmas Boxing Day. The origin of the term is supposed to come from the custom of exchanging gifts on that day, but I think it's more likely that it comes from the Celts, who had the habit of knocking seven bells of shit out of one another when they found who had been sleeping with whom the night before. Anyway, Boxing Day morning 1973, as I rose from my berth, still fully booted and spurred, was one of those mornings when even the seagulls looked like pterodactyls.

My session with Salomon had lasted until the small hours of the morning. I had been introduced to the delights of *chicha*, which makes Polish vodka taste like gnat's piss. We had eaten half an ox disguised as bowls of greasy beef stew. We had caroused with the ladies of the night, elegant and otherwise, discussed soccer with half the male population of Callao, covered each other's retreat from two of the bloodiest barroom brawls I had seen in ages, and closely escaped arrest by the Peruvian security police. I had sung "Spanish Ladies" as we had staggered to our beds, Salomon to his truck, me to *Sea Dart*. Now, in the morning, I paid the price, with a hangover like the House of Usher after its fall.

At seven, Salomon turned up, driving a 1954 Ford truck that showed unmistakable signs of having been driven back and forth across the Andes, over some of the worst roads in the world, for twenty years. There was only one mudguard, on which was painted a picture of Che Guevara; one of the windscreens was missing entirely; half the floorboards of the flatbed were absent; black liquid dripped ominously from the oil sump; and the whole truck had no more than a square yard of paint remaining. The rest was rust and bare wood. But desperate situations require desperate measures. I recruited, with the aid of five dollars worth of *sols*, some of the Yacht Club peons, rustled up two lifting cables, and, with the aid of the hand crane, slowly hoisted *Sea Dart* up in the air. Then, with a series of heart-wrenching jerks, for the crane had no handbrake, we lowered her onto the groaning flatbed of the truck, which promptly took on a good ten-degree list to starboard.

"A good marriage, no?" Salomon, looking like I felt, showed me a piece of paper—our permit to leave the docks with an *empty* truck!

"Marriage? More like a bloody funeral party! Hey, you got a paper? Well done, *amigo*!" I took it in hand. "But it's for an empty truck. We'll never get past the gate!"

"Ah *sí*, we'll get past the gate. My brother-in-law is over there now, giving them hell about not keeping proper control on what passes out. No problem, *amigo mío*!"

With Salomon's girlfriend safely stowed in the driving cab and me perched in *Sea Dart*'s cockpit, we were given a hearty send-off by a few Yacht Club *socios* who had turned up. They looked as if they were watching something that wasn't quite real; they were so astonished that none of them even mentioned the matter of import permits. Once out of the dockyard gate, through which we were politely bowed by his brother-in-law, Salomon tore off up the Callao waterfront. The load on his truck was so high that we finished up outside the town with *Sea Dart* festooned with Christmas street decorations—flags, streamers, electric lamp fittings, cables, lines, and wires. Why I didn't get electrocuted is a mystery.

After being held up outside the town by a roadblock (which we reached moments after I had managed to jettison the last of the Callao electric and telephone wiring system), I suggested to Salomon that we arrange a signaling routine. Everytime we were about to go under something too low for our passage, I would bang on the top of the driving cab with a broom. And so it was arranged. *Sea Dart* rested on the bed of the truck facing forward, with the bowsprit hanging over the cab. On the bowsprit I rigged the Red Ensign and just abaft of that, the Peruvian courtesy flag. Between the boat's side and the sides of the truck I had jammed in a few old auto tires. Some wooden battens nailed to what remained of the truckbed floor completed the ensemble. Hopefully, these battens would prevent the three keels from moving about too much. I wanted to pass through the towns inconspicuously, but on the other hand I was determined to wear the British mercantile ensign, for if there was any trouble there was a remote chance that the presence of the flag might bring it into the diplomatic realm. It was a long shot. Besides, I wanted the ensign to be the first to cross the Andes.

Lima, the capital of Peru, is only eight miles from Callao. We soon found ourselves threading a tortuous path through the narrow Spanish-colonial alleyways of the impressively beautiful city center. Everyone gaped as *Sea Dart* passed, flags waving merrily, Salomon waving from the cab on one side, his girlfriend on the other, and me sitting on top of this strange load wishing I could disappear. A traffic policeman courteously saluted our passage and even held up traffic in order that we might pass!

After an hour we eased out of crowded Lima into the suburbs of the south, following the modern Pan-American highway over the coastal desert. We made good time through Pisco and Ica, with Salomon driving hard all day. At Ica we had a meal of fine fish and a bottle of *chicha*. This gave Salomon enough energy to drive all night across the foothills to Arequipa, one of the prettiest places I've ever seen, a white colonial town nestled in a lush green valley at the base of the nineteen-thousand-foot volcano, Misti. We pulled into Arequipa at dusk on the twenty-seventh of December and parked in the main square, right outside the front door of the city hall. If the customs were looking for us, they'd never dream we were parked right on their doorstep! After a good meal and another bottle of *chicha*, we fell into a deep sleep. The easy part of the haul was now over, though there had been some very nervous moments on hairpin bends and along the edge of precipices.

Sea Dart was still in one piece, though the same could not be said of the truck. The oil sump leaked badly and we had to refill it.

In the morning we found the boat and the truck under a strong guard of heavily armed policemen! The picturesque, tree-lined main square of Arequipa was jammed with a crowd of several thousand people. I asked Salomon what the hell was going on.

"Maybe the mayor, *el Alcalde*! Give a speech!" he suggested, wiping the sleep out of his eyes. His girlfriend sat motionless in the cab like an Indian madonna, her bowler hat perched precariously on top of her braided hair.

"Speech, *nada, hombre*. No, man," said the nearest burly cop, kicking a tire. "They've come to see *you*! Goddamit, it's not every day we get a boat in Arequipa; the mayor's coming down to receive you any minute. *Dios mio*, make yourselves look presentable. You look like fucking gypsies!"

And so it was that the mayor of Arequipa, the second most powerful man in the Republic of Peru, received us into his city, on behalf of "all its citizens, on this historic occasion, bringing memories of our forebears, the conquistadors, bearing in mind the heroic labors of the Peruvian government-owned fishing industry, the Peruvian maritime tradition, reminders of which we, in this land-locked great city of ours, have so little opportunities to experience, etc. etc. etc." For two solid hours he spoke impassionedly, as television cameras whirred, for we were still on the outermost fringes of a remote pocket of TV society. Salomon had smeared his hair down and buttoned up his decrepit jacket to the throat to hide his shirt. He stood on one side of the mayor looking heroic and humble at the same time, while I stood on the other, wishing the boat, the truck, the mayor, Salomon, and myself could disappear. The mayor—proud, haughty, almost majestic in his power—intoned for over two hours, and all the time *Sea Dart* sat on the truck, contraband, smuggled, paperless, probably being searched high and low right now by the Peruvian customs service!

At the end of the interminable speech, the crowd roared and clapped. The mayor, speaking very rapid Spanish of which I could only catch the gist, violently shook my hand, patted my shoulder, and asked what I needed.

"Old tractor tires, *Señor Alcalde, por favor*."

He snapped his fingers at the nearest guard and barked,

"Tires, tractor tires. I want, how many, *Señor*?" He turned to me.

"Six, please, *Señor*?"

He snapped his fingers again. The cop jumped to attention.

"Six, right away, *immediatemente*!"

The cop ran to the corner, jumped on a motorcycle, and roared off. Ten minutes later the six tires were jammed between *Sea Dart*'s sides and the truck sides by a mob of eager Arequipa policemen, anxious to shine under the stern eyes of *el Alcalde*. Salomon winked at me as I hid my face from the mind-spinning burlesque. Eight burly, beefy-faced Arequipa cops, pistols clattering, machine guns laid aside on the truckbed, grunting, grinning, shoving, and pushing at the huge tires, aiding and abetting the smuggling of a bloody seagoing vessel through their country!

Later that evening the mayor invited me to dinner in the marvelous old banqueting hall of the colonial palace, redolent with relics of the rich Spanish colonial days and the War of Independence. The whole of Arequipa society was there, prosperous-looking landowners and manufacturers, prelates and councilors, jewelry-bedecked ladies, beautiful girls, handsome men-about-town. I was able to thank them for a splendid reception and for their assistance and even told them a couple of jokes, hoping that the holes in my only pair of socks were not too obvious.

At midnight, with Salomon weaving his way into the cab after a good session in the nearest bar, we set off to cross the Andes!

35
AMONG THE CONDORS

AST FROM THE MAIN plaza of Arequipa, serenely basking in eternally spring-like weather, a solid wall of mountains rose over twenty thousand feet into the sky; snow-covered peaks glistened in the sun, deep purple in the early morning, sparkling silver in the afternoon, rosy pink in the sunset. These were the snows which had defeated me almost two years earlier as they rushed in melting madness to swell the might Amazon. As we had stood in the plaza of Arequipa in front of the crowd of citizenry intently listening to the harangue of the mayor, my eyes had strayed up the distant icy peaks. The whole time that the rapid Spanish was being hurled at the mob, all the while that Salomon was basking in the reflected brilliance of the mayor, I prayed in my heart that we would beat the rains. Twenty-eighth of December! The rains should have already started, the snow must already be melting! I glared at the spread of the Andes, right across the eastern horizon, *willing* the rain not to fall, *willing* the snows not to melt!

Now, as we trundled off up the rough track leading east out of the city, we passed slowly upwards. Past the last straggling poor huts, past the last feeble glimmer of electricity, forever upwards into the black, drizzling gloom, bucking over potholes the size of miniature craters. Inside *Sea Dart*, trying to stay in my berth and protect myself from the increasingly cold night air, the movement was like being inside a well-shaken pepper pot. At times, *Sea Dart* canted at an unbelievable angle. When the moon shone wanly between the scurrying clouds, I peered out of the companionway and saw that we were on the edge of a shelf no wider than twelve feet cut into the side of a cliff. Over the edge I looked down—into nothing; it dropped straight down into a chasm! And *Sea Dart* canted over towards the

218

edge at an angle of twenty degrees and more! Well, I thought to myself, if she goes over, so do I—*I won't leave her*!

At dawn the next day we found ourselves on an incredibly rough surface, the Paso Cimbral, 4,300 meters above sea level! Over to port loomed the peak of Misti Volcano, 5,300 meters high! As we jerked and bumped along, the ensign fluttered in the cold breeze. The highest maritime flag in the world! Way up in the blue sky wheeled the condors, the highest living creatures on earth apart from man! And *Sea Dart* was among them!

All day the truck lumbered slowly over potholes, bouncing along over a corrugated surface worn to bare rock by wind and rain. Whenever we stopped to fill up the oil sump, we were either on the edge of a sheer drop, with six inches between the truck's wheels and a descent of well over a mile, or beside a roaring cataract rushing down through the rocky chasms far below.

Towards noon we approached the spot I had been dreading, the Pati tunnel, under one of the high peaks. At first it looked too low for us to pass, even with the truck tires deflated; but we managed to scrape through, with only a quarter of an inch to spare at some points on the rough, undulating roof, carved out of rock. Even so, we still had to deflate the tires to get through. At least I was spared from having to unship the cabin roof. Salomon kept on going, racing against time. If the rains fell now we would be stranded in the Andes passes for weeks, if not months, for there would be no going on, no going back. During this time, the road becomes impassable even to a man walking! Where landslides occur, the road is destroyed, and for four months the Puna Altiplano, the high valleys of the Andes, are completely cut off from surface transport with the outside world.

Some of the bridges we passed over looked as if they had been built by the Incas themselves, swaying, rickety, wooden structures slung over chasms a mile and more deep, with rivers thundering below. The country on the edge of the snowline was completely deserted; not a tree, not a bush, not a blade of grass was visible as we passed over the divide of the western cordillera. As we skirted the throat-lumping gorges, Salomon argued with his lady friend. The edge of the cliff was decorated with hundreds of crosses, erected to commemorate many a hardy traveler who, in his last moments, had also probably been arguing with his girlfriend.

Then, after a whole night of creeping up and down passes which made the Burma Road look like Broadway, we passed into real Indian country. There we saw many flocks of llamas tended by Quechuas in their chorros, pointed caps with earflaps, and ponchos made of llama wool, walking barefoot in the snow. We stopped at each wayside *pozo*, or bar, tiny, adobe-built hovels with squatting Indians and rooting animals seeking protection from the bitterly cold wind. Outside each bar a herd of patient-looking llamas waited, with their loads tied up in gaudily woven blankets. When the local braves became blind drunk on *chicha* or *pisco,* truculent and threatening, the local, usually elderly, peacemaker, would lead them to a ditch and lay them down to sleep.

At one *pozo*, with Salomon staggering around, I ventured to ask him why he drank so much, for I had felt all along that perhaps he shouldn't mix so much drinking with so much arduous driving.

"Drink, *amigo mio*, drink?" He lurched violently over to the battered wooden door of the hut, took a running jump at it with his left foot, and fell through the door into the snow outside. Belching, he rose slowly to his full height of five feet and pointed with a grubby finger at the snow-covered peaks spread before us.

"You see that road up there, *amigo inglés,* you *see* that road?" He was pointing up at a rocky, snow-covered gap between two frowning peaks, holding himself at an angle against the raging, freezing wind.

I replied, perhaps a little patronizingly, "What road? That's the bloody mountainside."

He belched, spat, farted, laughed, and hiccuped all at the same time, in the inimitable Quechua way, balancing himself again just in time to save himself from falling flat on his face. "Mountainside?" he shouted. "That's the *hijo de puta*, the son of a bitch of a road! Now you know why I drink this *chicha*, now you know, *amigo*. If I *didn't*, we wouldn't get one *fucking meter* up that shitty track!"

The haul progressed all day on the twenty-ninth, until we were bogged down by a particularly violent rainstorm that evening. We stopped, hung out a storm lantern, huddled in *Sea Dart*'s cabin, and waited. It *pissed* down. I have never in my life, anywhere, seen such heavy rain. When it finally stopped, around dawn, we slowly and carefully crept forward with the girlfriend and me testing the road ahead for any weakness, any tendency to landslide. On the thirtieth, we crawled exactly twenty-five miles, but by the thirty-first, the tracks had dried enough to enable us to wheeze forward at ten miles an hour over the high plain. That evening we encountered the road which leads from Cuzco to the Lake. We were over the worst; now it was a straight road to the Lake, and we roared along at twenty miles an hour, leaving a trail of oil spots along the way.

The night was brilliant, with a clear sky and an almost full moon. Everything was covered with dried mud, including me. Three old Indians slept on the truckbed and the boat was undamaged. We limped and wheezed our way into Puno at ten in the evening. For one unforgettable moment on the way into the town, I glimpsed the moon shining on Lake Titicaca. It was calm, inviting, welcoming. Unbelievable—I'd made it! I'd arrived on the shores of the Lake before the end of 1973—ninety minutes before. I'd smuggled myself and the boat across Peru. I'd done it! Whatever might happen, I'd made my destination. Almost, for we decided to spend the night in the main square, surrounded by a gaping crowd of Quechua Indians, descendants of the Inca, who stared at this apparition in utter disbelief. A boat from the sea!

I had a lot of trouble getting to sleep in *Sea Dart*'s cabin. It wasn't Salomon's snoring, it wasn't the lack of oxygen at almost thirteen thousand feet above sea level; it was out of thankfulness to all the Gods of the Oceans for my arrival at my destination after so long.

36

ANOTHER YEAR: ANOTHER WORLD

EW YEAR'S MORNING, 1974! Onboard *Sea Dart,* perched on top of an ancient Ford truck parked in the town plaza of Puno, I woke with the first light of dawn, put the kettle on the stove, and clambered down to shake my Quechua friend Salomon, who was sleeping off the effects of a bottle of *chicha* consumed straight after our arrival. I had not bothered to undress the night before, for the temperature in those parts, even during the southern summer, plunges from eighty degrees at 5:00 P.M. to below zero just an hour after the sun sets. I had slept in all my arctic gear and covered the berth with three thick blankets. Nevertheless, I had awakened often with the cold and lack of breath. This was caused by the shortage of oxygen at that height, which is 40 percent less than at sea level. The second phenomenon caused by this lack of oxygen was the time it took for the kettle to boil for morning tea!

All around the muddy plaza, Indians were rising from their sleep in the open. They come into Puno with small bundles of produce to sell, and they stay, sleeping in the freezing air, until the last tiny potato or piglet is sold, then return to their homes, which Salomon told me might be anything up to a hundred miles away. Some of them come in by truck, but most of them walk for days across the bitterly cold, wide open plain of the Altiplano.

By the time we had eaten breakfast, a great crowd of Indians, silent, barefoot, and very dirty, had gathered in front of the shabby but impressive cathedral, and were gazing expressionlessly at *Sea Dart* and the truck. We were too conspicuous to escape the vigilance of the local constabulary for long, so we set off, wheezing and dripping oil, down to the small jetty on the lake. Having smuggled my way across Peru, there was only one thing in my mind apart from the immense satisfaction of having reached such a remote target, and that was to get the hell out and gone from Puno before the Peruvian customs figured out what had happened. So far, so good, but the stir that our appearance had excited all along the route would surely, sooner or later, put the vultures on my tail. Once I'd actually sailed on the Lake, that would not be of such great importance; moreover, I knew that once I was on the Lake they would have to run to catch me, especially if I was near Bolivian waters.

As we crawled in and out of potholes, through a heavy downpour which caused the roads to stream with flood-waters, I was thinking that the way down from the Lake back to the Pacific would be comparatively simple. From Guaqui, in Bolivia, at the southern end of the Lake, a railroad runs across the Andes into Chile and to the Pacific coast port of Antofagasta. I would, after I had cruised the Lake for a few weeks, load the boat on the train and head down to Chile, back into the Pacific, then store up, either for a fast, easy run up the Humboldt Current to Panama, or, if funds were sufficient, across the Pacific for Australia, and then on, after a spell down under, back home to England.

Suddenly I was shaken out of my reverie, for there was the Lake, with great black thunderclouds streaming overhead and sheet lightning forking down on the far horizon. But even in the dim gloom of the thunderstorm it looked more beautiful than any other water in the world. The shoreline consisted of a short, broken-down jetty, a few miserable adobe huts huddled at one end with rainwater streaming off their thatched red roofs, an ancient steam-crane, and a shed, but to me it looked more heavenly than the Grand Canal at Venice and more impressive than the Thames at Tower Bridge. The tiny, whitewashed adobe church at the end of the jetty looked more magnificent than the Notre Dame; the small flotilla of ragged little Indian sailing vessels hugging each other along the jetty seemed more majestic than the whole power and glory of all the navies in the world combined.

I jumped off the truck and started to run to the Lake shore, but the lack of oxygen soon brought me up short, panting. Salomon stared after me as if I had gone crazy, then he laughed and shouted, "*Bueno, muy bueno*!" I kept walking to the water's edge and with all my arctic gear on, walked right into the freezing water of Lake Titicaca until it came up to my waist. Then I bent and cupped my hands, drinking in the clear, fresh water, giving thanks to God for letting me survive all the dangers and perils of the last few years long enough to live this moment. As I straightened up, the thunderheads in the distance faded and a bright rainbow, sharper and more vivid than any I had ever seen before, arched across the Lake, bridging the sky from the peak of Sorata to the gleaming silver heights of Illampu, way over in the south, more than one hundred miles away. Bands of brilliant color curved across the heavens, framing the Island of the Sun.

I stood in the cold floodwater, oblivious to the iciness in my seaboots, no longer weary with effort, no longer worried about shortage of money, no longer breathless with lack of oxygen. Sunbeams streamed through the rain clouds in golden shafts, illumining green, green islands, where before there had been only dark gray, shadowy smudges. As the clouds rolled apart, they revealed the bluest water in the world, and small green parrots flew overhead like emeralds thrown up into the sky. Then my legs and feet started to ache with pain and numbness.

I sloshed my way back to *Sea Dart*'s cabin and changed into dry pants and boots, then walked over to the harbormaster's office, trying to look as confident as I could before a crowd of gawping Indians. They just stood there in the rain, the water pouring off their blankets. Salomon was the only one grinning. "*Bien hecho, amigo inglés*! he crowed. "Well done!"

Half an hour later, *Sea Dart* was afloat in the Lake and Salomon was helping me raise the small mainmast and set up the standing rigging. As the rain recommenced, we rigged the sails, hoisted the burgee of the Royal Naval Sailing Association, and there she was, ready for the off, the world's highest burgee, at 12,850 feet above the ocean!

I looked around the jetty. Beyond a netted enclosure I spied two gray launches, one with a small gun mounted on its bow. I grabbed Salomon's arm and thumbed at them over my shoulder.

"Navy or customs?"

"Navy, *amigo*, but you got no problems. On one boat the gun doesn't work, on the other the engine is buggered. Anyway, they are too busy pissing about policing the town; there's rumors of a revolution in the air!" Again he managed to spit, grin, fart, belch, and scratch all at the same time.

Then I got the motor out of its unopened wrappers and rigged it up to move the boat out alongside the jetty. Unfortunately, because of the lack of oxygen and the watery gasoline, it would not start! I'd had the motor ever since Panama and never used it once. Now it was useless on the Lake, so I stowed it away in its wrapper. I had a long sweep oar, and I sculled her around to a berth which the harbormaster arranged for me after his palm had been suitably crossed.

It was raining as Salomon and I waded through two-foot-deep cataracts in the streets on our way to the town bar. We both agreed that *Sea Dart* had beaten the rainy flood season and the Andes snow melt by only a matter of hours. I paid Salomon two hundred dollars; the extra we agreed should go towards a new oil sump for his truck, plus a bottle or two of *chicha* for the terrible trip back down to the coast when the rains finally stopped in March. There followed an emotional farewell scene, during which Salomon made a curious remark: "*Amigo inglés, cuidado con los Aymaras!*" "Careful with the Aymaras!" Several weeks later I found out what he meant. But that afternoon, despite the floods and chaos, we were happy, and by the time I rolled back onboard *Sea Dart* I was in fine fettle, ready to sail off in the morning.

That night, with the oil lamp lit and the tiny cabin cozily warm from the heat of the kerosene stove and after a good, hot meal of bullybeef and potatoes, I lay down and listened to the rain strumming on the coachroof. I had no charts for the Lake, for at that time none existed, but I had garnered a little information from Adolph Bandelier's *The Island of Titicaca* in the British Museum Reading Room. In the morning, God willing, I would take off and hide myself away from the prowling customs officials of Peru. I had just over one hundred dollars; I was three hundred miles from the Pacific and two thousand miles from the Atlantic, but I had over three thousand square miles of fresh water to get lost in. Also, I had time to write and restock my depleted coffers.

It takes a few weeks to become accustomed to the lack of oxygen at the altitude of the Lake, and I often woke with a tight chest, gasping for breath. Then I would lie thinking of all I had overcome and endured to reach this magic Lake; and sometimes it all seemed like a dream. The first night afloat in Lake Titicaca was like that, and I had little sleep. I was fully awake at the first crack of false dawn; with the kettle singing slowly on the stove, I went out into the clear freezing dawn to let go of the mooring lines.

As I sculled *Sea Dart* with the long oar over the stern out of Puno in the darkness of the early dawn, I did not know that I was about to enter a world of superstition and fear, black magic and wonder, from which I would emerge only after a harrowing eight months. All I could think about was reaching the broad, sweeping miles of high, totora-reed water meadows and there hiding myself and my boat from the Peruvian customs!

By the time the sun rose over the black masses of the high Cordillera Real away to the east; by the time the mountain peaks had changed color to gray and the Lake water to startling turquoise under a low-lying mist; I was well out into the Lake, with a slight southwest wind. As I crowded sail and headed for the strange, low, floating islands of the Uro Indians, islands which, like living animals, move up and down with the Lake water level, islands which support one of the most primitive and pitiful tribes on earth, I thought of what I had learned thus far of the history of the Lake.

37

WHERE ANGELS FEAR TO TREAD

 HE SPANISH CONQUISTA-dors first arrived on the shores of Lake Titicaca in 1535, after subjecting the Quechua Indians of Ecuador and Peru. Pizarro and his tiny band enjoyed incredible luck, sailing south from Panama at the precise time when the Holy Child current had reversed the north-flowing Humboldt. Instead of struggling against the strong Humboldt in their awkward ships, they made a fast passage to Cape Santa Elena where they landed horses, guns, and stores.

The arrival of the Spanish centuries later on the same current which brought the mighty god Kon-Tiki-Vira-Cocha, the creator of plains and mountains, struck terror into the hearts of the Incas. The periodical change in direction of the current was in itself, to the superstitious Incas, evidence of the wrath of Kon-Tiki. This legendary white, bearded God, had according to their legends, after bringing light to the world of darkness, disappeared into the ocean, "walking away across the waters with his band of Saints."

Now came these other bearded white beings, perhaps the sons of Kon-Tiki, on the same current as the God himself. This was the mighty current which, when Kon-Tiki wished, changed direction, turning the sea blood red and killing all the fish in the waters. (In the nineteenth century this phenomenon was called by English seamen "the Callao Painter" because the ships' hulls were turned blood red by the discoloration caused by the millions of dead organisms in the water.) Then the climate would change, earthquakes and disasters would occur throughout the lands of the empire, from the hot jungle shores of northern Ecuador to the cold barren wastes of Chile. The wind and the rain would lash the mountain fastnesses with unbounded fury, flooding the lowlands, destroying the crops so that hunger and famine stalked the land every seven years. (Shades of Egypt!)

Then, relenting, Kon-Tiki had ordered the first Inca, Manco Capac, to build grain storages throughout the empire, thus establishing an iron hold over all the tribes. Now these strange men, white and bearded like Kon-Tiki himself, with their terrifying thunderbolts and four-legged monsters had stepped ashore at the same place where, the Indian storytellers later told me, Manco Capac himself had first stepped ashore!

In trembling awe, carefully concealed by a great show of pomp, the Inca king, Atahualpa, was carried in a magnificent litter to Cajamarca to meet the sons of Kon-Tiki. Word of the arrival of these gods had been carried swiftly to him for a thousand miles along the imperial highways. Atahualpa was accompanied by a mighty army of fierce warriors: the Quechua, stern and disciplined; the sly Oruro, fastest runners in the empire; and the murderous Aymara.

With incredible courage Pizarro thrust the Holy Bible of his God into the sacred hands of Atahualpa, who haughtily cast the object into the dust, and thereby sealed the fate of South America. In that moment the whole of Ecuador, Peru, Bolivia, and great tracts of Chile and Argentina fell into Pizarro's hands.

With his two hundred bold spirits, the Spanish commander, the bastard son of an Andalusian peasant, seized the Inca by the golden scruff of his neck and drove his assembled minions into screaming retreat. Then, after holding the emperor for ransom, he strangled him with a garrote.

Immense mountain ranges, fertile valleys, towns and cities, half a continent, roaring rivers and dusty deserts, as well as unimaginable treasures of gold, silver, tin, and lead fell into the grasping hands of Spain. For the Andes Indian time stopped from the moment of Atahualpa's seizure until now.

So fell the first, and most efficient, fascist corporate state the world has ever known. Ever since Atahualpa's death the Andes Indian has mourned him and awaits his return.

Such were my thoughts as I headed out for my first sail on

the Lake. I was heading toward the unknown, for in their zeal to get to the gold and silver of Bolivia the conquistadors had bypassed the islands leaving them practically unexploited.

For centuries now they had remained almost in the same state they had been in when Atahualpa died.

38

THE FLOATING ISLANDS

N MANY AREAS OF THE Lake an underwater tree, the *llachon*, grows. With a sturdy trunk rising from the Lake bottom, it grows to within inches of the surface; indeed, during the low-level season the tips of its branches rise above the Lake waters. The trees grow in groves, like a ghostly apple orchard underwater. As I headed for the main Uro island, where the smoke from the Indians' fires was rising in the early morning, I sailed straight into one of these groves. *Sea Dart* must have been making a good four knots on a broad reach, with the main and genoa drawing like dray horses in the fresh breeze, when suddenly she stopped, all standing, still heeled over and not moving an inch. Placing my mug of hot tea safely in the bottom of the bucket, I thought of the immortal words of Earl Jellicoe at the Battle of Jutland as three British cruisers, with all hands, were sunk by the German Imperial Fleet in the space of a half hour: "There must be something wrong with our bloody ships today!"

I eased the sheets right away and looked over the side, for I at first thought *Sea Dart* had run aground into soft mud. Instead I saw that I was deep into a mass of clinging tendrils, up to two inches thick, closely entwined around the keels. The water was clear enough to see down to about a fathom. I started to push the tendrils apart, using the long bamboo pole which I had brought along with me all the way from St. Helena, the island of Napoleon's exile. Within minutes my chest was aching with lack of oxygen and I was gasping for breath as though I were being strangled. I sat down to recover. It was obvious that I could not single-handedly part the clinging *llachon* tendrils and free the boat. The only way I could escape would be to cut the bloody tentacles with my cutlass. I drew it out of the scabbard, honed it, and set to work. It took until noon to cut a passage of only a few feet, lying down on deck, slashing away with the cutlass. Warm work, and with the thin oxygen, exhausting.

Free again, in clear water, I carefully conned the boat in towards the village. I thought it strange that no one had paddled out to see what was happening, until I arrived at the huddle of hovels and realized that these folk were so poverty stricken they did not even have a boat! I entered the cleared creek between tall totora reeds, about fifteen feet high, and poled the boat in, having first handed the sails. The Uros stared at me as if I was Christ Himself returned to earth. There was no comment, no noise, as I slid up alongside the huts and dropped the danforth anchor. All the kids were stark naked. All had the balloonlike bellies of severe malnutrition, plus the apathetic, staring eyes of famine and starvation. The men and women were skinny, cadaverlike creatures, dressed in incredibly filthy rags. I found out later their island was about a mile long and a half-mile wide. It was constructed of woven totora reed into a raft about two feet thick, on top of which soil from the mainland had been spread. In this soil they normally grew potatoes and yucca, oca and quinua, all roots. But they made me understand with sign language that the winds and the rains of the previous week had washed away most of their soil, ruining years of hard, backbreaking labor. I asked them why they did not move over to the mainland, waving my arms around and pointing first to them, then to the mainland. They cringed, horrified. I found out later that the Uros have been hunted and persecuted by the other tribes, the Quechua and the Aymara, for centuries. They had found refuge in this unique way, living on fish, potatoes, and wild duck. They are the only Indians who eat the giant eyeless toad which inhabits the lake bottom, a monstrous creature, two feet long from its snout to its webbed feet. I pointed to the next nearest island, floating about one hundred yards from theirs. The spokesman shrugged and pointed to *Sea Dart*, then gave me to understand that they had no boats, the wind had swept them all away.

I pointed a finger at four of the least cadaverous-looking

men and gave them to understand that they should help me. I dug out my hundred-fathom nylon storm line, which I carry for trailing astern in a bad blow, in a wide bight, to slow the boat down when running before the wind. I pulled over to the far floating island, took a round turn on a great clump of it, gave it two round hitches, and returned across the channel to the Uros. They understood what I was about and were pulling as heartily as a three-year-old girl by the time I landed on their raft. Slowly but surely, with the whole *ayllu*, or clan, pulling, the channel narrowed. By dusk we had the two islands tied together and the Uros had gleaned about twenty pounds of potatoes from the patches of earth on their recovered property. With this they made a stew of tiny *boga* fish, and when I added three of Charlie-boys's dried fish, all the way from the San Blas Islands, their eyes lit up as they eagerly accepted the food. By dark they were all sleeping, still in their filthy rags. The Lake Indians, Quechua, Aymara, or Uros, never take off a vestment until it falls off.

Next day, after another uncomfortable night of struggling for oxygen, I sailed out of the creek with two Uros and took them to another floating island where members of the same clan eked out a living. This other island had two balsa reed craft to spare, and these we towed back to my hosts, who were delighted that they could now get out into the clear water to fish and could sail over to the far mainshore to search for the toads.

I stayed with these Uros for three days, but running short of food myself and not being able to communicate with them very well, I decided to head for one of the high islands which I had seen far to the west. I would try to secure enough food to make for the little explored north coast of Titicaca, the country of the Colla Indians.

On the last night with the Uros, we experienced the full force of a mighty storm. These are frequent on the Lake from January to March. The wind howled at hurricane force, flattening the totora reeds with lashing rain and lightning. I had two anchors dug in and four mooring lines secured onto the floating island, which, in its turn, was surrounded by millions of tons of reeds, thick plants with roots two or three inches thick going deep into the mud of the lake bottom. Nevertheless, when I looked round in the morning, the whole lot, island, boat, and reeds, had dragged about half a mile! I decided to head for the island of Taquila, which the Uros pointed out to me as a good place.

With a good southwesterly I weighed the anchors, cast off the mooring lines, and, to the waves of about a hundred Uros, got under way. They didn't look much healthier, but they certainly seemed to be a bit more cheerful. One or two small children even managed to shout a goodbye.

When I got clear of the reeds into the nearly dead calm lake, it was mid-afternoon. The scene was fantastic. In the west the sun was shining on the silver peaks of the Cordillera Real and on the lofty peaks of Illampu and Illimani thrusting up over twenty thousand feet far in the west. Below the shining peaks, the glaciers, purple and violet, dripped like curtains down to the misty gray foothills and bright emerald green of the lakeshore. And all this was repeated upside down, for the whole of this spectacular spectrum of color was reflected in the calm waters of the Lake! It was the most exquisite sight I have ever seen. Away to the southeast, beyond the Strait of Chucuito, the Island of the Sun glistened a royal purple and seemed to be floating in a milk-pearl mist above the Lake.

Sailing close to the shore of Capachica Peninsula, I saw little stone houses clustered around the tiny harbor, neat, well-tilled fields set on the bottom slopes of the hills, and I heard the music of the *cuenas* or flutes, as boys called to the flocks of small, skinny mountain sheep in the gulleys. I passed three Quechua Indian luggers with their one huge mainsail, loaded down with totora reeds, heading for Taquila. The skippers and crew stared impassively as *Sea Dart* bowled along under a quartering wind, well heeled over. I disconnected the wind-vane steering gear and took over the tiller by hand. Once *Sea Dart* was out of the Chucuito Strait, the Peruvian customs could never locate me. To the south lay Bolivia and the Island of the Sun, where I'd be safe at last. It was doubtful the Indians would transmit any information to the Peruvian customs, for the

Quechua has no love for the Lima government. He lives in a separate world, oblivious to all the game-playing, posing, and musical chairs of modern politics.

Fifty yards offshore, Taquila Island seemed to be almost bare; then I entered the prettiest little harbor in the world, with an entrance channel between raw stone walls only ten feet wide and running in the shape of a dog's leg back into the cliffy shore for two hundred yards or so, terminating in a clear waterfall off the cliffs. There was not a soul about as I worked *Sea Dart* in and tied up.

39

SAILING ON THE ROOF OF THE WORLD

URING PASSAGE FROM THE Uros's floating island to Taquila, I had surveyed the Lake as best I could, using my sextant to measure heights and distances between prominent landmarks where I could not get close inshore because of the thick totora reeds and *llachons*. I measured the depths with my lead, a long line marked with knots and rag streamers with a lead weight on the end.

Taquila Island rises almost 1,000 feet over the level of the Lake. (This means, of course, that the peak of Taquila is 14,200 feet above sea level!) I got ready to climb the hill in the morning so as to take a careful survey of the northern half of the lake, known to the Indians as Chucuito. I cleaned my sextant and packed it in its carrying case and picked up my binoculars, my handbearing compass (to take the bearings of different points on the Lake islands and on the mainland), a set of air navigation tables (to see if, at this height, I could fix the position of the Island), a notebook, pencil, umbrella (rather tatty by now since I had used it innumerable times since I bought it three years before in Ethiopia). Also I packed a stopwatch, my portable transoceanic radio, so as to obtain an accurate time signal, a tape measure, in case I came across anything interesting to measure, a length of strong nylon line for emergencies, my seaman's knife, and my cutlass, tied to my waist.

The following morning I started up the eight hundred feet to the top of Taquila, clambering over the rocky path, which ascended along dizzying ledges. It was heavy work in the thin air, and I had to stop every few yards to catch my breath. About halfway up I saw my first Taquilan. He looked about seventy years old and he passed me at a fast run, springing from rock to rock with a live sheep strung over his back, kicking! Greeting me with a lively *"Buenas,*

Señor!" he was soon out of sight. Astonished, I gazed down over the edge of the precipice and saw that far below a boat had sailed in; the little port of Maynani was now crowded with people. I decided there was nothing I could do but carry on. It was unlikely that anyone would interfere with the boat; the Quechua Indians were too proud to steal. Anyway, on the companionway hatch I had painted a snake and above it a skull. (If there's anything an Andean Indian is scared silly of, it's a snake! This turned out, all through South America, to be a good ploy, for the boat was never boarded without my invitation.)

I finally panted to the top of the steep, conical mountain to find a fantastic scene. As the sun set, the long range of the Cordillera turned to pure shining gold, and the glaciers below the peaks became a deep turquoise blue; while below this vast sweep of glowing color, the Lake itself glistened emerald. Around me, on top of the ridge, were ancient ruins, watchtowers, storage houses, and a small necropolis with human skulls grinning out of tiny windows set in the vertical tombs, the skulls facing to the east. Human bones and pottery lay everywhere. Without touching anything, I returned to the top of the cone and awaited the arrival of the Indians plodding up the rough foot-track, weighed down with enormous loads. This is where I first met Machamachani, the ancient *Quipucamayo,* one of the most respected elders of the Lake Quechuas.

Of the thirty or so Indians climbing to the summit on their way to the settlement on the far side of the island, he was the only one not carrying a load. All of them, men, women, and children, were burdened with sacks, colorful blankets, and even a few boxes loaded with foodstuffs and grain, seed and roots. Even tiny, doll-faced little tots, with minute broken blue veins on their cheeks caused by the freezing nights, carried loads, even if only a dozen oca roots in a small blanket. The little girls, with their six petticoats, bare feet, and little derby hats, were perfect replicas of their mothers.

Machamachani, bent and looking as old as the hill we were meeting on, approached me with great dignity.

"*Buenas, Señor,*" I greeted.

"Muy buenas, Señor," he replied, coming straight up to me. He was around five feet three and wore the *chorro*, the pointed woolen cap with earmuffs. Over his upper body a brilliantly colored poncho blanket covered a red and white *unku*, or sleeveless, collarless shirt. Below that a pair of gray llama-skin trousers were rolled up to his knees, while on his feet were a pair of leather, thonged sandals. His face was as weatherworn as the rocks around us, a deep, shiny bronze. There was no sign of a beard on his cheeks, which, though wizened with age, were as hard and firm as those of a lad of twenty. His teeth were white and shining, and they were all his own. Later that night I saw him ripping away at the hind leg of a sheep as if it were made of paper. His hands were sinewy, graceful, and he made small, controlled gestures while he spoke.

Machamachani was a pattern for the average Lake Quechuan of around his age, which I figured was about sixty-five, though he wasn't sure himself.

I addressed him in Castilian Spanish, but this confused him. Turning quickly, he spoke rapidly to one of his companions, who dropped his load of *chuño* and ran off towards the village. (*Chuño* is the original "freeze-dried" food. It consists of potatoes, with all the liquid squeezed out, set out in the cold nights on woven mats to freeze. This food, though bland and tasteless, keeps forever and is the Indian staple during the winter months when there is nothing else to eat.)

The messenger came back in a surprisingly short time, considering that the village was a good two miles away, down a steep track. He was accompanied by a thickset youth of about twenty, dressed in a plain brown jacket and wool trousers, dyed black. He was barefoot. Machamachani approached the youth and, turning to me, said, smiling, "Huanapaco, Bolivia; Quechua, Castilian!"

Huanapaco spoke clear but slow Spanish. He told me he came from a small pocket of Quechuas who live on the south basin of the Lake, Unimarca, in Bolivian territory. His father was chief of the *Illacata* of the *Anan Saya* of Cachilaya! Each Indian *ayllu*, or clan, is separated into two factions, one of which is in power for one year, the other acting as the "opposition." The north faction is called the *Anan Saya,* while the south faction is called the *Ma-Saya.* His father was the constable, in charge of the distribution of land, an event which took place every autumn when his half of the clan, the north party, was in power. In the spring he would arrange and oversee the communal repairing of houses, communal sowing and reaping, the provision of an adobe hut communally built by the whole clan for newlywed couples, and the distribution of food to members of the clan too old or ill to work their share.

Huanapaco was a sturdy chap, about five feet eight inches tall, but with the broad chest and big lungs of the Andes Indian, which are about one third larger than those of people who live at sea level. At first sight he was so thick limbed he appeared fat; only later did I realize that it was, in fact, solid muscle. His face gleamed with intelligence; the basic education he had received during a short spell in La Paz, the capital of Bolivia, had given him a knowledge of the outside world. He was obviously looked up to by all the Taquilans as a man who had seen the white man's miracles.

A *Quipucamayo* is so called because he reads the *Quipu,* knotted strings on which the accounts and legends of the mountain Indians have been preserved for centuries. As dusk fell and a great fire was lit, a crowd of men and boys gathered around, while the women busied themselves with the cooking chores. With Huanapaco interpreting, Machamachani and I were able to converse, or rather I was able to listen to his tales of the dim and distant past of the Quechua, of the days of the royal splendor of the Incas, of the coming of Kon-Tiki-Vira-Cocha and Tunupa, another of their prominent gods.

He told me of the battle between the Collas, under the great warrior chief Chari who, while Manco Capac was busy raising cities and fortresses in Peru, had marched north from the far-off valley of Coquimbo away to the south, near the ocean, in Chile. When they reached the Island of the Sun, they found a race of white, bearded men, fierce and warlike, living on the sacred island. The Collas had defeated these strange bearded ones "from a far-off land across the ocean, away to where the sun sets."

Machamachani gestured to the west, to the last dying glow of day, over the western cordillera. I followed his wave in wonder.

As we ate caracha and yucca around the glowing fire, huddled in blankets against the cold night wind, Machamachani, his eyes dreaming, told me about the journeys and doings of Tunupa, "The Wise One," and Tunapac, "The Son of the Creator," both of whom, *white* and *bearded*, long before the Spanish arrived, had appeared from the steaming jungles of Brazil and preached to the population of Tarija, a province in the south of Bolivia. They had then journeyed north to Lake Titicaca. There Tunupa, after drowning in the Lake waters, had been laid out on a balsa reed craft and floated away, to the weeping of the tribes along the shore. Tunupa's balsa had swept away, very fast, to the south end of the Lake, where it crashed into the mountainous shore, which parted and let free the flooded waters of the Lake. These waters flowed south, carrying Tunupa with them, to the distant salt flats of Poopó. Tunupa's balsa raft carried on over the mountains, down to the sea, and disappeared over the ocean to the west! Again the *Quipucamayo,* carved face gleaming under his *chorro*, gestured towards the west. Again I followed his action, wondering.

"What about Kon-Tiki-Vira-Cocha?" I asked the old man.

"Kon-Tiki appeared twice," he replied. "Once to create the mountains and the sky, the rivers and the Lake, Man and the animals. But he forgot to make light, and so for a long, long time there was a world, there was life, but there was no light. All was darkness and cold." In the flickering light of the fire, as the women carried the now sleeping children into the adobe huts, to keep warm among the guinea pigs and piglets, Machamachani went on: "Kon-Tiki came back after a long, long time, to the Island of the Sun and, striking the Sun Stone, made the Sun, the Moon, and the stars rise out of it. The moment he did this Manco Capac emerged from a cave and, marching northwards, built Cuzco and many other towns, establishing the Inca Empire.

"Then Kon-Tiki went south and, coming to the city of

Tiahuanaco, found the people to be unworthy of the light he had brought them. So he turned them into stones. These are the great stones you will see when you visit that place, which you surely will, for all whom the Gods have touched visit Tiahuanaco." He smiled at me. "Long ago, the name of the great city of great temples to false gods had been Taycala, which means 'the between stones.' It commemorated the terrible wrath of Kon-Tiki, who caused the petrified folk to be suspended between heaven and earth, forever frozen in stone, hard and cold, as they had been in their wicked lives.

"But Manco Capac, contrary to what the ordinary people believe, was not born at the moment the sun appeared under the wand of Kon-Tiki. He came from an island off the coast of Ecuador, far to the north, called Guaya, where his ship had been wrecked. Struggling ashore he marched south along the desert shore to Ica, where many stories are still told of the miracles he wrought there. From Ica [just as *Sea Dart* did] Manco Capac had ascended the mountains and arrived at the Lake with four followers. Telling his companions to carry on north, he hid in the cave of the Island of the Sun until Kon-Tiki arrived and gave him the sign to emerge. He then became the first almighty Inca.

"This is the true story of Manco Capac," Machamachani declared, "but the common people are rarely told it in this way, for they will not understand. Most of them know nothing of the great limitless ocean which stretches away across the world to the birthplace of the Gods. They think that Manco Capac was born on the Island of the Sun!"

Into the late hours of the night Machamachani spoke, with Huanapaco fumbling for words in his basic Spanish and me listening carefully. The *Quipucamayo* later told me that he had never been further away from the Lake than La Paz, to the south of the Lake, high in the Andes. He could not read or write, and his Spanish was too poor to understand much.

By the time I stumbled down the steep, starlit steps of the hill of Amantini, my head was whirling. Eventually I went to sleep, still wondering if Kon-Tiki, "who made water spring from the mountains," was in fact a white man who knew the secrets of water divining and used this knowledge to gain dominance over the wild savages. Was Tunupa, "the Wise One," whose balsa craft had magically carved the river Desaguadero out of the southern mountains, an engineer who dug a channel to release the waters of the Lake to relieve the ruinous annual flooding?

Machamachani had told me that the name of the great temple city of Taycala had been changed to Tiahuanaco, which means "dry beach" in Quechua. Had the waters of the Lake, before the canal had been dug, extended to the mighty temples of a highly populated city? Had the water channel been dug by Tunupa to deprive his enemies in the stronghold of Taycala of their water supply, thus defeating them? Is this the origin of the tale of the "white, bearded God" turning the people of the city to stones? When I later visited the river Desaguadero, it appeared to me that it could be man-made, although time has worn away the rivage over the ages, with countless billions of tons of Lake water escaping to the salt flats of Poopó, to evaporate, to seek the Sun, the offspring of the Lake itself.

Machamachani's version of the arrival of Manco Capac, together with the arrival of Pizarro, plus the story of the departure of Kon-Tiki himself, all taking place in the same area of the coastline, indicated to me that there was regular traffic from *somewhere* to the three capes of Ecuador, and to Cape Santa Elena in particular. That "somewhere" was most likely Asia, probably the Middle East. From where else could white, bearded men have appeared and disappeared on the Pacific coast of South America with such regularity?

I later learned, from old accounts in the library of La Paz, that after the Spaniards arrived at the Lake there was a great volcanic eruption near Copacabana in 1600, which darkened the sky over the Lake for many days. Is it possible that centuries before 1600 other white men had used a propitious volcanic phenomenon to seize power over an intensely superstitious, ignorant, aboriginal population?

With these questions in my mind, I finally fell asleep, rocking gently to the night breeze.

The following day I spent pottering about the ruins on the island with Huanapaco as my guide. He explained to me that many of the stone buildings had been used for storing grain. He also showed me the ancient cemetery, where the bodies are still well preserved in baskets, with their knees tucked under their chins. By the time we returned to the Quechua village I was quite impressed with his intelligence.

That night, as Machamachani and other elders sat by the fire, telling tales of past hunting and fishing exploits, I beckoned Huanapaco over to me. He crossed over the circle of blanketed men, the flames of the fire reflected in their eyes.

"*Sí, Señor?*"

"Would you like to sail with me while I am on the Lake?"

His eyes lit up. He fell to his knees before the *Quipucamayo* and asked him in Quechua. The old man smiled and nodded. Huanapaco rose, grabbed my hand, turned to the fire, his mahogany face glowing, and shouted, "*Mi capitán!*"

And so it was arranged with Machamachani that Huanapaco would accompany me to Lake Chucuito, the northern half of Lake Titicaca, then through all the islands, to the Island of the Sun, and escort me into Bolivia. There he would seek out his father and ask for permission to accompany me for one year, until I returned to the mighty waters of the great ocean. Throughout the night the declamations of the *Quipucamayo* and Huanapaco went on, under the brilliant stars, until the moon rose slowly over the distant Cordillera Real, over Sorata Mountain, known to the Quechua as *Achacilla*, "the grandfather of snows!" I slept contentedly in the adobe of Machamachani, for tomorrow I would be able to survey the northern Lake from the vantage point of the peak of Taquila.

On that first night's sleep in an Indian dwelling, I learned that vicuña, llama, and *titi*, the jaguar, are not the only fauna that move by night. I was continually wakened by the chattering teeth of a dozen guinea pigs, which the Indians keep as pets in their one-room dwellings until they are ready to be killed for meat. The *Pulex irritans*, or human flea, and the bedbug were also extremely active, while the body lice just clambered onboard me.

Before we went back to *Sea Dart*, I soaked my head and

pubic hair in gasoline, then shaved them, then scrubbed and scrubbed under the waterfall for an hour or more, until I was sure there were no livestock on my body. I insisted on Huanapaco's doing the same, which he did, though reluctantly, for the Lake Indian usually does not wash from the day he is born till the day he dies. Whenever I joined their company, I made sure I was going on the windward side of them, for the stink was enough to fell an ox.

Despite all these precautions, however, before I had passed a month among the Lake Indians, the boat was crawling with fleas and bugs, which did not finally disappear until she was soundly disinfected at the Brazilian army post at Coimbra nine months later. At first these parasites were a living purgatory, but before many moons had passed, hunger, cold, and other privations had diminished their importance to a minor irritation.

When we finally settled into *Sea Dart* after a thorough survey of all that could be seen from the mountaintop, I was satisfied that the effort had been more than worthwhile, for I now had a good idea of the layout of the Lake. In the morning we would set off to explore the many islands and bays of the northern half of Lake Titicaca, the least known part, hardly ever traveled by Europeans.

In the early dawn, before the southwest day-wind piped up, we worked *Sea Dart* out by hand from the tiny harbor, between the worn, timeless stones of the mouth, and commenced sculling north. For breakfast we had dried fish and cold rice, with tea. Huanapaco turned out to be a very curious youngster, wanting to know everything about sailing a boat like *Sea Dart*. He had sailed often in the Lake in Indian boats and knew a little about it, but he was amazed that a sailing craft could actually go into the wind. The other thing that amazed him was the self-steering gear; he would stare at it for hours as it obeyed the wind direction and kept the boat on a straight and steady path.

For six weeks we cruised the whole northern half of the Lake, sounding for shallows, finding safe anchorages, exploring long fiords, communicating with the Colla Indians through Huanapaco. The most beautiful cruising ground in the whole world unfolded before us. At night we sailed full pelt into a reed patch and let the reeds hold the boat firm, no matter how strong the nighttime northwesters blew. Once at rest in the reed beds, there was no sound but the call of the *choca*, a black dipper with metallic plumage, or the *alka mari*, a chestnut-colored buzzard with bright yellow legs, who would strut along the shore as if he were an Inca. In the daytime, high, high above us soared the gray eagle and the condor, watching intently for smaller prey. Off the small, deserted Indian settlements huddled by the shore, the *tanta*, a green-feathered stork, perched on the abandoned roofs, while across the evening sky the pure white *huallatas,* or wild geese, flew home in perfect squadrons.

But six weeks was all I dared chance in Peruvian waters, for I was afraid that word would sooner or later get back to the bureaucrats in Puno about *Sea Dart*. I determined to head south for Bolivian waters and the fabulous Island of the Sun. On our way south we called at Taquila once more, to drink a memorable new-moon bottle of *chicha* with Machamachani and watch him divine the future with coca leaves thrown on the firelit floor under the moon.

"All will be well for you, *Macchu Cuito,*" said Huanapaco. I had a new name, the same in Aymara, or Quechua: "Thorny Bush"—this because of my beard!

40

THE ISLAND OF THE SUN

I T WAS NOW MID-FEBRUARY 1974 and the rainy season was more than half over. Our exploration of the Colla coast and the islands of Soto, Amantani, and (for want of any other name) Alpha, Baker, and Wight had found *Sea Dart*, Huanapaco, and me alternately soaked in bitterly cold showers and perspiring in hot sunshine. Now, as we left Taquila to head for the Island of the Sun, we were seen off by all the able-bodied people. The men wore their best caps, woolen and long, like a stocking with a bobble or pompon on the end. They had their fiesta clothes on, brilliant woven belts of llama wool and black llama wool trousers. Banging tambourines, they lined up along the miniature port and, with the *kena* flutes piping, played for all they were worth. The women and girls kept a discreet distance, laughing and joking among themselves. One of the prettiest looked long and hard at Huanapaco who, of course, pretended not to notice. The women wore black mantillas, *llicllas* they call them, fastened across the breast with a beautiful ornamental pin either of gold or silver, the *putu*, their most treasured possession. This was the only time in eight months on the Lake that I ever saw Indians actually change their clothes. Even for one of the frequent fiestas, they put their magnificent sequined dancing costumes, together with devils' masks and all the other paraphernalia, straight on top of their filthy rags.

Soon the morning breeze picked up *Sea Dart* and sent her dancing over the short chop of Lake Titicaca, heading south towards the Island of the Sun. While cruising the Colla coast, we had encountered some very wild storms indeed, with savage winds blasting down from the frozen Andes peaks onto the sun-baked Altiplano, where the difference in temperature between the sunny and shady spots

245

Prevailing Winds

DAY
NIGHT

N

DOLPHIN HEAD.

FOUNTAIN OF THE INCA.

YUMANI

Strait of Yampu-Pata

PUCARRA BAY

APACHINANKA VILLAGE

PUCARRA

KONA BAY

SEA-DART POINT.

Toetora Reef

WEED

ROCK

ROCK

ROCK

KEA 420 KOLLU

KEA BAY

KEA

Point Conrad

CHALLA BAY

INCA ROAD

ANCIENT INCA ROAD

KAKAYO-KENA RIDGE

WRECK BAY

MACHAPACHANI BAY

ARIA BAY

MIZZEN-TOP POINT

ACA HEAD

YOCKI

NORTH KONA

SAND & WEED

POINT BARBARA

Lake Titicaca

The Island of the Sun
Lake Titicaca
Bolivia
Tristan Jones.

Cachilaya, Bolivia
May 30th 1974

⊙ RUINS (PRE COLUMBIAN)
Ⓡ TITI-CALA, THE SACRED ROCK.
Ⓑ CHUCURUPI - SACRIFICIAL ALTAR.

★ No native name
⚓ Recommended anchorage
    night-time

Soundings in feet
Heights in feet (approx.)

was as much as seventy degrees! I was glad that I had curved the mast in order to spill the wind quickly, for often these devil winds would come out of a clear, sunny, blue sky, with absolutely no warning whatsoever. One minute *Sea Dart* would be ghosting along in a zephyr and the next be almost heeled over flat in a gust of a hundred miles an hour or more. It was exciting, exhilarating sailing, even though I was always short of breath, especially when working the sheets. When the going was steady it was gravy-sailing, and to the amusement of Huanapaco I would whoop and sing at the pure joy of sailing free on the wind across the roof of the world, bound for the Island of the Sun, the legendary Inca birthplace of the world!

There are several kinds of fish in Lake Titicaca; the *boga*, tiny and bony, similar to a pilchard; the *suchez* and the *amanto*, both somewhat larger, but much rarer; and the rainbow trout, huge, up to two feet long, but even rarer still. However, there was no point in trailing lines astern, for the rainy season had washed all kinds of foliage into the Lake, such as the branches of the *kenua*, the wild olive tree, which bears a tiny, bitter version of that fruit and which the Indians eat with the roots of the totora reed, stewed with green peppers and *boga* fish. To this stew they add *mancha*, a sort of red-clay soil! A noisome gruel, but filling when you're hungry. This ad hoc stew is usually cooked, by the Aymaras at least, on a fire fueled by *taquia*, the dried dung of the llama. The stench of the Aymara cooking area has to be imagined! In addition to which, neither the men nor the women ever move very far from the fire to relieve themselves!

As *Sea Dart* moved closer to Bolivian waters and the Island of the Sun, I felt better. As we passed the frontier line I felt easier at heart than I had since I loaded *Sea Dart* onto Salomon's wagon in Callao almost two months before. I also felt more than a mite triumphant, for I had been the first to reach Bolivia in an ocean-sailing vessel, or indeed ocean vessel of any kind, in almost a hundred years, ever since Bolivia lost her Pacific Ocean coast to the Chileans in the Bird-Shit War of 1879!

Just before dusk, as the wind finally dropped to a silent

calm, Huanapaco and I paddled the boat into Kona Bay on the south side of the Island of the Sun, well protected from the harsh, bitterly cold night winds, and anchored only fifty yards from the spot where Kon-Tiki is sworn by the Indians to have landed.

As the moon, waxing now, shone pale silver over the deep head of the Bay of Kona, we saw fires lit all along the sides of Yumani hill, where the Aymara settlement lay. Setting the snake-painted hatch cover in its place, we turned in to sleep in darkness, after allowing the flame from the kerosene cooker to warm up the tiny cabin. Before he dropped off, Huanapaco said to me, softly and seriously: *"Macchu Cuito,* I know this island. Let me speak to the Aymara; it is better that way. Let me speak to them before you go ashore, or they may not let you see the things you want to see."

"Right, you do that," I replied in English, for I was drowsy and already half-asleep, dreaming of green English cricket fields and foaming pints of beer, roast beef and Yorkshire pudding. It was almost spring in England, and everyone would be looking forward to April and the vernal burst of flowers. Here, in the remotest cruising ground imaginable, surrounded by primitive, alien mentalities, I was dreading the coming of winter. Meanwhile, I had fetched the Island of the Sun and would make a marine chart of its coast! The call of the *choca*, a night bird, finally lulled me to sleep, rocking away in Kona Bay.

After breakfast of fried oca and *boga* fish, caught on bottom lines overnight, Huanapaco paddled ashore in the rubber dinghy. Under the suspicious gaze of several Aymaras, he climbed the steep path leading to the main settlement, Apachinaca, a widely strung-out village of adobe huts, thatched with totora reed. Through the binoculars I followed his progress as he jumped from rock to rock, sure-footed as a mountain goat, until he finally disappeared behind a bluff and I was left to gaze at the surly faces of the Aymara gathered on the stony beach and the dozen or so pigs rooting in the ground around the huts.

After an interminable wait Huanapaco appeared again, this time standing on the bluff, waving to me to come ashore and up the hill. "Bloody fool," I thought, "does he think I can walk on water?" Finally he remembered the dinghy and dashed down the hill and paddled out to *Sea Dart*, grinning.

Once on the beach, he told me that the alcalde, or chief of the clan, had invited me up to see him. Huanapaco said that the alcalde seemed well disposed, but would probably expect a gift, for the Aymara has only three moving spirits— cupidity, alcohol, and bloodlust, in that order. I was to discover that although they were in the main highly intelligent people, for the most part their intelligence was employed in doing evil. There were striking exceptions, of course, but they only served to prove the rule about the Aymara in general. I do not believe that their viciousness is a reaction to ill treatment by the Spanish conquerors, because the Quechua do not share in this partiality to the evil arts. Neither do the other tribes, the Chibcha, the Colla, and the Uros. It is something in the genetic makeup of the Aymara, in their racial characteristics.

The assertion that the Spaniards killed millions of Indians in Latin America is not borne out by the historical records. Many spot censuses were taken by Jesuits in the mid-1500s, and if the figures are examined and computed, it will be found that the population of the Andes Indians has increased greatly since those days. Certainly they were exploited in the mines of Potosí and under the *Encomienda* system, which reduced them to serfdom under the great Creole hacienda owners; but the records do not bear out stories of intentional cruelty or genocide. It would have been to the Spaniards' detriment to have done this, for because there were so few whites or members of other races in the Andean countries, they would have deprived themselves of a strong, cheap labor force. The increase in population cannot be explained away by a high birthrate, because among the Indians inordinately large families are not the rule, and the natural attrition of disease and disaster, until recent times, has kept the population within reasonable bounds.

In a very large area, the Spaniards left the Andes Indians almost completely alone, with a great measure of autonomy; this was the case on Lake Titicaca. This is the reason that the *ayllus*, the clans, still exist just as they did under the Inca in 1532. Most of the Aymara were left alone completely; the argument that their hostility to strangers, their greed, their drunken savagery is a reaction to white exploitation just does not hold. The exploitation of Aymara by Aymara is far greater than anything imposed from the outside. The *llaycas*, or medicine men, have most of the clansmen in a grip of terror, and the *llaycas* wax fat. Although to the traveler they may seem poverty stricken and raggedly picturesque, I have been told that some of them could afford to retire to La Paz tomorrow if they wished, but they choose to live in rags, fleas, dirt, and disease.

The alcalde, a big man with heavy jowls and the face of a power-seeker, looked me up and down as if trying to weigh my worth from my appearance. He spoke rapidly in the slurring and guttural sounds of his language, the hardest of any to listen to, whether you understand it or not. Huanapaco explained to me that if I wanted to visit the sacred place I would have to give money to the *ayllu*. I said that I was a poor man who had sailed far to visit this island and that I wanted only to visit the holy places and that I could do this without a guide, for my friend Huanapaco knew the island and would guide me.

The chief said this would not do; many gringos (he was the only Indian on Lake Titicaca I ever heard use that word, as offensive to a white man as "nigger" to a black man) had come to the island but they never gave the *ayllu* anything. He said this to Huanapaco in Aymara, but I did not believe he could not speak Spanish, so I blurted out, "*Entonces no quiero ver esta isla de mierda!*" ("Then I don't want to see this island of shit!") I said it looking the alcalde directly in the eye. He faltered in the midst of a long spiel to Huanapaco and said, "*Qué dices?*" "What did you say?"

"I said that you are not a truthful man, *Señor*, because you have pretended to us that you do not speak Spanish, when, by my mother you do, so how can I believe anything else you tell me? If you do not let me pass to view Titi-cala, the sacred rock, then I will, when I see President Banzer in La Paz, inform him of your action and your attitude."

At this his face dropped and he spoke rapidly to Huanapaco, asking him if I really was going to see the president. Huanapaco, catching on quickly, swore that I was a personal friend of Presidente Hugo Banzer Suárez, an honored guest in Bolivia, and there would be all sorts of hell if I wasn't treated properly. The chief's expression changed to one of creeping humility. He turned to me and said, "*Señor,* I myself will escort you to the Titi-cala sacred stone. Not only that, but I shall also show you the fountain of the Inca on Yumani point, and the ancient Inca road on the ridge of Kakao Kena!" And so, with an expert guide anxious to please in every way, we viewed all day at our leisure the wonders of the Inca legends and later returned to *Sea Dart* heavily laden with gifts of oca, potatoes, and a great trout.

Now that *Sea Dart* was out of Peruvian waters, she was safe from the fifty percent import tax on her value, the iniquitous toll demanded by the rubber-stamp caesars of Lima. She was, at the Island of the Sun, not yet officially in Bolivia, although she was in Bolivian waters, for there were no entry facilities until Tiquina, well inside Bolivian territory.

Before sailing through the Strait of Tiquina, which separates the two parts of Lake Titicaca like the stem of an hourglass, into two semi-equal halves, Chucuito and Unimarca, I intended to explore the coastline of the Island of the Sun. The rain showers were becoming less frequent, the sun shone brilliantly in the daytime, the winds were easing off, and I still had enough food supplies to live, though modestly.

For eight days we worked our way around the Island and its nearby neighbors, Kochi, Pallaya, Chuyu, and Lauassani, small islands which support nothing but birds, mainly *chocas.* Huanapaco and I would sound the depths in the early morning from five until nine, before the wind had risen and while the Lake was like a smooth sheet of glass, with the early morning mist suspended thinly above it and the other islands seeming, in the distance, to hang in thin air, as in Chinese paintings. Huanapaco dipped the lead to the bottom and sang out the depths while I sculled the boat this way and that in the time-honored "square search" method. Often I would look up and see, far away in the distance to the north, islands beyond the horizon, Soto and

Amantani, apparently hanging upside down on the indistinct horizon, for it was impossible to see where the lake and the sky met. This was the fata morgana phenomenon, caused by the refraction of light waves by differences of temperature. The last times I had seen it were off Madagascar and Sicily.

About ten o'clock the wind would slowly increase, and during this time we would lay off, quite close to the Island, which is, all around, very steep-to (the Lake water is deep right up to the shores). I would set to work with the sextant and hand-bearing compass, fixing the different headlands and peaks in their correct relation to one another on the chart and calling out the numbers, in my turn, to Huanapaco, who would make note of them neatly on the chart.

Hove to, bobbing up and down in the short seas off the Island of the Sun, at early afternoon we would take turns making a mid-day meal. I would usually make fish and chips, while Huanapaco would come up with a Quechua concoction of totora reed roots, green peppers, and oca. By now I had run out of tea, except for a tiny amount which I was hoarding for use in case of a disaster.

From two in the afternoon until four we would sail round to the next anchorage. This was usually not far. We would arrive there at the full blaze of the sun. On the shore off the anchorage there would usually be a stream or a small waterfall where we could bathe and relieve ourselves of some of the ever-increasing livestock on our heads and bodies brought on board by visiting Indian fishermen and smugglers. There was no way we could refuse them aboard. They were very conscious of the rules of hospitality, and word passed quickly around the Lake. We had many interesting, sometimes funny, chats with the smugglers, who worked under sail, sliding through the Tiquina Strait at night under the noses of the Bolivian navy, carrying meat, flour, coca, and sugar to Peru and returning with clothes, *chicha*, beer, radios, and textiles. It is estimated that in 1973 seventy percent of Bolivia's imports were smuggled in and fifty percent of its exports were smuggled out! Most of this trade took place in the frontier waters of Titicaca, under sail! Very often a sailboat, with a great lugsail, would appear on the horizon, becalmed in the dawn. She would work her way in, come alongside, and the crew would greet us like lost friends, especially the Quechua boats from the north. They had heard of the strange "gringo" with the even stranger boat, which, like a bird, could actually sail *into* the wind. They would pull up shouting my Quechua name, "*Macchu Cuito*," and we would spend an hour or more gossiping through Huanapaco in the clear limpid light which the Lake, like a golden chalice, held cupped in its liquid hand until the sun rose over Copacabana Peninsula, forcing us to seek the shadows.

At dusk we would make another meal. The wind would drop, silence would descend all around us, except for the rustling of the reeds. Huanapaco would wrap his poncho around himself and fall asleep; I would light the oil lamp and work on the chart or write up my log. After that I would work on a magazine article to send off when we again returned to the twentieth century. About nine o'clock, after listening to the world outside and far below us over the radio, I would warm up the cabin with the kerosene stove and turn in.

Sometimes in the afternoon, after anchoring the boat safely, we would climb to the heights of a nearby island. Often this was to survey the surrounding area, but many times I would clamber up the steep, rocky mountainside and collapse, exhausted, at the top with the lack of oxygen. The view was astounding. Whenever the sun shone, which now was almost all day, the scenery from the heights of Titicaca was magnificent. We could see mountains, far to the east and north, 350 miles apart; and it seemed that we could just reach out with our hands and touch them, the air was so clear. Sweeping away at our feet, the azure blue Lake stretched on into the far distance, dotted with islands, most of them surrounded by beds of reeds, glistening emerald and gold as the breeze riffled across them. Far below in the bay, *Sea Dart*, like a tiny toy, bobbed in the wavelets, her red ensign fluttering on the stern, scaring the storks and dipper-birds, who loved to perch on the masthead and shit all over the topsides when there was no one onboard.

At this height there were two very obvious phenomena; the first was the effect of the sun's rays on color, which was much more dazzling in the sunshine and subdued in the shade. The difference between light and shade was much sharper than at sea level, and I came to the conclusion that a painter would find the color contrast on the Lake even more intense than Van Gogh found the country around Arles.

Another not so obvious effect in the thin, clean air was the difficulty in judging distance. As a navigator of small craft for many years, I can normally gauge a distance, especially from seaward, to within a few yards, even at six or seven miles' range. But up on Titicaca I found myself very often fooled, underestimating distances by anything up to three miles! It seems that the abnormal angle of the light rays, together with the magnifying effect of the clear, clean, dry air, causes this. When surveying I had frequently to pace the distance between two points of land, or actually sail between two islands to log the distance between them, instead of just taking a sextant angle.

The clearest night skies I have ever seen anywhere were over the Lake. Out in the ocean, well clear of the land, perhaps a thousand miles out, the skies are crammed with stars, but on Titicaca there was hardly room for the black sky among the stars! The bright planets and all the major stars were like small moons, their rotundity clearly delineated. The man-made satellites were immediately obvious, like taxicabs on the Epsom Downs course on Derby day. There were literally a million bodies in the sky. I cannot think of any finer place for an observatory to be erected. Many a time I would go topsides and be struck with wonder at the display of the heavens, beautiful beyond words, awe-inspiring in its magnificence. When the moon rose, I could see every crater and every blemish on its ravaged face.

On February sixteenth the survey of the Island of the Sun was completed, and I determined to make for Tiquina. There lay the Bolivian naval base, perched on a cliff overlooking the lovely, mile-wide Strait which separates Chucuito Lake from Unimarca Lake.

One may well wonder why a landlocked country like

Bolivia has a navy. It has very little to do with the contraband which passes over the frontier waters with Peru. It has, indeed, hardly anything to do with a naval threat from Peru, for none exists. The reason is that the region that in 1825 became Bolivia once had a seacoast on the Pacific; her national territory, as originally parceled out upon the conclusion of the wars of independence against Spain, included a large stretch of the Atacama Desert, in what is now northern Chile. On this most miserable and Godforsaken coast, dry and parched after centuries without rain, a small hamlet was built by a safe roadstead, a huddle of hovels among burning boulders and baking sand, with the grandiose name of the Port of Antofagasta.

For two centuries it was the territory's only outlet to the sea. Apart from a dribble of contraband, it was never used for international trade. Soon after the South American republics gained their independence, the Industrial Revolution in Europe caused an unprecedented burst in population growth. A means had to be found of increasing food production in Europe, for this was before the days of steamships and refrigeration. What better way than finding good fertilizer? On the west coast of South America were hundreds of square miles of barren shore, offshore rocks, and islets thickly covered, often to a depth of two or three feet, with guano, bird-shit.

In 1842 the only ocean-sailing vessel, apart from *Sea Dart* in 1974, arrived in Bolivia. *The only one on record, that is.* She was the *Hapsburg*, a four-masted brigantine out of Glasgow. She had sailed in 1841 laden with slate for roofing as ballast, crewed with the dregs of Barlinny Prison and the Gorbals, skippered and officered by the hardest men on the Clyde. By November 1841 she was beating her way around the Horn, where she lost three men, one washed over the side, one fallen from the top-gallant-royals, and one knifed in a brawl in the reeking forepeak. In January 1842 she fetched the roadstead of Valparaiso, Chile, and offloaded her slate, which can still be seen on the roofs of the fine, stately homes of that port. With no cargo for the voyage home, her captain, with true Scots ingenuity, bore away north to the coast of Bolivia. There, at Antofagasta, he met the Chilean bird-shit poachers and arranged with them to load the *Hapsburg* with the white gold of the Atacama. No bills of lading were made out, no entry was formalized, no crew-list was rendered to the Bolivian harbormaster.

Laden with six hundred tons of bird-shit, the *Hapsburg* weighed anchor after long weeks of shoveling dusty guano and wheeling tons of the stuff out to small barges and hoisting it on board. (Half the crew was sick with dehydration on that waterless desert shore. "Half a pint o' water, half o' whiskey" was the rule when taking on the Guano trade.) With a diminished crew she bore away for Cape Stiff, as they called the Horn. After losing two more crew in the savage April winds, she arrived home in Glasgow in August of 1842, working her way up the Clyde, weather-beaten, triumphant, and stinking for miles around of Bolivian bird-shit!

Meanwhile, word of the theft had leaked out to the Bolivian government in La Paz. Representations had been made to the British ambassador, who had swiftly transmitted to London word of the *Hapsburg's* unauthorized entry into Bolivian territory and, more seriously, the theft, in effect, of six hundred tons of Bolivian bird-shit. A messenger had been sent on horseback to Argentina and the dispatch carried back to Her Majesty's Government in London by a swift grain-carrier, a "greyhound of the seas," a three-sky-sail-yarder, bound direct for the Thames. The grain ship, with her cloud of stud sails and bucko skipper, made the distance back to England in no time at all and was sitting in the Isle of Dogs, with the dispatch delivered safely, long before the lumbering *Hapsburg,* short of crew, limped into the Glasgow docks. As the *Hapsburg* was warped alongside, the bobbies were waiting to board; the captain was seized, the crew returned to Barlinny Prison, and the cargo handed over to the Bolivian consul in London. This gentleman, whose name is unfortunately not preserved, promptly sold the cargo to a German firm in Hamburg and took off for Paris with the wife of his partner. For generations his memory was desecrated in Bolivia; he was known as the Benedict Arnold of that never-never land, the man who elegantly sipped absinthe for years in the cafes of the Champs Elysées with the proceeds from six hundred tons of bird-shit!

For three decades after this incident, the Bolivian government tried to remove the Chilean bird-shit poachers from her territory. Finally Chile, with the backing of England, whose ambassador to Bolivia had been tied backwards onto a donkey and displayed, fully and formally uniformed, through the narrow, winding streets of La Paz in revenge for the stolen bird-shit, lost her patience. Chile declared war on Peru and Bolivia. In a quick campaign lasting only a few days she beat the living daylights out of the Bolivian army and annexed the coastal province of Antofagasta.

The repercussions of this squabble are still felt in western South America. Peru, with millions of semi-starving peasants crowding into Lima, Arequipa, and Cuzco, squanders vast sums of money on jet fighter planes; the military of Chile murders the legally elected head of state; and Bolivia rattles a rusty saber.

41
ANOTHER SPLENDID RECEPTION

N FETCHING THE SOUTHERN end, the scene that met our eyes was paradisical. Lake Unimarca was even bluer than Chucuito. There were many small sailing craft of reed and wood, hundreds of them, some underway, some hove to, fishing. Their sails sparkled in the sunlight. The many green islands scattered around obscured the misty horizon; above them soared three majestic mountains, Sorata, Illampu, and Illimani, all over 20,000 feet high! Their glittering silver changed into purples, blues, and gray greens as our eyes followed the glaciers down to the hazy foothills.

It was arranged that Huanapaco would land on the eastern side of the Strait, at the tiny port of Tiquina. From there it would be easier for him to get to his home village and explain the situation to his father, Huanameni, the *Illacata* of the *Anan Saya* of Cachilaya. Meanwhile, I would work my way over the narrow Strait and enter the naval base to arrange a formal entry of *Sea Dart* and myself into the country.

Once Huanapaco was ashore, I bore away under main and genoa and in no time at all, with a good beam reach, was hovering off the flooded stone quay of the navy base. Several uniformed figures in rough serge blue suits, barefoot, all armed, gazed at me as I came alongside. A squat, dumpy mestizo, wearing the badges of a sergeant, pointed a machine gun straight at my solar plexus.

"*De dónde estás?*" His eyes shone malignantly; he looked as if the last water to touch him had been at his baptism. "Where are you from?"

"*Inglaterra*—England."

"That cannot be. Is that in Peru?"

"No, it's on the other side of Peru. Over the ocean."

"That cannot be, you have a red flag—a red flag!" He

pushed the muzzle of his machine gun into my stomach. *"Vamos, comunista!"*

"I'm not a com——" But I got no chance to explain; I was surrounded by grim-looking youngsters, none of them more than eighteen, all of them filthy and barefooted, with muddy uniforms. I was thrown into a tiny adobe hut with barred windows, and there I stayed all night long in the freezing cold, with no covering other than my sailing shirt and trousers, hunched shivering on a pile of reeds rustling with bugs. With the flooding of the Lake the water had risen, so that by now it was lapping over the cell floor. Through the tiny barred window I could just see *Sea Dart*, and I was relieved that no one seemed to be going onboard, although an armed sentry was posted alongside her all night. Apart from the intense cold and hunger, I was not too worried, for I imagined that in the morning the officer in charge would turn up and the misunderstanding would be solved. When the morning came around I waited with mounting anticipation. All that day, and the next, and the following night, I waited in frozen misery, but there was no sign of an officer. All I heard was the wind outside and the shouts as the sentries changed guard. They used a dialect I could not understand and I later ascertained that they hailed from Tarija and Potosí, far to the south of Bolivia. Whenever I tried to talk to them, they would stubbornly ignore me or crash their rifle butts against the metal door of the *calabozo*. By the afternoon of the second day in my cell, I was seriously trying to think of a way of breaking out, but all I could manage to do for myself was try to warm my freezing body in the narrow ray of sunlight which shone through the tiny barred window.

The third night in the cell, just after dusk, it started to snow. Finally, around ten o'clock, I was awakened from my frozen doze by the sound of a horse's hooves and the clanking and jingling of metal. I peered through the gap between the cell door and the warped wooden doorframe and saw a sight that almost made me burst into laughter.

Outside in the snow Huanapaco, still barefoot, was leading a black horse on top of which was mounted a fully booted and spurred Bolivian naval officer. The officer looked for all the world like Napoleon retreating from Moscow. In one hand he held an honest-to-God saber; on his head he wore a fore and aft commander's cap, complete with feathers and chinstrap. He was shouting at the top of his lungs to a dozen or so filthy, barefoot sailors, the sergeant among them. With some difficulty he dismounted the horse, getting his cape tangled on the lee side of the animal while descending on the windward side. The sailors were not only half frozen to death, they were scared stiff. Laying the flat of his saber against the sergeant's shoulder, he yelled at him to open the door. A second later a cold, snowy wind blasted in and I was a free man again.

"Commander Raimundo Antonio de Valdez, Bolivian Navy, at your service, *Señor.*" He grabbed my frozen mitt and shook it vigorously.

"Captain Tristan Jones, Liverpool Tramway Driver's Club, at yours," I replied. Then I collapsed into Huanapaco's arms.

Minutes later, when I had recovered enough, the officer addressed me again. "On behalf of the Navy of the Republic of Bolivia, it gives me great pleasure to welcome to our shores the first ocean vessel to visit them." On and on he went, ". . . our right to the sea is indisputable. . . ." Finally he wound up with something that really perked my ears up, "and it would give us ineffable pleasure if you would do the honor of dining with us in the officers' mess." Honor! Dine? If we had stood there much longer in the freezing wind, I would have eaten his bloody horse! I accepted as gracefully as I could, and he led me up to the barracks, which were lit by oil lamps, for there was no electricity!

Commander de Valdez clumped up the rickety stairs in his shiny riding boots with me following, half-fainting, hungry, and flea-ridden. I looked down at Huanapaco standing out in the snow, trousers rolled up to the knees below his poncho blanket, his pointed woolly cap making him look like a great bronzed elf, his bare arms folded in front of him, bare feet planted wide apart, and winked; he burst out laughing, winked back, and did something he had learned from me, held out his hand with the thumb turned up and the fist clenched. Then he turned on his heel and strode towards *Sea Dart*.

The scene inside the officers' mess was dazzling. There was a great long table with a snowy white tablecloth weighed down with silver and, above, three huge chandeliers, each with at least a hundred burning candles! There were fifty or so officers sitting at dinner, all in full uniform. Steaming tureens of soup sat on the table; a team of sailors carried other dishes into the room. At one side a group of sailors were playing guitars and dancing the *quenas* of Cochabamba, a round dance performed with a handkerchief in one hand and the other perched on the waist. It was a sight to see these shaven-headed, Siberian-looking sailors, real tough nuts, prancing around in their shabby rough blue serge as if they were the Royal Ballet Company.

I sat down at the place of honor, at the head of the table, every nerve in my weary body strained towards those steaming tureens, towards the smell of hot, cooked food. When the eating commenced I tore at each course, soup, fish, meat, cake, like a famished seabird.

After dinner (washed down with fine Chilean wines), speeches were made about the historic occasion. The Bolivians were honored to welcome me after such a tremendous voyage (they had known of my approach; the La Paz newspapers had been informed, belatedly it seems, by Reuters in Lima). Then the speeches of welcome tapered off and it became clear that I was expected to reply.

I stood up, rather groggily, and told them how gratified I was by their welcome and hospitality, how pleased I was that the first ocean vessel to visit them was British, and how I looked forward to cruising in their country for a few months before making my way back down to the Pacific Ocean. Finishing up with a rousing "Long Live Bolivia!" I sat down to enthusiastic applause.

The commander then approached me and asked if there was anything I needed.

"Yes, *Señor*, a good hot bath and a gallon of disinfectant!"

This brought the house down. The commander flicked his fingers at one of the sailors, who came running over at the double. Ten minutes later I was in a coal-scuttle bath, a genuine piece of Victoriana, probably made in Birmingham, soaking in hot water brought over in relays in huge kettles straight from the galley stove.

After my ablutions, back in the mess, the commander buttonholed me again. "Captain, about getting back to the Pacific Ocean through Chile, I'm afraid this may not be possible. You know that the political situation there is very tense since the demise of Allende?" I nodded. "Well," he continued, "the frontier has been closed tight for two months and I cannot foresee its opening again this year. You had better plan to go back down through Peru, the same way you came."

Peru! Where I was wanted for smuggling a bloody ocean-going vessel, where they demanded three thousand dollars import tax, where they would stick me inside a jail and lose the key! Jesus Christ, this was a turn up for the books! I couldn't go forward and I couldn't go back. I was stuck on Lake Titicaca; winter was approaching in five months, the terrible Altiplano winter of the upper Andes, three miles up in the air and ten thousand miles as the bloody crow flies from England. England, my England, I thought, as I staggered back to *Sea Dart*. Oh, to be in England, now that April's here. I fell asleep, exhausted, fucked to the wide.

42
STRANGE ENCOUNTERS

HE MORNING AFTER MY reception at the Bolivian naval base in Tiquina, I was awakened by a razzle-dazzle din of discord. There was such a clamor of noise topsides it made me think that the hosts of hell were descending on Lake Unimarca to claim their own. I quickly dashed for the companionway, still heavy with food, wine, and sleep, and peering through a rain drizzle, saw a remarkable sight. There, standing on the quay, inundated by the rising lake waters, barefoot and as dirty as the guard of the night before, was the *brass band* of the Bolivian navy, complete with bass drum and euphonium, blowing and banging away for all it was worth.

As I emerged, the band leader, looking over his shoulder, nodded his head in greeting so violently he almost shook his epaulettes loose from his shoulders. The bandsmen, amongst whom I spied several of my erstwhile captors, were tunelessly and enthusiastically blowing as hard as the oxygen content of the rarefied air would allow.

Forgetting the rain, forgetting the lack of tea for breakfast, I collapsed back into the cockpit, half with laughter, half in terror at the God-awful racket emerging from what seemed to be an excellent collection of pre-World War I German army orchestral equipment.

Huanapaco, stolid as ever, squeezed through the tiny companionway hatch to stare expressionlessly at the apparitions on the quay. Then, even he started to shake with laughter. Grabbing his arm, I indicated that we should shove off. With the brass band giving their rendition of either the "Dead March" from *Saul* or the "Washington Post" (I wasn't sure which), we slid away from the jetty, hoisted sail, and headed off into the fuzzy distance, where the water joined the sky. I looked back to see the band blowing and banging as heartily and as seriously as ever, with the shako of the conductor bobbing up and down like a cormorant pecking at worms on a mudbank—up, down; up, down; oom-pah-pah, oom-pah-pah. We laughed until noon, as we made our way to the southern extremity of the Lake system, to the port of Guaqui, where lay the office of the Bolivian customs service, almost *sixty miles* inside Bolivian territory! *Sea Dart* was, at least temporarily, legal again, for at the naval base the night before, the officer of the day, by the light of the single candle in the operations room, had written out for me, with a quill pen, a laissez-passer for Bolivian waters, until such time as I should arrive at the customs office.

Down in the great sprawling cities, there were millions of neon lights flashing, there were computers chattering, there were jet planes and telephones and taps with water running out of them, and subway trains, telegraph, and telex systems, and drains, and garbage disposal units and the thousand and one other miracles, good and bad, that make up the twentieth century. Meanwhile, in Bolivia, the only ship entry registered in all the time that country has been in contact with the rest of the world, the *permiso*, was written by *candlelight with a quill pen*!

As the sun climbed overhead, the rain cleared up. Soon *Sea Dart* was scooting along, with the wind on the starboard quarter, past the islands of Anapia, Taquiri, Suana, Suriqui, and Quebraya, overtaking sailing luggers loaded with produce heading for the market at Tiquina, the inter-island trading center.

We passed the beautiful headland of Santa Rosa, where the conquistadors had built a very pretty little church, one of the few still in good repair on the Lake. Near the shore we could see far off the snowy peaks of the Andes through the green leaves of the eucalyptus trees. These eucalyptus trees are not indigenous, but were introduced from abroad and were found to be the only nonnative tree which could withstand the sudden and profound temperature changes of the rigorous Altiplano climate.

When we reached the bay of Guaqui the wind failed us, and Huanapaco and I took turns sculling the nine miles into port. For me it was a lung-bursting exercise, but good for purging my system of the effects of the previous night.

Guaqui is the only other land access to the Lake apart from Puno, way back in Peru. Here, there was the same kind of tumbledown jetty as in Puno, the same kind of decrepit hovels, the same kind of mud-baked tracks; yet there was a difference, for this was Bolivia, so the jetty was even more tumbledown, the hovels even more decrepit, the tracks even muddier than in Peru. The town was at siesta, the main plaza deserted, the flag drooping listlessly from the town hall (which looked as if it had last been whitewashed during the Bird-Shit War). Indians, ragged as ever, slept in assorted doorways, while huge flies buzzed around the piles of horse manure along the road.

The customs office was open, but everyone inside was asleep, so Huanapaco and I settled ourselves on the windowsills to share the siesta. Eventually, after a good two hours of total silence, a cock crowed in the distance, a dog barked, a child cried, a man coughed, then, from somewhere up an alley, a drunken Indian whooped. Siesta was over. In the office all eight of us stirred ourselves, rubbed our eyes, stretched our arms, and recommenced the business of keeping the lifeblood of Bolivia flowing through the pulsing vein of Guaqui.

The large, fat man behind the desk was obviously the boss (only bosses wax fat in the Altiplano). He stared at me for a full two minutes, while clearing out his starboard ear, evidently with the intention of improving his understanding of what I might have to say. He then shifted his gaze to Huanapaco, who, wooden-faced as ever, returned his stare as only a Quechuan can return a stare. Another pause of a minute or so, the dead silence broken only by the buzzing of flies around the horse-shit along the street outside and a slight rustle as the boss changed the matchstick from one hand to the other and set in on the portside ear; then he spat. Not one of your sissy gringo spits, but a great big "macho" Bolivian gob, which missed one of his henchmen sitting by the door by no more than a millimeter, shot across the paving slaying two flies en route, wheeled over and over, green and glistening in the sunlight, and landed in the exact center of a pile of Bolivian cavalry horse-shit.

Gazing at the almost hypnotic gob of Bolivian phlegm, we ascertained that the horse-shit was, indeed, cavalry horse-shit, for just at that moment a platoon rode by, jingling their reins in the English fashion, gripping their sabers like Germans, fierce-looking, grim-faced, rapacious. After shuffling some papers, the boss looked up at us and snarled.

"*Qué quieres?*" "What do you want?"

"Entry for an English boat, *Señor*, permit to enter Bolivian waters." I shoved my naval *permiso* under his nose. He pawed it down onto the desk to read it, then scribbled his initials on the bottom.

"Very good, *Señor*," he said without glancing up, "you may proceed."

"But what about an entry permit, *Señor*?" He looked at me quizzically.

"What about an entry permit, *Señ*——"

"I said, YOU MAY PROCEED!" He pointed to the door. We shuffled out.

"You heard him, *amigo*, he said we might proceed. You're a witness, okay?"

"Ugh," said Huanapaco, which said everything. Still I had the naval laissez-passer, which was better than nothing.

Out of my diminished money supply, we bought potatoes, fish, tiny tomatoes, and even an onion! Then we headed back for *Sea Dart*, for I wished to sail back to the main lake of Unimarca and find a decent anchorage before nightfall. I did not fancy staying in Guaqui harbor, for the winds at night blow straight in, very strong, raising a bad sea. Pushing off, we started to row across the nine-mile channel to Santa Rosa. It was only four-thirty, and we had an hour and a half before sunset. Even then there was not much hazard, for the moon would be rising soon after the sunset, and there did not seem to be any off-lying dangers.

At six o'clock, after we had paddled our way out about five miles, we heard the noise of a powerful motor. It was the customs launch, headed in our direction. In a matter of minutes it was alongside of us, with the boss in the wheelhouse yelling, "Drop your sails, pass a line. You're going back in!"

I looked at Huanapaco, nonplused. "Do as he says,

amigo," I told him and in a trice all the sails were handed and a line passed quickly to a grim-faced henchman on the customs launch. Revving up her powerful engine, she set off with *Sea Dart* under tow astern, at high speed, twelve knots or so. All I could do was steer my boat in the wake of the launch, and hope the launch would not drag *Sea Dart*'s foredeck out of the boat. "What in the name of jumping Jesus am I arrested for *this* time?" I wondered.

Fifteen minutes later we arrived back in Guaqui. The launch cast off *Sea Dart* so that we could steer towards the jetty and tie up. Then we sat there on deck, awaiting the worst. The boss and four of his biggest henchmen approached us with heavy steps. A most alarming phenomenon in Bolivia, where an aimless shuffle is more the rule. Then the boss looked down at us. We looked back at him, and he broke into a wide smile and stretched his arms out towards me.

"*Señor*, a thousand apologies, I did not realize you were on a boat. All the way from England. Mother of God, you must come and have dinner with us tonight, and we will drink to your arrival, *carraco*! Shit!" He struck his forehead with his fist time and again, repeating *carraco! carraco!* Then he introduced himself and his assistants. Walking back to the office with his arm around my shoulder, he explained that this was the headquarters of the Bolivian Calvary Brigade, a fine army, although unfortunately they'd not won any of the five wars that poor Bolivia had been involved in. "But of course, you understand, *Señor*, wars are not all that armies are for, no?" He grinned as we trudged through the baked mud into the office.

There, until sunset, his assistants played guitars, while the boss, Huanapaco, and I knocked back *chicha*, beer, and made merry conversation, after which we went to dinner in a small, filthy restaurant nearby with peeling gray walls. The reception carried on into the night, ending up with toasts to our respective countries and a promise from the customs boss that we had no worries about papers or "*esta mierda*" in Bolivia. Was he not the boss? From me he extracted a promise not to sail the next day but to honor him with our presence for at least another twenty-four hours.

"Besides," he said mysteriously, "we have some business, you and I." I fell asleep, with the boat surging in a steep sea, wondering what the devil our "business" would turn out to be.

Next day the boss took me to the customs warehouse. There, among piles of rotting potatoes, cases of beer, bolts of cloth, and sacks of flour and sugar, all seized off craft trying to sneak into Bolivia from Peru, he showed me a brand-new diesel engine of American manufacture. He asked me if I knew anything about this particular make. Luckily I did, for I had worked on one just before I left Connecticut. I was able to give him hints on the installation and maintenance of the engine. This delighted him, and he listened as carefully as his pure Spanish blood would allow. He told me that he was going to install the engine in his own personal boat. It was being built with funds garnished from the sale of confiscated contraband, and he would use it for fishing trips. When I asked him how much the engine had cost him, he replied, "Oh, I didn't buy it here; *I smuggled it over from Peru!*"

Later that night, as we prepared to make the evening meal of fried *boga* and boiled yucca, one of the customs henchmen came onboard bearing a tray on which, under a napkin in the usual state of Altiplano hygiene, lay two succulent meals of chicken and boiled potatoes! For the first and, up to now, only time in over twenty-five years of cruising in over a hundred different countries, my dinner was sent onboard to me by the local customs service!

Before we sailed from Guaqui the following morning, the customs boss came down and, in the course of his long farewell speech, advised me to head for Huatajata, the site of the Bolivian Yacht Club. A yacht club at three miles above sea level? This I had to see. With a good stiff southwesterly breeze, *Sea Dart* returned to the main stretch of Unimarca Lake and headed east past many lovely islands scattered under brilliant sunshine. At Puerto Perez I anchored for lunch and dropped off Huanapaco, who started overland to see his father, Huanameni. He disappeared over the hill, still rigged in the same gear he had worn the night of the snowstorm at Tiquina.

After lunch, alone again, I weighed anchor with some difficulty, for it was fouled in a great tangle of sunken reeds. The run to Huatajata and the "Yacht Club" was short and fast. Bowling along on a beam reach, I soon arrived off the small jetty, nestled behind a thick bed of totora reeds, through which had been cut a passage wide enough to admit small craft. I worked my way in through the passage with the wind astern, under jib only, sheet and halyard ready to let go as soon as I was within drifting distance of the jetty. *Sea Dart* came alongside as sweet as a nut; I stepped off, trying to look casual, for there was an audience of white men, one of whom was standing on the jetty. He helped me tie the mooring lines, then rose and shook my hand. Bowing, he introduced himself in Spanish, with a very German accent.

"Dr. Boehm. On behalf of Bolivian yachtsmen, welcome to the Club. We heard that you were in Guaqui through the customs service in La Paz, and we persuaded the customs chief there to delay your sailing until today, Saturday, so that many of the members could come along and welcome you. Kindly step this way."

He led me up a flight of wooden steps, overgrown with weeds. As I pulled myself up the rough cedar handrail I looked around. At the top of the steps were about thirty men, all looking very German, with closely cropped heads, rimless glasses, sober yachting clothes, and the blue peaked caps so beloved by Teutons. They were drawn up in a line, the tallest at one end, the shortest at the other, like a set of rum measures. Around the grassy sward in front of the one-story club building with its barred windows was something I had not seen since the Panama Canal Zone—a chain-link fence. On top of that were six strands of barbed wire. Patrolling this Siegfried Line were two men with huge German police dogs on thick chromium-plated chains. The two patrolmen wore brown uniforms with jodhpur type trousers, peaked caps, and *jackboots*. Their costume was completed by a Sam Browne belt worn around the left shoulder and, dangling from a leather belt at the waist, a *dagger in a sheath*!

Astounded, I passed up the line of "Yacht Club members" with Dr. Boehm gripping my elbow. Each one, when introduced, bowed stiffly and clicked his heels. One or two of the handshakes had a touch of warmth, the rest felt like dead flounders. Every one of them had a heavy German accent, while several had beetling brows and looked something like Rudolf Hess. Near the end of this lineup, a particularly Aryan-looking creature grunted at me in English, "British navy, *nein?*"

"Yes, sir, pleasure to meet you and hear English," I replied.

"I killed many British sailors," he retorted.

"Oh, really, what ship were you in, sir?"

"*Scharnhorst.*" He drew himself up even more stiffly.

"Oh, I see. I was in H.M.S. *Chieftain* myself. Let's see, we sank you, in 1942, wasn't it?" His face showed a twist of hatred which would make an Aymara envious. I passed to the next member.

At the far end of the line, Dr. Boehm gave a speech, in Spanish, about how pleased they were to welcome the first boat ever to arrive from Europe in the Lake, etc., etc., and wound up inviting me to the German Club any time I should visit La Paz. In reply I gratefully accepted and reflected on how grand an experience it was for me to meet so many *Bolivian* yachtsmen so soon after my arrival in *their* landlocked country, and how I hoped that *their* country, Bolivia, would soon regain access to the sea, so unjustly lost to their aggressive neighbor Chile, which, egged on by a megalomaniac dictator, had invaded peaceful neighbors without warning, trampling on the sacred soil of Bolivia with jackboots and bayonets. Why, Chile was almost as bad as a certain European country which, thirty years ago, had run riot, a wolf among the lambs.

By this time the faces of the "members" were livid, but I continued in the same vein for a good ten minutes, to the vast amusement of the native Bolivian club staff, who had gathered to see the reception. I finished up by saying that I hoped that when Bolivia did return to the sea, she would not, as certain people in Europe had, use it to bring misery, death, and destruction to so many honest sailormen!

I left the panzer battalion glaring after me in dead silence
and descended the steps, followed by *Herr Doktor* Boehm,
who was now, in contrast to half an hour previously, somber
and silent. I thanked him for the welcome, climbed onboard
Sea Dart, and cast off. As I hoisted the sails outside the reed
bed, I looked back to see the "members" still lined up at
attention, listening to Dr. Boehm's harangue.

Later, I felt a bit guilty about my broadside, for I had
coldly lost my temper in reaction to the man's cruel remark
about the *Scharnhorst*. I have many very respected and ad-
mired friends in Germany. I have visited that country several times and have been treated with nothing but
camaraderie among the yachtsmen and friendlinesss from
the Germans as a whole. In Germany itself, such conduct as
this man had shown me would be totally unthinkable. All
those old wounds healed long ago in Europe, at least among
the seamen I know.

Afterwards, I found out that many of these men were
survivors from the German battleship *Graf Spee,* which scut-
tled herself in the River Plate rather than fight three much
smaller British cruisers. On weekends they roared around
that part of the Lake in their power-craft, looking for all the
world, with their pea jackets, riding boots, and peaked caps,
like members of the *deutsche Kriegsmarine,* vintage 1941.

As I worked *Sea Dart* into Cachilaya creek just before
dusk, I was astonished to see a mighty crowd of Indians
waiting on the foreshore and in boats at anchor. There must
have been a thousand of them, men in their *chorros* and
unkus, ponchos and bare feet, women in bright blankets and
bowler hats, and children dressed just like their parents,
little chubby dolls with blue-veined cheeks.

There was excitement in the air as I slowly sculled the
boat into a reed bed. On the foreshore, standing with a
group of elders, I discerned the figure of Huanapaco,
stolid, feet apart, arms akimbo, grinning, just as he had
looked when the Bolivian officer had released me from the
frozen fleapit of Tiquina! I remember thanking God the
wind was blowing onshore towards the Indians. Then
Huanapaco and the elders pushed off in a small boat towards me.

43

DANCES AND SKELETONS

UANAPACO WAS THE FIRST to clamber onboard. In the Quechua manner he ducked his head in greeting and grasped my forearm. "Captain, these are the headmen of my people; Manco Chenua, the alcalde."

A man of about forty-five stepped forward, smiling. He was wearing a western style jacket, ragged but fairly clean, over the usual rough-spun *unku* shirt. Around his waist was a woven llama wool belt of a dozen colors, tied like a sash. On one finger of the hand which he offered me was a gold ring; in the other hand he held a short whip. One of his teeth was filled with gold. "*Señor*," he said softly, "we have heard many stories of you and your flight, like a sea-bird, from the ocean, over the mountains, to our lake. Welcome to our *ayllu*."

"Welcome, *Señor*. My boat is your boat," I replied.

Next, Huanapaco introduced his father, Huanameni, a man slightly older than the alcalde. He wore the llama wool poncho, thick cotton trousers, and sandals. He shook both my hands, smiling, then looked urgently at Huanapaco. "My father is in the *Illacata* here," the boy said. "He is in charge of the organization of communal labor and the distribution of food and necessities to the old, the sick, and the orphans. He does not think his Spanish is good enough to address you, but he wishes you to know you are as his brother."

The third man was the *llayca,* the medicine man. On his head he wore a multi-colored *chorro* with ear flaps, on the ends of which dangled small silver ornaments, tiny figurines of men and animals, birds and fish. Around his neck was a rosary strung with the same kind of fetishes. Suspended from that was a leather bag, looking much like a Scotsman's sporran, with long streamers of horse-tail hair that dangled to his waist. He wore no poncho. Around his waist was a wide belt of many colors, featuring a pattern of dancing men, fishes, and animals. His trousers were sheepskin, or so they seemed, for the wool was too coarse a fiber to be llama. At his waist hung a dagger, flute, drumstick, and other implements.

All three sat down and courteously accepted a mug of tea. They were overwhelmed with curiosity about the gear in the boat—the echo-sounder, the compass, the galley stove, the oil lamp. They stared around with eyes shining, touching everything with gentle fingers, like Aladdin in the magic cave. When I showed them the chart of the Lake which I was constructing, they were astonished, then highly amused as I picked out the various islands and headlands which they could recognize. As Huanameni later put it, it was as if I had looked down at the world with the eyes of a condor, and written down what I had seen!

As the three headmen took their leave, Huanapaco thrust a basket into my hands, saying it was a gift from the *ayllu*. Uncovering it, I found it was half-full of boiled potatoes and fish! He then said that in the morning the entire clan was to hold a fiesta, and they would perform the *Chacu-Ayllu*, the clan hunting dance, the rain dance of the Quechua, a ritual as old as time itself!

In the morning, to the sound of toads croaking and *chocas* chirping among the reeds, we woke to find a brilliant clear sky. The sun rose like a king over the shoulders of Illimani, the White Water Peak, which was, in the early morning shadow, sitting like a ghost on the eastern edge of the roof of the world. As we ate breakfast, the remains of last night's feast, the silence of the morning was shattered by the noise of an engine. I looked ashore to see an ancient truck lurching down the rocky path, loaded with crates, on top of which were perched several of Huanapaco's fellow clansmen. "Beer, from La Paz" was all he said.

"This early?"

"Yes, they set off yesterday morning, as soon as I brought them news that you were coming."

"But that load must have cost a fortune!"

"We are not poor people. We have our methods."

By the time the black shadows of the mountains were

changing to purple and silver, all the beer had been unloaded on the grass clearing between the village and the
beach. Half an hour later the dancing commenced. There
was a band of flutes and drums, trumpets and tambourines,
cymbals, bells, a huge gong. The medicine man, recognizable even under his devil mask, rattled the llama bones.

Most of the men of the *ayllu* were rigged up in weird
costumes made of satin and sequins, with knee-high leather
boots—the finest I have ever seen—of calfskin, also white.
Their masks represented dragons, devils, and one Inca.
Some of the masks represented Spaniards and had little red
faces with white beards and wigs, and one or two had pipes
fixed in the mouths, below huge, round, staring blue eyes.

The first dances were like quadrilles, with the men lined
up opposite the women. They danced forward and back,
never touching, to a monotonous refrain. Then, as the day
wore on, they went into the round dances, the courting
dances, wherein a young man is given the chance to touch the
girl he fancies (and thus commit himself for life), while the
older men throw down the beer and *chicha* and the women
sit, very soberly, to one side, watching the girls and handing
out the food. In the early afternoon, the rain dance began,
with the medicine man, the *llayca*, taunting the devils in a
dance of great intricacy. It finished, after about two hours,
with the devil falling "dead" on the ground, the medicine
man triumphant, and all the other dancers reeling around
him in celebration. It was one of the most strenuous exer-
cises I have ever seen, hour after hour of wild gyrations. By
dusk all the men except the alcalde, who had a tremendous
capacity for *chicha,* were dead drunk, staggering around
cheerfully. Yet when the dance of moon-welcome started,
the *mamula*, almost all of them seemed to sober up enough
to dance the complicated steps in unison. Two hours after
the sun went down, there was not a sound to be heard
except for the snoring of the single men who had collapsed
in the clearing—the wives having carried the husbands
home.

Sozzled, Huanapaco and I waded out to *Sea Dart* and
poured ourselves onboard.

During the following weeks, *Sea Dart* cruised the islands

of Lake Unimarca, sounding the depths, exploring remote bays, and visiting different communities. April and May passed. On the island of Quebraya, difficult to reach in a reed-choked, shallow bay, Huanapaco and I explored an ancient necropolis crowded with stone tombs. The island was approximately three kilometers long by half a kilometer wide, and it was full of very old remains. The tombs were built of stones fitted closely together without mortar. They were three stories high, and the skeletons inside were *standing up*, most of them with their faces looking through a small window pointed directly, and very accurately, to the east.

Inside the tombs were many remnants of cloth preserved by the ultra-dry climate. There were little baskets, some containing small bronze figures, others *seashells*. In many there were bows and arrows, spears and other weapons, such as tiny axes and clubs.

The entrance to the tombs behind the door-stones was piled with clay pots, some of which still contained what looked like the remains of maize and yucca. I took bearings all around to fix the position of the island and its treasure. Huanapaco had been very reluctant to go ashore there, for the Indians have a dread of spirits. Later he told me that he had heard of this place and that no one had ever gone there since time immemorial. I personally believe that it is old enough to have been connected in some way with the Tiahuanaco civilization, because there is no sign of a burial place around the mighty stone temple.

Later, when I visited La Paz, I met the director of the National Museum. I asked her about the island of Quebraya. She'd never heard of it, nor of the necropolis. Excited by what I told her, she arranged for a party of archaeologists and historians to visit the site and for the government to set a guard on these priceless ruins. Quebraya is, in a straight line, only eighty miles or so from La Paz, yet among the urban Bolivians it was completely unknown. An island of about twenty-five square miles, full of pre-Inca treasures! (I took only one small bronze figurine.) So far as I know, it is the only place in South America where human remains are found in a standing position, at attention—at least until the "yachtsmen" of Huatajata are finally put to rest!

44

A TRIP TO TOWN

URING THE TIME *SEA DART* had been sailing among the islands of Unimarca, from mid-February until the end of June, I had been busy, apart from surveying the remote passages and bays, writing articles and sending them off to nine countries. These works started their journeys to England, Australia, Germany, and the United States on a reed balsa craft paddled or sailed to Cachilaya by Indians in *chorros* and ponchos! From Cachilaya the weekly truck would rattle over the rocky roads of the Altiplano, in the wan winter sun a bowl of limpid light, to the city of La Paz, eight hundred feet lower than the Lake, and from there they went on to the outside world.

By now, I had worked out a possible solution to the problem of getting back to the ocean. The frontier with Chile was still closed and the new military government there was showing signs of violent reaction. Any foreigner, regardless of political coloration or purpose, was liable to be thrown into the nearest concentration camp. Chile was out. Peru, also, was out. If I was to get *Sea Dart* back to the ocean, I would have to go *east, across the continent*!

Studying the map, I found two possible routes. Both involved hauling the boat, by some means, right across the high and mighty Cordillera Real. Once across that barrier, there were three alternatives. One was to try to get to the headwaters of the River Beni, and from there sail downstream for thousands of miles back into the Amazon via the Madeira River. Eventually this idea faded, for no one knew if there were rapids to negotiate or not. All the information that I could get was that the Beni and the Madeira were about the worst, wildest, most insect-ridden, hellish places in the whole South American jungle.

The second alternative was to haul to Santa Cruz, a town

800 miles away on the other side of the Andes, down at the edge of the Chaco Desert, and from there ship the boat by rail all the way south to Buenos Aires. But I ruled this out, for the cost was way beyond anything I could hope to earn in the short time before winter set in.

The third alternative seemed to be the only one that gave me a fighting chance of getting through at a reasonable cost. This was to ship the boat by rail from Santa Cruz east across the Chaco Desert to the Brazilian frontier in the state of Mato Grosso, and from there head downstream on the River Paraguay for about 2,000 miles to the Plate estuary.

No one could tell me for sure if this third alternative was practical, for no one had ever done it before. No one knew anything at all beyond Santa Cruz, though there were rumors. One of these rumors was that the railroad from Santa Cruz did actually arrive at the Paraguay, and that there was a small port on the river with a jetty and a crane. When I discussed these things with the embassy staff, or in the Bolivian railroad company's offices, or in La Paz or anywhere else, people answered politely, noncommittally, all the while looking at me as if I were completely crazy.

Once I had made the decision to try the Mato Grosso route, I set to work writing in order to get together the five hundred dollars or so that would be needed for the haulage costs and in dribs and drabs the money trickled into the bank in La Paz.

In the meantime, I spent very little on food and other necessities. As the winter crept in we just did without, apart from the odds and ends that Huanapaco could bring in from the meager stocks in Cachilaya. But, sparse as it was, it was enough to keep us alive. Potatoes, yucca, and, very rarely, for it was bitterly cold on the Lake, a small *boga* fish or some beans. Mostly it was potatoes and yucca, a root something like a turnip, which tastes like and has the same texture as the inside of a golf ball.

We sat in the boat, blankets over our shoulders, trying to warm up by the heat of a tiny oil lamp, me writing, Huanapaco dozing. Now and again we went out into the frosty air to tend the fishing lines hung over the side, but by now most of the fish were in the deeper waters. Many times there would be three feet of snow topsides, but that was welcome, for it helped keep the bitter wind off the marine-ply hull.

In the last week in July, I determined to go into La Paz to see how the funds stood at the bank. It was quicker to go myself along the arduous road, for a letter would take just as long and a reply might never reach me.

Leaving Huanapaco's father to guard the boat, we set off for the main road, about seven miles inland. There we waited for one of the few trucks to pass. With the snow flurrying down, there was small chance of a lift. The first day we waited by the trackside, and at dusk returned the seven cold miles to Cachilaya. In the morning we again waded and sloshed through the thick snow to the road and waited all day, but there was not one single truck. Again we returned to the boat. On the third day we were in luck, for around noon along came a wagon bristling with sailors grasping rifles. In charge was Commander de Valdez, the same officer who had released me so dramatically from the fleapit at the navy base!

He sprang out of the truck cab and greeted me with effusive warmth. "Of course we can carry you into La Paz, no problem, climb up, Tristan, *vamos*!" He was off, he said excitedly, to take this platoon of mariners down to the small port of Trinidad, on the River Mamoré, deep in the Bolivian jungles, on the other side of the Amazon. They would be there inside a week. Of course we could have a lift, were we not all sailors, with the comradeship of the sea? *Vamos*! He jumped back into the cab, out of the freezing wind. Huanapaco and I climbed onto the truck-bed, thick with driven snow.

Our fellow passengers were about forty shaven-headed, filthy, barefoot sailors. In charge was our old friend, the squat sergeant, who glared at me as menacingly as ever. I gave him a grin and a nod; he farted and spat over the side of the truck. Whenever we came to one of the few inhabited places on the bare, moonlike surface of the Altiplano, the sailors would growl and gesture with their rifles at any poor soul who happened to be out in the snow.

I pulled the earflaps of my tank-driver's cap down, and

hauled my scarf up around my ears and nose, but I was still cold. The wind, when the truck was moving, was like a thousand sailmaker's needles penetrating the three pullovers and thick Norwegian sailing jacket I was wearing. Huanapaco, with his blanket wrapped round him and his *chorro* pulled down, but with bare legs and feet, seemed not to notice. I was not surprised at this, for I had often seen him and many other Indians standing in the freezing waters of the Lake, fishing for hours on end, when I could barely keep my hand in the same water for more than a minute. In dealing with thin oxygen or cold, the Andes Indians surpass any other race I've ever been in contact with, including the Eskimos, for hardiness.

When the truck reached the escarpment overlooking the city of La Paz, it slowed to a crawl. Indians crowded the crossroads in a seething mass. Huanapaco edged closer to me. "I do not think the commander was telling the truth, Captain."

"About what?"

"The sailors."

"What makes you think that?"

"If they were going to the jungle they would carry much baggage, food, stores, clothes." He pointed at the heap of ammunition boxes piled at our feet.

"Maybe, Huanapaco, they have a depot in La Paz, where they pick up their stuff before they go on to Trinidad."

"Yes, Captain, and maybe the llama dances and the toad sings."

As we approached the airfield, the highest regular airfield in the world, all hell broke loose. The air force sniped away at us with rifle fire from behind huts and ditches. The truck whizzed away, with the sailors firing indiscriminately astern, for we were long past the airfield. Huanapaco and I lay flat on our stomachs on top of the ammunition boxes!

The squat sergeant smashed his rifle butt into the backs of several sailors who were still firing to make them cease. I turned to Huanapaco. "As soon as this fucking truck stops, my friend," I said to him, "off we go. You go over the stern, I'll go over the side. Then run like hell!"

"Right!" he whispered. We bounced down into La Paz

over the cobblestones, until the truck finally halted.

I went over the side of the truck in one bound, slithering on the icy pavement. As I ran for the nearest side street, I realized we were in the main plaza of La Paz. From the Air Ministry, a hundred yards away, firing was intense. The sailors were now firing more methodically, for the commander had clambered up over the side of the truck, revolver in one hand, saber in the other, shouting "*Hijos de putas, carraco!*" I ran straight up a narrow, cobblestoned alleyway between single-story cottages. How I managed to keep up the speed in the rarefied air of La Paz is a mystery, but the stray bullets ricocheting off nearby walls were certainly an encouragement. Right behind me came Huanapaco. Even though he was one of the fastest runners I have ever seen, I beat him to the top of the hill! We collapsed into an Indian *chicha* bar, laughing wildly, even though I could barely catch my breath.

Later, we found out that the Bolivian Air Force had attempted to seize power from the president, General Hugo Banzer Suárez. But he, a courageous man, had parachuted alone onto the air base and single-handedly quelled the rebellion! This outbreak was not out of the ordinary in Bolivia, where revolution has been, ever since Independence, the order of the day. In less than two hundred years there have been more than two hundred governments! In 1946 they hanged their president naked from a lamppost.

These revolutions are generally a matter of conflict among small groups of the ruling class and do not affect the lives of the Indians, except when they are drafted to do the fighting; but even then they scarcely know (or care) which side they are on.

We slept that night on benches in the tiny, dirty, Indian bar, along with a dozen or so others who were seeking refuge from the cold and uncertainty outside.

In the morning I called at the British embassy to pick up my mail. There, among a few letters from London, Sydney, and Boston, was a message. The president of the Republic had heard, through the Commission for Maritime Action, that I would probably be passing through La Paz shortly with my boat. Would I please send details and dates in order that a proper reception might be arranged? Would I! A man who would parachute alone into a nest of mutinous rebels was a man I had to meet!

Also at the embassy I picked up a long-awaited package, a box full of cricket gear—two bats, half a dozen balls, kneepads, wickets, and a hat for the umpire. All sent free by friends in Britain in response to an urgent request. Back at the Lake I had been showing the Indians how to play cricket. They were coming on very well, though now and again they would, when bowled out, try to bash the bowler's head in with the crude bats we were using. Still, they were slowly but surely learning the rules of the game, and the idea of fair play was seeping gradually into their skulls. Now we had the proper equipment!

At the bank I found I now had the amount necessary for the haul across to the Mato Grosso. I went back to Cachilaya elated. It took three freezing days to get back, but I had the dollars, I had some mail, we had escaped being shot, and I had the cricket gear!

45

TOUCH AND GO

RUISING AROUND THE ISLAND
I learned how the reed boats were
constructed. The reeds are bound
together, then pounded into the
shape of a lashed hammock. Three
of the bundles are then tied together with a cord made from *pala,*
a tough grass which grows only a few
feet from the beach. Into each balsa
goes a surprising number of reeds, something like half a ton
in weight. It takes, on average, three men one week, working all day, to make one balsa. Once made, it is about the
most stable and safest craft afloat. I have often seen a balsa
ride out a full storm with two or three people onboard,
remaining upright no matter how high the seas (and
Titicaca can at times blow up as rough as the English Channel in a southwesterly gale). One tale was told to me of a
balsa being cut in two by a Bolivian navy gunboat charging
at high speed across the Strait of Tiquina on a dark night.
The Indians merely clung to one of the hammock-like hull
members and held on. In the morning they were picked up,
safe.

While the hull is being made, another "balsa master"
makes the nets for catching fish, mainly the *boga*, which is
the staple food on the islands. Some of the women work on
the shelter, which protects the fishermen from the wind
and rain and is also made from totora reed, while others
make the mooring line and the line for the stone anchor
from *pacha*, another tough, hemp-like fiber. The balsas
have a life of about six months; after that they become
waterlogged. The lines and cords, if still good, are saved
and a new balsa is made. The old one is left on the beach to
rot and is later used as fertilizer.

Propulsion of the balsa is either by lattice sail, a square
contraption also made of reed, or by a single oar set in a
carved wooden rowlock. A good oarsman can achieve a

surprising speed.

More interesting and rewarding to me, however, was a visit to the island of Suriqui, where the lug-sailed sloops are built. I anchored in the beautiful bay and ran a long line ashore as a safeguard against the *supay*, the devil wind which comes down off the heights at enormous strength and can drag the anchor and blow the boat clear across the Lake. The Aymara of Suriqui have the curious habit, or maybe not so curious, of stationing one of the clan on the top of the mountain which comprises most of their beautiful island with a trumpet. When he sights the *supay* clouds way out in the distance, he blows the trumpet to scare the devil and make him change direction.

I had been in Suriqui several times to watch the construction of one of these sloops. They are about fifty feet long and built of cedar wood on eucalyptus frames. The cedar wood comes from the jungles of eastern Bolivia and is well seasoned. It makes an admirable building material. The frames are cut to shape using an adz. The work is very rough, but the hull shape is beautiful, except for the stern, which is a nailed-on, botched-up mess. Despite the surliness of the Aymara, I stayed on the island several times. During my talks with Quispe, their chief boat-builder (through Huanapaco, for he spoke no Spanish), I had been able to show him, as I had shown others on the Lake, how to rig the boats so that they would go to windward. After that we had got on together reasonably well.

One day in early May I returned from Quispe's hut to the beach and found that *Sea Dart*'s long mooring line, the safeguard against the *supay*, was missing. Someone had stolen it! This is about the worst crime anyone can possibly commit against a sailor. Rob him in port; charge him twice the going price for his stores; hit him on the head with a bottle; screw him to hell and back; but never, *never* steal his mooring lines!

My blood was up; Aymara or no Aymara, savages or no bloody savages, I was going to have this out. I struck out for the boat and retrieved my cutlass. Back on shore I strode up to the settlement. Huanapaco was worried and grabbed hold of my arm; "Captain, these are bad people; there are too many of them," he pleaded.

"The bastards have stolen my nylon line—*hijos de putas*!"

"Don't do anything, Captain, for the love of God. Let me go and call the *ayllu* together, *por favor*!"

"Fuck the *ayllu*, let me get at the sod who's got my line!" I broke free, shrugging him off, and carried on up the muddy path.

"But if they hurt you, then it will mean a war between Cachilaya and Suriqui!" he shouted after me.

"Oh, Christ, all right then, *carraco*! But you tell that mother-fucking chief, Manco Quispe, I want a clan meeting right now. I don't give a shit about the sun going down, I want that syphilitic *hijo de mariconita*, that son of a little fairy, down here on the bloody beach. Him, the *Illacata*, the *corregidor*, the whole blasted shooting match. But I don't want the fucking *llayca*. He can shove his bloody fetishes up his ass. Just keep him out of this!"

"But, Captain, they won't hold a clan meeting without the *llayca*!"

"Huanapaco, you get up that sonofabitch of a hill and get them down here. If you don't I'm going up there and if I catch the bastard who's got my rope, I'll have his bloody guts for breakfast!"

Huanapaco went, reluctantly. A crowd began to form in the village clearing, laughing and jeering.

Five minutes later he was back, accompanied by the *corregidor*, or constable.

"What do you want, *Señor*?" he asked in a whining tone.

"I want you to go back and tell Manco Quispe that I am waiting here for a clan meeting. Someone has stolen my mooring line, and I want that someone found and punished!"

"It is my job to deal with theft on this island, I am appointed by the *ayllu*."

"Then either bring the thief to justice or bring the alcalde to me!"

He turned on his heel and climbed up the road. I knew he was playing for time, hoping that he could delay me until the sun set, after which no meeting could be called.

Minutes later, with a face like a wet night in Aberdeen,

the alcalde appeared. Truculently, he asked what was the matter. I explained what had happened.

"None of my people have taken your line," he grunted.

"I want a meeting. I want a promise from the *ayllu* about strangers visiting this island."

"Impossible," he replied, stamping his feet on the ground.

I insisted, I cajoled, I threatened to go to the government in La Paz; I promised never to let this matter rest, even if I had to pursue it for the rest of my days. In the end, he gave way.

The Aymara gathered formally round the clearing in their tribal groupings, about five hundred of them. Many of them were glowering as we walked between them to the meeting stone, from which the chief would address them. Many carried the favorite Aymara fighting weapon, a wicked whip with a tomahawk in the handle, which they shook threateningly as we passed. Inside, I was shaking almost as much with apprehension as with anger, but I knew I had to brazen the thing out.

In the clear space at the center, surrounded by the Aymara, the four of us stood—the chief, the *Illacata*, Huanapaco, and myself. Speaking slowly, so that Huanapaco could translate from Spanish into Aymara, I told them that I had come to their island in peace. I wanted nothing from them; I had touched nothing on the island; I had taken nothing from the island; I had come to see how the boats were built. Huanapaco was my friend; he, too, had done nothing against the Aymara. We had not looked with covetousness on anything they had. We had not insulted their women; we had not walked abroad after sunset; we had respected their customs; we had saved two of their men from drowning when their boat overturned. Why, then, the theft of my line, the line which safeguarded my craft from the devil wind? Why the jeers? Why the insults? If any one of them, any one, wished to fight me alone, then let him speak up now. I had my weapon (I shook my cutlass in the air), and they had theirs.

There was silence. I looked around hoping to Christ no one would take me up, for a tougher mob of cutthroats cannot be imagined. Silence. I waited, then I demanded that the thief step out. No reply. I called the thief a coward, not fit to sit with the women. Their faces cracked when they heard this, some even grinned. I carried on, looking toward the group of women gathered to overhear us at the side of the crowd. "Maybe it *was* a woman. Maybe she wanted to tie her skirts up?" More of them broke out into guttural laughter. "Maybe she wanted to tie a man up to her, maybe she couldn't keep him any other way?" By now they were laughing uproariously. "Maybe she, this desperate woman, wanted to tie *two* men up; one man was not enough for her insatiable appetite?" By now Huanapaco could hardly get the Aymara words out for laughing; the whole place was ringing with mocking laughter. Suddenly there was a stir at the back of the assembled crowd and a man was pushed roughly through. He fell on his face at the feet of the alcalde, where he whimpered and groveled in the dried mud.

The alcalde spoke to the thief, then with a tremendous kick on the head, sent him rolling to one side. He then turned to me and told me that this man had admitted stealing my line and that he would be banished from the island forever. I asked about his family. The alcalde told me that they would be looked after by the *ayllu*.

It was touch and go as Huanapaco and I walked back through that armed crowd to the boat. When we got there I sat down and wrote out for them the last treaty made between American Indians and a white man in the Western Hemisphere.

> The community of Suriqui, united in assembly, has taken a promise not to molest any foreign citizen who is on this island.
>
> This promise is signed by the Secretary General, the *Corregidor*, and the Secretary of the Community, and the community as a whole promises never again to molest any person from outside this island.

They signed, and we sailed back to Cachilaya. I asked Huanapaco what the alcalde had said to the Aymara after the thief was given up. "He said that you were a true man. He has seen many strangers come to the island since he was a boy. Some had come in war, some in peace. Some had come in rags, some in suits of gold, with gold in their hands. None of these had he respected. But you had come only in rags, only in peace; you had only given, not taken. You had come on a voyage they could not even think of, through many dangers and perils. And you had not been afraid of all these warriors, even though they had laughed and jeered and shown anger; you are their Captain; and your feet will never be turned away from Suriqui!"

"Well, fuck him, kicking a man's head like that!" I grunted.

PART FOUR
And Not to Yield

Dear Mam,
   Life is a bastard.
Dear Son,
   So are you.
Dear Mam,
   I didn't know.
Dear Son,
   Nor does your father!

Excerpt from a traditional monologue of forty minutes duration which was always rendered by the oldest man present at the Royal Navy "Sods' Operas," or stag parties. It concluded as follows:

Leader: And now, gentlemen, we has the Fukawi Tribe.
Audience: The Fukawi Tribe?
Leader: Yes, gentlemen, the Fukawi Tribe; they lives in the deep jungles of darkest South America. Not one of 'em over four feet tall, an' the grass where they lives grows to eight feet, and they trots at a lopin' pace through the undergrowth on a circular course, an' every now and then the Chief sticks 'is ten-foot spear in the ground, climbs to the top of the shaft, shades 'is eyes from the sun with one hand, peers over limitless miles of sun-bleached eight-foot-high esparto grass, and shouts...
Audience: What does he shout?
Leader: He shouts, "We're the Fukawi!"
Audience: Groans. Then sings:
   Oh my, what a rotten song,
   What a rotten song, what a rotten song,
   Oh my, what a rotten song;
   And what a rotten singer toooo!

46

A RACE AGAINST NATURE

N THE EIGHTEENTH OF August 1974 we got *Sea Dart* underway in the teeth of a raging blizzard from the east. Despite the weather, the whole of the Quechua *ayllu* of Cachilaya turned up on the beach to see us off. They were all gathered around the shit-house I had built on the beach—a deep ditch with three adobe walls and a door around it; tiny, no bigger than a sentry box, with a wooden plank for a seat. It had a view of the Andes for hundreds of miles across the blue Lake. It was not exactly the best plumbing job in the world, but I often thought that it had the finest view of any shit-house on earth. The Indians had started to lay green tree branches around it before I left, and now, as they gathered around, I could see that olive branches and eucalyptus leaves were piled high all around the adobe walls. I asked Huanapaco about this. He told me that the Quechua thought I used the place to meditate on God and to get my ideas on making boats go to windward. They were treating it as a shrine! They thought the place was magic, and none of them would enter it or even look over the door! The women would not go near it. Sure enough, as we slid out from the reed bed, I saw that the women were all positioned well away from the men, who, to show their courage, approached to within a few yards of the shrine. Huanapaco said that only the *llayca* went near it to offer the branches and leaves.

To the shouted farewells of the Quechua, we slid away through the swirling snow and with a stern wind tore across the Lake the forty-odd miles to Guaqui, dead reckoning by compass courses, for I could see nothing through the flurries. It was a freezing cold trip, numbing to the hand, heart, brain, and lungs; but towards nightfall the sky cleared and we entered Guaqui by starlight.

In the morning I went to see the customs boss. I

explained to him that I had arranged for a truck to be sent up from La Paz to carry the boat to Santa Cruz, so that I could ship her by rail over the Brazilian border to the Mato Grosso.

"*Y?*" he said, in the Bolivian fashion. "And?"

"I need some papers to get across Bolivia, for technically I shall be importing the boat into the country while we cross over."

"*Carraco!* No problem, *amigo*. Look, I know you! You are my friend, no? What do you need papers for, eh? I'm the boss here! If I say you can go, then you go. Papers? Papers are for idiots! Besides, you have your naval papers; they'll be good enough, *amigo*. If anyone gets awkward just refer them to me. Hah! If anyone gets too awkward, I'll have him kicked in the ass! *Hijo de puta! Carraco!* Imagine anyone getting shitty with my friend!"

He put his gigantic arm around my shoulder. The garlic on his breath nearly knocked me sideways. Again, as before, he spat at the road, though this time the door was closed against the intense cold.

No matter how much I insisted, he dismissed the idea of an import permission as something beneath contempt. By the time the *chicha* bottle was half-empty, there was no more mention of papers.

In the afternoon the truck arrived from La Paz, bearing a load of tin ingots carried from Oruro, about 150 miles, as the crow flies, from La Paz, but on the Bolivian roads about twice that distance. It had taken the driver, who hailed from Cochabamba, eight days to make the distance because of the icy conditions and snowdrifts!

Compared to Salomon's over in Peru, the truck was positively modern—a Japanese Suzuki. It was in much better condition than the Peruvian Ford. Rather funny, I thought, a British sailing boat crossing the Bolivian Andes on a Japanese truck! The driver's name was Chanko, he was a *mestizo*, half-white, and a teetotaller. Chanko estimated that it would take us around five or six days to cross the mountains if the weather cleared up. By late afternoon on the following day, August nineteenth, we had dropped *Sea Dart*'s mast and lifted her, with the aid of an antique steam

crane, onto the truck. We had a last snifter of *chicha* with the
customs boss and his minions, then set off slowly along the
icy track which led past the immense ruins of Tiahuanaco
to La Paz.

Our first stop, unfortunately, was only 300 yards outside
the port. The truck slid on the ice into a deep ditch full of
snow and frozen mud. Lying at an angle of eighty degrees,
she waited there for two days until a tractor arrived from La
Paz to haul her out. Fortunately, the chocks on the truck-
bed held, so there was no damage to *Sea Dart*. However, it
was damned uncomfortable trying to sleep in her at that
angle, so I arranged a berth in the customs boss's office, on
the very same windowsill we had rested on when we had
first arrived, so many months ago, in the heat of summer.

While I waited for Huanapaco to get through the snowdrifts to La Paz and back with a tractor, I had time to weigh
the situation. *Sea Dart* had done what she had set out from
the West Indies to do—reach the destination of Lake
Titicaca. In addition, she had cruised the Lake for well over
a thousand miles. Now she couldn't get back to the Pacific
Ocean, so she had to go right across the continent to the
Mato Grosso and sail from there a long way down two
ill-charted and wild rivers, the Paraguay and the Paraná.
From the little research I had been able to do about these
two rivers in the library in La Paz and from the many
inquiries I had made of people, it appeared I had a problem. The rainy season in the vast jungles of central Brazil, in
the area of the headwaters of the three great rivers, the
Xingu, the Tapajós, and the Madeira, as well as in the area
where the vast swamp of the Mato Grosso lies, comes
around February and lasts until about the end of May. This
I knew from bitter experience on the Amazon. Now if May
was the height of the floods, then by August or September,
when I reached the Paraguay River, the level of the waters
should be going *down*. Would there be enough water to float
in so far away from the mouth of the river? It was almost a
thousand miles from where it joined the roaring white
waters of the Paraná, *"El Bravo"* as the Argentines call
it—"The Wild One." Already I had been seriously delayed
while getting together enough money for the haul; was the

snow going to delay *Sea Dart* further?

The only thing I could do was hope and pray that the snows would cease, the ice on the mountain tracks melt, and that the river, when we reached it, *if* we reached it over a thousand miles of rough track and railroad, would still be deep enough for *Sea Dart*. It was a desperate gamble, but this was a desperate situation. The great differences in temperature on the Lake between day and night were already beginning to open up the seams in *Sea Dart*'s marine-ply hull. Another year of this, even another few months, and she would be beyond repair!

Eventually the tractor, with Huanapaco perched on one of the mudguards, arrived, and slowly but surely the whole circus was dragged out of the ditch.

Huanapaco brought news from La Paz. The *Acción Marítima*, the Commission for Maritime Action, was waiting for *Sea Dart* to arrive in the capital. They were planning a reception for the first ocean-going vessel ever to visit their city! The *Acción Marítima* is a species of action group which agitates for, and keeps alive hopes of, Bolivia's recovery of her seacoast, lost to Chile in the Bird-Shit War of 1879–84. Now they were going to use the occasion of *Sea Dart*'s passage through the city as an opportunity for propaganda! Well, after that there would clearly be *no* chance of our getting through Chile, even if they did open the frontier!

The members of the *Acción Marítima* would be making speeches in the plaza; there would be a band; the whole thing would be in the newspapers; there would even be a dinner! But I did not get too excited. First of all, we had to *get* to La Paz; second, I was getting to know Bolivia too well to become excited by any kind of intention or promise.

When all was ready, there was another emotional farewell scene, with promises of undying friendship and emphatic denials of the need for import papers. Off we went, to the cheers and guitar-strumming of the whole customs Mafia of Guaqui, plus an assortment of ragged Indians, staring impassively.

By this time the roads had improved, for the ice had melted. I say "improved"—instead of slithery deathtraps they were muddy deathtraps! Most of the time the truck was axle-deep in thick mud. As we arrived outside the main gate of the enclosed temple ruins of Tiahuanaco, the truck slid straight into another ditch! It was the first time an ocean-going vessel had ever capsized within sight of those august ruins, as old, seemingly, as history itself. While a gang of Indians awkwardly levered the truck back onto the road for the agreed-upon price of two dollars, Huanapaco and I wandered around the richly carved temples, awestruck by the artistry, the engineering knowledge, and the faith of the ancient, unknown peoples who erected their temples among the barren rocks of the Andes Altiplano!

After the truck was on the road again, we slid and slithered towards La Paz until, hearts in mouths, perched atop the boat, we descended down into the chasm wherein nestles the city, clinging to the steep gulleys of tiny brooks, which roar away to eventually join my old enemy, the Amazon!

47
HIGH COMEDY

ACH TOWN AND CITY IN Bolivia has its own entry and exit control. Every car, every bus, every truck, every llama that passes in or out has to stop at these *aduanas* to be scanned, prodded, and searched. A gang of men in nondescript civilian clothes, with two-day beards and pistols, comes onboard under the protection of heavily armed, uniformed soldiers. The few cars which are allowed straight through have "respectable" occupants, which in urban Bolivia means prosperous-looking and well dressed.

The buses, too, if they have a gringo onboard, will escape intact and get through with a full cargo. The trucks, however, with their loads of Indians heading for the market with sacks and boxes of produce, must pay the tolls. On three occasions when I traveled into La Paz huddled down in blankets and cargo on the back of a truck loaded with Quechuas or Aymaras, the *aduaneros* came onboard with long pointed spikes, bayoneted the potato sacks, and opened the boxes. On each occasion they extracted a handful of produce, no matter what it was, and simply confiscated it. The Indians watched dourly, saying nothing. Shocked at the brazenness of the stealing, I asked them what they were going to do about it. They shrugged their shoulders, as if to say, "What can one do against acts of God, war, pestilence, fire, and the *aduaneros?*"

The Suzuki truck, with *Sea Dart* sitting atop, screeched to a grinding halt outside the northern gate of La Paz. Out came the local mob, looking like the cohorts of Genghis Khan. The man in charge was dressed in a long, very dirty, green overcoat with a fur collar. It was buttonless and tied across his chest with a rough string. I jumped down onto the icy mud in front of the *aduana* hut; inside, a roaring fire blazed in an ancient-looking potbellied stove. The smell of cooking assailed me.

"What's that?" the *aduanero* asked.

"A boat, English, heading for La Paz, then to Santa Cruz, *Señor*, to get to Brazil," I replied.

"I can see it's not an airplane, *carraco*! Neither does it appear to be a railroad engine, *mierda*! Where are your papers?"

"The customs chief in Guaqui said that I needed no more than this permission from the Bolivian navy." I handed over the document which had been so laboriously scrawled out by candlelight in Tiquina.

The *aduanero* grasped it with grubby fingers and looked at it perfunctorily. "*Este no vale nada, hombre*! This is no good. Where is the entry permit for this boat? *Madre de dios,* you're really in the shit!"

"Look, *Señor*, the customs chief in Guaqui told me that I needed no other papers to cross over. He said that if there was any problem, he was to be contacted."

The *aduanero* slit his eyes. "He said *what*? That *hijo de puta*. He runs Guaqui, he doesn't run La Paz! That dog-shit–eating mother-fucker, who does he think he is! You get the hell back to Guaqui and tell him I, Pedro Francisco Dominguez Lopez, need *papers*!" He pounded his chest with each name.

"But wait a minute, *Señor* Lopez, we have to be in La Paz tomorrow morning. The *Acción Marítima* is organizing a reception for this boat to further the cause of the recovery of the seacoast. The Army is going to stage a parade, there's going to be a crowd of bigwigs there—why even President Banzer himself might turn up!"

"I don't care if Donald Duck and Pancho Villa are coming. You don't get past here!" He was adamant. I put my hand in my inside pocket. His eyes followed it, gleaming. I brought out a hundred-peso note. His paw closed over it. "Well, considering the special circumstances of the case..." He turned his head and addressed Chanko and Huanapaco, who by now were listening intently, along with a crowd of Indian men, women, and children. "Considering the special circumstances, and the fact that *el jefe* himself may want to see you, this time I'll let you through. But next time you come through here with a foreign boat, be damn sure you have your papers!"

We hopped onboard the truck and were off before the *aduanero* could change his mind. As we rumbled over the steep, cobblestone street into the Prado, the main thoroughfare of La Paz, I wondered how long it would be before the next foreign boat passed that particular *aduanero*.

Even as I sat there half-angry, half-relieved, the front end of the truck collapsed. *"Mierda!"* shouted Chanko. *"Carraco!"* spat Huanapaco. The front offside chassis spring had collapsed! Right in the middle of the Broadway of the highest city on earth! Screeching and squealing, the truck pulled over to the side of the road, directly in front of the marvelous old pile of the Spanish colonial cathedral. The usual crowd of silent Indians soon gathered, as well as a vast number of townspeople, all talking ten to the dozen.

"We'll have to stay the night here, Captain," said Chanko, wiping his hands with a rag after he had crawled out from under the chassis. "I can't move it. It'll ruin the axle. I'll take off and stay at my relatives' house. You make sure the truck is guarded, eh?"

"If I guard the boat, I have to guard the truck, eh, Chanko?"

"Ah, *sí*, well, see you tomorrow, *Señor Capitán, amigo* Huanapaco, *buenas noches, hasta mañana!*" In the Bolivian manner he shook hands and was off, leaving us with a broken down truck and *Sea Dart* heeled over at an angle of about fifteen degrees by the cant of the rough cobbled road surface, which looked as if it had been laid by Pizarro himself.

I turned to Huanapaco. The crowd watched and listened intently. The *Pazenos* are probably the most attentive audience in the world. "Huanapaco, if you want to visit your uncle here, off you go. I'll stay with the boat, but on the way back, call at the British embassy and see if there are any letters waiting there for me, yes, *amigo?*"

"Sí, mi Capitán!" Now, in front of the crowd, he saluted, touching his hand to his *chorro*. He was a great one for

building up a situation, especially before an audience, more
so if there were Indians to impress. He turned smartly, in
his ragged blanket and bare feet, shouting, as he touched
his *chorro* again, "*Buenas noches, Dios bendiga, Capitán!*"

The crowd, suitably impressed, stared after him as he
disappeared up the steep hill, glistening with rain in the
thin drizzle.

After an hour of fending off questions from the citizenry
of La Paz, I turned in. The questions from the Creoles were
always the same—they asked them as if by rote. First, where
was I from, where was the boat from? Was I married? Did I
have a family? Did I get lonely? Did I get sick? Where was I
going? Was I a Catholic? How did I manage for money?
Was I rich?

Half an hour after I turned in, a knock came on deck.
Rising, I found a lad of about fifteen, Indian, with bare feet,
chorro, and poncho, peeping over the truck's side, balanced
on the rear wheel.

"*Qué quieres, amigito?*" I asked him.

"*Buenas noches, Señor*. My uncle has sent me down to look
after the truck; I can sleep in the cab."

"Who's your uncle?"

"Chanko."

"How do I know that?"

He dragged out from under his poncho a crumpled piece
of paper. He handed it to me with a filthy, muddy hand.
The fucking Bolivian navy permit! My only protection in
the topsy-turvy land of Bolivia! Chanko must have taken it
with him; then I remembered that when I'd jumped on
board at the *aduana*, I had placed it on the cab front windowsill. Jesus Christ, I'd better be careful! This rarefied air
had a way of affecting one's defense mechanisms!

"Right, *amigito*, into the cab you go! Do you need a blanket?"

"No, I usually sleep outside. *Buenas noches, Capitán!*" He
scrambled into the cab. The temperature was below freezing by now; it was well past midnight.

Up with daylight to make a cup of tea for myself and the
lad. We sipped tea and ate an empanada, small pastries
filled with meat that are sold at little street stands, the

hygienic standards of which would cause apoplexy in the United States. Sitting up in the morning sunshine in the cockpit, out of questioning range, I spied Huanapaco thrusting his way through the gawking crowd of bowler-hatted women, blanketed men, and silent, doll-faced children. He climbed up the side of the truck and dropped heavily into the boat.

"*Buenas*, Huanapaco, what news?"

"*Buenas, mi Capitán*, bad, bad."

"What in the name of Jesus Christ is the matter now?"

"The customs are searching for us. The *aduanero* at the northern control must have told them we have no papers! *Carraco, hijo de puta!*" he spat.

"So what? Look, *amigo*, nip down to the headquarters of the *Acción Marítima* and tell them that we need their assistance. Many of their members are bigwigs. They can pull some strings and get the customs off our backs, no?"

"Good idea, *Capitán*, I'll go now." He jumped down to the cobblestones. I wouldn't leave the boat myself. What would happen if the customs seized her? Where *she* went, *I* went. The *aduaneros* might even be watching her at that moment, waiting for me to leave.

An hour later Huanapaco was back in the cathedral square with the secretary of the *Acción Marítima*, an antediluvian gentleman who looked like Noah. He stared shortsightedly at the truck, then at *Sea Dart*'s bowsprit, poking over the tailboard, then at me, muttering, "*Maravilla, maravilla, el océano, el océano!*" Then he stumbled off into the crowd, poking Indians out of the way with his walking stick.

"What now, *mi Capitán*?" asked Huanapaco.

"We wait, *amigo*."

And wait we did, for *five* days, until Chanko reappeared. With no sign of apology, he gaily informed us that he had been to his home in Cochabamba by bus, over four hundred miles across the Andes and back, to collect money for toys and clothes, which he intended to smuggle back to his hometown for sale!

How the customs never woke to the fact that we were stuck right outside the cathedral main door, on the biggest plaza in La Paz, I will never fathom. During these five days of waiting there was no sign of any action on the part of the *Acción Marítima*.

As Chanko, with a mechanic, worked on the spring repair, a full-scale army brass band turned up. While the front end was being picked up and the greasy, shattered axle-spring replaced, the band blared away in the thin sunshine of August; naval officers in full-dress uniform gave speeches; and President Banzer, a small, middle-aged man who looked like a bank clerk except for his piercing soldier's eyes, presented me, still suffering from shock, with the one and only Bolivian maritime ensign—silk, huge, with red, yellow, and green stripes. Written across it in big, black letters were the words *Bolivia Mayllcu*—Condor of Bolivia!

Still in a state of bewilderment, I asked one of the high naval officers if he could give me a note to take to the customs so that they would write out a permission for *Sea Dart* to pass over Brazil. Certainly, no problem! In a minute it was done. Handshakes all round, and in a trice they were off to do whatever presidents and naval officers do in Bolivia.

I sent Huanapaco off with Chanko's small nephew and the new permit to the customs headquarters. Down came the truck, off the jacks. I paid the mechanic, it being my liability (this was Bolivia), and we were ready to tackle the Andes. The snow had cleared, and we stood a good chance of making Cochabamba, four hundred miles to the east in a wide valley between two massive ranges of snow-covered peaks, in two or three days. I smoked a cigarette, contented.

Within an hour, Chanko's nephew came running back to the cathedral plaza, poncho streaming behind him, *chorro* askew. He was shouting breathlessly, "*Capitán, Capitán!*" He almost ran straight into me.

"*Qué pasa, amigito?*"

"The *aduaneros* have arrested Huanapaco. They're on their way for you and the boat, now. When can you get the truck started?"

"*Madre de dios*," murmured Chanko, crossing himself.

I grabbed him, "*Vamos*, Chanko! Let's get this fucking

circus moving. At least we'll give them a run for their bloody money!"

"And Huanapaco?" he asked, quietly.

"God helps those who help themselves, *amigo*. He'll be all right. It's not the first time he's been inside, I'll bet. Anyway, my duty, as always, is to defend the vessel. He can manage alone; she can't!"

"Right, *Capitán*, then off we go. But *mierda*, what will happen to me and my truck when those *hijos de putas* find my toys and clothes? *Carraco*! *Esos maricones tan gordos, tan feos*! Those fat, ugly queers!"

We climbed onboard and the truck roared off, spewing exhaust into the misty air of the cathedral plaza, rumbling away over the rough, jagged road surface and out onto the Prado. At the end of that scenic avenue, with its park running down the center, we could see the gigantic mass of snow-covered Illimani towering over the town, more than twenty thousand feet high. We sped down the most beautiful main street on earth, hoping no one would see us.

As we pulled out of the town, Chanko was muttering, "*Dios mio, esperamos que el control al sur no sabe nada*! Let's hope the southern *aduana* doesn't know anything!"

48

THROUGH THE CLOUDS

N AMAZING SIGHT MET OUR eyes as the Suzuki rounded the bend at the bottom of the steep hill out of La Paz and screeched to a stop outside the customs control hovel. There stood a Bolivian navy truck. Around the *aduana* sailors armed with rifles were covering the *aduaneros*. In command, gripping his saber in one hand, a pistol in the other, smiling courteously, as befits an *hidalgo* descendant of the conquistadors, stood none other than Commander de Valdez.

Before the truck had stopped, I was walking toward him. He put his pistol away and grasped my hand. "We knew you were having some difficulties, and so we decided to render some small assistance," he explained. "Who knows, one day perhaps you will see on the ocean a Bolivian boat who needs your help. I know you would give it; that's why we are here. You can pass on your way to Cochabamba. When you get there, see my friend, the British consul. She has been in this country most of her life, a formidable English lady. The *aduaneros* will not interfere with you; they are terrified of her."

I told the commander about Huanapaco. He promised to see what he could do about springing him from the customs jail. Over his shoulder I could see my old friend, the squat sergeant, still scowling, not at me this time, but at the *aduaneros*, who, in turn, were scowling at me! I thanked the commander kindly and clambered back to *Sea Dart*'s cockpit. The truck engine started. As we slowly moved away, the commander walked alongside, shouting up to me, "We heard what happened on Suriqui! Bravo! See you in London!" He clasped both his hands over his head, then, remembering the sailors, dropped them and saluted as we pulled away.

I waved at them, holding onto the Bolivian maritime flag,

303

until they dropped out of sight astern and we were off along the modern road that follows the old Inca silver trail from La Paz to Oruro. We were free, at least until Cochabamba.

The road as far as Yaco was smooth, and we rolled along in the cold, sunny weather. It was such an easy ride that I cooked a meal in the tiny boat's galley for Chanko and myself (his nephew having returned to La Paz with the navy). As soon as we turned off the Oruro highway, we were again on rough mountain tracks, bumping, banging, twisting, canting, heeling, and sliding into potholes and fissures where the recent snowfalls had churned up the rock. Up, up we went, along narrow trails out on the cliff faces. Sometimes, on the way up, we had to wait for another truck; we would see it far below, climbing straight up what seemed to be a sheer cliff face. The higher we went, the colder it became, and I was soon wrapped up in two blankets as well as my three jerseys and the Norwegian sailing jacket, still crawling with vermin. I had obtained some bug exterminator in La Paz, and for five days had diligently put it to use, but to no avail, for as soon as any of my friends came onboard, the livestock came with them.

The passage over the first range of mountains took two days. The scenery was magnificent, the cold debilitating. I sat inside the little cabin of *Sea Dart*, for it was far too cold to stay in the cockpit, and thought about my situation.

My railroad freight charge I had already paid in La Paz—a total of $180. The truck haulage to the railroad station at Santa Cruz was also paid—also $180. The bribe I had paid to the *aduanero* to get into La Paz and the new axle spring had amounted to $80, which meant I was now left with $40. This would have to suffice until I reached the Paraguayan capital of Asunción, 1,400 miles downstream from my embarkation point in the Mato Grosso. With the river levels dropping, I could not afford to wait around for any money to arrive. I would have to press on alone, for it looked as if I had lost Huanapaco. I would not be able to employ anyone to come with me, and my food supplies, rice and corned beef, would last only five weeks at most, ten weeks if I was alone.

Chanko said that the road we were navigating had not

existed before 1968. Before that, Cochabamba had been completely cut off, except for a very rough trail.

"Rough trail! What the hell does he call this?" I thought, as we bounced along. "If he thinks this is a good track, what in the name of Jumping Jehoshaphat was the old trail like?" I was to find out on the other side of Cochabamba.

After two hair-raising days we finally started down into the Cochabamba valley, which is only 7,000 feet above sea level. As we descended to the flat floor of the pretty, fertile valley, with its wonderful, springlike climate, the road improved, and we soon pulled into the small colonial-style town. On the way in we were not challenged by the *aduana*. The streets were deserted, for it was siesta time, except for a few mangy-looking dogs lying in the sun-drenched streets. We pulled into the main square, hoping to find a bar open. Finding one, we stopped outside. There, sitting at one of the tables, calmly fingering a cup of coffee, was *Huanapaco*!

"*Buenas, Capitán.*" He looked as out of place in this semitropical town, in his poncho and *chorro*, as a Mongolian tank driver at a president's reception in the White House. I grabbed his hand.

"Huanapaco! *Buenas*! What in the name of every *puta Pazena* happened to you?"

"The *aduana* bastards put me inside, but I was only in for a few hours. Commander de Valdez showed up with an order from the president himself for my release, so the *hijos de putas* had to let me go. They didn't want to, and they wouldn't have, but the commander had a pretty roughlooking squad of *marineros* outside!" He grinned, his bronze face lighting up.

"*Carraco, hombre*! Come, let's drink to the Bolivian navy!" Huanapaco had caught the express bus, which had left that night on its weekly safari to Cochabamba. He had fallen asleep while watching for the Suzuki, and the bus had passed us on the mountain track!

"*Bueno*; we came into town at siesta time, we'll go out at siesta time, no, *amigo*?" I observed, downing my beer.

"*A buen seguro*," he replied. "Sure!"

I did call on the British consul and that dear old lady, an archaeologist, presented me with a huge British Union Jack to drape over the boat. Crippled with arthritis, she gazed at the apparition from England and instructed me that if I had any problems with those *"aduanero* scoundrels," I was to make sure she was informed immediately, if not sooner. After a lively evening, she sent us all off with a big kiss, and we strode back through the moonlight to the grove of trees where the Suzuki, with *Sea Dart* onboard, lay in hiding, ready to slide past the *aduana* in the heat of the morrow's siesta. I slept better now, for I was not alone. Now I had a faithful friend working with me again, even if it did cut the food supplies in half.

In the morning we readjusted the wedges and tires which held *Sea Dart* in position on the truck-bed, and after lunch we were ready to run the gauntlet of the worst customs service in the world. We took off from the shadow of the trees, waving to the consul as we passed her house on the outskirts of town, our giant Union Jack, along with the even bigger Bolivian maritime flag, fluttering away in the breeze. It was three o'clock in the afternoon and, sure enough, as we passed the *aduana* there was not a soul to be seen. Chanko put the engine out of gear and we rolled past in silence, except for the quiet squeak of the new spring. We were through. A hundred yards past the customs hut, Chanko gave her the gun and off we went like greased lightning. I couldn't swear to it, but as we hurtled away along the straight, flat road, bumping like a pea-sorter, I thought I saw someone step out of the hut.

The trail between Cochabamba and Santa Cruz was by far the worst of the three mountain crossings *Sea Dart* endured. The track consisted of ruts left by the wheels of Spanish ox-carts. For miles it was nothing but bare, bumpy, naked mountain rock. The heights were greater; the narrow shelves climbing the cliff faces at dizzy angles were narrower; the sheer drops, deeper. The road twisted and turned as it climbed and descended the steep slopes. Sometimes we were above the snow line, sometimes below; sometimes it was freezing, sometimes warm. Sometimes we could make over twenty miles an hour, sometimes we slowed to a crawl; other times we waited, seemingly for hours, for an ascending convoy of heavy trucks to crawl past us going the

opposite way. Sometimes Chanko put the truck in reverse
and headed backwards uphill for a mile, along narrow
paths cut out of the bare cliffs, to allow an oncoming truck
or bus to pass. At each bend there was a plethora of small
wooden crosses, marking the spots where trucks or buses
had plunged over the precipices to the rocky stream-beds
below.

The highest point we reached on this passage was
memorable—the Paso Siberia, over 16,000 feet above sea
level. The trail snaked and curved its way up a mountainside; then at a tremendous height, way up among the clouds
bearing the evaporated water from the Amazonian jungles,
it passed along a shoulder, a col, between the first peak and
the next. The trail ran for about five miles along the top of
this col, on a narrow ledge no wider at any point than twelve
feet, the edges marked by small, whitewashed boulders. On
either side there was a sheer drop of over a mile!
Huanapaco crept along one side of the truck just within
range of Chanko's vision, which, because of the fog, was
about ten feet. I crept forward on the other side, often on
hands and knees, feeling for the edge of the path, slowly
waving the truck on through the fog. It was freezing cold,
with the clouds flying across that pass at thirty or forty miles
an hour. When the clouds cleared, we looked down through
the gaps at a terrifying sight! On each side, a mile or more
below, a roaring torrent, white and furious, crashed over
rocky cataracts. Every now and then a splash of color down
below indicated where a truck, a bus, or a car had gone over.
Mountain Indians with impassive faces, on foot or dragging
llamas, squeezed their way past the slow-moving truck.
Above them rode an ocean-going yacht, with the Union
Jack crackling in the wind, 16,500 feet above sea level! The
place is so remote and the visibility so bad that an accurate
calculation of its height has not yet been made!

Freezing cold and weary with rain and mountain dust, we
gradually dropped from the Paso Siberia down the winding
trail. Down, down, slowly but surely, missing the edges by
inches, until we finally arrived in the foothills of the Andes
and the flat sand and scrub desert of the Chaco—only seven
hundred feet above sea-level. For the first time in eight

months I could breathe a good lungful of air, even if it was scalding. In the space of two hours we had dropped from freezing arctic weather to a temperature of 120° in the shade!

As we bowled along the flat road to Santa Cruz, level but still very bumpy, we cast off our cold-weather gear. Soon I was down to one vest and dungaree pants with deck shoes, or what was left of them. Huanapaco took off everything but his poncho, *chorro*, and trousers. To my amazement, all he discarded was his shirt! He had shown no sign, up in the subfreezing Paso Siberia, of feeling the cold, yet all he had on was one shirt, one thin cotton shirt!

There was no *aduana* on the way into Santa Cruz. Perhaps the pickings were not good enough. We rolled into the outskirts of the sunburnt settlement, hot and dusty, looking like beggars, mud-caked, flea-bitten, and burned almost black from the neck up and the elbows down. Then, only six kilometers from the railroad, the Suzuki went into another ditch and broke the front axle! But at least we were down almost at sea level!

49

OUT OF THE FRYING PAN

ETTING THE TRUCK OUT OF the ditch was no easy matter, but we finally did it with six horses heaving on my nylon mooring lines while we ran the truck engine astern at the same time. The rear wheels spun uselessly for several minutes in the hot sand before they finally dug in. Huanapaco and I helped the horses pull on the lines. When the truck emerged from the ditch, it was severely damaged, the front axle snapped clean in two. Chanko stood there in the blazing heat, scratching his head. Huanapaco sat by the side of the truck, exhausted with the heat, swatting away a cloud of flies.

I went up to Chanko, put my arm on his shoulder, and said, "*Amigo*, it's no good moaning. Lend me your jack; I will get the boat off the truck while you go into town and find a mechanic, and perhaps a tractor." Off he went, downcast, in one of the farm carts. My main concern now was to get the boat to the railhead by Sunday night, when the weekly train was due to leave for the six-hundred-mile run over the Chaco Desert to Corumbá, in the Mato Grosso of Brazil. It was now Friday, the sixth of September. We had two days, forty-eight hours, in which to settle the matter. If we were not on that train, it would cost money in postponement fees and bribes to catch the next, and we would lose a week getting to the river, where the level was dropping fast.

In the afternoon sun, we slowly jacked the boat up on the bed of the truck, first forward, then aft. In between the three keels and the truck-bed we placed, athwartships, three big balks of timber which Chanko had fortunately carried with him. From a nearby farmhouse I bought eight tree trunks, cut by the peons. When the trunks were delivered we stacked them two by two, alternately crosswise, so as to form a platform the height of the truckbed. Then, with the aid of a mule, we slid the boat over from the truck to the top of the pile of trunks, which had been secured in position by long stakes driven into the sandy ground. At last we had *Sea Dart* off the truck and on a free-standing platform. The trick now was to get her down to ground level. By the time Chanko returned she was almost there. Turn by turn, we jacked her up on the lower trunk, slid out the upper trunk, and lowered her down again. Finally, *Sea Dart*'s three keels were resting on the two bottom trunks, ready to roll.

Chanko had bad news. There was no crane in town. There was no tractor. Tomorrow was Saturday; all the mechanics were off work until Monday. Good news; he had been able to borrow another truck jack! A "click-click" he called it.

I made a deal with him. I had unloaded the boat, which was included in the price he had given me, so he was spared the expense of a crane. I would pay him ten dollars for his "click-click," which would help repair the axle, for in this case I was not liable; it was his fault we had run into the ditch. This he agreed to, and Huanapaco and I started rolling *Sea Dart*, with the aid of two mules, slowly but surely over the desert towards the railroad station. By dusk it was blowing a full sandstorm, called in those parts a *surazzo*. We hauled away through the night, breaking off only for a short meal at eight in the evening and again for breakfast.

In the blazing noonday sun of Saturday, we were within sight of the railhead. By four o'clock, after pulling through sand-drifted streets, we were within the gates. By dusk the boat was sitting on the flatbed truck of the only train that connects Bolivia with Brazil. We had moved her by muscle and mule power over six kilometers, four and three-quarter miles, through a sandstorm, over a rough, undulating track, in twenty-four hours! All three tons of her. We had lifted her down five feet off the truck and raised her onto the train four feet! All with the aid of two mules, eight small tree trunks, and two truck jacks! We secured her to the uprights on the railway flatbed and wedged her well and truly; then, exhausted, we sank down on the bed of the car and fell asleep. Before we collapsed I shook Huanapaco's hand. We were across the Andes—two ranges of them— and now all we had to do was ride easily to the railhead on the river, Ladário, in the Mato Grosso. There we would find water leading to the ocean, and to England.

In the morning, about ten o'clock, the stationmaster and his staff appeared. He walked over to us.

"*Qué es eso?*" he asked. "What's this?"

"A boat, going to Brazil, to Ladário."

"*Muy bien*, but there's one thing wrong, *Señor Inglés*," he replied.

"What's that, *Señor Maestro?*"

"You're on the wrong train, this one goes south to Argentina!"

"*Dios mio*, can't you disconnect this car and join it to the right train?" I beseeched him.

"Impossible, *amigo*, it's a completely different system, different rail gauge. The two railroads are in no way connected."

"Then where, *Señor Maestro*," I asked wearily, "is the train for Brazil?" I tried to keep despair out of my voice.

"It hasn't come in yet. It should arrive about noon—over there!" He pointed to a railway line about 500 yards away across the sun-baked parade ground. The rails on the Brazilian line, so far away, shimmered in the heat. I swatted a mosquito and turned to Huanapaco.

"*Amigo*, go back to the truck and fetch the 'click-click' again. I will start to get her off this train with the one I have here."

"*Muy bien, mi Capitán.*" He strode wearily off, but was soon back with the "click-click." This time, however, there were no mules, and we moved her over to the Brazil line by kedging the anchor, that is, by taking the anchor ahead of her on a long line, digging it into the sandy station yard, and hauling away on the sheet winch, using a block and tackle to lessen the load on the winch. A "handy billy" it's called. By this means we rolled her over with the trunks, which the farmer had left lying in the sand.

By three o'clock, almost dead in a temperature of over $125°$ (the thermometer in the cabin showed that in the shade), we had pulled, sweated, and grunted until *Sea Dart* was sitting comfortably as before, only this time on the right train.

I looked at Huanapaco, my face caked with sandy grime. He grinned just as he had in Tiquina and showed the thumbs-up sign. "Come on, *amigo*," I said, "let's get a beer. Fuck it, we've earned it!"

"*Es verdad, no?*" he replied.

That was the last cool beer we saw for 2,000 miles! When we got back to the train, half an hour later, it was crowded with people. The few ancient carriages, which looked Victorian, with no glass in the windows and with wooden seats in all but one car, were jammed with people sitting, standing, leaning out of windows, even perched on the roofs, and the carriage steps. They were claiming places on our flatcar, marking out their own territory. They were Bolivians, mostly from Chuquisaca, the area which borders the frontier of Bolivia and Argentina. But there were also peasants from northern Argentina heading for the Brazilian town of Corumbá, where they could buy provisions such as sugar, flour, canned butter, and canned meat. These they would smuggle back over the borders after a dreary, hot railway journey of over a thousand miles in foul conditions—two weeks of jolting, mosquito-ridden misery!

If we had not just experienced the nerve-racking trek over the Andes mountains and the torture of hauling three tons of boat five miles through a sandy, windblown hell, the train journey over the Chaco Desert would have been a nightmare. The boat was constantly twisting and bumping, continually working out of the wedges; the train movement was violent enough to break nylon lines; the heat was stifling; we were attacked by hordes of insects; and there was nothing to see for three whole exhausting days but featureless sand and scrub stretching away into infinity. Huanapaco and I took watches, day and night, below the boat on the swaying flatbed, ready to drive the wedges back in when they worked loose. During the day we repaired damage to the counter at the back of the boat, which had been smashed in when the truck fell into the ditch outside Santa Cruz.

It was not all misery, though, for there were plenty of lasses on the train; and though our appearance must have alarmed them somewhat, enough escaped the vigilance of their sleepy mothers and drunk fathers to walk back, balancing on the train roof like veterans of the Wild West, and join us on the flatbed car, flirting and laughing in the cool evening. Sometimes, too, their brothers would come back to the rear of the train, bringing hot beer and cool music on their guitars. The port of registry of the boat was Liverpool, and they sat around for hours talking about the Beatles.

The railroad track was unbelievable. The heat of the Chaco distorted the lines so much that the train often had to wait while a gang of plate-layers dismounted to work on the track ahead, straightening the line or repairing a broken wooden bridge over a dry ravine.

Eventually we reached Puerto Suárez, the Bolivian frontier town. The *South American Handbook* states that it is "fit for neither man nor beast." I will go further and say that it is the asshole of the Americas, north and south! It consists of a few unpainted, rotting wooden shacks slouched around railroad sidings, the lines of which are overgrown with jungle and alive with mosquitoes. On each side of the siding is a noisy fog-ridden swamp of fetid, stagnant water that stinks to high heaven. During the twilight hours millions of mosquitoes rise off it, crowding the night air so thickly that there is hardly room between them to see the giant moths, which smash headlong into every light they can find. Over all this hovers a smothering, dank heat, making for an experience rather like putting your head into an oven full of rotting rats.

Here we arrived on the tenth of September. Here we were abandoned by the train. The stationmaster, who looked as if he had crawled out of the swamp, insisted we had paid to go to Ladário, not to Corumbá. There was now no train to Ladário, and the track had long been uprooted; so we must somehow get ourselves to Ladário.

"Señor Maestro, is there a road?"

"Hah, road! Where do you think you are, gringo?"

"Look, Señor, I have come with the blessing of the president; he told me that all the Bolivians would help me."

"*El presidente*? What is that to me? He's a thousand

kilometers away. La Paz? What's La Paz to do with this place?"

He was adamant. There was no way I could fight him. I had neither the money nor the time to delay, for the river was dropping. Word had filtered back from Corumbá to this effect—the river was dropping fast! The cost of shipping *Sea Dart* from Puerto Suárez to Corumbá was fifty dollars, and I had but thirty-five left in the world.

I turned to Huanapaco. "*Vamos, amigo*, get the 'click-click' out!"

We commenced unloading the boat from the flatcar, using heavy sleepers lying about in the yard; they were great balks of heavy timber, thick with melting creosote and grease. We got her down on the ground, which was carpeted with dead moths to a thickness of an inch or two, and started hauling the *sixteen* miles to the river, along an old, now overgrown, railless railroad track.

50

INTO THE FIRE!

N SEPTEMBER ELEVENTH WE commenced hauling the boat to the River Paraguay, which we ultimately reached on the second of October. For over sixteen miles we sweated, heaved, hauled, pushed, and shoved until it seemed that we had never done anything else but this. For twenty-one days the two of us hacked and slashed at the thorny creepers that barred our passage along the railroad cuttings and embankments. How many men, I wondered, had died here to drive this forlorn hope from Bolivia to a waterway which finally might, or might not, lead to the sea? Before we were allowed to leave, the *aduanero*, in cahoots with the stationmaster, charged us twenty dollars in exchange for a worthless permit to pass over the border. The way we were going there was no border, and he knew it! The bloody bastard sent us into the Green Hell of the world with only fifteen dollars and enough food to last a month! For my twenty dollars I got no receipt, no acknowledgment, just a wave of a fat, sweaty hand to send us on our way. It is quite possible that a desire to tell the world of the *aduanero*'s action was one of the main motivations for carrying on during the next few weeks.

Once out from the station, heaving the keels over the greasy sleepers, we came to the scrub. First we would hack a clear way about eight feet wide for a hundred yards or so, then run a long mooring line, my old storm-running line, to a thick scrub bush ahead, then haul in with the handy-billy rig. At the same time the brush and grass had to be beaten continually to guard against snakes. We saw many cascabels, deadly giant rattlers, and frailesca, poisonous little vipers which live in the long grass. We wrapped our legs and feet, over shoes and trousers, with torn strips of blanket to guard against possible bites. The agony of being wrapped up in thick blanket material in that temperature can hardly be imagined, but we dared not take it off until we were safely inside the stifling cabin with all the exits, hatch, and ventilators tightly closed against entry by serpents or vampire bats, which were numerous.

We hacked away, Huanapaco and I, with cutlass and ax, from dawn until about two in the afternoon in the thicker growth. Then we hauled forward, always watching for snakes. Compared to them, the insects, *biting through several layers of cloth*, were a mere nuisance.

Sometimes we would come to a comparatively clear patch, and we would think we were doing extraordinarily well. I dared not empty the water tanks to lighten the load until we were nearer to the River, for I didn't know if there was an alternative supply. On the uphill stretch, of which, thank God, there was only one, about two miles long, we went at a snail's pace. It was all we could do, even with a four-purchase block, to heave her up inch by inch, slight though the old railroad gradient was. But eventually, after rounding a curve on this uphill Calvary, we came within sight of the River. There it was, in the distance, about five miles away as the crow flies, gleaming silver in the misty green of the Mato Grosso! It seemed to be so wide as to stretch beyond the horizon, but I realized that, in fact, we were looking at a number of small streams running parallel. We redoubled our efforts as well as our watch against snakes. As we neared the River, I was concerned about jaguars and anacondas for they, too, like a drink of water; but we saw none, though we did hear, three or four times, a distant roar and many screams of terror.

Going downhill was as hard as, if not harder than, going up; we had to rig not only the forward hauling gear, but another block astern in order to check her when she started to slide.

The heat was suffocating from about ten in the morning until around four in the afternoon. We once tried working after dusk, but without any lamps it was hazardous work indeed. And so we suffered the heat in preference to stumbling onto an anaconda or falling prey to a hungry jaguar looking for a tasty morsel. Besides, Huanapaco didn't like to work after dark. The mountain Indian is very superstitious and hates the dark; unless he's asleep his mind is full of evil demons.

By the thirtieth of September we were within easy walking distance of the River. The brush had thinned out somewhat. *Sea Dart* was in more or less clear country, with only a few bushes scattered around on each side of the old railroad embankment. Leaving Huanapaco to dig in the anchor and rig up blocks, I made my way to the River to spy out the land, or rather, the water. It took me about four hours to get to the bank, for we had both been on a meager diet for days, each eating only a handful of rice and half of a seven-ounce can of corned beef per day. Huanapaco found some white grubs under a rotting tree and mixed these, fried, with his corned beef. He pronounced them delicious. For a day I was wary of eating them, but when he didn't die or fall writhing to the ground, my hunger overcame my squeamishness, and after that we had grubs daily. They were about an inch or so long and half an inch round. They tasted, when fried, something like scampi (at least they did to me then). At any rate, they added tremendously to our protein intake.

What I found at the River almost broke my heart. For the first time in many years I was tempted to sit down and cry. The jetty was completely rotted through, eaten away by ants! Balanced on the end of it was an old British steam crane, built at Gateshead on Tyne, with the date "1878" on the door. It was a solid block of red rust! Inside the boiler generations of birds had built nests. In the eerie silence of the jungle afternoon, I carefully made my way back, trying to avoid the rotten planks which might give way and drop me forty feet into the swirling brown waters below.

If I could have sat down, I would have. Whether I would have cried or not is a moot point, for the hordes of ants crawling around, billions of them, discouraged any sitting and probably made the act of crying superfluous anyway. As I made my way back to the boat, I worked out a plan to get her down the steep riverbank. When I arrived, Huanapaco lifted his sweaty head, his almond eyes dull and listless with exhaustion.

"*Buenas, Capitán,*" he puffed. Nothing if not polite, the Quechua.

"*Buenas, amigo,* good news; I'm pretty sure there's enough water for *Sea Dart* to be able to navigate, at least in the stretch we're aiming for."

His face lit up, his white teeth flashed.

"Now the bad news, *amigo*; the jetty is useless, so is the crane; we have to get there fast, and then we have to carve a track down the bank to launch the boat."

"How far is that, *mi Capitán?*"

"Twelve meters." I didn't have the heart to tell him yet that we couldn't go straight down the bank, that we would have to slash, beat, and dig our way at an angle down the bank for *eight hundred meters*!

It took us another three days to reach the riverbank. On the morning of the second of October, *Sea Dart* was separated from the Atlantic only by 2,000 miles of wild river and a forty-foot drop. Down below, the swirling waters flowed rapidly on their way to the Plate estuary, that great brown scar through which flow the waters of half a continent.

I considered dropping the boat down the bank directly, on her side, controlling her by blocks and tackles, but the risk of straining the hull was too great. I considered erecting a sheer-legs, a sort of crane made from straight tree trunks, and trying to lever her out over the waters and lower her in, but this would take several days to construct, and I wasn't absolutely sure that the rope blocks, severely strained by now after all the heaving they had done, could do the job. There was only one course—dig at an angle down the riverbank!

We slashed, cut, burned, dug, beat, and lowered for eight days, sometimes with the boat leaning at so acute an angle over the river I felt sure she would capsize. I safeguarded against this by taking a complete turn with a heavy rope around her hull and digging in the anchor to secure it.

For eight days we worked like maniacs, watching the river level drop. We had no time to spare; I had learned, back in Santa Cruz, that seven hundred miles downstream, on the southern edge of the Mato Grosso, the River rushed over a shallow rock ledge—the Paso de Moros! If we could not get past the Paso de Moros, we would be trapped in the Mato Grosso. There we would have three choices—die of disease, die of hunger, or be eaten alive by the insects.

Little by little we forced her down the bank, transforming it as we went from a mass of scrub into a scarred slipway. We threw the soil as hard as we could into the bushes to save beating them with a stick to scare away serpents and other dangers.

At the bottom of the slope, keeping a wary eye out for alligators, we eased her in. I went out in the dinghy and dropped both anchors. Over the wet sleepers she slid inch by inch, and finally she floated. The swirling current grabbed her and sent her downstream, but the anchors held. And would you believe it? She didn't leak one fucking drop of water!

"*Maravilla!*" said Huanapaco.

"Bloody marvelous!" said I.

51

THE GREEN HELL

INCE *SEA DART* HAD ARRIVED on the banks of the River Paraguay, or rather on the bank of one of the numerous streams which comprise the so-called River—a maze of winding, twisting, muddy canals, stinking like a midden with the smell of rotting jungle—we had not gone short of protein. Now we had *fish*! True, it was mainly piranha fish, but it was meat, for all that. From my Amazon days I knew just how to catch them; each morning Huanapaco and I performed the drop of blood and bucket trick. The piranhas on the Paraguay River are smaller, skinnier, and bonier than their Amazon cousins, but to our hungry eyes they looked like succulent salmon. They were a lot fiercer, too, and jumped ten feet in the air for five minutes before they grew still enough for us to poleax them.

As we hauled up the mast and rigged the sails, I realized that the variety of life here was even more prolific than in Amazonia. In the high trees at day time hung huge bats, called *andiras* by the Guaicuru Indians. Some of these bats were up to eighteen inches across with their clawed wings extended; evil-looking monsters, vampire bloodsuckers. At night we heard the clicking of their little feet and the sound of their wings trailing on the deck above the stuffy little cabin as they tried to find a way through the hatchboards and windows. Through the tiny windows in *Sea Dart*'s doghouse, by the light of the tiny oil lamp, we saw their beady eyes and watched them scratch at the Perspex window screens.

There were birds, too, by the thousands: the hornero bird, which builds a hanging nest, something like a wasp's nest, that dangles from the branches; and the uratau, which sings the most plaintive song I have ever heard from a bird, a sort of low, infant whisper of complaint. Cutting through

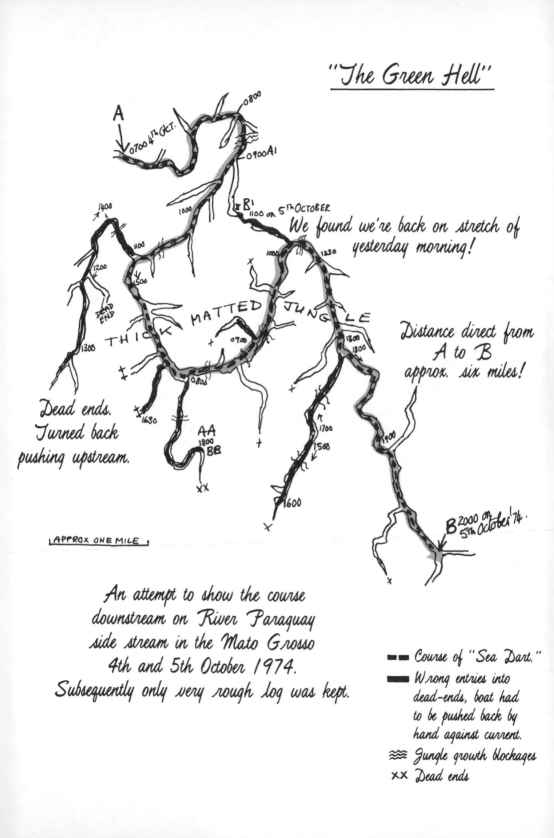

"The Green Hell"

A

0700 4TH OCT.

0800

0900A1

1400

1000

B¹ 1100 on 5TH OCTOBER

We found we're back on stretch of yesterday morning!

1100

1000

1230

1200

1500

DEAD END

THICK MATTED JUNGLE

0900

1300

1300

1800

1800

Distance direct from A to B approx. six miles!

0800

Dead ends. Turned back pushing upstream.

1630

AA
1800
BB

1700

1900

XX

1500

APPROX ONE MILE

1600

X

B 2000 on 5th October '74.

X

An attempt to show the course downstream on River Paraguay side stream in the Mato Grosso 4th and 5th October 1974. Subsequently only very rough log was kept.

▬▬ Course of "Sea Dart."
▬▬ Wrong entries into dead-ends, boat had to be pushed back by hand against current.
≋ Jungle growth blockages
xx Dead ends

the brush ashore, we had noticed the strange habits of the macagua, an inveterate snake fighter. The macagua attacks ferociously any snake it sees, rushing at it with one wing covering its head and its long beak poking through like a bayonet. If the snake bites it, the macagua rushes over to the bushes and pecks away at berries also called macagua, which are a snakebite antidote!

The trees along the banks were generally not as tall as those on the Amazon, but the tall ones, few though they were, grew much higher than anything I had seen on the northern river. The lapacho is immense, anything up to 250 feet high, and 50 or 60 feet around the base. There were wild pineapples in the undergrowth, and great bunches of passion flowers, the plant whose beautiful blooms reminded the old conquistadors, when they first saw them, of the crucifixion. They have a blood red flower with a golden stamen in the form of a cross. Along the banks of the streams grew the izpa tree, something like a weeping willow, which gives off a misty, pine-smelling vapor.

The rest of the flora was unknown to me, mostly dead or half-dead trees strangled by creepers. The branches of the trees would often overhang the narrow streams, and we would have to either shin up the mast and cut a way through or lower the mast to pass them. The distance to Paso de Moros and the main stream was only some 200 miles from Ladário, our miserable embarkation point, but by the winding course of the stream it came to nearly 600 miles! Often we would follow a stream around an immense bend, maybe for an entire day, and after we had completed the circle, would find ourselves looking over a narrow peninsula, a few yards wide, at the spot we had passed early in the morning!

The heat was intense, suffocating; and yet the sunshine was not strong, for the vegetation gave off a continual mist, day and night, forming rainclouds overhead which blew away to the west to break over the Andes. But hidden away in the narrow channels between thick clumps of high trees or grass fourteen feet high, crawling with snakes, we hardly felt the breeze. In the upper reaches, where we started sailing, or rather drifting, downstream, caimans were numerous, and we would often see hundreds of them sliding through the water. When they lashed into a shoal of fish, the water would boil and their ugly snouts would open and their loathsome eyes rise about the surface. Some were about twelve feet long from the tip of the tail to the snout.

Many a time (and this we dreaded more than anything), the stream would divide into two or three channels. If we chose the wrong one, we might not realize it until we had drifted some miles and found ourselves at a dead end, with solid brushwood and thick branches denying further passage. Then we had to jump over the side, into water about 4½ feet deep, sometimes deeper, sometimes too deep to stand up in, and take turns, one of us beating the water to scare off lurking piranhas, water snakes, and caimans, while the other pushed and dragged the boat back upstream. Periodically, we would climb onboard and run a kerosene-soaked, lighted rope over our bodies to burn off the great, black, shiny leeches, some of them five inches long. I do not know how much blood we lost in this manner, as well as to the piúm flies, mosquitoes, and bichus, but it must have been plenty, for by the time we emerged at Paso de Moros we were both as weak as children. I weighed 80 pounds against my normal 120, while Huanapaco weighed 100 against his normal 180!

As the awful days went on, we got yellower and yellower. We had now found, by testing, which leaves we could chew safely, hoping for vitamin C, but I don't think they did us any good. At the end of a day, swept up against a bank of tall swamp grass, we were too exhausted to do anything but shut all the inlets to the cabin, fall back on our berths, and sweat all night. By the end of the second week, the fresh water in *Sea Dart*'s tanks was running very low, and we had to resort to river water, much muddier than in the Amazon, strained, as before, through fine cotton wool. We must have ingested a whole laboratory of biological specimens that would have been of great interest to the London School of Tropical Medicine.

The whole period of the passage up to Paso de Moros merges together in my memory; each day for three weeks we fought tooth and nail for our lives. Each second of every

minute we struggled forward—if we stopped, we were dead
men. There was no doubt in our minds about that. We
could not go upstream against the four-knot current, we
could only drift down with it, barely maintaining steerage
way with the sails; there was no fuel for the engine. Even if
we'd had fuel it would not have done us any good, for the
little four-horsepower outboard could never have bucked
the swift current when we were forced back upstream.
Moreover, we would have used up a ton in a week, and
where could we put a ton of highly explosive gasoline in a
twenty-foot boat with an inside temperature of 130°?

Again, writing about this more than a year and a half later
in the safety and comfort of Manhattan, it is difficult to sort
out the days. My log is very terse on the period; there was no
time, no energy to write anything but the estimated distance
"sailed" on any particular day. All my thoughts, all my will,
all my deteriorating energy went into moving the boat
downstream. I explained to Huanapaco that we had to keep
going as hard as we could, and that if we did not we would
certainly die. Fortunately, as well as being very strong to
start with, as well as having grown up in one of the toughest
environments on earth, the pitiless Altiplano, Huanapaco
was also a stoic. He would keep going until he dropped. In
addition to a sense of humor, he had the patience of Job—*he
had never known anything else but the eternal struggle against
nature*. He'd been at it all his life. If I'd had with me a young
man of Huanapaco's age from a so-called advanced society,
I am sure he would have given up long before we finally
broke through.

Time and again, day in, day out—wet, sweaty, stinking,
miserable, hungry, hot beyond explanation—I wished I was
back in the arctic ice, even in a force-ten storm, even on a lee
shore. The sea could never be as cruel as this rotting, evil,
malignant inferno, with its millions of insects descending on
us every hour. I even, God help me, wished I was back in
the Amazon, pulling from tree to tree! Compared with this,
the Amazon was like a weekend on Coney Island!

Anacondas dangled from trees to the river's surface.
Their evil heads dove under the water and swallowed fish
without even chewing them. We saw one big brute whose

belly wriggled with live fish still kicking as they were being digested! Another time we saw a dying anaconda. It had eaten a mass of flesh, probably a capybara, a big rodent similar to a water rat which swims in the streams. The snake had lain on the bank in the sun to digest the animal and had stayed there so long that maggots were still eating the belly with the half-digested rotting flesh of the capybara still inside. The anaconda was feebly thrashing.

Inside the Mato Grosso for three weeks we saw no sign of any human life. It was only nature gone wild—a mad biological riot. We could have been on some faraway planet in another universe, or on earth five billion years ago. Awful in the true sense of the word, and very, very frightening. It was as if every malignant spirit on earth was pitting its evil intelligence against us. The plant life was so thick we could not see more than six inches away from the river's edge! Even now, almost two years later, I can hardly bear to go near a green plant in someone's apartment. I cannot even look into a florist's window and see an array of household plants without a shudder passing through me. I can hardly bear to look at grass or a tree, unless it is surrounded by all the impediments of urban civilization. A zoo, if I could find the courage to visit one, would shock me rigid.

Day after day we hacked our way along the river. Time out of number we dropped the mast to pass under some impossibly thick overhanging branch. Twice a day we would gulp down raw piranha fish and tree leaves, along with maggoty flour from the emergency stock. Once a week we would drool over the special Sunday treat of cold corned beef, of which we had four cans when we left Ladário. We could not cook, for we had to save the kerosene for the ropes and for painting the anchor or mooring lines to keep the snakes off and to stop the ants from marching onboard to eat the marine-ply hull from under our feet. The kerosene was vaporizing with the heat, too. When we finally arrived at Forte Coimbra we were down to the last dregs. We used to lay the piranha fish out on a metal tray and try to heat them up in the pale sun. The idea was to dry them out, but we both got severe cases of tapeworm anyway. The one taken out of me in Buenos Aires was four feet long and waxing roundly.

By the time we joined the main stream of the Paraguay, we were near the state of wild animals. The veneer imposed on us by our respective upbringings was practically gone. I would grab a piranha and start chewing it, head, eyes, tail, everything. We would scoop up maggoty flour and swallow it in handfuls. Huanapaco eyed everything that moved, including me. If it moved, it was food! We did, in fact, make an agreement that if one us died, the other would eat as much of him as he could stomach. At that moment even the thigh muscle of a dead Quechua would have been acceptable fare. Starvation knows no morals!

52

THE VALLEY OF THE SHADOW

NE OF THE MAIN DIFFI-culties in the Mato Grosso lay in finding out where we were. By the compass and the sun I could tell that we were drifting in a more or less southerly direction; but there were several occasions when *Sea Dart* headed north and kept going in that direction with the flow of the stream. In our hunger and desperation this was terribly discouraging. I couldn't trust the compass too much, in case there were iron deposits under the river or some other magnetic aberration. Instead, I watched the sun, pale above the ever-rising swamp-steam, as it swung over us high in the heavens.

As we hacked and slashed at yet another obstacle, I remembered that the same sun, as it rose to noon over us, could be seen back home in Wales. There, in another life, another world, people were getting to go home after a day's work, life was easy and comfortable, the threat of death by nature was hardly ever thought of. Mankind had, many millions of years ago, hacked and slashed, struggled and fought, dreamed and wept its way out of the primeval swamp, just as we were doing. They started from nothing; they had no previous experience to guide them, nothing to go back to.

"Why?" I asked myself as I attacked another tangle of creepers hanging over the river. "Why bother? Why pit ourselves against the torments that cruel nature piles up against us? Why not just lie down and accept the inevitable?" For days I racked my being with this question, in real hunger now, for the piranha had completely disappeared at the end of the second week. Our worm-ridden flour, too, was gone. We had eaten the last of the rice, soaked in muddy river water to soften it. Every edible thing onboard was gone, even the olive oil, the sailmaker's wax, the linseed oil, the candles! In desperation, we soaked the skull of a llama, which I had hung in the cabin as a souvenir, and drank the "stock."

Why did we carry on against such impossible odds?

The answer, when it came at last, was simple. By *not* struggling we would simply be going against nature! We were *made* to fight against nature by the very thing we were fighting, *nature itself*! Here was Man's destiny. To strive, to seek, to find; and *not* to yield! Not to give way to sentimental claptrap, insidious temptations, not to retreat into ourselves, hoping to find a reason. *Nature knows no reason*! Not to be content to sit in a mental or spiritual cave, while all around us nature, the very reflection of ourselves, runs riot! We are *here*. This is our situation. If we don't like it, then Jesus Christ almighty, let's claw and struggle and *bite* our way out of it, because it will not change itself! That is the game, and we must play or go under!

I looked at Huanapaco as he patiently, steadily hacked away, determined to survive. He was in a bad way, haggard, his Indian eyes dull, seeing nothing but the blockage ahead. Only when he raised the cutlass or the ax to *attack* did his eyes come alive! As we drifted down a comparatively clear stretch, I dismantled the galley, searching for something edible. Behind the stove I found a treasure—a handful of beans resting on one of the stringers. Hard, black, sprouting. I staggered along the deck to where Huanapaco was resting, exhausted, awaiting the next onslaught of creepers. The boat was bows to the current drifting stern first. Clapping him weakly on the shoulder, I passed him the beans. "*Vamos a comer, hombre*! Let's eat, man!"

He looked up, the sweat pouring off him, his *unku* shirt a tattered rag, stripped down to his *kuana*, the long scarf which the Quechua wrap around their loins. He grinned wanly, then extended his fist in the thumbs-up sign!

Five minutes later we saw the caiman. He was floating in midstream, about a hundred yards ahead of us; floating, not swimming. He must have left the banks because of the lack of fish. In this open stretch there was enough breeze to steer the boat. Dropping into the cockpit, I grabbed the sheets and tiller and brought Sea Dart around until the breeze filled the mainsail. Huanapaco grabbed the ax. The hammer, a fourteen-pound sledge, he laid beside him, along with the cutlass. I bore straight down on the caiman, still lying there, drifting with the current. As we drew closer we could see he was about nine feet long. Then *Sea Dart* hit him full on, with her bows, broadside. He spun around, lashing with his tail and wicked jaws. The shock to the boat was enough to jerk the knife drawer out of the galley cupboard! From the bow, Huanapaco smashed the ax right into the middle of the caiman's belly, so hard the ax stuck! The caiman twisted over onto his belly, blood and guts trailing away from his underside. Moving fast, for one in such puny condition, Huanapaco fumbled for a moment, got his brown hands on the sledge, and, taking careful aim, crashed it down on the caiman's skull. In the cockpit, steering the tiller carefully, peering over the side to keep the animal hard against the bow, I heard the crunch as the alligator's skull was smashed to a pulp in one blow. After one last, mighty lash of his whole body, he went completely dead in the water.

I threw the grappling hook to Huanapaco, who, with some difficulty, finally stuck it into the caiman's belly. We dropped the anchor right away. With a jerk the boat came up all standing and swung quickly around to face the current and the wind.

We pulled the caiman up alongside, turned him over, and hacked the ax out with a knife. Inside the belly we found four small fish only half-digested; these we made short work of. The caiman's blood was cold and tasted fishy. Our knives could not penetrate his armor scales, so we slashed away from the inside of his belly, delving down towards the tail, and extracted a good four or five pounds of very stringy meat, which we first soaked in water, then hung up to dry in the sun. We were now in a fairly open spot, and we carefully scanned the banks for a tiny clear space in which we might start a fire to cook the meat. After several hours of drifting, we found one—on top of a huge tree trunk which had fallen into the stream. It was crawling with ants, but we didn't care. Keeping an eye out for snakes, we built a fire and feasted on alligator meat. It was like eating tarred rope and with sore gums was very hard going; but it was one of the best meals I have ever had in my life, and it gave us enough protein to crash, smash, and bash our way for another few days.

At the end of the third week, we were nearing the end of the hellish maze, although we did not know it. Little by little, the banks cleared of overhanging trees and creepers. Little by little the streams got wider, the current slower. On the last night in the jungle, before we emerged into the swamp-lands, we had one of the most frightening experiences I have ever known. With the river fairly clear, we anchored midstream, away from the vegetation, for the night. In order to sleep we covered the hatch, not with the boards, which we left lying in the cockpit, but with the old British army mosquito net I had brought along from the West Indies. The idea was to try to get more air into the swelter-ing cabin. In the early hours of the morning, as a full moon swung pale and wan above the jungle mist, I woke to a loud noise. It was as if a large outboard motor or a motorcycle was running in the cockpit! I jumped up, shaking Huanapaco. Shuffling back to the companionway, I was aghast to see that the mosquito net was being eaten! It was actually collapsing into the boat under the weight of hun-dreds of moths, each about ten inches wide. As I watched, horrified, paralyzed at first, I could see their mouths chew-ing away at the *plastic* net! Coming to my senses, I grabbed the frying pan out of the galley rack and started to bang them away. Huanapaco, stupefied with sleep and terror, grabbed the cricket bat. We beat and beat the net for four hours, until the light of dawn brought the strange onslaught to an end. In the morning, with only a few of these monstrous insects left, we saw, to our astonishment, that the whole topsides of the boat was carpeted with their corpses to a depth of four inches!

On the twenty-second of October we sighted smoke away in the distance. There was no chance of its being a forest fire, for the jungle is much too humid and dank to burn. Smoke meant fire; fire meant humans. Now, the question was, what kind of humans? I knew that the southern Mato Grosso was the home of the Guaicurus, aboriginal primi-

tives, very savage, very aggressive, and very, very
dangerous—probably the most dangerous savages in the
whole of the Americas. Warriors to a man. Well, we could
understand that, all right, so long as we were not the intended victims! Even so, at the sight of smoke our spirits
rose. We were near humans! Even though they might be the
most dangerous animals of all! They ate together, they slept
in groups, they talked, they sang, they made music, even if
only by banging two human jawbones together, they had
the spark of an idea about superior spirits, they loved in
their fashion, and they *dreamed*! They were our kind, our
kindred!

Keeping the Very flare-pistol and the harpoon gun
handy in the cockpit, we pushed on downstream. Apart
from the ax, cutlass, sledgehammer, and our knives, they
were our only weapons, and we were determined to use
them should the need arise. We had discussed this
thoroughly. There was no doubt, no hesitation on our part.
The first savage to come within yards of *Sea Dart* would get a
harpoon straight through his chest. If that did not stop him,
he would find a distress flare, a great blob of flaming phos-
phorescence, right in his face, a sledgehammer crashing
down on his skull, and a cutlass slitting him up the gizzard!
We had fought too hard for our own lives not to respect
other men's right to life, no matter how savage they were.
On the other hand, we were determined to survive. We had
fought tooth and nail for our lives and we were damned if
somebody was going to deprive us of our *earned* right to live!

Rounding a bend in the 200-yard-wide stream, we saw the
first human we had sighted since leaving Puerto Suárez,
five weeks before. At least almost human! He was standing
in a dugout canoe about twelve feet long. He was poised
over the river, looking like the statue of Eros in Piccadilly
Circus, with an arrow in his bow pointing down at the water.
The surprise on both sides was complete. We had passed
him and shot out of sight round the next bend before
Huanapaco could get the harpoon gun in his hand or I the
Very pistol. The savage, too, went bone rigid. He stood
there, in a state of utter astonishment. His head was
smothered in what looked like red clay. He seemed hairless,

even around his loins, for he was stark naked, although around his thighs he wore a bracelet of yellow feathers.

The red clay, I found out later, was actually blood, animal or human, mixed with earth and dung. The grown men smear it over themselves. The Guaicuru *pluck* all their hair out, even their eyelashes. Before the age of fourteen, they paint themselves completely with blue dye. From fourteen to sixteen, or until they kill their first human, they paint themselves red, after which they smear blood and earth over their heads. When not engaged in killing something or someone, they spend their time plucking each other's hair out.

They have always been feared, they have always been a terror to a vast area stretching from the eastern side of the Mato Grosso for a thousand miles and more over to the western edge of the great Chaco Desert. I was told later that long before the Spanish penetration into the Chaco, these savages had crossed the burning, waterless Chaco for a thousand miles to attack Tahuantinsuyu, the mighty Inca empire itself, and in the Bolivian province of Chuquisaca had inflicted a severe defeat on the (until then) invincible armies of that far-flung civilization. Now here they were, in 1974, in the same state of utter savagery, still unconquered, fighting tooth and nail for every inch of their fetid swamp, for their right to bash others over the head.

After seeing the Guaicuru brave, we kept an even sharper lookout until finally we emerged into the main stream of the Paraguay River, a half-mile wide and deep. But we still had to negotiate the rapids at Paso de Moros. With bleeding gums and loose teeth, we pressed on until, on the twenty-fifth of October, we saw white water through the rising heat-mist ahead.

It stretched clear across the river. As we drifted closer we could see the river humping over the great rock shelf, then breaking into foam as it rushed over, boiling, spuming, spitting in a mighty cataract, the water of half a continent squeezing inexorably over one of the ribs of the spine of South America! We headed straight for the seething cauldron.

53

BESIDE THE GREEN PASTURES

 SCANNED THE WHITE WALL of foaming water ahead. Three hundred yards upstream from the rapids I sighted, to one side, off the bank, a passage of less disturbed water. Shoving the tiller over, I headed for it, hoping we had enough speed over the current to reach the gap in time. Out of one corner of my eye, I saw a great lone hump covered with greenery, like a mountain in an old Chinese painting, the mist from the cataracts hovering around its base. This was the Pão de Azucar, the Sugar Loaf, and it looked like one too. All alone, with only a small cluster of foothills to keep it company, it sticks out of the Brazilian Mato Grosso like a sore thumb. This is the only landmark, the only high ground in millions of square miles of flat, dreary swamp and low scrub. It marks the utmost point, or very nearly, of Portuguese penetration into the southwest hinterland of Brazil.

We rushed into the rapids and suddenly were in the gap. It all happened in less than a minute, yet it seemed to take a year. One minute we were in calm yet swift-running water; the next, in the middle of a roaring cloud of foam so thick we couldn't see anything. The eddies, brutal and determined, gripped the rudder as if trying to turn the boat sideways to the fifteen-knot current. Wet through with spray and sweat, Huanapaco and I strained against the tiller to keep little *Sea Dart* on her course. I prayed the rudder would not break loose from the pintles, the hinges which hold it to the rudder post. If it did we were dead men, for in that fierce, savage maelstrom there would be no chance for either of us, both nonswimmers. Besides, in the state we were in, at three-quarters of our normal weight, and with nothing left to go on but will power, we would have gone straight down. If she turned broadside on to that wall of rushing spume, thousands of tons of water would lift her up

333

as if she were a paper boat in a rain gutter and throw her in the air, right over.

In the 200 yards or so of rapids we *hit the bottom* with the three keels at least twenty times. We didn't float, we were *pushed* over the flat stone bottom, sliding on the keels with a terrible jarring shudder. Each time she banged the bottom the shock passed right through my feet, up my legs and spine, to my already loose teeth.

The last three bumps were the worst—Slam! Bang! Crash! The whole boat shivered and shuddered, the hull, the mast, the keels, the deck—if anyone had told me that a boat of her size and construction could withstand this encounter, I would not have believed it. But *Sea Dart* did! As we roared over the rapids, I didn't think of anything at all. All I remember is *willing* her over with every fiber of my mind, heart, soul, spirit, and body. I do not recall having any thought of death or drowning or being battered to pieces on the rocks; all I thought about was beating this last fucking bastard of a barrier.

Then, we were through! As if by magic. One second we were in a wet hell of mad, murderous movement, the next we were in calm, deepening waters, moving sedately down to the southern edge of the Green Hell of the Mato Grosso.

With only a few minutes to go before nightfall, we rounded a narrow, swift-running bend and sighted the Brazilian army fort of Coimbra, old and white, looking just as it had when the hardy Portuguese *bandeiras* built it 200 years ago!

The Brazilian soldiers thought they were seeing a mirage. They could not believe their senses as a filthy, bedraggled, blistered sailing yacht, wearing the British Union Jack from the masthead, sailed into their riverfront as smartly as two ragged, yellow, haggard half-skeletons could manage her.

Quickly, a boat loaded with soldiers and officers came out to us. We were helped ashore, where we were bathed and disinfected, fed a little, and put to bed under sedatives. When we woke up next day, the Brazilians had de-bugged the boat with a gas exterminator and their soldiers were, even as we talked with the *comandante*, scrubbing her inside and out.

"Where in the name of God have you come from?" asked the *comandante*.

"Bolivia, from the north. We hauled to the river from Ladário."

"Good God Almighty!" He spoke Portuguese slowly enough for me to understand. "The way you came—our army has been trying to penetrate that area for forty years! We've only gotten into the outer fringe of it! The Guaicurus, we've been fighting them off and on ever since Brazil was first brought out here! But *Senhor* Tristan, when you feel better, you must tell us your story. Feel free to go anywhere you wish in the fort. Stay in bed if you care to. You both have open house, and you will dine with myself and my officers as soon as you feel well enough to do so."

The few days we spent at Forte Coimbra seemed like a dream. Even though we were still surrounded by the Mato Grosso, we had reached safety! Even though we had almost 1,500 miles to go downstream to the sea, it looked like child's play compared to what we had been through.

At Coimbra we were cosseted in the sickbay for three days; then, as soon as we could hold down solid food, we messed with the army officers. Out of his own scant supplies, the medical officer gave me mosquito repellent. The little outboard motor was taken ashore and tested. Five gallons of gasoline were put onboard, along with a gunny-sack full of jerked beef.

After another two days I was itching to continue south. Even though we were still shitting green liquid, we pushed off, because the river was still dropping and soon there might not be enough depth for *Sea Dart* to navigate. In a small gesture of gratitude for the Brazilians' hospitality before we left, I managed to shin up the eighty-foot flag-pole in front of the gates and repair a broken sheave.

Fifty miles downstream from Forte Coimbra, a hot, sticky finger of Bolivia pokes through a Godforsaken stretch of putrid swamp and humming jungle for a hundred miles, to touch the River Paraguay at Puerto General Busch. Trust the Bolivians to name their only viable outlet to waters leading to the sea—a tiny, insect-ridden, primitive, ramshackle camp of rotting wood grouped around a raft—after a president who blew his brains out after an all-night orgy in the palace of La Paz! Here we stayed one night, tied up alongside the raft. There were only two Bolivian soldiers. They were dressed exactly the same as the sailors who had arrested me on Lake Titicaca in the freezing cold of the Altiplano—rough, dirty, blue uniforms, trousers tied up with string, shaven heads, filthy bare feet—and they had the same charm, the same courtesy to the traveler, the same curiosity, the same *simpatía*. This place was Bolivia's last outpost, and it looked it! From here we finally took our last farewell of the one country which in all my travels stands out most clearly in my mind. I wore the Bolivian maritime ensign, the only one, all the way to the ocean.

A few miles downstream, on the swampy riverbank, a lone monument pokes up into the sky. This is the point where three countries meet—Bolivia, Brazil, and Paraguay. Nothing else marks the frontier. No customs post, no tanktraps or barbed wire; only the jungle and the cement post. It is probably the only place on earth where you can sail between three countries without challenge, without paper inspections or tax impositions, or any of the rest of the legalized extortion that has crept into international travel. In my grandfather's day you could sail around the world, showing nothing more than a five-pound note or a gold sovereign! But of course that was in the days before the "little Hitlers of the filing cabinets," with their proliferating piles of paper and the Himmlers, with their beady eyes behind rimless glasses, started creeping around in the shadows behind their ever thickening barriers of bullshit.

Within a day's sail of the frontier monument lies the first outpost of Paraguay, a row of neat, clean, wooden buildings perched on top of stone columns. The reason for this is to allow a breath of cool air to come up from the river and ventilate the houses through grilled holes in the floors. Also, of course, to keep out ants, snakes, jaguars, and all the rest of the crawling life of the Chaco.

There was no bullshit here, in Bahía Negra. No papers to riffle and stamp, no mean minions sitting behind desks, no rubber stamps, none of the paraphernalia of the potbellied, bullet-headed, myopic pen-pushers. This particular place was too hot, too remote, too bloody dangerous; piles of forms don't mean a fucking *thing* to a hungry jaguar!

The man in charge of the place was a naval commander. When he had recovered from his astonishment, he treated us royally. All the people in the tiny settlement of about five hundred turned up on the toy jetty. The first thing I noticed about the Paraguayans was how very *handsome* they are. So different from the poor Bolivians. It was a pleasant change to be surrounded by pretty women and good-looking men. The mixture of Guaraní Indian, Spanish, German, and other assorted European strains through centuries of miscegenation has resulted in what is probably, along with the Madagascan Polynesian, the best-looking race of folk on earth. Also the happiest, friendliest, and most hospitable, as well as the jolliest and most musical, always ready to play the guitars and dance.

The whole population of the town made merry at sunset—the young men played guitars and the girls, in long petticoats, danced intricate steps. The *comandante*, Huanapaco, and I ate wild duck shot that day, washed down with warm, sweet, Paraguayan beer. We were still out of range not only of bureaucratic bullshit, but also of refrigeration.

While the dancing and other festivities went on, the older people walked up and down on the grassy sward of the river's edge, flicking themselves with huge handkerchiefs to keep the pests away. To save our precious mosquito repellent, we adopted this idea and it became an unthinking habit, so much so that when I finally returned to England I would involuntarily grope for my mosquito-flicker as the sun went down.

By mid-evening the *comandante*'s house was choked with people, old, young, men, women, children, dogs, chickens. At one stage even a horse wandered in!

In the morning, amidst cheerful farewells and hand-shakes from the men and wistful looks from the women (for Paraguay has a great excess of females), we slipped the moorings and headed downstream. We used our four-horsepower outboard motor for the first time since I had bought it in Panama, ten months and over 7,000 miles ago. We used it infrequently, because the noise and fumes from the motor, added to the intense heat of the Chaco, made life a misery. We made four knots on the current, to which we added perhaps two knots with the sails; in this way, now we were out in a clear, wide river with few hazards, we made our way downstream.

Sea Dart called at many hamlets and villages in the Chaco, and very often we ate with the Paraguayans ashore. A lot of these people are hunters who ride out into the bush far away from the river to shoot wild deer, so we thrived on a diet of venison and fish. By the time we reached Asunción, the capital, we were almost back to our normal weight, though still debilitated from the heat. Once out of the thick jungle of the Mato Grosso and into the open country of the Chaco bush desert, the sky was clear, for there is little mist. The sun beat down so hard that by nine o'clock in the morning it was impossible for us to touch any metal on deck without burning our hands. Hiding in the shade was also difficult, because as the river twisted and turned in great winding loops, the attitude of the boat to the sun changed. The same with the wind; one minute we would be close hauled with the sails and sheets in tight and the next we would be on a broad reach, with the wind blowing from the side of the boat, running free, with the wind dead astern. This meant continuous work for Huanapaco, shifting the sails, as I could not leave the tiller for one second for fear that the current, a swirling brown mass of eddies, might grasp the keel and spin *Sea Dart* around like a toy top, ripping the sails to shreds. It was hard work every day, from the time when the sun rose above the pampas on the eastern horizon until the last dying embers of the day sank into the parched, dreary wastes of the Chaco thorn desert in the west.

54

THE CRUCIFIED LAND

HE HISTORY OF PARAGUAY is fascinating. When the first explorers beat their way up the mighty river, they found the Guaraní Indians, a fairly advanced tribe of cultivators and gatherers, on the eastern bank of the Paraguay. On the western side of the river, in the thorn bushes of the Chaco, an area three times the size of Texas, the savage Guaicurus roamed in merciless fury, naked and plucked, their bodies smeared, then as now, with blood, dung, and clay. On the river itself lived the fierce Payaguas, a tribe of cannibalistic river pirates who paddled in great war canoes carved out of the *lapache* tree. Some of these immense dugouts were long enough to carry a hundred warriors. Naked, with wooden disks in their earlobes several inches in diameter, they were gruesome-looking creatures. The women accompanied the men on their bloody forays, wearing silver ornaments suspended from the lower lip. Any poor sod unlucky enough to be captured by these ladies died in the most excruciating agony, forced to eat his own testicles, roasted slowly before his eyes, then his tongue and ears, his fingers, and finally his toes, hands, feet, and last, his eyes. Whatever was left was consumed by these female gourmets.

In the northern parts of the country, in small roaming bands, lived (and still do) the wild and aggressive Chiriguanos, who several times crossed the immense barren stretches of the Chaco to attack the power and pomp of the mighty Inca empire. So successful were they that even now a small band of their descendants lives in the remote province of Chuquisaca, in the far south of Bolivia, where for several centuries they have successfully resisted the sustained efforts of the Incas, the Spaniards, and, after independence, the Republicans to dislodge them.

Around Bahía Negra, our first port of call in Paraguay,

339

live the Itatines, in villages now, for they have given up headhunting except, it is said, on special occasions. They now hitch themselves to crude plows and try to till the thin, dusty earth of the Chaco.

Pizarro was not, in fact, the first conquistador to reach the Inca empire. This honor belongs to a little-known Portuguese by the name of Aleixo García, who had been with Juan Díaz de Solís, the discoverer of the huge estuary of the Plata, when that intrepid seaman had been eaten by the Indians in Uruguay. In a journey which for pure courage and daring surely excels any other made until Shackleton's magnificent Antarctic exploit, García ascended the Rivers Paraná and Paraguay alone for a thousand miles or more, gathered together an army of the Chiriguanos and Itatines, then led them through the Mato Grosso. From Corumbá, in 1525, García crossed a thousand miles of Chaco desert and penetrated the eastern Andes as far as Chuquisaca *seven years* before Pizarro entered the empire from the north, which makes one wonder at the truth of the alleged belief that Pizarro was a god.

With his savage Indian allies, García fought three pitched battles with the Incas, winning the first two and losing the last, after which he was forced to retreat along the same terrible trail by which he had come. But before he left Tahuantinsuyu, the Inca empire, he looted several temples and towns. The gold and silver from these enterprises he carried back to Paraguay. Once back on the river, after unimaginable hardships, García was promptly roasted and eaten by the Chiriguanos and the silver distributed among the tribe. The gold, not being to the Chiriguanos' fancy, was thrown into the river, where it lies to this day, under the black, silky mud washed down from the heart of this wild continent. The silver ornaments were later sighted by Sebastian Cabot, who led the first organized expedition into Paraguay. Thinking that the Chiriguanos, or some other nearby tribe, had made the trinkets and that there must be silver mines in the country, Sebastian, an egotistical glory-seeker, named the river *Plata*—the River of Silver. Hoping to be appointed viceroy, he founded Asunción, the capital, and sent news to Spain of his discovery. As soon as the name

"River of Silver" reached the ears of the avaricious Spanish, colonists poured into the country by the thousands, mixing with the peaceful, gentle Guaranís. Later, these Spaniards were joined by Germans from the Hanseatic ports on the Baltic, who were attracted by accounts of Paraguay given by returned Spanish sailors.

Asunción, then, is much older than any other city in the south of the continent. It was a thriving town when Buenos Aires was a collection of the Spanish bones left after the pampas Indians had made a meal of the first settlement.

With independence came *el Supremo*, José Gaspar Rodríguez de Francia, a megalomaniac dictator who held power for twenty-six years and never slept in the same bed two nights running. He threw thousands of his opponents into the foulest dungeons imaginable and exiled many thousands more to forced labor in the Chaco. During his reign of terror all frontiers were closed. All music and dancing were forbidden under penalty of imprisonment for life (music meant a gathering, a gathering meant people, people meant a plot), and for twenty-six years the country was like an undertaker's waiting room. When the weight of Francia was lifted by his death, the country went wild with joy for about two hours. It then fell into the hands of the López family. The first López was not too bad—at least he allowed guitars to be played—although he still kept the enemies of Francia rotting in the stinking cells below the palace. But his son, who succeeded López *père* in 1862, really stands out as far as South American dictators go! Francisco Solano López—Napoleon of the pampas!

An admirer of Bonaparte, he studied the military arts in Paris. There, he met an Irish courtesan by the name of Eliza Lynch from Dublin. Back in Asunción she changed her name to the more sonorous sounding Elisia Alicia. Meanwhile, Francisco ordered the construction of a new post office, a new palace, a new customs house (always be suspicious of a poor country that has a grand customs house!), and, of course, a new opera house. There under the scornful gaze of the Creole descendants of the conquistadors, she fluttered her fan in their faces as they waited for her to enter. After that, Francisco built a great arsenal.

Unfortunately, the English architect hired to build all these places died before work on them had scarcely begun. No one knew how to put a roof on the huge new theatre or how to construct window arches in the great railway station (only a single line, leading nowhere, but as big as Pennsylvania Station). To this day these buildings, with the exception of the palace and customs house, remain unfinished!

Next Francisco tried to expand his little country into the rich pampas west, south, and east of Paraguay. Unfortunately, there was only one problem, or rather three; these pampas were owned by Brazil, Uruguay, and the Argentine. So Francisco started a war in 1865 which lasted for five years. Great armies were put into the fields and jungles. The Paraguayans, natural fighters, made their reputation for bravery ring around the world. More than three-quarters of the male population died in the war, and the total population fell from one million to 221,000. Young lads of thirteen to old men of eighty were wiped out by the booming cannons of the Triple Alliance. Attacking in massed regiments, eighteenth century style, they presented an easy target for their enemies; chained missiles cut wide swaths through their ranks, but they fought back bravely, tooth, claw, nail, bayonet, for the sick ambitions of a megalomaniac dictator. In the end, Francisco lost too. After a last, desperate, bloody stand at the gates of Asunción, he fled into the jungle at a wounded hyena's pace, loaded down with looted treasure. Legend has it that, as the pursuers closed in, he buried the treasure, chest by chest, along the trail. With the chests, of course, went the buriers. To this day men dream of finding the trail of buried gold coins that dripped their way bloodily across the southern end of this country, abandoned at last by her crucifier. To this day, Francisco López's name is worshipped by the Paraguayans. His name is on almost every street corner; his statue can be found throughout the country. At the end of a trail in a foul-smelling swamp, not far from the Argentine frontier, his pursuers found the remains of his body, gnawed at by fat, white, jungle grubs. After kicking and spitting on the heap the victors headed back to their pampas and homesteads. Paraguay was left in mourning, a land of widows and orphans, a disaster from which she did not recover for two generations, just in time to lose the flower of her manhood again in the senseless Chaco War of the 1930s. Out of that debacle emerged the present tyrant of Paraguay, General Alfredo Stroessner, who, with the aid of the most pervasive secret police system in the world, has held power for over thirty years. Today, Paraguay's main source of income comes from drugs and fake scotch whiskey, American cigarettes and Japanese radios; it is the smuggling cross-roads of the world, a country where twenty-five percent of the native-born people are in political exile!

Despite all this misery and bloodshed, the Paraguayans meet life with great humor and courage. Poor, uneducated, hardworking, courteous and well-mannered, they eke out their humble lives in a place they honestly believe to be the paradise of the world. One day, perhaps, it may be; I hope so with all my heart!

55

WHERE THE OCEAN MEETS THE PAMPAS

E LEFT BRAZIL AT THE steaming banks of the River Apa, a black stream of mud which flows into the Paraguay at a miserable collection of palm-thatched hovels slowly collapsing into the riverbank—San Lazaro. This "town" was one of the main causes of contention during the Paraguayan War of the Triple Alliance. I looked at the rotting wooden shacks, overgrown with creepers from the ever-advancing forest. I looked at the poverty-stricken inhabitants, with not one glimmer of hope in their eyes, and I thought of 304,000 men dying on the blood-soaked ground of the jungles around Humaita, their legs blown off, their stomachs oozing. I thought of little boys dressed up in men's uniforms far too big for them, trousers rolled up on their thin brown legs, charging at the cannons with rifles almost too heavy to carry, bayonets fixed, straight into a wall of death. I thought of them being blown to pieces in the hundreds and thousands—for San Lazaro! For this stinking, steamy, sweltering, rotting collection of huts on the edge of the screaming jungle! And I thought what assholes get into power (Hitler's father, remember, was a customs official). How these bastards work their way up by stages, like woodworms eating through furniture, like teredo worms gnawing through a rotten keel, from behind their anonymous desks, where they gradually build their secret little empires and weave their sticky webs of intrigue until suddenly, almost unnoticed until the very last minute, they are *in control*. Then there we are, under the heel of fucking maniacs like Stalin, Mussolini, Hitler, Franco (he was in charge of supplies), Perón, Trujillo, Stroessner, Kadaffi, and Idi Amin. The list goes on and on. And the only reason these buggers ever get on top is because few people will stand on

344

the rooftop and shout, "Hey, look what's happening! Look at this little asshole crawling his way up!"

As we sailed down the widening river, turning and twisting through Paraguay, the land on the eastern side changed gradually, first from thick jungle to sandy, thorny desert, then to scrub brush, until at last we were sailing alongside the sun-scorched light brown grass of the pampas, that great fertile plain which stretches for thousands of miles across Paraguay, Uruguay, and northern Argentina. A vast expanse of prairie bigger than all of Europe put together! One day, soon after we had reached the northern edge of the pampas, I looked over at the horizon, many miles away over the glistening, waving grass. There, in the far distance, was a trail of dust. I thought at first it was a car; this alone would have been remarkable, for the only car we had seen since Santa Cruz, almost 2,000 miles away, had been an old Ford Model "T" in the Chaco.

Gradually, the dust came towards us accompanied by the sound—bumpity, bumpity, bumpity—of horses' hooves. Transfixed with wonder, Huanapaco and I saw a sight we will never forget. Six men came galloping up on magnificent, fast horses, Arab stock captured from the Moors in Spain and brought over to America by the conquistadors. The men were dressed in black slouch-hats, the brims turned up by the wind. On their shoulders they wore red and blue waistcoats, decorated with silver buttons that flashed in the sun. On their legs they wore baggy, Turkish-looking trousers; they were shod in leather riding boots with silver spurs. They reined in on the bank to watch us pass by, close enough for us to see their sunburned, incredulous faces, gleaming eyes, thick mustachios, and red handkerchiefs around their necks. Their rough hands calmed the nervous horses. The Gauchos! Apart from sailors, the only truly free men on this earth. Roamers of the vast ocean of the pampas who live in the saddle as they drive thundering herds of cattle, kill their food on the hoof, and roast the meat at night under a million stars. They stared at us in amazement as we drank in the sight of their magnificent horses, their sparkling stirrups, their weather-beaten riding gear, their blankets lashed across the saddles; and there was a moment of pure wonder as our eyes met and they recognized in us the same spirit and freedom as we saw in them.

We encountered many bands of gauchos on our way downstream. We watched them catching wild steers with their *bolas*, three wooden balls containing lead weights and lashed onto three joined lines. They flung these missiles at the steer's legs and down it came, helpless but unharmed. It was always a remarkable display of skill and horsemanship.

Later that evening we found out how remarkably friendly, curious, and hospitable a fellow the gaucho is— full of movement and a compulsive sharer of everything he has, except for his horse and riding gear, which he holds sacred. As we tied up to the bank at sundown, we spied a group of them dismounted, lighting a fire. They called us over to join them. We waded through the thick, long grass above the riverbank and found them digging a shallow pit in the ground. Into this they piled small pieces of dried driftwood and a sack of dried cow-dung. Soon they had a good, hot, ember fire glowing. Meanwhile, one of them had killed a young steer, simply by sticking a long knife right into its heart (just as a matador kills a bull), and was cutting the flesh into long, thin strips. These he stretched over a frame of sticks stuck in the ground close to the fire, and, while they shared their wine and maté with us, the meat cooked by the fire's reflected heat. It was a memorable experience—to eat Paraguayan beef that had been on the hoof half an hour before, to share wine with the gauchos, to hear their stories and laugh with them as the moon rose full out of the horizon towards the bright stars in the black night sky, out of the wide sea of gently waving grass, with the whispering warm breeze easing down from the north.

The gaucho has a great sense of humor, with not much obscenity. He is too gentle a man for that. He usually cannot read or write and is more or less born in the saddle. His wages are a pittance, but the perquisites of freedom and beef whenever he wants it suit him down to the ground. Many of them told me that they eat twenty pounds of beef a day! Ten kilos! I can believe it, too, as I have seen six of them demolish a good-sized calf. I am not a big meat-eater, but here on the pampas there was nothing else. Just *tons* and *tons* of rich, juicy steaks, costing *nothing!* I had so much beef going through the pampas that when I reached Buenos Aires I couldn't even bear to look at a piece of meat.

I did not know at the time that I had a tapeworm, though something was obviously wrong, for my stomach was aching and I felt feverish. What concerned me more was a small spider which had penetrated the skin on the back of my right hand. This little sod, another denizen of the Mato Grosso, had claws or hooks on the end of its legs. It also secreted a deadly poison in a sac under its belly. At Forte Coimbra my hand had swollen to the size of a coconut and turned a deep red color. Holding or handling anything was painful in the extreme. I showed the swelling to the fort's medical officer and told him about the little crablike spider I had actually seen burrowing his way, very fast, under the skin. He was so fast that before I could scratch him *out*, he was *in*. The doctor told me that if I had burst the poison sac of the spider, a *chicuru*, he called it, I would have been dead in a matter of seconds. He dared not operate on it, for fear of letting the poison out. The recognized course of treatment was to leave the thing alone and wait for it to die. Then, for some strange reason known only to the God of Insects, the poison is neutralized and the swelling subsides. All the way downstream, the whole 2,000 miles, the little bugger gnawed away inside my hand, creating a terrible itch, enough to drive a man crazy. Because of this, I had to be very careful not to bang my hand, which by now was a swollen mess, oozing yellow pus day and night through the tiny entrance hole left by the *chicuru*. For nine months I acted as host to the little sod, until he finally croaked, surfeited with my flesh and blood. Then the swelling went down, and in Uruguay the small black corpse was finally extracted and consigned, as many a time he had consigned me, to a bottle of alcohol.

We sighted our first car in 2,000 miles (except for the Model "T" in the Chaco) at Concepción. Concepción is, with the exception of the one car and an ancient bus, the rear end of which has been cut down to make a truckbed, about in the same stage of development as (I imagine) an American frontier town in the 1850's. There was one main street, along which the gauchos jingled, eyeing the girls, on their way to the few saloons down by the river front. Outside the saloons they tied up their horses to hitching posts, then swaggered in and stumbled out. The electric light plant was very erratic, and the power went on and off at various intervals until around midnight, when it failed altogether and oil lamps were lit throughout the town. On the cobblestone streets grass grew, chickens fluttered as horse-drawn carts rumbled by, and pigs grunted in the gutters, scoffing the garbage thrown out of the low, thatch-roofed cottages.

At each corner stood a policeman or soldier, while outside the town's one and only bank three armed guards smoked and hooted after the passing women and glared at all the men. Now and again a pure Guaraní Indian passed by in a long black cloak, a sort of "Pilgrim Father" hat, and trousers rolled up to the knees, barefoot, tall, and wide shouldered.

The girls were very pretty, blondes, redheads and brunettes (not necessarily in that order), and they were about the most sociable and friendly females I have ever come across anywhere. But we were not in a fit state to stay in Concepción for long, being both physically and financially exhausted, two conditions we hoped to change in Asunción. On the eighteenth of November, by the grace of God, we arrived at the capital of Paraguay, having, on the way, sighted two momentous things. One was a British merchant ship, registered in Liverpool, the same as *Sea Dart*, an ocean-going vessel which had ascended the river for 1,000 miles! As we passed under her stern, we received a tremendous barrage of cheers from her officers and crew. The other thing was an Argentine river vessel. This was our first realization that we were nearing that country and that we were near the end of our long, long crossing!

The first thing we did after tying the boat up alongside the customs house was to navigate a tedious, devious route from one bloody pen-pusher's lair to another for three hours, in order to enter the country. *Enter the country?* We'd been in it for a whole 700 miles! We'd been feasting on *their* bloody beef with *their* gauchos, sitting on *their* pampas for weeks! But the paperwork brigade was in full force in Asunción; any protest would have been squashed by a slap in the teeth from Stroessner's bully boys, who stood guarding every doorway, every window.

The next thing we did was walk over to the main plaza of the town and look up the British embassy, where I expected to find many weeks of mail waiting for me. As I walked the mile from the boat to the embassy, I kept a record of what was offered to me by the hordes of pimps and hustlers on the main road. Fourteen *shoeshines*, although I was wearing sandals made of rope; twelve *religious calendars* for 1974, although it was November of that year; eight bottles of *scotch whiskey*, mainly Johnnie Walker Black Label, looking exactly like the real thing because of expertly forged labels; ten *transistor radios*, with a famous, high-quality Japanese name, fumblingly put together down near the port; fifteen bottles of *scent;* innumerable packets of *cigarettes* in phony containers; six *dancing dolls;* three packets of *plastic hair curlers* (!), which I suppose were intended for my beard; three rides to the *Botanical Gardens*, by shifty-looking cabbies of horse-drawn hansom cabs, the motive power of which, in any state of the union, would be the subject of an immediate investigation by the Society for the Prevention of Cruelty to Animals; seven grubby little baskets of *tawdry flowers*; *sixteen women* of differing age, from around fourteen to sixty; and *five adolescent youths*, for reasons which can only be left to the imagination, though I'm pretty sure it wasn't to teach them cricket!

Sweating in my torn but clean rags, trying my utmost to look more like a British sailorman and less like a survivor of the Klondike gold rush, I walked up the stairs to the embassy.

There was one letter, a bill from the Income Tax Authority in London! I was back in the twentieth century.

56
EL SUPREMO

URING THE NEXT FEW DAYS, while *Sea Dart* was moored off a tiny jetty near the palace of the president, we talked with many people. One was an old Guaraní Indian pie-seller, who sold us lunch because it was too hot to cook on the boat. He could neither read nor write, his Spanish was very poor, and he must have been about eighty. He certainly looked it. One day, in the heat of the siesta, we sat in the cool shade of a tree, talking about Guaraní legends. He told me the tale of Isarki, a young warrior many ages ago. Isarki was a fidgety, unsettled youth, never satisfied with his lot. One day while wandering around the forest, he met an old Indian witch, a medicine woman, a very powerful figure in pre-Spanish Paraguay. Isarki was a treacherous lad and therefore admired the jaguar, who was even more treacherous. He asked the witch to change him into a *yaguarete*, which was what the Guaranís called a man who turned into a tiger. The old witch did his bidding, and for many weeks Isarki terrorized the forest, until one day a fox outwitted him. Back he went to the witch and asked her to turn him into a fox, because the fox was even more cunning than the jaguar; again she complied with the wish. As a fox Isarki roamed the settlements killing all the fowls, until one fine day he met a snake, which slithered from his grasp. Back to the witch he went, to become a snake. As a snake he was stung by a wasp, and so he changed into a wasp. As a wasp he stung a man who was trying to steal his honey; the sting, of course, remained in the man's flesh and the wasp died. Isarki returned to human form, as a human spirit must do when living in an animal body. Sadly he went back to the witch and asked her to make him into an animal more ferocious than a tiger, more cunning than a fox, more loathsome and deceitful than a snake, more vicious than a wasp. So the witch changed Isarki into a *Spaniard*!

I had a good laugh at that one and many others like it, some funny, some unutterably sad. The old pie-seller also told me of the Guaraní religion, which had no temples, no priests, no organization, no sacrifices or bloodletting, as did the religions of such "advanced" Indian societies as the Incas, the Aztecs, and the Mayas. He told me that *Tupan,* the God of Thunder, was the creator of all things good. *Ana,* the creator of all things bad, took refuge in the waning moon. *I-Yara,* the Master of the Waters, the God of the River was sent by *Tupan* to fetch two clumps of mud. These *Tupan* molded into two men. When he gave them a spark of life from the sun, they became alive. They were *Pita,* who was bronze or red, and *Moroti,* who was white. But after a time the two brothers called sadly to *Tupan* for mates. *Tupan* then ordered *I-Yara* to perform a task which was too mean for the creator of all things good. He ordered him to scoop up two more clumps of mud and make two women! That was how the Guaraní, the distant cousins of the Carib Indians of the coast of Venezuela, thought of the beginnings of man.

One day while I was napping in the noonday heat, I heard a voice say to Huanapaco, "I wish to come onboard your vessel!" It was a peremptory order, not a request. Huanapaco, as instructed long ago on Lake Titicaca, replied, in his broken Spanish, "*Señor*, this is a British registered vessel. The Captain is asleep below. No one is allowed onboard without his permission, for which you must wait."

"My name is Alfredo Stroessner," replied the voice stridently. "I am coming onboard."

I woke out of my doze, jumped up, and ascended the companionway as if a rocket was up my ass. "*Buenos días, Señor*. My name is Tristan Jones. What can I do for you?"

"*Buenos días, capitán*, I wish to come onboard to see your vessel."

A thin, slight, ascetic-looking figure, with a stern, very Germanic face, he was surrounded by a bodyguard of eight secret policemen, all holding submachine guns. This was a surprise indeed!

"Very good, Your Excellency. Please step onboard over the pulpit."

He climbed up, with the aid of one of his guards, who

started to clamber after him. I looked at the guard and said, "Sorry, no arms onboard, please." He continued to climb over the pulpit, ignoring me. I said to Stroessner, "I am extremely sorry, Your Excellency, I cannot allow any arms onboard this vessel. She is British territory. It is against the laws of my country to allow armed men onboard unless I specifically request them to come onboard. Quite apart from that, if all that lot comes onboard, it will sink the boat!"

At first he frowned, nonplused, but as the humor of the situation dawned on him, he turned to his bodyguards and told them to wait on the jetty. Then he came down into the cockpit to talk. Most of the discussion was about small craft, in which President Stroessner was interested. I told him my stories of the Arctic, of Africa, and of this voyage, and after listening very civilly for an hour, he wished me good sailing and promised to keep the customs off my back, for which I thanked him kindly. In Paraguay everything goes through *el Supremo*! Even a scruffy little sailing boat!

The missing mail soon turned up, as did two hundred dollars—a fortune! We wandered around the market stalls of Asunción picking up food—luxury items like canned meat, canned milk, canned butter even—and for two days we wallowed in an orgy of fresh green vegetables, good clean bottled water, and *ice cream*! Unimaginable delights. As for the other amenities of Asunción, there was no shortage of cold beer and women, pretty, fresh-faced lasses. We shoved off from Asunción like giants refreshed, following the stream down south to the mouth, 300 miles from Asunción as the crow flies, 400 with the winding bends.

I was in a hurry now to escape the blazing heat of the sun, for in the latter half of November, we were coming into the full southern summer of heat and humidity. Also I was determined to get to Buenos Aires by Christmas.

We passed the fabled River Bermejo, where the conquistadors had struggled through incessant dangers and hazards to drink of the water, which they believed contained the elixir of life. At the end of the first week in December, we emerged at long, long last from the River Paraguay, passing the ruins of Humaita, a tiny jungle clearing which the mad Francisco López had once fortified so strongly it was known as the "Gibraltar of the Jungles" and where most of the manhood of Paraguay had bled to death a hundred and more years ago.

As we swept into the Paraná River, it was obvious that this was indeed very different from the River Paraguay, which all the way south from the Brazilian frontier had been comparatively easy to navigate, despite the intense glare of the sun, the *bichus*, the mosquitoes, swift, swirling eddies and bends in the river which seemed to flow in every direction but the one we were trying to make.

57
THE WILD PARANÁ

HE PARANÁ LIVED UP TO its South American name, *Paraná Bravo*, the Wild Paraná. A much wider river than the Paraguay, it is, until the city of Paraná, very wide, up to five miles, and correspondingly shallow, littered with shifting sandbanks and uncharted rocks, against which fallen trees carried down from the jungles of Brazil pile up. Rusting hulks of river steamers bear evidence at almost every turn of the penalty for neglecting to keep an unremitting lookout. On this stretch the winds would sometimes blow upstream at a terrific rate, setting up a very dangerous short sea that threatened to swamp the boat. After the placid, enervating passage down the Paraguay, this was like coming off the lake in Central Park and going straight into a winter gale off Cape Hatteras!

When we arrived in Paraná, we were lucky enough to find a vacant berth alongside an old barge in the center of the city. Soon after *Sea Dart* was tied up, a crowd of citizens gathered on the barge to stare at the boat, at Huanapaco, at me, and at the red ensign. We cleaned up the boat as we waited for the harbor police to arrive. I was not concerned about entering Argentina, as I had made sure, at the Argentine embassy in Asunción, that this time we had valid entry papers.

After a while two policemen arrived, along with an Argentine naval officer.

"*Buenos días, Capitán*. Where have you come from?"

"From Paraguay, *Señor*."

"Do you have your exit papers from Argentina?"

"No. This is our first port of call in this country."

"*Cómo*? You cannot get to Paraguay unless you pass through Argentina; there is no other way." The naval officer was obviously suspicious of us.

"We arrived in Paraguay from Bolivia; see, here are my papers." I handed him a sheaf of entry and exit papers going back to Callao, Coimbra, and Asunción.

"*Dios mío! Carraco!*" The naval officer turned to the policemen. "They have crossed the continent. It's incredible! Phone the press right away!" Then he turned to me and said "*Señor*, you are a hero; no one has ever done this before. You have put yourself among the conquistadors!"

While we were waiting for a reporter to arrive from the local newspaper, we exchanged yarns about sailing in different parts of the world, for this lieutenant had trained with the American navy and spoke English quite well. He also gave me some hints as to the lively spots in town.

The reporter soon turned up and took our story. He was especially interested in Huanapaco, for mountain Indians are rare indeed in that part of Argentina. His story came out quite well, and he told us that it would be published the morning of the following day. Everyone was very courteous, and both Huanapaco and I looked forward to visiting the town.

That evening we made our way to a small restaurant, where we had a huge feast of beef and rice, salad and tomatoes for about fifty cents U.S. each. The cost of living in Argentina then was very low; Isabel Perón was in power and she, while embezzling all the money she could get her hands on, was trying to keep the masses quiet by subsidizing consumer goods. In the restaurant, full of workers, we were entertained by guitar players and accordionists, which delighted us so much that we decided to stay for a few beers. Everything was so cheap we could have stayed there every night for a week for the equivalent of ten dollars U.S.

Finally, with Huanapaco beginning to weave about a bit, we made our way back to the waterfront. He was still dressed in his *chorro* and poncho, still barefoot. He had tried to wear a pair of shoes in Asunción, but after half an hour of intense discomfort had finally given them away to a beggar.

As we emerged into the main square of the town, a car pulled up alongside of us. A black nondescript car, unmarked. The door flew open and in seconds we were surrounded by four men pointing automatic pistols straight at our heads. I was too astonished to say anything.

"Move and you're dead! Hands up!"

Up went our hands.

"Security police!" The leader spat this out. He, like the rest, was dressed in ordinary street clothes and, apart from the brutal, ruthless expression in his eyes, looked much the same as anyone else we had seen that night.

"Papers!"

"We're off a boat—he's Bolivian." I gestured with my chin at Huanapaco, who was standing motionless, glaring at the police through half-closed slits. "I'm British. We don't carry our passports with us in case we get robbed, but they're back on the boat." I gestured with my chin toward the mooring barge, where *Sea Dart*'s mast was in full view, the huge Union Jack drooping lazily from the masthead.

"*Mierda*. Shit!" The leader waved his gun at the car. "Get in!"

We got carefully into the car, saying nothing, but I was wondering whether these were police or terrorists. What the hell was happening? They all looked so desperate and nervous that I was sure that with one wrong word I'd have my head blown off.

They very quickly drove us to the police headquarters, where, after our names had been registered very laboriously by a sergeant, we were slammed into a cell crowded with people. The cell was about twenty feet long by maybe fifteen feet wide. Inside there were thirty-two men and boys, plus one crouching over the crapper in the back corner. Immediately after the cell door slammed, we were asked for cigarettes, and right away handed around all we had. This supplied about fifteen men with a smoke, then the butts were handed over to the other fifteen. I spied close to me a sad-faced man of about forty, soberly dressed, wearing spectacles, with an air of resignation about him straight from a painting by Goya.

I addressed him, "*Hola, amigo*. Look, I'm English and my Indian friend over there, he's Bolivian, and we don't know what the hell goes on, *qué pasa?*"

"You're in for a security check; how long have you been in Argentina?"

"Only one day."

He laughed. "Oh, if you're clean you've nothing to worry about. This happens to everyone here. They just come and pick you up off the street, keep you inside for three or four days while they check your record at Central Register, then, if you're clean, off you go. It's nothing. It happens to everyone."

"Where did they pick you up?" I asked him.

"Outside my house; I'd just gone over the road to buy some cigarettes."

"What happens if you're not clean?"

"If you have a criminal record, you get maybe six weeks inside the 'local.' "

"What for? I mean supposing you haven't done anything wrong since you were released?"

"*No importa*; you get six weeks anyway, for being picked up!"

"And if you are a *político*?"

He passed his finger over his throat. "Then you get roasted!"

"What about the judges, don't they say anything?"

"You're not in the *Estados Unidos* now, *amigo*." He looked around nervously, then said, "Do you have any money?"

"A bit, about five dollars."

"And your friend?" He pointed with his chin at Huanapaco, who was in serious conversation with a raffish-looking youngster on the other side of the crowd.

"About the same," I replied.

"Will you pay for my food until I can get out and repay you? See, I'm a widower, and my kids are all down in Rosario, working."

"They don't feed you here, eh?" I asked.

"What do you think?" He smiled, throwing his hands in the air.

"Sure, I'll get you a meal whenever I get one." I patted his shoulder.

"*Dios bendiga, gringito,* I've been in here for two days with very little to eat, we're all poor here. I'm only a waiter, you see."

"Oh, really; where do you work?"

"God forgive me, *amigo*, and you won't believe me—at the *hijo de puta* Police Social Club!"

"What? And they don't know you? How long have you worked there?"

"Twenty-eight years, but the *maricón* who picked me up has only just arrived from Córdoba. A real bastard he is, so they booked me!"

"Cor, stone the bloody crows," I said, in English.

"What's that?" he asked.

"Bad luck, *amigo*!"

"*Seguro.*" He laughed, quietly.

The following morning, early, money was collected by the guard, who after a delay returned with about forty percent of its value in food and cigarettes. These were distributed around the cell, which by now contained about forty-five people, all standing, except for the one whose turn it was to use the toilet facility. The place stank like a sewer. The inmates of the cell were all ages, from around fourteen to one poor old chap of about eighty, whom Huanapaco had taken under his wing.

At about ten o'clock we were all lined up for a roll call. When my name was called out, just recognizable in the Paraná accent, I was perfunctorily beckoned to one side. So were Huanapaco and two others. I quickly slipped my remaining money to Ramón, the Police Social Club waiter, and stepped to one side. He murmured, "*Qué hombre tu eres!*"

We were taken out into the front office, where a gold-braided officer was waiting. He smiled broadly at me, shouting as he grabbed my hand, "*Carraco!* Why didn't you tell us who you were? All this is completely unnecessary. Welcome, welcome to Paraná! You know, we are renowned throughout Argentina for being the friendliest, the most hospitable city in the whole country!"

"Yes," I replied, "so I see. Can we go now, please?"

"But, of course, of course, you may go, you and your friend here." He patted Huanapaco's shoulder.

"Thanks a lot, *Señor!*"

"Stay as long as you wish!" he shouted, as we walked out of the grimy doorway.

"We will, *Señor,* we will!"

"Jesus Christ!" murmured Huanapaco.

"Let's get the bloody mooring lines slipped, *amigo.* We're off!"

Four times on the River Paraná we were forced to take refuge from the howling *pampero* wind, which drove upstream holding back the wide river, piling up greeny-gray waves, blowing the tops of the steep seas until the whole surface turned into a mass of seething white water. Even the five-knot current was stopped, and on one memorable occasion it was actually reversed. Swooshing out of a low, cigar-shaped cloud, the dusty *pampero* flattened the greeny-gray grass and forced cattle to kneel with their heads bowed, as if in homage.

A cold wind, it blew all the way from Patagonia, almost 2,000 miles to the south. A sudden hush, fraught with tension, heralded its arrival; birds grew silent, wild horses galloped for refuge in the hollows of the riverbank. Then, on the southern edge of the curved world of grass and water, a long black line rose into the sky. Under the cigar-shaped cloud, between it and the pampa, loomed a band of dirty brown weather, the underside of which shone silver white over the wide river. Quickly, we secured *Sea Dart* to the sandy river bed with two anchors and to the pampa foreshore with six mooring lines firmly bent onto as many heavy wooden stakes of *palo blanco*, the toughest wood in the world. Huanapaco and I had driven the stakes, about ten feet long, into the ground until there was only a foot of wood showing before securing the mooring lines. Even so, when the roaring *pampero* arrived, it turned everything around us into dust and white water. It was strong enough to send derelict trees floating back upstream! Over the banks the gray water rushed backwards, shifting the bank's position and turning the river to a sandy yellow under a sky as black as night in the bitter cold wind. The temperature dropped *seventy degrees in four minutes*! Hoar frost formed on the pampas grass minutes after we had been sweltering in a humid heat of over a hundred degrees!

The Paraná is a roving river, continually shifting course, splitting off into shallow streams, with islands growing and dying from week to week. At some parts it is as wide as thirty miles, at others, as narrow as one. Here there is little time to view the scenery or birdlife. As *Sea Dart* rushed headlong downstream in the heat of the north wind or the bitter cold of the south, we caught quick glimpses of swamp backed by the edge of the pampas. From there flat grassland stretched way over to the far Andes, a thousand miles to the west.

Santa Fe, about 250 miles upstream from the delta of the River Paraná (an area about half as big as England), was the first true ocean-shipping port we encountered going downstream. Here there were great stone docks and cranes. On the walls of the jetties the names of visiting ships have been painted in big letters by the crews, showing dates decades old. Here, as *Sea Dart* crept in through the long, man-made canal which joins the small city to the river, we worked our way over to the stone wall and wrote, *British Yacht Sea Dart, Liverpool, arrived here December 17th, 1974 from Callao, Peru, by way of La Paz and Mato Grosso.*

We also encountered here our first real Yacht Club since leaving the Pacific shore, 3,000 miles sailing and 2,000 miles hauling ago. Our arrival caused astonishment, then incredulity, then when they realized who we were, an uproarious, wonderful welcome. The good people of Santa Fe took us under their wing and treated Huanapaco and me royally, with a reception attended by around five hundred people, in return for which I entertained them with a short account of the voyage. During the two days *Sea Dart* was moored off the club, the members came onboard and offered to drive us around town, so that we could see the beautiful cathedral and the colonial parts of the friendliest town, with the best folk, in the Argentine. The young lads, who were sailing the first dinghies we had seen in South America, a flotilla of Snipes, even took Huanapaco out for a spin, which he enjoyed no end. Imagine, a mountain Indian, a Quechua, doing something for pure enjoyment! This was the real breakthrough; for an Andes Indian to make any effort which does not result in food or booze or intoxication is a complete heresy!

South, ever more south, headed for the ocean. We sailed from early dawn until the last flickering red in the sky disappeared at night. We anchored wherever we could, for I wanted more than anything to arrive at the Argentinian town of San Nicolás before Christmas, and at Buenos Aires by that festival day.

I had a gift to bring to San Nicolás. When I had been on the coast of Turkey back in 1970, I had visited the ruins of the church of Saint Nicholas, or Santa Claus, as he is more familiarly known. The good patron saint of sailors, children, thieves, and shoemakers, as well as Russia, is buried in that church. I had taken a colored photograph of his tomb and picked up a tiny sliver of stone from the ancient church walls. These I carefully kept, with the intention of taking them to the town named after the saint by the conquistadors in far-away Argentina, as a sort of thanksgiving for surviving the long voyage between two very distant, very different places. Stowed away in my little ditty box, these two gifts had come through all the storms and hazards of the voyage. I was determined to complete my little pilgrimage before Christmas.

Hardly stopping at any one place for more than an hour or two, sailing hard and continually now, our passage closely watched by the international news agencies, though I did not suspect this at the time, we made it to San Nicolás on the twenty-first of December, tired, weary, and pooped out. The tapeworm was waxing and the *chicuru* still gnawed away at my hand, while Huanapaco suffered terribly from the heat and humidity, for which his Quechua body and big lungs were not designed.

I anchored by the flashy yacht club jetty and went ashore, bearing my precious gifts. They were accepted graciously by the commodore of the club, who then extended an invitation to attend the club Christmas dinner, which was to take place that very night. Excitedly, I rushed back to the boat to tell Huanapaco. The remaining hours of daylight we spent making ourselves and our clothes as presentable as we could in the circumstances. We showered in the club and tidied ourselves up, for the Argentines are very conscious of appearances. They are incredibly bourgeois about this— with two cents in their pockets, they will dress like millionaires.

Long before the dinner commenced we offered our services in helping to arrange furniture. For hours we worked gladly at the preparations, for the Argentines dine late. Then the members and guests started to arrive. You would have thought it was a reception at the White House. They were all dolled up in formal dinner suits and long gowns, with diamonds and pearls asparkle.

Back in the kitchen, where Huanapaco and I were helping to stack plates and cart napkins off trucks loaded down with gear, word arrived that the commodore wanted to speak with Huanapaco. Out he went, happy and excited, full of high humor.

He came back looking like the world had fallen around his ears and came over to me, taking my elbow in his gentle way. His almond eyes were wet with tears. "*Mi Capitán*; I'm going back to the boat. The commodore says that I cannot attend the dinner because I am too *dirty*." I thought he was joking, until I looked into his eyes.

"What?" I said, as the shock hit me. "What the fuck is this, a joke?"

"No, *mi Capitán*. He says that the ladies will all be wearing their ballgowns, the gentlemen, *los caballeros*, will be in their best clothes, and if I go in wearing these clothes they will be offended. The ladies will be wearing scent and," a tear dropped down his cheek, "they don't want me; he says because I am dirty, but you know, *mi Capitán*, you *know*, *tú sabes*, that I washed and washed today, to come here, and as I have no clothes of my own left, I have to wear these shirts we bought in Asunción, which are a bit too small for me, and these trousers. You know I did my best to look respectable, *aparacer gentil, no?*" Another big tear dropped down his bronzed face.

I just stood there, shocked beyond belief. *Fucking Huanapaco in tears? What in Christ's name was going on?*

I turned to look through the kitchen door where the middle class of the Argentine was about to indulge in yet another orgy of cramming itself with beef from the underpaid labor of brave gauchos. As I started for the door, I heard Huanapaco say in a quiet voice broken by sobs, "But you also know, *mi Capitán*, it's not for this, *no es por eso*; *es porqué soy Indio,* because I'm an Indian." As soon as the phrase came out, for I knew it was coming and I was waiting for it, my mind blew. Every Celtic sinew in me exploded; I felt again, if only in my brain, the bite of every fucking insect in the Mato Grosso, the strain of every bloody push and shove through that Green Hell, every effort that this man had made to help me away from a rotting death. I marched into the dining room straight to the commodore.

"Pardon me, *Señor,* may I speak with you a minute, please?" Smirking, he left a group of local prominents and came over to me.

"What is it, *Capitán?*"

"What is this about my friend Huanapaco not being allowed to attend the dinner?"

"Well, you know how it is; look around, this is a formal occasion, the highly placed people from all around, some even from Rosario, are here tonight and the ladies," he gestured with a beringed finger at some ancient, horse-faced hag dripping with pearls, "the ladies are not used to—well, you see, they are all in their gowns; all dressed for the occasion. We know it's difficult for you, for that reason we don't mind *your* joining us. We can, after all, make arrangements for someone to take some food over to the boat for your Indian sailor. Or if you prefer, he can eat in the kitchen."

I could smell the eau de cologne wafting up from his silk-faced jacket!

I looked him straight in the eye; I stared him down until his guilty eyes dropped to the floor. Then I said, slowly and clearly, so that there could be no possible chance of misunderstanding, "*Señor Comodoro,* you are a liar about your reasons for excluding my friend and comrade from your dinner. *Señor,* you can take your dinner, and your yacht club, and the gifts I brought to you across thousands of miles of ocean and which we rushed down the River to present to you before Christmas—and you can stick them right up your ass!" I flung away the club burgee that he had so patronizingly offered. "And what's more, I'm taking off right now into the River at night. I don't care about floating logs or sandbanks, or whatever else son-of-a-whoring thing there is out there; I'd rather be dead in that dogshit-eating, mother-fucking river than alive in your goat-shagging club!"

With that, I went over to the kitchen door and shouted to Huanapaco, "*Vamos, amigo, hay casas de putas en Buenos Aires!* Come on mate, let's go, there are whorehouses in Buenos Aires!" We walked out looking them straight in the eyes, all the shocked old women, all the well-fed men. I slammed the door hard on the way out, causing a pane of glass to fall out and shatter on the ground.

Right away we weighed anchor and took off into the dark night, into the swirling mist of the River Paraná. An hour later we anchored again in a calm, insect-ridden side-stream and ate canned Paraguayan beef, which to us tasted better than all the San Nicolás Yacht Club goodies put together. We never mentioned the episode again, either of us.

58

SOME BOTTLE! SOME CORK!

PART FROM THE INSULT AT San Nicolás, our reception and treatment along the Paraná were, in the main, kind and friendly. A river policeman from the patrol boat at Rosario presented me with a hand-driven siren in return for which I gave him my Swiss railroad guard's horn. Many offers to show us the sights were made, but we took only a few of these, as we were both still suffering from the effects of the heat, the humidity, and the effort to keep going along the strong current of the Paraná.

As we drew closer to the huge delta of the River, we saw more and more pleasure craft, and we were escorted some distance downstream by one of them. By now the whole of the Argentine knew of our arrival; our progress was being reported daily in the press and on the radio.

The pleasure craft, fast outboard-motor boats usually, fascinated Huanapaco. When he saw the first one, north of Asunción, he gawped as it flashed by, throwing up a tremendous wake. He stared after it for two minutes or so, until it disappeared. Then he turned to me with a questioning look on his surprised face.

"It's a speedboat, very fast, probably belongs to a *hacienda* owner." (Later, in southern Paraguay, we saw quite a few *haciendas* where the owners live in a splendor that would shame the Agha Khan; great rambling estates with two planes standing on the small airstrip outside the house and luxury speedboats moored up to the riverbank.)

"Why does he go so *fast*?" asked Huanapaco, after another moment.

"He's in a hurry. Wherever he's going he wants to get there *fast*."

His bronze face furrowed deeply in thought.

365

"Why does he want to go so fast?" he asked me, half frowning.

"Oh, Jesus Christ, to save *time* of course!" I replied testily. The hot sunshine was not conducive to long discussions on the obvious.

After another pensive moment, he asked quietly, *"What does he do with the time he saves?"*

For that there was no answer. I asked him to go forward and set up the anchor line.

In the towns and cities where we went ashore, Huanapaco was all eyes, watching everything. Rosario, for instance, is a much greater city than La Paz. The highest building above street level in La Paz is about fifteen stories high, standing all alone. Here they were skyscrapers fifty or sixty stories high! I knew that Huanapaco compared everything to Bolivia and that this was disturbing him, making him unhappy, for obviously every time he compared his beloved country with anything here, in a modern industralized land like estuarial Argentina, he found Bolivia severely wanting. As he gazed at the skyscrapers, I tried to cheer him up.

"But they are so *big*. In La Paz——*pobre* Bolivia!" he moaned.

"*Pobre Bolivia* nothing, *amigo*! Look, how far above the sea do you think we are standing, you and I?"

"*No sé*, I've no idea."

"Right, well, let's see; there's the river wall, that's 20 feet high, then there's the distance to the sea at the delta, that's about 200 miles; call it 50 feet; so we are 70 feet above the level of the ocean, yes?"

"If you say so, *mi Capitán*."

"So that building, that one you're so envious of, how far above the ocean is it, the top of it?"

He craned his neck and shook his head.

"Let's say it's 500 feet, right? Then the top is 570 feet above the ocean, yes?"

He nodded.

"And how high is fucking La Paz above the ocean?" I asked him.

He knew this one. "12,800 feet!"

"*Bueno, amigo*. And what's 570 feet from 12,800?"

This one took him some minutes, writing figures on the back of a cigarette pack. Then he replied, smiling, "12,230 feet."

"And how high is that? Go on, look up in the sky, tell me, point to me where the top of the La Paz building would be if it was here!"

He grinned in happiness for a few seconds, then his face dropped again. "But all that height is the height of the mountains. It wasn't built by Bolivians."

"And who built that building over there?" I gestured at the one he was staring at.

"Argentinos."

"*Bueno*, and who built the mountains of Bolivia?"

"God."

"Are you comparing the *hijo de puta Argentino* to *God*?"

He laughed uproariously, patting my shoulder. On the way back to the boat he said, "*Mi Capitán*, I guess that men, too, are like buildings. Some already start off on top of the mountains?"

"*Sí, amigo,* especially the Quechua." He was silent, pleased.

"*Y los marineros ingleses,*" he said quietly, after a while.

"*Tal vez*, perhaps," I murmured as we climbed onboard.

As we approached the delta of the Paraná, the land again changed, from open, grassy plains to thick scrub and then to jungle, a low, bushy jungle that covers the hundreds of islands which compose the 200-mile-long water maze. On the other side of this last obstacle was the Mar del Plata, the great estuary of the waters of the Paraná, the Paraguay, the Bermejo, and the Uruguay, half the waters of the continent, from as far away as the Andes in the west, the infested Mato Grosso in the north, and even further north than that, right from the very heart of the huge continent. From all over southern Brazil came the rushing torrent, to sweep ever onwards out into the estuary, and so into the Atlantic Ocean. Our job was to make sure that *Sea Dart* went with the deep water and did not end up being washed onto one of the many islands, rocks, sandbanks, sunken trees, or wrecks as she charged forward in the lively breezes.

At last, on the twenty-third of December, we reached the

small but busy fishing port of San Isidro. After staying there overnight, we were off again in the early morning light, down the branch of the delta known as El Tigre. At ten o'clock, on the morning of the twenty-fourth, straining to see beyond the long, dreary stretches of river, weaving our way around the obstacles, at long, long last I sighted, way ahead, a clear horizon—the Mar del Plata, gleaming clear and silver along the horizon, under the rising sun! An hour later *Sea Dart* shot out of the Tigre like a cork out of a bottle! "Some *Bottle*! Some *Cork*!" I thought as we heaved in to close-haul her llama-skin sheet ropes and headed for the port of Buenos Aires, the biggest city in the Southern Hemisphere! At their invitation, we dropped anchor right in front of the Yacht Club Argentino. In the center of one of the busiest seaports in the world, with ocean steamers moored by the dozen, tiny *Sea Dart* crept in on the weakening evening breeze, her grubby, patched sails only just edging her forward, her worn hull blistered by the hot sun of the pampas, her mast scarred and scratched by the cruel overhanging jungle thorns of the Mato Grosso, and anchored at the guest-of-honor mooring. She crept in like a wayward child and quietly settled down only yards from the haughty clock-tower which sticks up like an admonishing finger in the center of the Buenos Aires docks.

I shook Huanapaco's hand. He looked up at the Bolivian ensign drooping from the starboard spreader and stuck his thumb up, grinning. I pointed at the red British ensign, now bleached an anemic pale pink, torn and tattered, hanging slackly from the stern, then poked him in the ribs and stuck my thumb up too. We'd done it! We'd reached the bloody ocean!

It was Christmas Eve, and everything except the bars and restaurants was closed. The British embassy, the banks, and the post office were all shut up as tight as a drum. The Yacht Club was deserted. Huanapaco and I, still in our worn and torn, but carefully repaired, rags, celebrated our feat with corned beef and six bottles of cold beer obtained on the slate from the friendly club barman.

We'd done it! For the first time ever in recorded history a sea-going boat had crossed right through the middle of

South America! We had sailed *Sea Dart* thousands of miles where no sail had ever been before!

I had taken the ocean to Bolivia and had brought Bolivia back down to the ocean! I had seized for Britain the altitude sailing record of the world, unbeatable until man finds water on a star! I had reached three *impossible* destinations—the Dead Sea, Lake Titicaca, and then the Atlantic through the living death of the Mato Grosso! Slowly, little by little, as *Sea Dart* progressed down the populated areas of the Argentine, she had become a living legend.

In the warm, sticky cabin, among the damp-rotted rags of clothing and the stained charts and papers, was the brightly dyed llama wool blanket which Manco Quispe had given me "to show to the ocean sun" as he made me *padrino* of Suriqui! Honorary Chief of the Aymara! I sat on it, as the boat danced at anchor in the ocean tide, weary, exhausted, sick to my stomach, trying to grasp the fact that it was over, and feeling humble before the terrible majesty of all that we had seen, all that we had overcome.

"What do you do now, *mi Capitán*?" asked my Quechua brother.

"Get back home, of course, *amigo*."

"Me too."

"After Christmas?"

"Yes, after Christmas!"

"*Feliz Navidad*, Huanapaco, *jok'halla*! Merry Christmas, mate!"

"*Feliz Navidad, Capitán* Tristan!" He slugged at his beer.

I carefully made my way up the tiny companion ladder for a piss into Paraná waters, and a first one into the Atlantic, under the gleaming bright stars of Argentina. Acrux was winking away in the south to one side of the luminescent night sky of Buenos Aires, a reflection of the glow of a billion electric lights. As I stood there a big ship hooted on her way out to the ocean. She was out of London, her red ensign showing clearly in the light of her stern steaming lamp. It fluttered. I saluted thumbs up across the black, gleaming waters of the night harbor and turned in, thinking of Christmas Eve in Bethlehem four years and forty lives before.

59

TRIUMPH—AND DISASTER

ITH THE MONEY I COLLECTED at Buenos Aires, Huanapaco and I received medical treatment. We were poked and prodded in the modern seamen's hospital, and my tapeworm guest of the past few months was extracted, but nothing could be done about the *chicuru* in my hand. He lived to a ripe old age of nine months, well fed and chewing happily.

In the last week of January, Huanapaco left *Sea Dart* and returned home to the Lake in the Sky. Silently we went together in the bus to the airport and shook hands.

"You coming back to Bolivia, *mi Capitán?*"

"One day, Huanapaco, one day."

"With another boat, a big one?"

"Not on your bloody life, *amigo mío*. Next time I come in a fucking balloon!" In his new clothes he strode out to the exit, laughing. As he disappeared through the door he turned round one last time. He winked, grinned, and stuck up his thumb, just as he had done in Tiquina so long ago when I emerged like the Count of Monte Cristo from the frozen bug-pit of the Bolivian navy!

In February I moved to the small port of Olivos to refit. It is much more peaceful and quiet than Buenos Aires harbor, where the frequent swells from the wash of rushing tugboats and great, lumbering ocean vessels made any kind of work impossible. Here, little by little, I started to feel better. I worked onboard or at writing articles during the hot, humid days. In the cool evenings, I took a stroll around the city. In early 1975 Argentina was a very cheap place to live. After changing my dollars or pounds on the black market, I found that it was almost impossible to spend five dollars in a good night. I would have a three-course meal with wine, visit a cinema or a night club, stay until around one in the morning, and go back with change from the five dollars!

The political situation had deteriorated, and the police made life very awkward for the average citizen. They picked him up off the street and stuck him inside a filthy cell, with no food except what friends or relatives could bring. Then, after his identity had been checked, they released him or sent him to another filthy cell. This happened to me three times during the five months I spent in Buenos Aires. Each time I spent two full days and nights cooped up with all kinds of people, from respectable businessmen to the riffraff of the red-light district. There was a lot of brutality. A continual war was going on between various factions in the country, and police were being knocked off regularly by the left-wingers. I don't blame them, especially after seeing one of the cops kick out the eye of a lad of eighteen, and after seeing others pick up an old man having an epileptic fit on the filthy floor of the cell and punch him until he bled. In fact, I'd have a go at knocking off those particular sods myself! Especially the fair-haired bastard of a pig-fucking detective in civilian clothes, red shirt, and grey pants, who, in Station 13 of the Buenos Aires Police Prefectura, kicked out the boy's eye on March fifteenth, 1975, at five o'clock in the morning. *Hijo de puta!* Talk about savages!

By mid-May the boat was ready enough to tackle the passage over to Montevideo, and by mid-July I headed north, after having puzzled and perspired my way through a tangled web of forms and papers, entry certificates, exit permits, rat control certificates. In Argentina, as in all police states, the desk dictators have a field day raising paper obstacles, the overcoming of which would test the ingenuity of Thomas Edison, the logic of Bertrand Russell, and the mathematical capacity of Albert Einstein! In the end I gave up the struggle, stocked up a two-week's supply of food, and silently slid out of Olivos, under the nose of the sleeping naval sentry, at two in the morning, with clouds obscuring the crescent moon. Even after what happened, I'd still rather tackle the Plate Estuary than the Argentinian customs and Nautical Control Authority!

Keeping to the buoyed channels, I sailed out as best I could into the dark, breezy sky of the night. By dawn I was over toward the Uruguayan shore, nearing Montevideo, the chief port and capital of that small country. All the next night I kept going, alone on the helm, for the wind was too shifty to trust the wind-vane steerer in the narrow channels. The following day, the sixteenth of July, I was sliding nicely along, about a mile off the Uruguayan coast, about the prettiest in all of South America, sandy beaches with craggy rock outcrops and green hills, as in England, behind the beaches. There was a fresh northeaster blowing off the shore. All round was a clear blue sky. The wind was chilly, for this was the southern winter. I had only eight miles or so to make Montevideo harbor. I was feeling triumphant. After crossing the continent, *Sea Dart* was once again in true saltwater. I was looking forward to making preparations for the passage north to Rio Grande do Sul, a matter of 600 miles or so against the prevailing wind and current. This prospect, however, did not worry me unduly, for *Sea Dart* was a witch going to windward, though the state of her sails was a cause for concern. I had not been able to find any Dacron in Argentina, and the cost of getting it through the customs, or for that matter, of getting *anything* through the customs and into Argentina from abroad, was plain daylight robbery. Uruguay was the same. There are very few manufacturing industries in that predominantly agricultural country; but in any case I intended to wait for two or three weeks in Montevideo for the winds and the hard, southerly running Falkland current to ease off, before heading north.

The estuary of the River Plate is an awful mess of shallows and wrecks that are not always marked by buoys. In the middle are vast, shifting banks of mud and sand, while the coast of Uruguay (my lee shore) is a ghastly maze of rocks.

"Never put yourself on a lee shore unless you are 100 percent certain you can claw your way off" is the first rule in coastal pilotage under sail. "If you can see a lee shore, it's too close" is an elaboration of the same tenet. But this is all very well when you have enough sea-room to get out of trouble. In the Plate, however, the channels are narrow and run close to the shore. There is no possibility of standing off the Uruguayan shore much more than two miles, as the way further out is blocked solid with sand and mud.

The first sign of trouble came in the early afternoon with the sudden appearance in the southern sky of the *cigarro,* the *pampero* wind cloud—a long, black line like smoke, menacing and devilish. I looked towards the shore. "Holy fuck!" I thought, "I've only got a mile of sea-room." I clambered up to the foredeck, handed the big genoa, thrust it below, and hauled up the number two jib. Then, grabbing the tiller, I headed away from the shore as fast as I could, towards the edge of the great mudbank that lies parallel to the coast.

As the ominous cloud moved closer, the wind increased, rising from ten knots to seventy in ten minutes! The mainsail, reefed down to one-third its full extent, blew out like a toy balloon. The jib, in good shape, held as long as I held the course on a broad reach. By now the shallow Plate was like a seething cauldron from one horizon to the other. Little *Sea Dart* was bouncing around like a landed piranha!

If I'd had a clear run ahead, I think I'd have made it into Montevideo with no problem, but directly ahead lay a group of jagged rocks sticking out a mile from the beach. I could not avoid them if I maintained the course. And I could not gain into the wind with only the working jib. The tiny four-horsepower engine stood no chance against the wind and sea. It was not even powerful enough to hold the boat in a fixed position against the *pampero.*

Then, to add to the agony, a thick fog suddenly surrounded *Sea Dart,* caused by the *cigarro* cloud's descending to sea level. There I was, with the visibility nil and a storm force wind! I bounced up to the foredeck, clutching at the rigging, and *dropped the hook.* I anchored! There was nothing else for me to do, risky as it was in that raging sea. With the boat bucking like a wild horse, it was quite a feat to anchor at all, but somehow I managed to get the twenty-eight-pound danforth out on a twenty-fathom, 1½-inch nylon line, the same line that had hauled us out of the ditch beside the ruins of the temple at Tiahuanaco! Then I slithered down below and delved into the tiny foredeck to extricate my great, heavy "hurricane" hook, a sixty-pound fisherman anchor that, in comparison to *Sea Dart,* looks as if it could hold a bloody battleship.

Cursing in four different languages, dragging out chain, anchor, rope, spare sails, ragged shirts, I heard a crack like doomsday overhead and knew right away that the anchor line had parted. *Sea Dart* began to drift swiftly ashore before the wind! Down below all hell broke loose as she broached and started to slam sideways. I staggered up through the tiny cabin dragging the huge anchor and chain and rope, all at one go, as fast as I could, thinking, "Fucking hellfire and damnation! She's going! She'll touch!" I bulldozed the anchor out into the bouncing cockpit like a maniac, sheer willpower moving me on. Then she touched!

With a force that shook her small frame to the very keel-bolts, she crashed against solid rock. Somehow, God only knows how, I managed to drag the genoa out of the cabin and jam it under her bilge keel, which was buckling as it smashed into the hidden granite fist of South America, an underwater menace that had been waiting here for her all this time, within half a mile of the blue, safe, deep Atlantic Ocean! By now the wind had dropped to about thirty-five knots. *Sea Dart* pounded on a smooth, rounded rock. I rammed the genoa bag between the keel and the rock with the long bamboo pole brought all the way from St. Helena. As soon as the pounding eased, I went back in the cockpit and started on the bilge pump. The stern, badly splintered, was taking water fast.

I never considered the possibility of abandoning her. It would have been impossible to think of that after all we had been through together. I was not going to leave my bloody boat on a fucking South American rock. I had to get her off. She didn't belong here; she was British, and, by Christ, back to Britain she'd go, regardless! Her destination was home, and by the bleeding Pope of Gozo, that's where she was going.

We must be able to exclude fear and despondency from our calculations at sea (or on shore) for the very simple reason that these two emotions do not serve any constructive purpose. They interfere with reaching a conclusion, finding a viable solution. But on that night off Santa Lucía, with the wind still blowing seven bells of shit at thirty knots,

in fog and knifing cold, I almost lost my reason. For one of
the few times in my life, I was tempted to give way, to give
up. Then I recalled what my old friend Tansy Lee had said,
many years before, when *Second Apprentice* ran aground on
the Hailsborough sands in a very stormy North Sea. "What
the hell do we do now, Tansy?" I cried.

"Do?" he replied, "why make a fucking cuppa tea, you
silly little nit, and make it bloody strong, too—it might be
your last!" And we'd done that. The storm had died fast, so
that by the time the tide refloated her, she sailed off nice as
pie, and Tansy and I pumped her all the way back to
Yarmouth.

Pumping away, cold and tired, wet and hungry, I smiled
at the memory of Tansy. I alternated between pumping out
water and pumping air into the rubber dinghy. Then, heaving the dinghy over the side, *I piled it up with the hurricane
anchor,* chain, and the hundred-fathom storm line. Then,
somehow, I rowed the dinghy out against the raging seas, a
ticklish job, and dropped the fisherman anchor about
twenty fathoms, maybe two hundred feet, away from the
pounding vessel. Back to *Sea Dart* in that awful sea, a quick
pump-out, then I clapped the anchor line on the jib-sheet
winch and started heaving in, all strength gone now, only
will power left, right down to the bare nerve threads.

It took two hours of hard, heavy heaving, cursing, groaning, and pumping before *Sea Dart* finally started to inch out
to the anchor, pounding and bouncing all the while, with
me cold, desperate, and wet through.

Towards the false dawn the wind dropped completely,
and with it, the awful sea. I handed the tattered remnants of
the mainsail below and bent on the storm trysail. Then I
waited, pumping out and eating cold corned beef out of the
can. The working jib was still good, still in one piece. In the
early forenoon the wind came up again, but this time from
the north, from off the land. Slowly I hauled in on the
anchor line and, with some difficulty, weighed the anchor;
Sea Dart started to head out slowly at first, then, as I grabbed
the tiller, she gathered speed. On she went against the
heavy swell, as I steered her carefully and delicately, all the
while pumping her out.

She was still afloat! She would make it! If she stayed afloat for twenty-four hours she'd make port!

By late forenoon *Sea Dart* had tacked her way laboriously right into Montevideo harbor. She had reached salt ocean water! She had done what she set out to do! I ran her hard right up onto a dry mudbank, kicked the anchor over the side, and fell into the deepest sleep I can remember.

In the morning, after another customs formalities round, I took stock. I did not have the resources to refit her in the next few months. Even if I could get the necessary gear into Uruguay, I would need about a year to recoup and to earn enough money to get *Sea Dart* back in shape. I could not leave her in South America, I could not work in South America. There was only one solution; she would have to be shipped home!

After the necessary arrangements had been made, I hoisted her onboard the British steamer *Hardwicke Grange*, bound for England. As she sat on deck, looking forlorn but cocky, I walked away, thinking, "Lionhearted, courageous little bitch. Well, South America tried to get you a thousand times, but in the end, you little bugger, you beat it, you won! You beat a continent!" Through the winter rain of the Montevideo docks, feeling both victorious and bereft, and very, very lonely, I walked on towards the main gate. Cold wind swept along the wide, wet, deserted acres of cobblestones; rain streamed off the roofs of the blank-faced warehouses. As I trudged toward the bright loom of the port control gatehouse, a ship's siren mourned, soft and low in the distance. I knew it was the *Hardwicke Grange;* she was due to leave within the hour with *Sea Dart* onboard.

Cold and shivering, with icy water seeping through the holes in my only shoes, I turned around to stare over towards the big, brightly floodlit ship. There *she* was, far away through the sabering rain, a small dark hump on the deck. I turned and ran back towards her, scrambling over the railroad freight lines glistening in the pale lights, along the black alleyways, stumbling over crates and soggy piles of garbage, until at last, breathless, I stood on the departure mole. Under the doleful light of the mole lamps, I waited for the *Hardwicke Grange* to pass. Through the rain I searched for *Sea Dart,* and as the ship passed majestically by, I saw her, abaft the after deckhouse. She was on her way home, the ragged ensign fluttering on her stern.

I stared after her, wet through, with wet eyes, until the last glimmer of the ship's lights disappeared. Despondently, I turned towards the sad city and my cheap room.

A docks policeman stood under the next lamppost, rifle in hand under his streaming cape. His leather chinstrap dripped water, a damp cigarette drooped from his mouth. He waved his free hand lackadaisically as I passed.

"*Buenas noches, Señor.* You have a friend onboard going to England?"

"*Buenas.* Yes, she's going to England."

"She must be very beautiful for you to stand out there in the rain all this time?"

"*Sî, Señor,* the most beautiful in the whole wide world!"

He grinned. "Some people have all the luck!"

POSTSCRIPT

ONRAD JELINEK IS SAILING his yawl *Carousa* in the West Indies. He and his family take groups of "guests" out among the remoter islets in these beautifully blue waters. Every Christmas I hear from him; every year he said he would come to the West Indies and now he has finally made it.

Huanapaco is back on Lake Titicaca. In the dark, cold winter nights of that strange world, he sits with the Quechuas, wrapped in blankets, *chorros* pulled down low over their dreamy eyes, and tells them long, poetic stories from his saga, while small children and dozy guinea pigs nestle together in the totora reeds on the floor of the adobe. Through the glassless windows sweep the bitter cold winds of the Andes. Above, in the clearest sky in the world, the stars in their millions listen and remember. The condor rustles his wings softly as he stirs in his sleep, dreaming of brave sails under his wings. The ancient *Quipucamayo*, fingering his knotted strings in the corner by the gleam of the smoldering llama-dung fire, smiles to himself, adding the epic to his strings. Old women with nut-brown faces stir the *chicha*. The haunting music of a flute echoes in the distance. On the Lake gleaming under the moon, the wavelets dance and the reeds shiver. A toad croaks. A *choca* bird flutters abroad, on the bare mountains which soar from the fabulous Lake on the Roof of the World. The ghosts of Kon-Tiki, Manco Capac, Tupac Amaru, Atahualpa, and Pizarro wander under the moon amid the ruins of temples known only to the hearts of the Quechua, the Aymara, and the Uros. By the light of the flickering oil lamp inside the adobe, they talk of Macchu Cuito, the one from the great ocean, and his strange game, played with a flat stick and a ball.

In the Mato Grosso and the Chaco, the track we hacked

378

has disappeared completely under the creeping jungle. It is as if *Sea Dart,* Huanapaco, and I had never passed. The jaguar roves hungrily, the snakes and caimans slither, the clouds of insects hum, and the passion flowers bloom bravely, awaiting the next poor lost souls.

Sea Dart sits in a dockside shed, home again, in Sussex, England, in the custody of Her Majesty's Customs, who wait to seize her in default of an import tax of twelve and a half percent of her estimated value!

As for me, I sold my sextant, charts, outboard motor, mooring lines, and dinghy in Montevideo. The proceeds paid for my fare to London, where, bereft and unable to rescue *Sea Dart,* penniless and still half-crazy from the Mato Grosso, I slept under a tree on Hampstead Heath for a week, until my wandering, mourning spoor was picked up by good friends. Then, I went to work again in Harrod's boiler-room, where I had worked out the courses and navigational problems of this incredible voyage six years before. After a month a message came from across the western ocean—but that's another story.

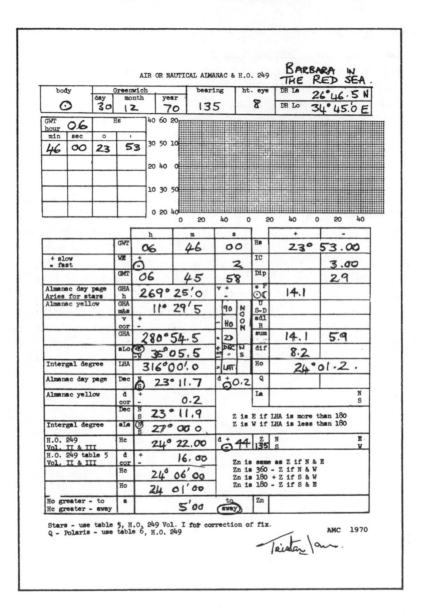

AIR OR NAUTICAL ALMANAC & H.O. 249					*BARBARA* IN THE RED SEA.	

body	Greenwich			bearing	ht. eye	DR La 26° 46.5 N
	day	month	year			DR Lo 34° 45.0 E
☉	30	12	70	135	8	

		Hs					
GWT hour 06		40 60 20					
min	sec	°	'	30 50 10			
46	00	23	53				

		h	m	s		+	−
	GWT	06	46	00	Hs	23° 53.00	
+ slow − fast	WE	+ ☉		2	IC		3.00
	GMT	06	45	58	Dip		29
Almanac day page Aries for stars	GHA h	269° 25'.0	v + −		* P ☉☾	14.1	
Almanac yellow	GHA m&s	11° 29'5	90 N O O N		U S−D		
	v + cor −		− Ho		ad1 R		
	GHA	280° 54.5	− Z)		sum	14.1	5.9
aLo ⓔ		35° 05.5	+ DEC " S		dif	8.2	
Intergal degree	LHA	316° 00'.0	LAT		Ho	24° 01.2.	
Almanac day page	Dec N Ⓢ	23° 11.7	d + ⊝0.2		Q		
Almanac yellow	d + cor −	0.2		La		N S
	Dec N S	23° 11.9	Z is E if LHA is more than 180				
Intergal degree	aLa N Ⓜ S	27° 00 0	Z is W if LHA is less than 180				
H.O. 249 Vol. II & III	Hc	24° 22.00	d + ⊝44	Z 135	N S		E W
H.O. 249 table 5 Vol. II & III	d cor + −	16.00	Zn is same as Z if N & E				
	Hc	24° 06' 00	Zn is 360 − Z if N & W				
	Ho	24 01' 00	Zn is 180 + Z if S & W Zn is 180 − Z if S & E				
Ho greater − to Hc greater − away	a	5' 00	to away	Zn			

Stars - use table 5, H.O. 249 Vol. I for correction of fix.
Q - Polaris - use table 6, H.O. 249

AMC 1970

A typical navigation working sheet from *Barbara,* showing the working out of a sun sight on the thirtieth of December 1970 in the northern part of the Red Sea.

Letter of thanks from the Imperial Navy of Ethiopia. Five officers went to sea for the first time in the *Barbara*. Part of it is in the Amharic language but they've also put it in English.

Voyage of the Yawl 'Barbara', May 1969 to May 1972.

Ports visited.

Left Westport, Connecticut, USA.		Yugoslavia (cont),	Split, (2)	
Bermuda,	Hamilton.		Merta,	
	St Georges.		Pula.	
		Italy	Venice.	
Azores,	Fayal.	Yugoslav.	Mali Losinge	
	Ponta del Gada.		Jadi	
			Zadar,	
Portugal,	Setubal,		Pagman,	
	Lisbon,		Zibenek	
	Portimao		Trogir,	
Spain,	Cadiss.		Supetar,	
			Sobra,	
	Gibraltar. (3)		Broce,	
			Ston,	
Spain,	Estepona,		Sumartin,	
	Marbella,		Loviste,	
	Malaga, (2)		Cavtat.	
	Motril	Italy	Brindisi.	
	Adra,	Greece..	Corfu	
	Almeria, (2)		Paxos,	
	La Garrucha, (2)		Atheni,	
	Aguilas, (2)		Patras,	
	Cartagena, (2)		Tristonia,	
	Alicante, (2)		Aspra Spiti,	
	Ibiza, (4)		Corinth,	
	Palma, (3)		Piraeus,	
	Formentera,		Kithnos,	
	Port Andraixt,		Mykonos,	
	Calpe,		Bokanouea,	
	Torreveija,		Astapalia,	
Morocco,	Tangier		Rhodes.	
	Casablanca,	Turkey..	Fethiye,	
	El Jadida,		Kas,	
	Safi,		Kakava,	
	Mogador, (2)		Myra,	
	Agadir,		Fineke,	
Canaries,	Arrecife. 1970.		Antalya,	
	Las Palmas(2)		Side,	
	Santa Cruz		Alanya,	
	Christianos		Anamur,	
	Gomera	Cyprus	Kerenia (refused)	
		Israel.	Haifa,	
Madeira,	Funchal.		Acre,	
			Jaffa,	
Morocco,	Mellila.		Ashdod, -EWGEDI.	
Spain.	Porto Colom,		Eilat,	
	Port Mahon.		Mrs el At.	
Corsica,	Bonifacio.	Ethiopia	Massawa 1971	
			Assab.	
Sardinia,	Madelena,		Edd.	
	Olbia	T.F.A.I.	Djibouti,	
Sicily,	Trapani	Kenya	Mombasa, (2)	
	Mazala,		Malindi,	
	Empadocla,		Wassin. (2)	
	Gela.	Tansania	Tanga,	
			Mwaze,	
Malta,	Valetta,		Zansibar	
	Sliema,		Dar es Salaam.	
			Kilwa Kivenge.	
Italy.	Otranto		Kilwa Kisiwani.	
		Comoros.	Moroni	
Yugo-slavia.	Dubruvnik (4)		Mutsumudu.	
	Slano	Seychelles	African Islet,	
	Korcula,		Victoria(Mahe)(2)	
			La Digue(2)	
			Praslin Is.	
			Coetivy Is.	
		Madagascar	Nosy Vahilla.	

List of ports visited by the *Barbara* on her way round from
Westport to the West Indies and then in search of *Sea Dart*.

Voyage of the Yawl 'Barbara' Ports visited 1969-72(cont)

Madagascar(cont)
    NOSY MANAROVO— NOSY KALAKAJARO
    Hellville,
    Majunga.

~~Mozambique.~~   ~~Inhambane.~~

South Africa.   Durban
                Port Elizabeth,
                Mossel Bay,
                Capetown.
                        1972.

St. Helena.   St. James.

Brazil.   Recife,
                Fortaleza,
                Salinopolis,
                Belem do Para.
                Abetatuba,
                Boa Vista,
                Breves,
                Gurupa,
                Almeirim(2)
                Aquiaqui,
                Preana(2)
                Monte Alegre,
                Santarem(2)
                Juruti,
                Barreirena,
                Eva,
                Manaus.
                ~~Itacaitara~~(2)
                Urucurituba,
                Jurupari,
                Parantins
                Obidos,
                Paricaratuba,
                Santana,
                Macapa.
                Curea.
Fr. Guiana.   Cayenne.
                Ile Royale(Devil's Is)

Brit. West Indies. ~~Grenada.~~ ST VINCENT, ANTIGUA, ST THOMAS(U.S.VIRGINS).

TOTAL MILES SAILED IN 'BARBARA' ~~30,417~~

WESTPORT TO ST THOMAS . . . . . 31,242 .

                                    Tristan Jones.

PLUS, IN BANJO II LOOKING FOR "SEA DART" 1,420

                        TOTAL 32,662

PORTS OF CALL ON SEARCH FOR SEA DART :- IN BANJO II.

BARBADOS --. BRIDGETOWN	PUERTO-RICO SAN JUAN
ST VINCENT BEQUIA,	ST CROIX
ST LUCIA (2)	ST THOMAS
MARTINIQUE (2)	TORTOLA
GUADALOUPE (2)	ST MARTIN
ANTIGUA (2)	ST BARTS
ST KITTS	BASSETERRE
NEVIS	DOMINICA
ST JOHNS	MONTSERRAT
	BEQUIA .

Atropellos del DAS denuncia extranjero

El ciudadano inglés Tristan Jones, escritor y navegante, fue víctima de atropellos propinados por detectives del DAS, luego de haberlo capturado, por no tener papeles, a pesar de haberles explicado que se los habían robado la noche anterior en un atraco.

Tristan Jones, quien desde tiempo atrás se dedica a la navegación, recorriendo los mares del mundo, para luego escribir sus experiencias que son publicadas en varias revistas europeas, llegó en uno de sus tantos viajes a Santa Marta, en donde logró una visa por 3 meses, con la cual se dirigió a Cartagena; allí el motor de su embarcación sufrió averías irreparables, que lo obligaron a trasladarse a Bogotá para comprar uno nuevo.

Sin embargo, no acababa de llegar a la capital de la República, cuando fue atracado, en los alrededores del Hotel San Francisco, en donde se hospedó, por cuatro sujetos que le quitaron 2.000 pesos en efectivo.

Al día siguiente, decidió trasladarse a una oficina de cambios para adquirir más dinero colombiano, pero con tan mala suerte que al salir; lo abordaron tres sujetos que le quitaron 3 mil pesos en efectivo, 250 dólares, cheques viajeros, el pasaporte y un reloj de pulso.

Ante la inseguridad de que estaba rodeado, Tristan Jones, puso en conocimiento de la Policía de Turismo los hechos ocurridos los dos días anteriores, sin que allí le dieran respuesta alguna.

Tristan se puso en contacto con el consulado de su país y allí le expidieron una certificación en la que constaba que había sido víctima de los ladrones y que por lo tanto carecía de los papeles de identificación y de extranjería.

La situación del escritor inglés se agravó por lo que decidió comprar pasajes para viajar a Cartagena, pero cuando salía del edificio de Avianca en la carrera 7ª con calle 16, fue notificado por dos detectives de que debía seguir con ellos por no tener documentos de identificación. Jones, les mostró la certificación del consulado, pero esta no fue razón suficiente para que los detectives desistieran de su propósito.

Manifiesta Tristan Jones que lo llevaron a la "casa pequeña", en donde lo encerraron en unos sótanos por dos horas, más tarde lo llevaron junto con otros extranjeros a la sala de encapuchados, en donde uno de los policías, dirigiéndose a uno de los norteamericanos, le dijo que lo había visto fumando marihuana.

De allí los sacaron y los hicieron meter en unos calabozos subterráneos, sin permitir que el ciudadano inglés diera explicación alguna, a pesar de haberles solicitado que lo dejaran comunicarse con el consulado de su país.

El escritor y navegante pasó tres días de tortura en los calabozos del DAS, en donde no se le permitió defenderse, ni mucho menos explicar de quién se trataba, ni por qué estaba en Colombia. El viernes en la tarde lo soltaron, permitiéndole únicamente una visa de un mes para abandonar el país, sin que para el efecto haya explicación alguna de parte de las autoridades.

Tristán Jones

Otro Caso de Anti-Turismo

(Continuación de la Pág. 1-A)

abordado por dos agentes del Departamento Administrativo de Seguridad (DAS), que es la policía secreta, quienes lo detuvieron por no tener sus documentos de identidad, a pesar de que les había presentado la certificación expedida por el consulado.

Jones afirmó que en las dependencias del DAS, fue incomunicado y llevado a un calabozo, donde permaneció tres días, hasta que el viernes último fue dejado en libertad, sin que se le diera explicación alguna.

Otro Caso de Antiturismo

- BOGOTA, mayo 14. (UPI). El escritor y navegante inglés Tristan Jones denunció hoy aquí que fue víctima de atropellos por parte de las autoridades colombianas.

Jones dijo que entró al país por el puerto de Santa Marta, con visa de tres meses. La semana pasada llegó a esta capital y en dos días consecutivos fue víctima de ladrones que le quitaron sus documentos de identificación y una considerable suma de dinero.

Manifestó que, en estas circunstancias, se dirigió al consulado de su país, donde se le expidió una certificación en la que constaba que sus papeles le habían sido robados.

Sin embargo, cuando se disponía a comprar pasajes aéreos para viajar a Cartagena, al norte del país, fue

(Continúa en la Pág. 12-A Col. 1ª)

A newspaper report of imprisonment in Bogotá, Colombia.

384

Señor Capitán de Puerto de Puno

S. C.

TRISTAN JONES, de nacionalidad Inglesa, con Pasaporte N°.C 281164, mayor de edad; ante Ud. con el debido respeto me presento y digo:

Que, debiendo realizar estudios en el Lago (Huiñamarca) y para lo cual necesito trasladar la embarcación denominada "Velero-Yate", con motor Jonsoen, y para lo que necesito contar con la Licencia expedida por su digno Despacho; a Ud. recurro señor Capitán de Puerto para que tenga a bien autorizar el sarpe de la citada embarcación con destino al Puerto de Guaqui (Bolivia), para cuyo objeto acompaño los siguientes documentos:

- Certificado de Importación Temporal N°. 150 de fecha 28 Diciembre 1973 del Yate-Velero "SEA DART" s/n.

- Certificado de matrícula del Yate-Velero "SEA DART".

- Permiso especial de la Capitanía de Puno.
- Tarjeta de Turismo Nro. 327832 de la República de Bolivia
Por lo expuesto:

Ruego a Ud. acceder a mi petición por ser de justicia.

Puno, 11 Marzo 1974

Puno, 11 Marzo 1974

Vista la solicitud que antecede se decreta:

1.- Autorizar el sarpe por 50 días de la citada embarcación. Hágase saber y archívese

El Capitán de Puerto de Puno

CAPITAN DE FR-GT A.P.
JORGE RAZ PEGORARI

Permission to enter Peru, not a customs document, just permission, and to navigate on Lake Titicaca.

385

Tiquina, 16 de Marzo de 1.974

A la solicitud anteriormente expuesta, el sus-
crito Alferez Capitán de Puerto de Tiquina, autoriza el zarpe del Velero- Yate "SEA-DART" su
para cumplir la misión indicada.

Alf. Gonzalo Sanchez Carranza
CAPITAN DE PUERTO TIQUINA.

Guaqui,19 de Marzo de 1.974

A la solicitud anteriormente expuesta, elsuscrito
Alferez Capitán de Puerto Mayor Guaqui, autoriza
el Zarpe del Velero- Yate "SEA-DART" para cumplir
la misión indicada, a las localidades de Huatajata
y Tiquina.

Alf. Juan Lopez Montaño
CAPITAN DE PUERTO MAYOR GUAQUI

RECEBIDO   Capitania dos
PORTO MURTINHO
10 / 10 / 1974 Portos do Estado
1469   de Mato Grosso
Agente
Antonio B. de Aquino
2° Ten (A - CP)

Overleaf the permissions to navigate on Lake Titicaca, the first
one ever given.

Page 3 is the permission given by the Bolivian navy, written by candlelight with a quill pen on the fifteenth of April, 1974. This also was permission to navigate on the lake. Down below there are stamps from the Mato Grosso, and the only port of any size, about five houses, Porto Murtinho—the first time that this stamp has ever been used.

A Suriqui.

3 de Mayo 1974.

La Comunidad de Suriqui reunida en assemblia
a tomado un accuerdo de comprometerse de no
molestar a todo cuidano extrangero qui estare
en la isla;
esta compromisa le firman el Secretario de Comunidades
Central Senor El Nestor Salas, Secretario General
Gregorio Esteban, el Corregidor Mario Arratia:
el Secretario de Justicia Miguel Suxo y la
Comunidad en total comprometiendo c e a no molestar
a ningun persona de fuera de la isla,

SECRETARIO   _SECRETARIO GENERAL_

CORREGIDOR   _...RIO JUSTICIA_

The treaty made with the Aymara Indians on the Island of
Suriqui the third of May, 1974. "The community of Suriqui
united in assembly has taken an agreement to promise never to
molest any strange citizen who is on the island. This promise is
signed by the Secretary of the Community, Central *Señor* Nestor
Salas, the Secretary General Gregorio Esteban, and the Corregidor Mario Arratia: the Secretary of Justice Miguel Suxo and
the community as a whole promises never to molest any person
from outside the island." This treaty was made after the fracas
caused by the stealing of *Sea Dart*'s mooring line.

388

```
NUCLEO ESCOLAR CAMPESINO
DE ISLA: "SURIQUI"
PROV. LOS ANDES
LA PAZ - BOLIVIA.

                              Isla Suriqui, 8 de julio de I.974

        Al Señor

        Tristan Jones

                        Ref: Nombramiento de Padrino.-
        Huatajata.-

Muy Señor nuestro:

                Mediante el presente, nos es grato saludarlos muy
cordialmente augurándole éxitos en su trabajo Lacustre.
                El propósito único que nos induce a dirigirles a
su distinguida persona, como Autoridades de la comunidad y escuela;
Director del Núcleo, Sindicato Agrario, Central Agrario. Pdte. Junta
de Vecinos, Oficial de Registro Civil, Corregidor Auxiliar, Comité
de Festejos, Junta de Auxilio Escolar y padres de familia, hemos
acordado honrarte con todo respeto, nombrando como:

        PADRINO DE 300.oo $b. PARA LOS PREMIOS

                Por la buena acogida de nuestros intereses, tendrá
el honor de entregar en presencia del público en un acto cívico, que
se realizará la Segunda Fiesta "DIADEL INDIO BOLIVIANO", en la que nos
visitarán las Escuelas Séccionales pertenentes al Núcleo, que se lle-
vará a cabo el Iro. y dos de agosto, en la Escuela Central.
                Con este motivo y esperándole su buena acogida, nos
despedimos reiterándoles una vez más nuestros saludos y al mismo
tiempo suscribiéndonos como sus más atentos servidores.
```

"POR LA EDUCACION BOLIVIANA"

SINDICATO AGRARIO
CENTRAL SURIQUI

PROVINCIA LOS ANDES
LA PAZ - BOLIVIA

Sr. Gregorio Estéban Huarina   Sr. Nestor Sálaz A.
STRIO. GENERAL DEL SINDICATO A.   CENTRAL AGRARIO

Sr. Mario Arratia Huarina   Sr. Andres Sálaz Suxo
CORREGIDOR AUX.   OFICIAL REGISTRO CIVIL.

Sr. Cornelio Arratia   Sr. Fructuoso Quispe
ALCALDE ESCOLAR.   STRIO. DE EDUCACION.

Sr. Gregorio Corani Bautista   PDTE. COMITE DE FESTEJOS.
JUNTA DE AUXILIO ESCOLAR.

NUCLEO PILOTO ESCOLAR CAMPESINO
" SURIQUI "
DIRECCION
Prov. Los Andes
LA PAZ - BOLIVIA

Prof. Juan Huañapaco C.
DIRECTOR NUCLEO ESCOLAR

Nombramiento de Padrino. Tristan Jones was appointed as a
Padrino of the school on the Island of Suriqui. "We have the
honor to invite you to be present at a civic act at which we are
realizing the second Fiesta of the 'Day of the Bolivian Indian' in
which we will be visiting schools on different islands presenting
prizes. We hope that you will be able to attend these and subscribe
to your attentive servants." Note that the chief of the school
service has signed this with his thumb prints because he couldn't
write.

389

A letter written by the chief of the security police for the river and communications at Corrientes in the Argentine on arrival in that country, passing Tristan Jones down to his friend at a place called Paraná:

"Lieutenant Mieriz: The carrier of this letter is an English writer, Tristan Jones, navigating from Lake Titicaca. As he does not know this zone nor the river Paraná, try to treat him with all possible aid. If you can, find him some fish. He's going to be with you approximately one day. From here I thank you for what you can do for him."

Tristan Jones was born at sea aboard a British ship, *Star of the West,* off one of the most remote islands in the world, Tristan da Cunha in the South Atlantic. It was a fitting birthplace for a man who would one day hold nine world sailing records, including the title of "the world's longest distance sailor." He is from a long line of Welsh sailing people—even his grandmother was first mate on a wool-trading ship.

At age thirteen he left school and signed on a sailing barge exporting scrap iron to Germany for wages of five cents a week—and he's been at sea ever since. When World War II broke out, he joined the Royal Navy and was sunk three times before he was eighteen. After the war he transferred to the Royal Hydrographic Service and served on convoy duties to the USSR from Iceland, then later in Far Eastern waters. His service ended in 1952 in Aden when an in-shore survey vessel he was on was blown up by guerrillas. He suffered a severe spinal injury that left him paralyzed. He was told he would never walk again and given a physical discharge.

Today Tristan Jones has sailed a record 345,000 miles in small boats under 40 feet in length (well over the distance to the moon). He sailed 180,000 miles of this distance single-handed. He has crossed the Atlantic eighteen times under sail, nine times alone.

Tristan is currently working on another book, *Saga of A Wayward Sailor.* It is about his first solo adventure, in which he circumnavigated Iceland and reached the furthest point north ever touched by a sailing craft.

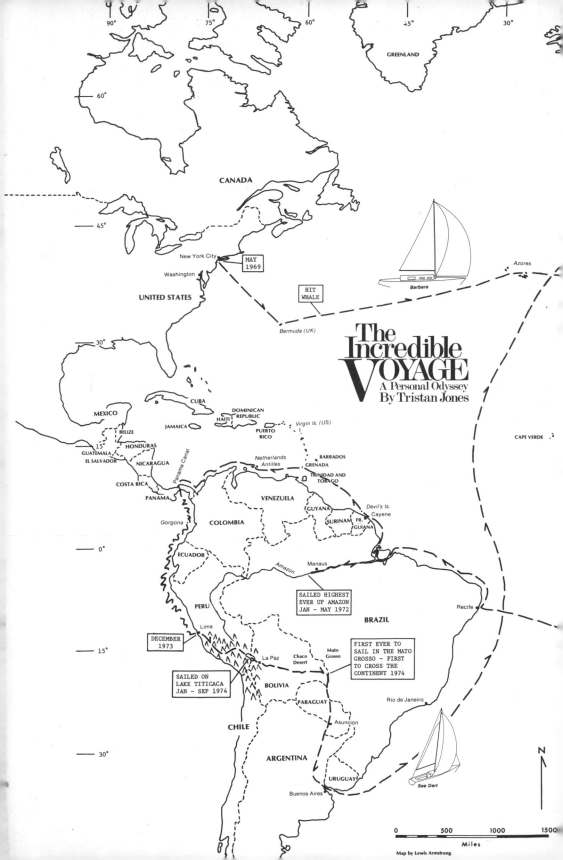

The Incredible VOYAGE
A Personal Odyssey
By Tristan Jones

90° 75° 60° 45° 30°

GREENLAND

60°

CANADA

45°

New York City
Washington

MAY
1969

Barbara

Azores

UNITED STATES

HIT
WHALE

Bermuda (UK)

30°

CUBA
DOMINICAN
REPUBLIC
HAITI
MEXICO
JAMAICA
PUERTO
RICO
Virgin Is. (US)

CAPE VERDE

15°
BELIZE
GUATEMALA
HONDURAS
EL SALVADOR
NICARAGUA
Panama Canal
Netherlands
Antilles
BARBADOS
GRENADA
TRINIDAD AND
TOBAGO
COSTA RICA
PANAMA
VENEZUELA
GUYANA
SURINAM
FR.
GUIANA
Devil's Is.
Cayene

Gorgona
COLOMBIA

0°
ECUADOR
Amazon
Manaus

SAILED HIGHEST
EVER UP AMAZON
JAN – MAY 1972

Recife

PERU
BRAZIL

DECEMBER
1973
Lima

15°
La Paz
Chaco
Desert
Mato
Grosso

FIRST EVER TO
SAIL IN THE MATO
GROSSO – FIRST
TO CROSS THE
CONTINENT 1974

SAILED ON
LAKE TITICACA
JAN – SEP 1974
BOLIVIA

Rio de Janeiro

PARAGUAY

CHILE
Asuncion

30°
ARGENTINA

N

URUGUAY
Sea Dart

Buenos Aires

0   500   1000   1500
Miles

Map by Lewis Armstrong